"Carries the very useful procedures of *Feeling Good* into many other important areas of life. Clear, systematic, and forceful."
—ALBERT ELLIS, PH.D.
President, Institute for Rational-Emotional Therapy, and author of *A New Guide to Rational Living*

"Dr. Burns has done it again. He has provided us with clearly described and practical guidelines for dealing with fears, anxieties, panic attacks, procrastination, and communication problems. . . . invaluable."
—MARVIN GOLDFRIED, Professor of Psychology and Psychiatry, State University of New York at Stony Brook

"This book makes a difference. Anyone who experiences emotional distress (that is everyone) will find this book invaluable. Dr. Burns presents dozens of helpful exercises in his inimitable, lively, and self-revealing style."
—JACKIE PERSONS, PH.D., Assistant Clinical Professor, Department of Psychiatry, University of California at San Francisco, and private practitioner

(for more extraordinary praise, from professionals and readers, please turn the page . . .)

Dr. David Burns graduated magna cum laude from Amherst College, received his M.D. from Stanford University School of Medicine, and completed his psychiatric training at the University of Pennsylvania. He is a clinical associate professor of psychiatry at the University of Pennsylvania School of Medicine, and practices at the Presbyterian Medical Center of Philadelphia. He lives in Gladwyne, Pennsylvania. The bestselling *Feeling Good: The New Mood Therapy* is available in a Signet edition.

"Dr. Burns seemed to be talking directly to me . . . he took me by the hand and led me step by step to an understanding of *why* I feel the way I do and *how* I can feel better about myself."

—N.C.S., Caldwell, New Jersey

"THIS IS MY BIBLE! IT'S AMAZING! IT'S WONDERFUL!"

—F.G., San Diego, California

"These techniques are for anyone who doubts his own self-worth, falls prey to anxieties, desperately strives to be perfect, or just feels bad but can't figure out why. This book can truly change your life and give you back the ability to enjoy it."

—J.K.S., Chadsford, Pennsylvania

OTHER BOOKS BY DAVID D. BURNS, M.D.

Feeling Good: The New
Mood Therapy
(1980)

Intimate Connections:
The Clinically Proven Program
for Making Close Friends
and Finding a Loving Partner
(1985)

THE
FEELING GOOD
HANDBOOK

DAVID D. BURNS, M.D.

A PLUME BOOK

PLUME
Published by the Penguin Group
Penguin Books USA Inc., 375 Hudson Street, New York, New York 10014, U.S.A.
Penguin Books Ltd, 27 Wrights Lane, London W8 5TZ, England
Penguin Books Australia Ltd, Ringwood, Victoria, Australia
Penguin Books Canada Ltd, 10 Alcorn Avenue, Toronto, Ontario, Canada M4V 3B2
Penguin Books (N.Z.) Ltd, 182–190 Wairau Road, Auckland 10, New Zealand

Penguin Books Ltd, Registered Offices: Harmondsworth, Middlesex, England

Published by Plume, an imprint of Dutton Signet, a division of Penguin Books USA Inc.
This is an authorized reprint of a hardcover edition published by William Morrow and
Company, Inc.

First Plume Printing, September, 1990
20 19 18

 REGISTERED TRADEMARK—MARCA REGISTRADA

LIBRARY OF CONGRESS CATALOGING-IN-PUBLICATION DATA
Burns, David D.
    The feeling good handbook / David D. Burns.
        p.   cm.
    "Reprint of a hardcover edition published by William Morrow [New York] . . .
c1989"—T.p. verso.
    Includes bibliographical references.
    ISBN 0-452-26174-0
    1. Cognitive therapy.   I. Title.
[RC489.C63B87   1990]
616.8914—dc20   90-7130
                                                                            CIP

Printed in the United States of America
Set in Garamond No. 3
Original hardcover designed by Richard Oriolo

PUBLISHER'S NOTE
The ideas, procedures, and suggestions contained in this book are not intended as a
substitute for consulting with a mental health professional.

All names and identities of individuals have been disguised to protect their anonymity.

This book is dedicated to my colleagues
Tony Bates and Sheila Flynn,
who are very dear to me.

Acknowledgments

I owe a debt of gratitude to many people who have contributed to this book in so many ways. First, I want to thank my colleagues Tony Bates, Sheila Flynn, and Dr. Peter Druian for their thoughtful review of the manuscript and their guidance in its revision. Their vision and creativity were crucial to the birth of this book and have been a constant source of joy to me. I would also like to thank Drs. Jim Luebbert and Alan Schatzberg, who provided valuable suggestions about the chapters on the chemistry of mood disorders. In addition, many of my patients, who wish to remain anonymous, read and critiqued various chapters of the *Handbook* while it was being written and edited. This feedback was absolutely essential in showing me what was genuinely helpful and what was not. The result was the development of a much stronger manuscript. Thank you!

I would like to thank Retta Jo Bender, Mary Lovell, Wendy Brusick, and Sharon Barksdale for the huge volume of meticulous word processing that was necessary in the creation of this book. I also want to thank my editors, Arnold Dolin at New American Library and Maria Guarnaschelli at William Morrow, for their enormous patience and generous support of my efforts.

I would like to thank the thousands of readers who have written to me after reading my first book, *Feeling Good: The New Mood Therapy*. Sharing your personal experiences about the help you received from that book has meant more to me than you will ever know. Your ideas and suggestions helped in the development of this *Handbook*. I also want to thank the many psychiatrists, psychologists, clinical social workers, nurses, clergymen, and counselors who have recommended *Feeling Good* to the clients they work with. I know of no higher possible endorsement than yours!

Finally, I want to emphasize that I am not the sole creator of the many ideas and techniques in this book. Cognitive therapy has been a team effort, with hundreds if not thousands of talented clinicians and researchers throughout the world contributing to this important movement, which has revolutionized our understanding and treatment of depression, anxiety, and marital discord. Although I could not begin to acknowledge each contributor, I want to emphasize that much of the early pioneering work was done by Drs. Albert Ellis and Aaron T. Beck. The field of mental health owes much to their vision and leadership.

Contents

Introduction

In *Feeling Good: The New Mood Therapy* I described a revolutionary, drug-free treatment for depression called cognitive therapy. The word *cognition* simply means thought or perception. Cognitive therapy is based on the simple idea that your thoughts and attitudes—and not external events—create your moods.

When you are upset, you may have noticed that you think about yourself and the world in a pessimistic way. If you feel depressed you may think, "Everything seems so hopeless, I'm such a loser. I'll *never* feel good again." If you feel anxious and panicky, you may think, "What if I lose control and crack up?" During an argument with your spouse, you may tell yourself, "That SOB! What a jerk!" Although these negative thoughts are often distorted and illogical, they can seem deceptively realistic, so you believe things really are as bad as you think they are. Cognitive therapy can help you break out of these mood slumps and develop more positive and realistic attitudes.

Although cognitive therapy was largely unknown at the time that *Feeling Good* was first published, it has exploded into one of the most widely practiced forms of therapy in the world. Extensive research sponsored by the National Institute of Mental Health at universities and medical centers throughout the country has proved that cognitive therapy is as effective and fast-acting as antidepressant medications in the treatment of depression. Even more exciting are recent studies showing that patients treated with cognitive therapy stay free of depression longer than patients treated with drugs alone. This means that the treatment can help you feel better in the here-and-now and deal with future periods of stress and disappointment so you can feel better about yourself and others for the rest of your life.

I wrote *Feeling Good* because I was tremendously excited about how helpful these methods had been to my patients, and I wanted to share these exciting developments with as many people as possible. However, I did not know whether my book would really be helpful to people who were not receiving therapy. I had intended *Feeling Good* to be a supplement to therapy, thinking I would assign chapters to my patients to read between sessions.

Soon after the book was first published, I began to receive heart-warming letters—hundreds at first, then thousands of them—from readers who were kind enough to share their experiences with me. I can recall a man from Oklahoma who described his decades-long unsuccessful struggle with depression. He wrote, "God bless you. Because of your book, I have had my first happy Christmas in over twenty years!"

Many of those who wrote suggested I prepare a sequel that would illustrate how to apply the new mood therapy to the entire range of everyday problems, including low self-esteem, anxiety and panic, and personal-relationship problems. To these many people I owe a debt of gratitude. Your vision inspired the creation of this *Handbook*. I hope it will be equally helpful to you.

People often ask me, "Do you still believe in this approach? Have your methods or theory changed since you wrote *Feeling Good?*" Although there is much that is new and different in this *Handbook*, the vision and techniques described in *Feeling Good* are like pure gold. There's not a day in my office when these ideas do not surprise and enlighten me and my patients, just as if I had discovered them for the first time.

However, there have been many exciting developments since I wrote *Feeling Good*. I have discovered that the new mood therapy can be tremendously helpful for the entire range of mood problems that we all encounter in our daily lives. These include feelings of insecurity and inferiority, procrastination, guilt, stress, frustration, and irritability. Recent door-to-door surveys of thousands of American households sponsored by the National Institute of Mental Health have indicated that nearly 20 million Americans suffer from chronic nervousness, panic attacks, or phobias. You may be afflicted by some type of anxiety such as the fear of heights, public speaking anxiety, nervousness in social situations, agoraphobia, or test anxiety, to name just a few. In this *Handbook* you will discover why you are plagued by these irrational worries. You will also learn how to confront and conquer your worst fears without having to rely on addictive tranquilizers or alcohol.

Another important development has been the application of the new mood therapy to personal-relationship problems. Cognitive therapy has sometimes been criticized as being too self-centered and preoccupied with personal happiness and fulfillment. There is nothing wrong with wanting to grow as an individual, but it is equally important to learn how to get closer to other people so you can resolve conflicts and enjoy greater intimacy.

For the past ten years I have been doing intensive research on the causes and cures for marital and personal relationship problems. I have discovered that certain attitudes cause people to get stuck in endless cycles of blame, hostility, fear, and loneliness. I will show you how to express your feelings more effectively and to listen and really hear how the other person is thinking and feeling during a conflict. The goal is to help you feel closer to the people you care about the most.

As you read the *Handbook*, I will ask you to complete a number of self-assessment tests once a week, just like my patients do. These tests will help you monitor your progress as you read the book. I will also ask you to write down how you might think, feel, and act in a variety of situations that typically make people angry, sad, frustrated, or anxious. Then I will suggest some new and different ways to communicate or think about the situation. If you want to make actual, tangible changes in your life as you read this book, these exercises are vital. Some people may neglect them. They may tell themselves, "I don't need to fill this out. I'll just read what he has to say and that will be enough." I strongly urge you to resist this temptation!

Many of the people who read *Feeling Good* emphasized the importance of these written exercises. They told me that they did not actually began to experience a profound transformation in their moods and outlook on life until they picked up a pencil and paper and did the exercises that I described. I have taken this feedback seriously and substantially improved and simplified these exercises in the *Handbook*. Although I will ask more of you than most authors or therapists, the potential rewards are great. I want you to enjoy better self-esteem, greater productivity, and enhanced intimacy for the rest of your life as a result of reading this *Handbook*.

Some people have told me, "You seemed to be writing specifically with me in mind. I don't understand how your descriptions of depression and anxiety could be so accurate. It's almost as if you had experienced these mood slumps in your own life." And a few have boldly asked if I have.

Let me share an experience when my son, David Erik, was born. . . .

He was born around 6:00 P.M. on October 13, 1976. While his birth was a normal one it was obvious that he was having difficulties breathing. He was bluer than a healthy baby should be and he was wheezing and gasping for air. The obstetrician reassured us that the problem didn't appear to be serious but explained that they were sending him to an incubator in the premature intensive-care unit as a precautionary measure because he wasn't getting enough oxygen into his blood. I panicked and thought, "God! He needs oxygen for his brain cells. What if he ends up with brain damage or is mentally retarded?"

As I walked through the hospital corridors, frightening thoughts raced through my mind. I developed tunnel vision and I felt as if I were floating across the ceiling. I had fantasies of taking him to clinics for the rest of his life as he struggled with various handicaps. As the night wore on, I was flooded with wave after wave of panic and I felt like a nervous wreck.

Then I asked myself: "Why don't you do what you tell your patients to do? Aren't you always suggesting that distorted thoughts—and not realistic ones—upset people? Why don't you write your negative thoughts down on a piece of paper and see if there's something illogical about them?" Then I told myself, "Oh, that wouldn't work because this problem is real! A silly paper and pencil exercise wouldn't do me any good at all!" Then I countered this with "Why not try it as an experiment and find out?"

The first thought I wrote down was "Other people might think less of me if I have a mentally retarded son." I'm a little ashamed to admit that my own ego was already caught up with the accomplishments and intelligence of my own son. But that was how I was thinking! This is such a common trap. We're programmed to believe that if we're number one in athletics or scholastics or in our careers, then we're no longer "average" or "ordinary" but "special." Our children incorporate this value system as they grow up and their feelings of self-esteem get connected with how talented, successful, or popular they are.

Once I wrote my negative thought down and thought about it, I began to see how distorted and unloving it was and I decided to look at it this way instead: "It's not very likely that people will evaluate me based on how intelligent my son is. They're more likely to evaluate me on what I do. Their feelings about me will depend more on how I treat them and how I feel about them than on my own or my son's success."

The more I thought about it, the clearer it became that my own feelings of happiness and my love for my son didn't have to be connected with his intelligence or career at all. And then a rather sweet realization came to mind. It dawned on me that even if he was only average or below average, it didn't need to diminish the joy we would share by one iota. I thought of how wonderful it would be to be close to him and to do things together as he grew up. I had the fantasy of going into the coin-collecting business with him when I was old and ready to retire from psychiatry. I had always had an interest in coin collecting, and my daughter, who was five years old at the time, was quite bright and independent. She had always developed her own interests and hobbies and never had much interest in coins. The fantasy of going to coin shows with my son and wheeling and dealing Lincoln pennies and buffalo nickels was so exciting that my anxiety vanished entirely.

By this time it was around 3:00 in the morning. I had the sudden urge to go to see him so I drove back to the hospital. Since I was on the hospital staff, the nurses were kind enough to let me visit him. As he lay in the incubator he was still bluish and his nostrils flared with every labored effort to move air in and out. He was crying, frightened, struggling, and exhausted. My heart went out to him. I wanted to touch him. I put on a surgical glove and reached through the hole in the side of the incubator. As I placed my hand on his forehead I felt all the love I had for him. He seemed to settle down and it appeared that his breathing became more relaxed.

When I got home I had the impulse to call the intensive-care unit to see how he was. The nurse said that right after I left he began to breathe normally and his skin turned pink. The order had already been written to discharge him to the regular nursery so he could be with his mother!

Ultimately it turned out that he had no deficiencies or brain damage due to his breathing difficulties. My negative thoughts were quite unrealistic. This crisis helped me learn to love and cherish him as he is, and not because of his intelligence or talents. The joy he radiates every day is my reward.

The story shows that all of us succumb at times to feelings of doubt and despair. These vulnerabilities are universal, and are part of what makes us uniquely human. As you read this book, I will illustrate numerous methods that have helped hundreds of thousands of people to break out of their bad moods and experience greater joy, greater self-esteem, and greater intimacy. But *changing* the way you feel is only one of our goals. The other goal is *self-acceptance*. I want you to learn to accept and love yourself as a flawed and imperfect human. I want you to accept your strengths as well as your weaknesses without a sense of shame or embarrassment.

One of the spiritual principles at the root of cognitive therapy is a paradox: Your weaknesses can become your strengths. Your shortcomings can become your greatest assets, your windows of opportunity, once you surrender and accept them. The fear and desperation that I experienced when David Erik was born have given me the opportunity to develop unconditional love for him and to reach out to you. Perhaps you and I can also form a more meaningful bond because you can see that I am not a guru who knows all the answers but simply a flesh-and-blood human being like yourself. I often hurt and experience irritability, anxiety, and disappointment, just like you do. I believe that sharing these feelings can make us feel closer. It's our shortcomings and not our successes that give us the opportunity for genuine caring.

That's what I mean when I say that your weakness can be your secret source of strength. I hope that you will come to comprehend this and to discover a profound sense of self-acceptance, compassion, and joy as you read this book.

PART ONE

Understanding
Your Moods

♦

You Can Change *the* *Way You* Feel

Many people believe that their bad moods result from factors beyond their control. They ask, "How can I possibly feel happy? My girlfriend rejected me. Women always put me down." Or they say, "How can I feel good about myself? I'm not particularly successful. I don't have a glamorous career. I'm just an inferior person, and that's reality." Some people attribute their blue moods to their hormones or body chemistry. Others believe that their sour outlook results from some childhood event that has long been forgotten and buried deep in their unconscious. Some people argue that it's realistic to feel bad because they're ill or have recently experienced a personal disappointment. Others attribute their bad moods to the state of the world—the shaky economy, the bad weather, taxes, traffic jams, the threat of nuclear war. Misery, they argue, is inevitable.

Of course there's some truth in all of these ideas. Our feelings undoubtedly are influenced by external events, by our body chemistry, and by conflicts and traumas from the past. However, these theories are based on the notion that our feelings are beyond our control. If you say, "I just can't help the way I feel," you will only make yourself a victim of your misery—and you'll be fooling yourself, because you *can* change the way you feel.

If you want to feel better, you must realize that your thoughts and attitudes—not external events—create your feelings. You can learn to change the way you think, feel, and behave in the here-and-now. That simple but revolutionary principle can help you change your life.

To illustrate the important relationship between your thoughts and your moods, consider the many ways you might react to a compliment. Suppose I told you, "I really like you. I think you're a neat person." How would you feel? Some people would feel pleased and happy. Others might feel sad and guilty. Some people would feel embarrassed, and some would react with anger and annoyance. What explains such different reactions? It's because of the different ways they might *think* about the compliment. If you feel sad, you're probably thinking, "Ah, Dr. Burns is just saying that to make me feel good. He's just trying to be nice to me, but he doesn't really mean it." If you feel annoyed, you might be thinking, "He's flattering me. He must be trying to get something from me. Why isn't he more honest?" If you feel good about the compliment, you're likely to be thinking, "Gee, Dr. Burns likes me. That's great!" In each case the external event—the compliment—is the same. The way you feel results entirely from the way you think about it. That's what I mean when I say that your *thoughts* create your moods.

This is also true when something bad happens. Suppose someone you respect criticizes you. How would you feel? You may feel guilty and inadequate if you tell yourself you're no good and the problem is all your fault. You will feel anxious and worried if you tell yourself that the other person is looking down on you and is going to reject you. You'll feel angry if you tell yourself that it's all their fault and they have no right to say such unfair things. If you have a good sense of self-esteem, you might feel curious and try to understand what the other person is thinking and feeling. In each case, your reaction will depend on the way you think about the criticism. The messages you give yourself have an enormous impact on your emotions. And what's even more important, by learning to change your thoughts, you can change the way you feel.

The powerful methods described in this book have helped thousands of people take greater charge of their emotions, their careers, and their personal relationships—and they can help you. It's not always easy. Considerable effort and persistence are sometimes required to snap out of a bad mood. But it *can* be done! The techniques are practical and straightforward, and you can make them work for you.

This new approach is called "cognitive behavior therapy" because you learn to change the way you *think*, the way you *behave*, and the way you *feel*. A "cognition" is simply a thought. You may have noticed that when you feel depressed or anxious you are thinking about yourself and your life in a pessimistic, self-critical way. You may wake up feeling discouraged and tell yourself, "Ugh! What's the point in getting out of bed?" You may feel anxious and inferior at a social gathering because you tell yourself, "I don't have anything witty or interesting to say." Cognitive therapists believe that these negative thinking patterns actually *cause* you to feel depressed and anxious. When you think about your problems in a more positive and realistic way, you will experience greater self-esteem, intimacy, and productivity.

If you want to break out of a bad mood, you must first understand that every type of negative feeling results from a specific kind of negative thought. *Sadness and depression* result from thoughts of loss. You think you have lost something important to your self-esteem. Perhaps you were rejected by someone you cared a great deal about. You might have retired or lost your job or missed out on an important career opportunity. *Frustration* results from unfulfilled expectations. You tell yourself that things should be different from the way they really are. For example, "That train shouldn't be so late when I'm in such a hurry. Darn it!" *Anxiety and panic* result from thoughts of danger. Before you give a speech in front of a group of people, you feel nervous because you anticipate that your voice will tremble and your mind will go blank. You imagine that you'll make a fool of yourself. *Guilt* results from the thought that you are bad. When a friend makes an unreasonable request, you may feel a twinge of guilt and think, "A really nice person would say yes." Then you may agree to something that isn't really in your best interest. *Feelings of inferiority* result from the thought that you're inadequate in comparison with others. You think, "She's so much better looking than I am" or "He's so much smarter and more successful. What's wrong with me?" *Anger* results from feelings of unfairness. You tell yourself that someone is treating you unjustly or trying to take advantage of you.

The list on pages 6–7 illustrates the connection between your thoughts and your feelings. Study this table carefully. It will help

YOUR THOUGHTS AND YOUR FEELINGS

Emotion	Thoughts that lead to this emotion
Sadness or depression	Thoughts of loss: a romantic rejection, the death of a loved one, the loss of a job, or the failure to achieve an important personal goal.
Guilt or shame	You believe that you've hurt someone or that you've failed to live up to your own moral standards. Guilt results from self-condemnation, whereas shame involves the fear that you'll lose face when others find out about what you did.
Anger, irritation, annoyance, or resentment	You feel that someone is treating you unfairly or trying to take advantage of you.
Frustration	Life falls short of your expectations. You insist that things should be different. It might be your own performance ("I shouldn't have made that mistake"), what someone else does ("He should've been on time!"), or an event ("Why does the traffic always slow down when I'm in a hurry?").
Anxiety, worry, fear, nervousness, or panic	You believe you're in danger because you think something bad is about to happen—"What if the plane crashes?" "What if my mind goes blank when I give my talk in front of all those people?" "What if this chest pain is the start of a heart attack?"
Inferiority or inadequacy	You compare yourself to others and conclude that you're not as good as they are because you're not as talented, attractive, charming, successful, intelligent. "She's really got what it takes. She's so cute. All the men are chasing her. I'm just average. There's nothing very special about me."
Loneliness	You tell yourself that you're bound to feel unhappy because you're alone and you aren't getting enough love and attention from others.

Emotion	Thoughts that lead to this emotion
Hopelessness or discouragement	You feel convinced that your problems will go on forever and that things will never improve. "I'll never get over this depression," or "I just can't lose weight and keep it off," or "I'll never find a good job," or "I'll be alone forever."

you understand why you're in the mood you're in, and this can make it easier to change the way you feel.

What you will learn here is that even though you are convinced they are valid, most of the negative thoughts that make you feel bad are distorted and unrealistic. Example: Following a romantic breakup or divorce you tell yourself, "It's all my fault. I must be unlovable. I'll never be close to anyone." You feel so rotten that it seems absolutely true, and you think your life is over. Months later you begin to date and you start to feel close to people again. It suddenly dawns on you that you are lovable after all, that you *weren't* entirely responsible for the breakup of your relationship. You wonder how in the world you could have believed all the put-downs you were heaping on yourself. But at the time, your negative thoughts seemed completely valid.

That's one of the peculiar things about bad moods—we often fool ourselves and create misery by telling ourselves things *that simply are not true.* And the strange thing is that we usually don't have the vaguest suspicion that we're being conned by our misery and self-doubt.

The ten forms of distorted thinking that lead to negative moods are listed on pages 8–11. Study this list carefully, because you will refer to it frequently as you do the exercises in the book. Many people have told me that this list changed their lives.

One disclaimer is necessary. There are many times when negative feelings are healthy and appropriate. Learning when to accept these feelings and how to cope with a realistically negative situation is just as important as learning how to rid yourself of distorted thoughts and feelings. If a loved one is seriously ill, you will feel concerned. These sad feelings are a sign of caring. If the house you had your heart set on is sold to someone who made a slightly higher offer, it is natural to feel disappointed. If you're having an argument with your spouse, you will probably feel angry and hurt. If you have to give a speech or

THE TEN FORMS OF TWISTED THINKING

1. All-or-nothing thinking

You see things in black-or-white categories. If a situation falls short of perfect, you see it as a total failure. When a young woman on a diet ate a spoonful of ice cream, she told herself, "I've blown my diet completely." This thought upset her so much that she gobbled down an entire quart of ice cream!

2. Overgeneralization

You see a single negative event, such as a romantic rejection or a career reversal, as a never-ending pattern of defeat by using words such as "always" or "never" when you think about it. A depressed salesman became terribly upset when he noticed bird dung on the windshield of his car. He told himself, "Just my luck! Birds are *always* crapping on my car!"

3. Mental filter

You pick out a single negative detail and dwell on it exclusively, so that your vision of all of reality becomes darkened, like the drop of ink that discolors a beaker of water. Example: You receive many positive comments about your presentation to a group of associates at work, but one of them says something mildly critical. You obsess about his reaction for days and ignore all the positive feedback.

4. Discounting the positive

You reject positive experiences by insisting they "don't count." If you do a good job, you may tell yourself that it wasn't good enough or that anyone could have done as well. Discounting the positive takes the joy out of life and makes you feel inadequate and unrewarded.

5. Jumping to conclusions	You interpret things negatively when there are no facts to support your conclusion. **Mind reading:** Without checking it out, you arbitrarily conclude that someone is reacting negatively to you. **Fortune-telling:** You predict that things will turn out badly. Before a test you may tell yourself, "I'm really going to blow it. What if I flunk?" If you're depressed you may tell yourself, "I'll never get better."
6. Magnification	You exaggerate the importance of your problems and shortcomings, or you minimize the importance of your desirable qualities. This is also called the "binocular trick."
7. Emotional reasoning	You assume that your negative emotions necessarily reflect the way things really are: "I feel terrified about going on airplanes. It must be very dangerous to fly." Or "I feel guilty. I must be a rotten person." Or "I feel angry. This proves I'm being treated unfairly." Or "I feel so inferior. This means I'm a second-rate person." Or "I feel hopeless. I must really be hopeless."
8. "Should statements"	You tell yourself that things *should* be the way you hoped or expected them to be. After playing a difficult piece on the piano, a gifted pianist told herself, "I shouldn't have made so many mistakes." This made her feel so disgusted that she quit practicing for several days. "Musts," "oughts" and "have tos" are similar offenders. "Should statements" that are directed against yourself lead to guilt and frustration. Should statements that are directed against other people or the world in

general lead to anger and frustration: "He shouldn't be so stubborn and argumentative."

Many people try to motivate themselves with shoulds and shouldn'ts, as if they were delinquents who had to be punished before they could be expected to do anything. "I shouldn't eat that doughnut." This usually doesn't work because all these shoulds and musts make you feel rebellious and you get the urge to do just the opposite. Dr. Albert Ellis has called this "*must*erbation." I call it the "shouldy" approach to life.

9. Labeling

Labeling is an extreme form of all-or-nothing thinking. Instead of saying "I made a mistake," you attach a negative label to yourself: "I'm a loser." You might also label yourself "a fool" or "a failure" or "a jerk." Labeling is quite irrational because you are not the same as what you do. Human beings exist, but "fools," "losers," and "jerks" do not. These labels are just useless abstractions that lead to anger, anxiety, frustration, and low self-esteem.

You may also label others. When someone does something that rubs you the wrong way, you may tell yourself: "He's an S.O.B." Then you feel that the problem is with that person's "character" or "essence" instead of with their thinking or behavior. You see them as totally bad. This makes you feel hostile and hopeless about improving things and leaves little room for constructive communication.

10. Personalization and blame	Personalization occurs when you hold yourself personally responsible for an event that isn't entirely under your control. When a woman received a note that her child was having difficulties at school, she told herself, "This shows what a bad mother I am," instead of trying to pinpoint the cause of the problem so that she could be helpful to her child. When another woman's husband beat her, she told herself, "If only I were better in bed, he wouldn't beat me." Personalization leads to guilt, shame, and feelings of inadequacy. Some people do the opposite. They blame other people or their circumstances for their problems, and they overlook ways that they might be contributing to the problem: "The reason my marriage is so lousy is because my spouse is totally unreasonable." Blame usually doesn't work very well because other people will resent being scapegoated and they will just toss the blame right back in your lap. It's like the game of hot potato— no one wants to get stuck with it.

start a new job or ask your boss for a raise, you will probably feel a little nervous. It's often best to accept these negative feelings.

I don't believe that you should try to be happy all the time, or in *total* control of your feelings. That would just be a perfectionistic trap. You cannot always be completely rational and objective. Certainly I'm not! I have my share of shortcomings, my dark moments of self-doubt, my periods of irritability. I believe these experiences give us the opportunity for growth, for intimacy, and for a deeper comprehension of what it means to be human.

Self-Awareness Exercise

Let's summarize the most important ideas in this chapter. First, you learned that your thoughts, and not external events, create your moods. Second, you learned that specific kinds of negative thoughts cause specific kinds of negative emotions. For example, the belief that you are in danger will make you anxious or frightened. Third, you learned that the negative thoughts that make you depressed, anxious, guilty, angry, or frustrated are frequently distorted and unrealistic, even though they seem absolutely valid. Recognizing the vital connections between your thoughts and your emotions is the first step in breaking out of a bad mood. This exercise will make you more aware of the kinds of distorted thoughts that are most frequently associated with different kinds of negative feelings, including anger (page 12), anxiety (page 17), stress (page 19), and depression (page 23), as well as for bad habits such as alcoholism (page 25).

ANGER

Think of a time when you were angry or irritated. Write down a brief description of the situation that made you angry. What actually happened? Were you upset with yourself or someone else?

_____

_____

_____

_____

_____

Did you fill that out? I have found that some patients—and some readers—do the written self-help exercises that are so crucial to the success of cognitive therapy. Others do not—they seem to be along for the ride. Research has indicated that people who actually do the written exercises improve far more than those who do not. Do you want to feel better and change your life as a result of reading this book? If your answer is yes, then I want you to fill in the description before you continue reading.

Now I want you to tell me about the negative thoughts and feelings you were having in the situation you described. Did you feel hurt? Annoyed? Frustrated? What messages were you giving yourself? Did you tell yourself that the other person was a self-centered bum or that they were being unfair to you? Describe your negative thoughts and feelings here:

_____

_____

_____

_____

A common irritating situation is when someone is late. The later they become, the angrier you get. By the time they finally show up you feel as if you could strangle them. When George was late coming home from work, Marge felt angry and had these thoughts: "He's *never* on time. What a jerk! If he cared about me, he wouldn't be so late. He should be home by now."

Let's examine these thoughts and see if they contain any distortions. Her first thought is "He's never on time." Review the list on pages 8–11 and see if you can find the distortion in this thought. This one is fairly easy. Put your ideas here before you read on:

_____

_____

It's an example of an "overgeneralization," because Marge sees this negative event as a never-ending pattern of defeat. George may *sometimes* be late, or he may be *frequently* late, but he's not *always* late. If you called it the "mental filter," you would also be right. Marge is concentrating on all the times George is late and ignoring or filtering out the times he's on time.

The problem with overgeneralizing is that it will make the situation seem worse than it really is. This may trigger a pointless argument when George comes home. Marge might accuse George of "always being late." He will feel indignant and insist, quite rightly, that he isn't "always late." They'll get into a frustrating argument that misses the point entirely. They'll both feel misunderstood and absolutely convinced that the other one is to blame. Do you recognize this pattern? If you've ever been involved in a marital squabble; I'm sure you know how exasperating this type of interaction can be.

Marge's second thought is "What a jerk!" What distortions are there in this one? Put your ideas here after you review the Ten Forms of Twisted Thinking:

_____

_____

This is an example of "labeling," because Marge is attacking George rather than what George did. You might also view it as an example of "all-or-nothing thinking" since Marge is writing him off entirely. Being late may have been thoughtless or it may have been due to factors beyond George's control, such as a traffic jam on the expressway. Either way, it doesn't make George "a jerk." Contrary to popular opinion, there are actually no "jerks" in the United States at this time. There's certainly plenty of jerky behavior, however!

What is the main distortion in Marge's third thought, "If he cared about me, he wouldn't be so late"? Put your ideas here:

_____

The major distortion in this thought is "mind reading" or "jumping to conclusions." Marge is automatically assuming that a lack of caring explains why George is late. Although he may not care, there could be other explanations for why he's late. Can you think of any possibilities?

List them here:

1. _____

_____

2. _____

_____

3. _____

_____

Here are several possibilities: George might be working late because his boss is pressuring him about a deadline. He may be
working overtime so he and Marge can save up enough money for a
down payment on a new house. Or he may be annoyed with Marge
about something. If so, it may mean that George and Marge don't
deal with conflicts openly and directly. This wouldn't mean that
George "doesn't care"—his anger would probably mean that he *does*
care and he feels hurt. If this were the case, George and Marge could
benefit from some communication training so they can learn to share
their feelings more openly instead of acting them out through nagging and arguing.

Marge's last thought was "He should be home now." What is the
distortion in this thought? Check the list on pages 8–11 and put your
ideas here:

_____

This is a classic "should statement." It might be better for Marge
to tell herself that she'd *like* George to be on time. This would sound
less judgmental and it would create a less antagonistic atmosphere for
discussing the problem.

Some readers may feel that I am attacking Marge. You may want
to defend her and think, "What if George *is* a jerk? Maybe he's
having an affair with someone. Maybe she has the right to be angry!"
Certainly there are times when anger is healthy and appropriate.
There will be other times when your thinking is way off base and
your anger is not particularly valid. And even when someone is
treating you unfairly, your feelings will still result from the way you
think about what's happening. When you think about a genuinely
upsetting situation in a distorted way, your feelings will get blown
up out of proportion so much that the real problem becomes harder
to resolve. If you're willing to think about the problem more realis-

tically, you'll find it far easier to express your feelings in a constructive way so that the other person will listen and not get so defensive.

Marge just doesn't have enough information yet. She hasn't found out the facts, but she has already convicted and sentenced George. This attitude of blame will guarantee that there will be a fight when George gets home. Her thoughts are so inflammatory that she'll overreact. This will simply make the problem worse. She may pout and cry or accuse him of being a thoughtless jerk. I can't imagine that this will lead to a productive exchange of feelings. Can you?

What *could* Marge say when George comes home? Put your ideas here:

_____

_____

_____

_____

_____

She might say, "George, I was really worried about you, and I'm angry because you're so late and you didn't call. I cooked this great meal for you because I love you, and when you didn't show up on time I felt really hurt. Can you tell me what's going on? Did we have a misunderstanding about when you were going to be home, or what?" This statement is far more powerful than telling him off, because she is sharing how she feels without hurling accusations or putting George down. She invites him to explain what the problem is instead of acting as if she already knew.

Now review the angry thoughts you wrote down at the beginning of this section. See if you can identify any of the distortions that are most frequently associated with anger. Look for:

- **Should statements:** "He shouldn't have said that" or "She's got no right to feel that way."
- **Labeling:** "He's an S.O.B."
- **Mind reading:** "She obviously doesn't have any respect for me."
- **Blaming:** "This is entirely his fault."
- **All-or-nothing thinking:** "I'm right and she's wrong about this."
- **Overgeneralization:** "All she ever thinks about is herself."

ANXIETY AND FEAR

Think of a time when you felt anxious or worried. What was happening at the time? Were you nervous about an important test? An airplane flight? A talk you had to give? Perhaps you were worrying about your health or a bill you forgot to pay. Describe the situation that made you feel nervous:

_____

_____

_____

_____

Next, try to identify your negative thoughts. What were you telling yourself? What were you thinking? Perhaps you were thinking that something bad was going to happen or were worrying about what other people would think of you. Record your negative thoughts here:

_____

_____

_____

_____

Henry felt anxious before an important job interview. I have listed his negative thoughts in the left-hand column. Cover up the right-hand column and see if you can identify the distortions in each of his thoughts. You can refer to the list on pages 8–11.

Negative thoughts	Distortions
1. I'll probably blow it. My mind will go blank and I won't be able to think of anything to say.	1. This thought is an example of "fortune-telling," because Henry is predicting that something bad will happen. Fortune-telling is the commonest distortion that leads to anxiety.

Negative thoughts	Distortions
2. He's probably just giving me the interview out of courtesy because he knows my father.	2. This is an example of "mind reading." Henry is assuming he knows how his prospective boss is thinking.
3. I don't really have anything to offer. He probably has a lot of applicants who are much better than I am.	3. This is an example of "disqualifying the positive," because Henry is overlooking his positive qualities. He's also "jumping to conclusions" since he's assuming that all the other applicants are more qualified than he is. Henry has no information about this.
4. I'll probably make a fool of myself.	4. This is an example of "labeling," since Henry is calling himself "a fool." We all occasionally say or do foolish things, but this makes us human beings, not "fools." This is also an example of "fortune-telling" since he's predicting a bad outcome.
5. That would be terrible.	5. Henry's last negative thought is an example of "magnification." Henry is blowing the importance of this particular interview way out of proportion. The Holocaust of World War II was "terrible." If you have a bad interview and you don't get a particular job, it isn't "terrible," it's simply "unfortunate." Not getting the job could still be a good learning experience. Henry may need to go out on as many as ten interviews before he finds the job that's right for him. His entire future does not hang on any one interview.

Now review the anxious thoughts you wrote down at the beginning of this section. See if you can identify any of the distortions that are most frequently associated with anxiety, panic, or nervousness:

* Fortune-telling: "What if I get so nervous that I pass out or crack up?"
* Mind reading: "People would look down on me if they knew how nervous and insecure I feel."
* Should statements: "I *shouldn't* feel so panicky. This is abnormal. What's wrong with me?"
* Emotional reasoning: "I *feel* frightened. Therefore it must be very dangerous to be on this airplane."
* Magnification: "This is *awful*! What if I lose control?"

Write down the distortions in your negative thoughts here:

1. _____

2. _____

3. _____

4. _____

STRESS

Harry is a successful attorney who feels tense the moment he walks into his office each morning. He can't seem to relax or enjoy his work. The following negative thoughts flood his mind when he sits down at his desk. Cover up the right-hand column and see if you can identify the distortions in them, using the list on pages 8–11 as your guide.

Negative thoughts	Distortions
1. This is awful! Just think of everything I have to do! I just have too much work.	1. This is an example of "all-or-nothing thinking," because Harry's dwelling on everything he has to do rather than the specific things he has to do this morning. You could also call this "magnification."

Negative thoughts	Distortions
2. There's always so much work left at the end of the day!	2. The second negative thought is the "mental filter," since Harry thinks about all the things he hasn't done and overlooks the many things he has done.
3. I'll never catch up.	3. This is an example of "all-or-nothing thinking." Harry is actually on schedule in his preparation for the majority of his cases. A busy and successful attorney is not supposed to be completely caught up. The reason he has so much work is that he has a prosperous practice with a constant flow of new clients. It's actually good that he's never completely caught up!
4. I'll make a mistake or forget to do something important.	4. This is an example of "fortune-telling," because he's telling himself that he's going to foul up. He'd feel better if he told himself that he was doing well and was going to have a productive day.
5. What if I lose this case?	5. This is another example of "fortune-telling." Every lawyer wins some trials and loses others, but Harry's track record has been excellent. Since he has prepared a strong case for this particular client, it would be more realistic to tell himself that the odds are in his favor and that things will probably turn out well.
6. My client will be teed off at me if I lose.	6. This involves "mind reading" and "fortune-telling." Harry's assuming that he will lose and that if he

Negative thoughts	Distortions
	does his client will be dissatisfied. The majority of Harry's clients have told him they were pleased with his work. Harry told me that when he has lost, his clients have usually been even more appreciative because they recognized that Harry did the best possible job in a difficult situation.
7. Then I won't get any new cases.	7. This thought is an extreme example of "fortune-telling." In fact, Harry's had so many referrals recently that he can hardly keep up.
8. Then I'll lose money and end up destitute.	8. I'm sure it's obvious to you that this is one more example of "fortune-telling." Harry's income has been growing substantially. He will continue to enjoy a comfortable standard of living, and he will not end up in the poorhouse!

See if you can think of a time when you felt stressed. You may have been pressured by your boss about a deadline at work or overwhelmed by all your commitments to your family, your church, or your friends. Describe that stressful situation here:

_____

_____

_____

Now I'd like you to tell me what kinds of negative feelings you had when you felt stressed. Simply check "yes" or "no" for each of the following:

Yes	No	
1. _____	_____	Sad or depressed
2. _____	_____	Nervous, panicky, worried, anxious, or fearful
3. _____	_____	Annoyed, irritable, resentful, or angry
4. _____	_____	Frustrated
5. _____	_____	Pressured, tense, or stressed
6. _____	_____	Guilty or ashamed
7. _____	_____	Hopeless or discouraged
8. _____	_____	Inadequate or inferior
9. _____	_____	Exhausted, tired, drained, or overwhelmed
10. _____	_____	Bored, unmotivated, or uninterested
11. _____	_____	Lonely, unloved, or alone
12. _____	_____	Other (describe any additional emotions): _____

Now write down several of your negative thoughts in the left-hand column like the example on pages 8–11.

Negative thoughts	Distortions
1. _____	_____
_____	_____
2. _____	_____
_____	_____
3. _____	_____
_____	_____

Review Table 2 and see if you can identify the distortions in each negative thought. Record the distortions in the right-hand column. Look for:

- **Fortune-telling:** "I'll never get everything done."
- **All-or-nothing thinking:** "I've got to do a perfect job."
- **Should statements:** "I shouldn't make any mistakes."
- **Disqualifying the positive:** "I didn't get anything done today."
- **Mind reading:** "My boss will think this is crummy."
- **Magnification:** "I've got so much work to do."

DEPRESSION

Joanne is a 28-year-old woman who lives in New York and works as an options trader. As you probably know, options traders buy and sell futures on stocks, and they can make or lose vast amounts of money in incredibly short periods of time. The profession can make you or break you, and either way, it's enormously stressful.

Joanne recently formed a partnership with a man who put up $100,000 as capital for her to invest. They agreed to share the profits. Joanne decided to pursue a conservative, low-risk investment strategy. For the past three months, Joanne made $4,000 a month in profits. For several months before that, she had averaged $12,000. She was distraught because of the decrease in profits and felt suicidal.

I was curious why Joanne was so despondent and asked her to write down the negative thoughts that made her feel so bad. They included, among others, the thought that she was a failure and the belief that when her partner found out about her shoddy performance he would be terribly disappointed and fire her. Can you identify the distortions in her thoughts? Check the Ten Forms of Twisted Thinking and put your ideas here:

1. _____

2. _____

3. _____

4. _____

5. _____

One of the distortions is "all-or-nothing thinking": Joanne thinks that if she isn't doing stupendously and making a fortune every single month, then she's a total failure. This may seem ridiculous to you, since $4,000 profit per month is hardly a "failure." However, it feels like a failure to Joanne because of her perfectionist attitude. She reasons, "I feel like a total failure, therefore I must really be one." This illustrates a second distortion, "emotional reasoning," since Joanne assumes that her negative feelings necessarily reflect the way things really are.

A third distortion is "fortune-telling," since Joanne is predicting that the return of the investment will continue to be mediocre. There's no real evidence for this. You could also call this an "overgeneralization," since she imagines that the low-profit months will continue endlessly.

A fourth distortion would be "should statements." Joanne is telling herself she should always make big profits. But if you look at her overall performance, this is clearly an unrealistic expectation. She's had some $12,000 months and she's had some $4,000 months, so her average monthly profit is actually $8,000. That's not bad—it actually amounts to an annual rate of appreciation of nearly 100 percent. She simply hasn't accepted the fact that market conditions are inherently unpredictable, and that her income will fluctuate greatly from month to month. There's no such thing as an investor who *always* scores big. Joanne would do well to stop demanding so much of herself and to make her expectations more realistic.

She's also involved in "mind reading." She assumes with absolutely no evidence that her partner will be as angry and disappointed as she is, and that he will fire her. As part of her psychotherapy homework, I insisted that she talk things over with her partner. Joanne was quite reluctant to do this and procrastinated for weeks.

I twisted her arm and she finally agreed. Joanne was amazed to learn that her partner was quite satisfied with her performance. He told Joanne she could feel free to take even greater risks, and that even if she lost the entire $100,000 she'd still have a job.

You can see that the solution to Joanne's depression involved a combination of self-acceptance and change. Joanne had to *change* her distorted thinking patterns so she could assess her situation more realistically. She wasn't making an absolute killing, but she wasn't a complete failure either. At the same time, she had to *accept* the fact that she wouldn't always be a big winner, and that good months would be followed by bad ones—and vice versa. Sometimes more humble and modest expectations can be tremendously liberating. Although it may stimulate our egos to think we're so brilliant and hardworking that we will always succeed, carrying the burden of having to be so great and so perfect can be overwhelmingly frustrating and lonely.

TEMPTATIONS

Many people have problems controlling their impulses. They can't resist temptations like overeating, smoking, gambling, drinking too much, using drugs, or having sex with the wrong person. Can you think of a time when you succumbed to a temptation? The thoughts that tempted you to give in to these bad habits probably contained positive distortions that are mirror images of negative ones listed on pages 8–11.

Frank had the habit of eating and drinking too much. His family physician advised him that his drinking was a serious problem and that he was in the early stages of cirrhosis of the liver. Frank was overweight and had elevated triglycerides and blood cholesterol levels, along with increased blood pressure. This meant that he was in a high-risk group for a heart attack. He was chronically stressed and irritable, and overeating and drinking were his way of coping with the tension in his life.

Although every morning his "rational self" felt it was a good idea to diet and to quit drinking, Frank's "emotional self" would decide to have a drink—and then another, and another—every night when he came home from work. This urge to drink was caused by positive tempting thoughts. I've indicated the positive distortions in each thought in the right-hand column.

Positive thoughts	Distortions
1. Gee, I'll really feel good if I have a beer now. And it will taste so good.	1. This is an example of positive "fortune-telling," since Frank is predicting something that isn't entirely true. Although Frank usually experiences a brief mood elevation when he starts to drink, he

Positive thoughts	Distortions
	nearly always ends up feeling worse because his drinking gets out of hand. After three or four beers he gets angry and depressed and starts to argue with his wife. He ends up flying off the handle and feels guilty. He wakes up with a hangover and a lack of self-respect the next morning.
2. I really shouldn't have that beer.	2. This is a "should statement." The problem with saying "I shouldn't" is that it sounds moralistic and controlling. This makes Frank feel rebellious and it increases his urge to have a beer.
3. I'll only have one beer. That won't hurt me.	3. This is another example of positive "fortune-telling," because Frank is predicting something very unrealistic. While it's true that an occasional beer is harmless, Frank won't stop after just one. Once he starts drinking, his inhibitions will disappear and he will quietly devour one or two six-packs.
4. Life is so boring. I deserve a little fun.	4. This is "emotional reasoning." Frank may deserve a little fun, but his life won't be much fun if he keeps drinking. His alcoholism makes him chronically depressed and bored with his life and keeps him from getting close to his wife.
5. Gee, that beer tasted good! I think I'll have another one. I'll feel even better!	5. This is more "emotional reasoning" and "fortune-telling." One drink may be relaxing, but five or ten drinks will make Frank irritable and unhappy.

Can you think of any temptations that you succumb to, such as smoking, overeating, drinking excessively, using drugs, or shoplifting? Describe the problem here:

_____

_____

_____

_____

_____

Can you think of the positive thoughts that cross your mind when you feel tempted to do this? Write them down in the left-hand column and number them. Then see if you can identify the positive distortions in these thoughts and record them in the right-hand column.

Positive thoughts	Distortions
_____	_____
_____	_____
_____	_____
_____	_____
_____	_____
_____	_____
_____	_____
_____	_____

OTHER EMOTIONS

Distorted negative thoughts can be associated with any emotion such as loneliness, guilt, jealousy, depression, or frustration. Maybe you're mad at yourself because you snapped at a friend during a moment of irritability and fatigue. Maybe you feel depressed because you didn't do as well on a test as you had hoped. Write down a brief description of any situation that upset you. It could be a recent problem or something that happened many years ago:

_____

_____

_____

_____

How did you feel? Record your negative feelings here:

	Yes	No	
1.	_____	_____	Sad or depressed
2.	_____	_____	Nervous, panicky, worried, anxious, or fearful
3.	_____	_____	Annoyed, irritable, resentful, or angry
4.	_____	_____	Frustrated
5.	_____	_____	Pressured, tense, or stressed
6.	_____	_____	Guilty or ashamed
7.	_____	_____	Hopeless or discouraged
8.	_____	_____	Inadequate or inferior
9.	_____	_____	Exhausted, tired, drained, or overwhelmed
10.	_____	_____	Bored, unmotivated, or uninterested
11.	_____	_____	Lonely, unloved, or alone
12.	_____	_____	Other (describe any additional emotions): _____

Now, write down your negative thoughts and number them. Then look for the distortions in these thoughts, using the list on pages 8–11 as a guide.

Negative thoughts	Distortions
1. _____	_____
_____	_____
2. _____	_____
_____	_____
3. _____	_____
_____	_____
4. _____	_____
_____	_____

I don't expect you to be able to *change* your thoughts and feelings yet. I just want you to practice tuning in with your "third ear" so you can begin to learn more about the vital connection between the way you think and the way you feel. This is the crucial first step.

Answers to Questions Most Commonly Asked About Cognitive Therapy:

Doesn't cognitive therapy just lead to intellectual change without changing how a person really feels on a gut level? No. The purpose of cognitive therapy is to transform your emotions and your perceptions of yourself and your life. Providing rationalizations or intellectual excuses for things is not a part of cognitive therapy. The purpose of the treatment is to develop profound feelings of joy and happiness.

What kinds of problems does cognitive therapy work best for? When does it not work well? Cognitive therapy is an excellent treatment for mood problems such as depression, anxiety, panic attacks, phobias, anger, guilt, and feelings of inferiority. The therapy can be exceptionally helpful for the kinds of problems that we all confront in the course of daily living. These include personal relationship problems, rejection, criticism, procrastination, and the fear of failure. The techniques can be extremely effective and often work rapidly, even without the use of medications.

Cognitive therapy alone is not especially effective for severe psychotic disorders such as schizophrenia or the manic phase of manic-depressive illness. As described in Chapter 3, manic-depressive illness is a cyclic mood disorder characterized by abnormal highs and episodes of deep depression. Manic-depressives frequently need treatment with medication. Effective psychotherapy is also a crucial aspect of the treatment. Cognitive therapy can help manic-depressives develop greater self-esteem so they can cope with personal problems more effectively.

Isn't it normal to feel depressed and angry? Isn't it ridiculous to think that people should be happy all the time? One of the greatest misconceptions about cognitive therapy is that you should try to feel happy all the time. Negative feelings are frequently healthy and appropriate. Sometimes it's best just to accept bad feelings and pamper yourself and ride things out until the clouds pass and you feel better again.

Isn't cognitive therapy just a little bit too simplistic? Just too good to be true? This sounds like the "Power of Positive Thinking"! The principles of cognitive therapy *are* extremely simple. The treatment is based on the idea that your thoughts and attitudes have a huge impact on the way you act and feel. The actual procedures to change your negative thinking patterns, however, are quite sophisticated and require hard work.

Do cognitive therapists promote the idea that you should make yourself happy and ignore other people's feelings? Some pop psychologists have created the impression that you should "do your own thing" and ignore how other people react to you. My own position is quite different. I believe that if you ignore other people's feelings, you will set yourself up for enormous problems in your relationships.

Many people are self-centered. They don't seem to care about people and they use others to achieve their own goals. They often appear to be extremely happy, and they sometimes achieve a considerable level of fame or success. In spite of the external trappings, however, they may feel lonely and insecure because they never learned how to accept themselves or to get close to others. I do not envy them.

By the same token, there is a profound difference between *wanting* other people's love and approval and *needing* their love and approval. If you *need* love and approval, you may be too dependent on other people and feel terribly afraid of conflict or criticism. When someone is angry with you, you may be too threatened to express your own feelings, because you are afraid the other person won't like you if you do, and you cannot truly hear what they say because their anger is so upsetting to you. Like the narcissist who cares only about himself, people who need too much love and approval may be unable to develop mature, open, caring relationships with others. They end up feeling desperate and alone because they have not learned to love themselves.

How does a cognitive therapist deal with subconscious attitudes and feelings? About two thirds of the patients I see in my practice have straightforward problems that can be dealt with in a fairly short time—say, fifteen to twenty-five sessions. These patients find the cognitive methods helpful, and they usually get excellent results. About one third appear to have subconscious fears that cause them to resist therapy. On one level they want to feel better, but on a deeper level they are afraid to change. They ask for help, but soon they resist the therapy. They complain that they aren't getting better, and yet they appear to sabotage the therapeutic process so that progress is extremely slow. For example, some patients refuse to do any of the self-help assignments between sessions, even though these assignments have been helpful to them.

These patients can be a real challenge. When they become more aware of the subconscious fears that are holding them back, they often develop the courage to move forward with their lives. When they finally recover, it's a real cause for celebration. One of my goals has been to learn more about this puzzling phenomenon of resistance and to develop more effective treatment. Part VI illustrates techniques that can help therapists motivate these patients and facilitate greater feelings of trust and rapport.

2
·
How to Measure Your Moods

In this chapter, you will find out if you have been feeling depressed or anxious, and how severe these problems are. In addition, you will learn the answers to the questions people most frequently ask about the causes and treatments of mood problems.

To help you determine if you are suffering from depression or anxiety, I have developed two mood tests, the Burns Anxiety Inventory (BAI) and the Burns Depression Checklist (BDC). Think of them as emotional thermometers that will show whether you have a mood "fever." You can complete and interpret either one of them in under two minutes. I want you to repeat each test weekly to chart your progress while you are reading this book. If you are in therapy, you may want to show your weekly scores to your therapist, just as the patients at my clinic do. When your scores go down, you have proof that you are feeling better. When your score on either mood test is 4 or less, you'll be feeling terrific.

The Burns Anxiety Inventory lists 33 common symptoms of anxiety. Fill out the BAI now. All you have to do is check off how much each symptom has been bothering you in the past week. Each symptom is scored 0 for "not at all," 1 for "somewhat," 2 for "moderately," and 3 for "a lot."

THE BURNS ANXIETY INVENTORY*

Instructions: The following is a list of symptoms that people sometimes have. Put a check (√) in the space to the right that best describes how much that symptom or problem has bothered you during the past week.

Symptom List CATEGORY I: ANXIOUS FEELINGS	0–NOT AT ALL	1–SOMEWHAT	2–MODERATELY	3–A LOT
1. Anxiety, nervousness, worry, or fear				
2. Feeling that things around you are strange, unreal, or foggy				
3. Feeling detached from all or part of your body				
4. Sudden unexpected panic spells				
5. Apprehension or a sense of impending doom				
6. Feeling tense, stressed, "uptight," or on edge				
CATEGORY II: ANXIOUS THOUGHTS				
7. Difficulty concentrating				
8. Racing thoughts or having your mind jump from one thing to the next				
9. Frightening fantasies or daydreams				
10. Feeling that you're on the verge of losing control				
11. Fears of cracking up or going crazy				
12. Fears of fainting or passing out				
13. Fears of physical illnesses or heart attacks or dying				
14. Concerns about looking foolish or inadequate in front of others				
15. Fears of being alone, isolated, or abandoned				

	0–NOT AT ALL	1–SOMEWHAT	2–MODERATELY	3–A LOT
16. Fears of criticism or disapproval				
17. Fears that something terrible is about to happen				

CATEGORY III: PHYSICAL SYMPTOMS

	0–NOT AT ALL	1–SOMEWHAT	2–MODERATELY	3–A LOT
18. Skipping or racing or pounding of the heart (sometimes called "palpitations")				
19. Pain, pressure, or tightness in the chest				
20. Tingling or numbness in the toes or fingers				
21. Butterflies or discomfort in the stomach				
22. Constipation or diarrhea				
23. Restlessness or jumpiness				
24. Tight, tense muscles				
25. Sweating not brought on by heat				
26. A lump in the throat				
27. Trembling or shaking				
28. Rubbery or "jelly" legs				
29. Feeling dizzy, lightheaded, or off balance				
30. Choking or smothering sensations or difficulty breathing				
31. Headaches or pains in the neck or back				
32. Hot flashes or cold chills				
33. Feeling tired, weak, or easily exhausted				

Add up your total score for the 33 symptoms and record it here: _____

Date: _____

After you have completed the BAI, add up your total score. It will be somewhere between 0 (if you answered "not at all" on all 33 symptoms) and 99 (if you answered "a lot" on all 33 symptoms). Use this key to interpret your score:

Total score	Degree of anxiety
0–4	Minimal or no anxiety
5–10	Borderline anxiety
11–20	Mild anxiety
21–30	Moderate anxiety
31–50	Severe anxiety
51–99	Extreme anxiety or panic

There is an extra copy of the Burns Anxiety Inventory on pages 43 and 44, along with an answer sheet. You can use the answer sheet to record your answers each week when you take the test. At the bottom, add up your score and put the date in the box provided. You can use the score to monitor the effects of drug therapy, psychotherapy, or the self-help exercises in this book.

If you like, you can take the BAI more frequently than once a week. If you take the test when you're feeling especially nervous and insecure, put a note to indicate this at the bottom of the answer sheet. For example, if your score was 67 during a panic attack, that would indicate an extreme level of anxiety. You could write "when at my worst" next to your score. Similarly, you may want to take the test when you're feeling your best. By comparing your best and worst scores, you will see the range of moods that you have recently experienced.

The Burns Depression Checklist can also be completed and scored in under two minutes.* As you can see, the BDC lists 15 common symptoms of depression. All you have to do is put a check to the right of each symptom to indicate whether it has recently bothered you "not at all" (scored 0), "slightly" (scored 1), "moderately" (scored 2), or "a lot" (scored 3).

---

*Some readers may recall that in Chapter Two of *Feeling Good: The New Mood Therapy,* I presented the Beck Depression Inventory (BDI). The BDI is a slightly different but excellent self-assessment test for depression. I developed the Burns Depression Checklist because the wording of several items on the BDI was not as clear to my patients.

THE BURNS DEPRESSION CHECKLIST*

Instructions: The following is a list of symptoms that people sometimes have. Put a check (√) in the space to the right that best describes how much that symptom or problem has bothered you during the past week.

	0—NOT AT ALL	1—SOMEWHAT	2—MODERATELY	3—A LOT
1. **Sadness:** Have you been feeling sad or down in the dumps?				
2. **Discouragement:** Does the future look hopeless?				
3. **Low self-esteem:** Do you feel worthless or think of yourself as a failure?				
4. **Inferiority:** Do you feel inadequate or inferior to others?				
5. **Guilt:** Do you get self-critical and blame yourself for everything?				
6. **Indecisiveness:** Do you have trouble making up your mind about things?				
7. **Irritability and frustration:** Have you been feeling resentful and angry a good deal of the time?				
8. **Loss of interest in life:** Have you lost interest in your career, your hobbies, your family, or your friends?				
9. **Loss of motivation:** Do you feel overwhelmed and have to push yourself hard to do things?				
10. **Poor self-image:** Do you think you're looking old or unattractive?				

*Copyright © 1984 by David D. Burns, M.D., from *The Feeling Good Handbook*, copyright © 1989

	0-NOT AT ALL	1-SOMEWHAT	2-MODERATELY	3-A LOT
11. Appetite changes: Have you lost your appetite? Or do you overeat or binge compulsively?				
12. Sleep changes: Do you suffer from insomnia and find it hard to get a good night's sleep? Or are you excessively tired and sleeping too much?				
13. Loss of libido: Have you lost your interest in sex?				
14. Hypochondriasis: Do you worry a great deal about your health?				
15. Suicidal impulses†: Do you have thoughts that life is not worth living or think that you might be better off dead?				

Add up your total score for the 15 symptoms and record it here: _____

Date: _____

†Anyone with suicidal urges should seek immediate consultation with a qualified psychiatrist or psychologist.

After you have completed the test, add up your total score. It will be somewhere between 0 (if you answered "not at all" for each of the 15 categories) and 45 (if you answered "a lot" for each one). Use this key to interpret your score.

Total score	Degree of depression
0–4	Minimal or no depression
5–10	Borderline depression
11–20	Mild depression
21–30	Moderate depression
31–45	Severe depression

There is an extra copy of the Burns Depression Checklist on pages 46 and 47, along with an answer sheet. You can use the answer sheet to record your answers each week when you take the BDC. At the bottom, add up your scores and enter the date. Ultimately, I would like your score on the BDC and the BAI to be under 5, but any reduction will be a positive sign of progress.

Many people are unclear about the difference between anxiety and depression, since the two feelings often go hand in hand. If your score is elevated on the anxiety test, it will probably also be elevated on the depression test, and vice versa. *Depression* is the feeling of loss. You feel defeated and discouraged because of something bad that's already happened. Maybe you feel you failed at work or were rejected by someone you loved. *Anxiety* is the feeling of fear. It has more to do with the future—you believe that some disaster is ready to strike at any moment. Anxiety is like hanging from the edge of a cliff by the tips of your fingers. Depression feels more like you've already fallen and you're lying at the bottom of the ravine with your arms and legs broken beyond repair.

Suppose you have an elevated score on one or both of these mood tests. Does this mean you're sick or neurotic? Absolutely not. Feelings of anxiety and depression are nearly universal. Almost everyone feels this way from time to time. While one of my main goals is to show you how to deal with these feelings more effectively, I also want to encourage you to *accept* your negative feelings. You will need to understand this paradox to overcome your anxiety. When you fight your negative feelings and refuse to accept them, they become more and more intense. In contrast, when you *accept* your feelings, they become far easier to deal with. You will learn more about this "acceptance paradox" as you read this book.

Some of these questions about anxiety and depression may have crossed your mind:

How accurate and reliable are the mood tests? Do people try to make themselves look better or worse than they really feel? Not in my experience. Even a small change of a few points from week to week is an indication that a person is feeling better or worse. Most people answer honestly, and the tests continue to be remarkably accurate over time. You can take them as frequently as you want.

You can monitor the effectiveness of your progress as you read this book if you take the depression and anxiety tests in this chapter once a week. If you are in therapy, show the results to your therapist. If the scores go down, you are improving. If the scores go up or stay the same, you haven't started to move forward yet. This is crucial information—I cannot imagine how therapy could be successful without this kind of "quality control." I ask my patients to show me their scores at the start of every session so I know how they're doing.

What is the difference between depression and healthy sadness? When a friend dies or you fail to achieve an important goal, it's normal to feel sad. These feelings are a part of life. Your grief shows that you're human. Depression is different from healthy sadness in many ways:

- Depression involves a loss of self-esteem.
- Depression goes on and on.
- People who are depressed may not function productively.
- Depression is not realistic, and always results from distorted thoughts.
- Depression is an illness.
- Depression feels hopeless, even though the prognosis is excellent.

When should a person seek professional help? You should seek professional help if you have been unsuccessful in your own efforts to overcome a mood problem and you feel stuck. We all get upset when something disappointing happens, but we generally bounce back and feel good again in a few days. For some people this natural recovery can be very delayed, and the feelings of depression and anxiety may persist for weeks, months, years, or even decades. A good psychiatrist or psychologist can often speed up the process of healing.

What can I do to help a loved one who feels depressed? The techniques in this book are intended to help you with your own emotional problems. If you are not a therapist, do not attempt to apply these methods to someone else who is upset. Your efforts will probably backfire.

The best thing you can do to help someone who feels anxious or depressed is to show that you care. Try to understand them. Learn to listen so you can understand their problems and their feelings, using the three listening skills described in Chapter 19.

What can I do if a friend or family member needs psychiatric treatment? If someone is severely disturbed, you can recommend they go for therapy. If they resist, it's not your job to sell them on the idea or to force them to go. If you show concern and understanding, they may change their mind. Ultimately, people have the right to decide whether or not to seek treatment for themselves.

One exception would be if your child is depressed. As a parent, you have the right to bring them to a therapist. However, keep in mind that part of the problem may be a conflict between you and your spouse. Frequently when the parents are treated, the child gets better.

If someone is actively suicidal and threatening to kill themselves, you can bring them to a hospital or to a community mental health facility for evaluation. If that is impossible, you can call the police and ask for guidance.

How can I know if someone is suicidal? The answer to this question is simple: you ask them. Some readers may wonder, "But won't I push them over the brink if I ask?" No. The biggest mistake is *not* to ask. If a friend or loved one appears despondent or discouraged, ask these questions—in the same order—to find out if they are seriously considering suicide:

- **"Have you been feeling sad or unhappy?"** A "yes" will confirm that he or she has been feeling some depression.
- **"Do you ever feel hopeless? Does it seem as if things can never get better?"** Over half the people with depression feel hopeless. Feelings of hopelessness are often associated with suicidal thoughts.
- **"Do you have thoughts of death? Do you ever think you'd be better off dead?"** A "yes" indicates suicidal wishes but not necessarily suicidal plans. Many depressed people say they think they'd be better off dead and wish they'd die in their sleep or get killed in an accident. However, most of them say they have no intention of actually killing themselves.
- **"Do you ever have any actual suicidal impulses? Do you have any urge to kill yourself?"** A "yes" indicates an active desire to die. This is a more serious situation.
- **"Do you feel you can resist these impulses, or do they sometimes tempt you?"** If the person feels tempted, the situation is much more dangerous.
- **"Do you have any actual plans to kill yourself?"** If the answer is "yes," ask about their specific plans. What method have they chosen? Hanging? Jumping? Pills? A gun? Have they actually obtained the rope? What building do they plan to jump from? Although these questions may sound grotesque, they may save a life. The danger is greatest when the plans are clear and specific, when they have made actual preparations, and when the method they have chosen is clearly lethal.

- **"When do you plan to kill yourself?"** If the suicide attempt is a long way off—say, in five years—the danger is clearly not imminent and you have plenty of time to get the person into treatment. If they say they plan to kill themselves soon, the danger is grave and you must take immediate action.
- **"Is there anything that would hold you back, such as your family or your religious convictions?"** If they say that people would be better off without them and if they have no deterrents, suicide is much more likely.
- **"Have you ever made a suicide attempt in the past?"** Previous suicide attempts indicate that future attempts are more likely. Even if a previous attempt did not seem serious, the next attempt may be fatal. All suicide attempts should be taken seriously. If someone takes fifteen aspirin tablets in front of his or her spouse, they clearly don't have a strong desire to die at that moment. If someone scratches their wrists superficially and then calls the local hospital, they have mixed feelings about dying. These unsuccessful suicide attempts that are not immediately dangerous are sometimes viewed as "gestures" or manipulative attempts to get attention. This is often true, since suicidal individuals often feel unloved and angry. They frequently have a subconscious desire to get attention or to get back at lovers, family, and friends for not loving them enough. However, these suicidal "gestures" can be more dangerous than they seem, since many of these people ultimately do kill themselves.
- **"Would you be willing to talk to someone or seek help if you felt desperate? Whom would you talk to?"** If the person who feels suicidal is cooperative and has a clear plan to reach out for help, the danger is less than if they are stubborn, secretive, hostile, and unwilling to ask for help.

The answers to these questions will give you an idea of how severe the problem is. In my experience, people who feel suicidal are usually quite honest. If you discover that a friend or a loved one is actively suicidal, then they will need immediate emergency intervention. You may have to bring them to the emergency room of a local hospital or to a community mental health facility. If they refuse, you can call the police and ask for help. They can direct you to an emergency mental health facility where you can sign a warrant instructing the police to bring the person to a hospital to be evaluated. If the person continues to threaten suicide, he or she may be committed involuntarily for a three-day evaluation in most states.

This action will frequently anger the person who feels suicidal, but you could save a life! Bringing the anger to the surface may be intensely uncomfortable, but it's not nearly so horrible as the anguish and tragedy of a needless death. In addition, there is some evidence that people who express their anger may be less likely to make a sudden suicide attempt than people who keep their feelings bottled up.

My doctor did a blood test and said I had a chemical depression. Does this mean I need to be treated with drugs? Although people who are depressed often have abnormalities in their levels of a number of hormones, this does not necessarily mean that the depression is caused by a chemical imbalance, or that only medications should be used in treatment. (See Chapter 23 to learn more about the medications that can be used to treat anxiety and depression.)

I believe that good psychotherapy enhances the treatment of mood problems, and that people should never be treated with drugs alone. Ultimately the decision of whether or not to use medications is an individual one that needs to be discussed frankly with your therapist or physician.

THE BURNS ANXIETY INVENTORY*

Instructions: The following is a list of symptoms that people sometimes have. Put a check (√) in the space to the right that best describes how much that symptom or problem has bothered you during the past week. If you would like a weekly record of your progress, record your answers on the separate "Answer Sheet" instead of filling in the spaces on the right.

Symptom List	0–NOT AT ALL	1–SOMEWHAT	2–MODERATELY	3–A LOT
CATEGORY I: ANXIOUS FEELINGS				
1. Anxiety, nervousness, worry, or fear				
2. Feeling that things around you are strange, unreal, or foggy				
3. Feeling detached from all or part of your body				
4. Sudden unexpected panic spells				
5. Apprehension or a sense of impending doom				
6. Feeling tense, stressed, "uptight," or on edge				
CATEGORY II: ANXIOUS THOUGHTS				
7. Difficulty concentrating				
8. Racing thoughts or having your mind jump from one thing to the next				
9. Frightening fantasies or daydreams				
10. Feeling that you're on the verge of losing control				
11. Fears of cracking up or going crazy				
12. Fears of fainting or passing out				
13. Fears of physical illnesses or heart attacks or dying				
14. Concerns about looking foolish or inadequate in front of others				
15. Fears of being alone, isolated, or abandoned				

*Copyright © 1984 by David D. Burns, M.D., from *The Feeling Good Handbook*, copyright © 1989

	0–NOT AT ALL	1–SOMEWHAT	2–MODERATELY	3–A LOT
16. Fears of criticism or disapproval				
17. Fears that something terrible is about to happen				

CATEGORY III: PHYSICAL SYMPTOMS

	0–NOT AT ALL	1–SOMEWHAT	2–MODERATELY	3–A LOT
18. Skipping or racing or pounding of the heart (sometimes called "palpitations")				
19. Pain, pressure, or tightness in the chest				
20. Tingling or numbness in the toes or fingers				
21. Butterflies or discomfort in the stomach				
22. Constipation or diarrhea				
23. Restlessness or jumpiness				
24. Tight, tense muscles				
25. Sweating not brought on by heat				
26. A lump in the throat				
27. Trembling or shaking				
28. Rubbery or "jelly" legs				
29. Feeling dizzy, lightheaded, or off balance				
30. Choking or smothering sensations or difficulty breathing				
31. Headaches or pains in the neck or back				
32. Hot flashes or cold chills				
33. Feeling tired, weak, or easily exhausted				

Add up your total score for the 33 symptoms and record it here: _____

Date: _____

THE BURNS ANXIETY INVENTORY*
Answer Sheet

Instructions: Put a 0, 1, 2, or 3 in the space to the right after each of the 33 symptoms from the "Symptom List," depending on how much it has bothered you in the past week: 0 = Not at all; 1 = Somewhat; 2 = Moderately; 3 = A lot. Then add up your total score for all 33 symptoms at the bottom.

1.	1.	1.	1.	1.	1.	1.
2.	2.	2.	2.	2.	2.	2.
3.	3.	3.	3.	3.	3.	3.
4.	4.	4.	4.	4.	4.	4.
5.	5.	5.	5.	5.	5.	5.
6.	6.	6.	6.	6.	6.	6.
7.	7.	7.	7.	7.	7.	7.
8.	8.	8.	8.	8.	8.	8.
9.	9.	9.	9.	9.	9.	9.
10.	10.	10.	10.	10.	10.	10.
11.	11.	11.	11.	11.	11.	11.
12.	12.	12.	12.	12.	12.	12.
13.	13.	13.	13.	13.	13.	13.
14.	14.	14.	14.	14.	14.	14.
15.	15.	15.	15.	15.	15.	15.
16.	16.	16.	16.	16.	16.	16.
17.	17.	17.	17.	17.	17.	17.
18.	18.	18.	18.	18.	18.	18.
19.	19.	19.	19.	19.	19.	19.
20.	20.	20.	20.	20.	20.	20.
21.	21.	21.	21.	21.	21.	21.
22.	22.	22.	22.	22.	22.	22.
23.	23.	23.	23.	23.	23.	23.
24.	24.	24.	24.	24.	24.	24.
25.	25.	25.	25.	25.	25.	25.
26.	26.	26.	26.	26.	26.	26.
27.	27.	27.	27.	27.	27.	27.
28.	28.	28.	28.	28.	28.	28.
29.	29.	29.	29.	29.	29.	29.
30.	30.	30.	30.	30.	30.	30.
31.	31.	31.	31.	31.	31.	31.
32.	32.	32.	32.	32.	32.	32.
33.	33.	33.	33.	33.	33.	33.
TOTAL SCORE						
TODAY'S DATE						

*Copyright © 1989 by David D. Burns, M.D., from *The Feeling Good Handbook*

THE BURNS DEPRESSION CHECKLIST*

Place a check (√) in the box to the right of each of the 15 symptom clusters to indicate how much this type of feeling has been bothering you in the past several days. Make sure you answer all the questions. If you feel unsure about any, put down your best guess. If you would like a weekly record of your progress, record your answers on the separate "Answer Sheet" instead of filling in the spaces on the right.

	0—NOT AT ALL	1—SOMEWHAT	2—MODERATELY	3—A LOT
1. **Sadness:** Have you been feeling sad or down in the dumps?				
2. **Discouragement:** Does the future look hopeless?				
3. **Low self-esteem:** Do you feel worthless or think of yourself as a failure?				
4. **Inferiority:** Do you feel inadequate or inferior to others?				
5. **Guilt:** Do you get self-critical and blame yourself for everything?				
6. **Indecisiveness:** Do you have trouble making up your mind about things?				
7. **Irritability and frustration:** Have you been feeling resentful and angry a good deal of the time?				
8. **Loss of interest in life:** Have you lost interest in your career, your hobbies, your family, or your friends?				
9. **Loss of motivation:** Do you feel overwhelmed and have to push yourself hard to do things?				
10. **Poor self-image:** Do you think you're looking old or unattractive?				

*Copyright © 1984 by David D. Burns, M.D., from *The Feeling Good Handbook*, copyright © 1989

	0—NOT AT ALL	1—SOMEWHAT	2—MODERATELY	3—A LOT
11. **Appetite changes:** Have you lost your appetite? Or do you overeat or binge compulsively?				
12. **Sleep changes:** Do you suffer from insomnia and find it hard to get a good night's sleep? Or are you excessively tired and sleeping too much?				
13. **Loss of libido:** Have you lost your interest in sex?				
14. **Hypochondriasis:** Do you worry a great deal about your health?				
15. **Suicidal impulses†:** Do you have thoughts that life is not worth living or think that you might be better off dead?				

Add up your total score for the 33 symptoms and record it here: _____

Date: _____

†Anyone with suicidal urges should seek immediate consultation with a qualified psychiatrist or psychologist.

THE BURNS DEPRESSION CHECKLIST*
Answer Sheet

Instructions: Put a 0, 1, 2, or 3 in the space to the right of each of the 15 symptoms to indicate how much it has bothered you in the past week: 0 = Not at all; 1 = Somewhat; 2 = Moderately; 3 = A lot. Then add up your score for all 15 symptoms at the bottom.

1.	1.	1.	1.	1.	1.	1.
2.	2.	2.	2.	2.	2.	2.
3.	3.	3.	3.	3.	3.	3.
4.	4.	4.	4.	4.	4.	4.
5.	5.	5.	5.	5.	5.	5.
6.	6.	6.	6.	6.	6.	6.
7.	7.	7.	7.	7.	7.	7.
8.	8.	8.	8.	8.	8.	8.
9.	9.	9.	9.	9.	9.	9.
10.	10.	10.	10.	10.	10.	10.
11.	11.	11.	11.	11.	11.	11.
12.	12.	12.	12.	12.	12.	12.
13.	13.	13.	13.	13.	13.	13.
14.	14.	14.	14.	14.	14.	14.
15.	15.	15.	15.	15.	15.	15.
TOTAL SCORE						
TODAY'S DATE						

3

◆

How to Diagnose
Your Moods*

In the last chapter you learned whether you are feeling depressed or anxious. If you have ever been to a psychiatrist or psychologist, your therapist may have used terms like "manic-depressive illness" or "panic disorder," which could frighten or confuse you. You may also have wondered whether words like "neurosis," "psychosis," "mental illness," or "nervous breakdown" applied to you. This chapter will demystify psychiatric diagnoses. Once you understand how professionals classify emotional problems, you will no longer feel intimidated by these terms.

In 1980 the new *Diagnostic and Statistical Manual of Mental Disorders* was published by the American Psychiatric Association. Based on years of research and clinical experience, this manual has had a remarkable impact on mental health professionals, providing them with a common language for talking about disorders such as depression and anxiety. In 1983 work was begun to revise and improve this manual, culminating in the publication in 1987 of a new manual, the *Revised Diagnostic and Statistical Manual.*

*The descriptions of the disorders in this chapter are based on the *Diagnostic and Statistical Manual of Mental Disorders* (Third Edition, Revised), published by the American Psychiatric Association, Washington, D.C., 1987.

The diagnostic categories you will read about in this chapter, such as "major depressive disorder" or "social phobia," are based on this new diagnostic system. As you will see, these terms do not refer to mysterious entities like "neuroses" but simply describe clusters of familiar symptoms such as sadness or nervousness.

The difference between your score on a mood test, such as the Burns Anxiety Inventory (BAI) or the Burns Depression Checklist (BDC), and the diagnostic categories described in this chapter is similar to the difference between a photograph and a movie. The two mood tests show how bad you are feeling at any given moment. If those same symptoms persist over a period of time or in certain situations, then they are given a diagnostic label. For example, if you get nervous around other people at social gatherings, your score on the anxiety test (BAI) would be very elevated in those situations. The diagnostic name for this would be a "social phobia."

As you read about the symptoms for each diagnostic category, you will probably know whether or not you have experienced those symptoms. Keep in mind that the occasional experience of one or two of the symptoms is quite normal. To qualify for a diagnosis, nearly all the symptoms for that disorder must persist over a period of time. Check "yes" or "no" for that disorder in the table on page 51. When you finish the chapter, you will have an overview of where you fit into the diagnostic system.

As you read this chapter, remember that self-diagnosis with the help of a book like this can never substitute for a professional evaluation by a qualified psychiatrist or psychologist. In my professional practice, all new patients undergo a formal diagnostic procedure much more detailed than this chapter, along with psychological testing. My goal is not to turn you into your own doctor, but to make you more familiar with the diagnostic process.

Anxiety and Panic

Clinicians diagnose several types of anxiety. If your score on the Burns Anxiety Inventory is elevated, see if any of the following fits your symptoms. These categories are not mutually exclusive; there can be considerable overlap between them.

DIAGNOSTIC SUMMARY
Anxiety and Panic

Yes	No	
——	——	Generalized anxiety disorder
——	——	Social phobia
——	——	Simple phobia
——	——	Panic disorder
——	——	Agoraphobia
——	——	Obsessive-compulsive disorder
——	——	Hypochondriasis

Depression and Mania

Yes	No	
——	——	Major depressive episode
——	——	Dysthymic disorder
——	——	Bipolar disorder (manic-depressive illness)
——	——	Cyclothymic disorder

GENERALIZED ANXIETY DISORDER

People with phobias feel frightened in specific situations. For example, if you have a snake or a spider phobia, you'll feel anxious only when you're around those particular creatures. If you feel anxious and tense all day long, regardless of where you are or what you're doing, and if these symptoms persist more or less continuously for six months or longer, the problem is called generalized anxiety. This problem often first occurs between ages 20 and 40 and is equally common among men and women.

Some people with generalized anxiety harbor the superstitious belief that anxiety and worry will help them. You may think that if you worry enough about a test or paper you're writing, you'll do a better job on it. This attitude is usually not realistic. It may be true that a little anxiety can motivate you to hustle and try your hardest, but a lot of anxiety will simply get in the way and make the job more difficult. In fact, I find that I do my best when I'm not at all anxious.

Chronic worriers frequently believe that anxiety will protect their family and friends from danger. A woman named Anne got agitated whenever her children were five minutes late. She worried that something terrible had happened to them. When her daughter visited a friend in Florida, Anne constantly obsessed about traffic accidents and hurricanes.

Anne was reluctant to give up this habit of worrying because she was afraid that something terrible would happen to her kids if she stopped. There may be another deeper reason why Anne worries constantly about her kids. She may be unhappy about some problem in her life she's afraid to face, such as a marital conflict, or ambivalence about completing college and pursuing a career. She manages to avoid dealing with these frightening issues when she uses up all her energy worrying about her family.

If you have had symptoms of chronic worry and nervousness for at least six months, check "yes" in the Diagnostic Summary table now.

SOCIAL PHOBIA

A social phobia is the fear of other people. Social phobias are tremendously common and afflict both sexes, but they are more widespread among men. People with social phobias feel shy and are afraid of looking foolish in front of others. They don't want to be in any situation where people will notice how anxious they are. You may have a social phobia if you are afraid of public speaking, being with groups of people at meetings or social gatherings, introducing yourself to others, going out on dates, eating in front of others, saying foolish things at parties, or urinating in a public restroom.

A 24-year-old woman with a social phobia was talking to a handsome man at an office party. She grew more and more self-conscious because of her thought, "What if he notices how ill-at-ease I am?" This thought made her unbearably uncomfortable and tense. She got so flustered that she had to excuse herself and go home. Then she felt humiliated and began to berate herself.

SIMPLE PHOBIA

A simple phobia is the fear of something specific like heights, a certain animal, flying in an airplane, choking, thunder, driving, darkness, closed spaces, being buried alive, elevators, blood, dirt or germs, or bridges. Many phobias have Greek names. For example, the fear of heights is called acrophobia; the fear of closed spaces is called claustrophobia; and the fear of being buried alive is called laphephobia.

These terms create the impression that phobias are dreadful and dangerous and that scientists understand a great deal about them. Nothing could be further from the truth. Phobias are uncomfortable, but they are not symptoms of severe mental illness or a weak character. They can usually be treated effectively and quickly, but there is surprisingly little scientific knowledge about what causes them.

Simple phobias are extremely common. Between 10 and 20 percent of the population will develop phobias during their lives. Phobias can occur at any age but often first appear in childhood. They are about twice as common among women as among men.

PANIC DISORDER

A panic attack is a burst of intense, overwhelming anxiety that generally lasts for a brief period—sometimes for as little as a few minutes and rarely for more than several hours. The attacks seem to come out of the blue for no apparent reason. During a panic attack you will notice at least four uncomfortable sensations like dizziness, a pounding of your heart, a lump in your throat, racing thoughts, lightheadedness, trembling or shaking, tightness in your chest, palpitations, diarrhea or upset stomach, rapid breathing, a choking or smothering sensation, shortness of breath, numbness or tingling fingers, hot flashes, chills or sweating. You may feel strange and think that you are unreal or the world may seem unreal.

These symptoms develop suddenly and increase dramatically in intensity within ten minutes. At the height of the panic attack, you may be terrified by one or more of these fears:

What if I lose control?

What if I go crazy?

What if I have a heart attack?

What if I faint?

What if I die?

After a short time the episode wears off. You were hanging on for dear life and you think it's a miracle that you didn't crack up entirely. You don't want anyone to know what happened to you because you feel ashamed, abnormal, and weird. You live in dread of another attack. Your life becomes a constant vigil as you look for some sign that this terrible experience is about to hit again. This leads to the fear of fear itself.

If you've had at least four panic attacks in a four-week period, it's called panic disorder, but this definition is somewhat arbitrary. If you've had only one panic attack but you felt upset about it for a month, you would also qualify for this diagnosis.

Some people who have panic attacks worry that they are "going crazy"—becoming schizophrenic. But the symptoms of schizophrenia are quite different from the symptoms of anxiety. People with schizophrenia may hear nonexistent voices; they may believe that electrical forces or secret radio waves are controlling them; they may think that their thoughts are being broadcast over the television networks and radio stations; or they may feel that God Himself is sending them messages. People with schizophrenia rarely worry about going crazy. They're convinced that they're normal and they believe their delusions are completely real. If you're terribly worried about cracking up, you're not! Anxiety, not insanity, is your problem. Although panic attacks *feel* terrifying, they're quite harmless and very treatable.

AGORAPHOBIA

Agoraphobia is the fear of being in open spaces alone or traveling away from home. A 47-year-old married agoraphobic woman had an overwhelming dread of leaving her house alone. When she drove her car, she would worry that the car might break down and she'd get mugged. This fantasy was so frightening that she refused to drive or leave the house unless her husband came along. She became housebound and insisted on being with him any time she was away from home.

People with agoraphobia are afraid of being in situations where help might not be available in the event they develop frightening or embarrassing symptoms, such as dizziness or fainting, losing bladder or bowel control, having a heart attack, smothering, or cracking up. As a result of these fears, agoraphobics restrict their travel and may need a trusted companion when they travel away from home. Feared situations include being in a crowd, standing in line at the grocery store, being on a bridge, or traveling in a bus, train, or car.

Agoraphobia is one of the most common phobias, affecting an estimated 1 million Americans, and is far more common among women. The problem usually develops during adolescence or early adult life. Because agoraphobics are afraid of leaving home, many of them often have difficulty going to a clinic for therapy. As a result, they often do not receive the treatment they so desperately need to overcome this affliction.

OBSESSIVE-COMPULSIVE DISORDER

Obsessions are persistent, intrusive, nonsensical thoughts that you can't shake out of your head. For example, you may worry that the dirt on your hands will contaminate your children and give them leukemia, even though you know rationally that this is not realistic. A compulsion is a ritualistic act that you feel compelled to repeat over and over in order to ward off the danger. Thus, the obsession is the repetitious, frightening *thought* and the compulsion is the repetitious *action* that results from this thought.

According to the *Diagnostic and Statistical Manual*, the most common kinds of obsessions concern violence, contamination, or doubt. An example of a violence obsession would be a patient of mine who was troubled by the belief that he would suddenly throw his child out of the window or jump out in front of a car in heavy traffic. He had no real intention of doing these things, but was terrified by the irrational fear that he would suddenly lose control and act impulsively. An example of obsessive doubt would be a housewife who worried that the house would burn down because she forgot to turn off the stove at night, so she would get up to check the stove repeatedly. The most common compulsions include hand washing, cleaning things, counting, checking things, or touching things. The compulsive act is logically connected to the obsessive thought. For example, a physician obsessed while driving that he might have inadvertently killed a pedestrian and then forgotten about it. He felt the urge to stop his car and look around for a body to make sure that he hadn't hit anyone. Even though he realized intellectually that it was exceedingly unlikely that he had hit anyone, his fears were so emotionally charged that he couldn't resist the urge to stop and look around for a body.

HYPOCHONDRIASIS

People with this disorder are preoccupied with the idea that they are suffering from a serious illness such as cancer or heart disease. They usually go from doctor to doctor, getting repeated examinations and reassurances that they are in perfect health. Hypochondriasis can occur at any age but often begins when people are in their twenties, and is equally common among men and women. It is one of the most common problems seen by internists and physicians in general practice. Hypochondriacs usually resist the idea that stress or psychological problems may create their symptoms. Because they insist on finding a medical explanation, they can be a great source of frustration to physicians.

Hypochondriasis, like all the other forms of anxiety described in this chapter, is nearly always caused by other problems that the individual is ignoring. I recently treated a businessman who worried constantly about his health. He felt that every little bump, ache, or pain was a sign of some dreadful disease. He constantly ran from doctor to doctor for examinations, which invariably turned out to be normal. His anxiety was not caused by any real illness, and his frequent trips to doctors were simply a way of reacting to the conflicts in his life.

His wife, who was much younger, had recently received her MBA degree and had started her own business. She was working hard at her new career. Although he "rationally" saw that this was a wonderful idea, inside he felt insecure and resentful. They were already financially comfortable, and he wanted to retire and spend more time with her so they could enjoy the fruits of his labor. But she was so busy that he felt lonely and abandoned. He had trouble admitting that he felt this way because he thought he should be "strong." He was ashamed of his negative feelings and tried to ignore them. When he brought in his wife for some couples therapy and they learned to share their feelings more openly, his aches and pains went away as mysteriously as they had come.

Depression and Mania

Clinicians diagnose several types of depression. If your score on the Burns Depression Checklist (page 36) is elevated, see if any of the following fits your symptoms.

MAJOR DEPRESSIVE EPISODE

In a major depressive episode, a person feels sad or experiences a loss of interest in pleasurable activities for at least a two- to four-week period. In addition, there are several of the following symptoms: loss of appetite (or eating too much), trouble sleeping at night (or sleeping too much), feelings of agitation and extreme restlessness (or feeling dull, fatigued, and slowed down), feelings of worthlessness or guilt, difficulties concentrating, and thoughts of death. Many people with these symptoms do not realize they are depressed. They may feel convinced they are inferior and that life is not worth living.

Major depressive episodes occur twice as often in women as in men, but the reason for this is not known. Between 10 and 25 percent of all adult women have had at least one major depressive episode. The estimates for men are between 5 and 12 percent. These figures indicate that at least 15 million Americans have suffered from this affliction. Of course, the number who have experienced milder mood swings is substantially higher. Small wonder that depression is often referred to as the common cold of psychiatric disorders.

DYSTHYMIC DISORDER

This is an extremely common milder form of depression which lasts for two years or more. People with this problem tend to be chronically unhappy for much of their lives, but their depression is not severe enough to qualify as a major depressive episode. Dysthymic disorder usually begins somewhere between childhood and young adult life and is more common among women. It has sometimes been called depressive personality, or depressive neurosis, because chronic unhappiness and pessimism seem to be a part of the individual's personality and view of life.

BIPOLAR DISORDER

Recurrent depressions are sometimes called "unipolar depressions," since they have only one pole—the depressed side. In contrast, "bipolar depressions" have two poles—highs and lows. A person may go down into a deep depression, and then at other times may suddenly develop an abnormal and potentially dangerous mood elevation. The bipolar disorder has also been called manic-depressive illness, because it swings from mania to depression and back again.

There are two kinds of abnormal mood elevations, which differ in severity. Severe mood elevations are called manic episodes or mania. They can be extremely serious and often require hospitalization. Milder mood elevations are called hypomanic episodes, or hypomania.

Manic episodes usually develop rather unexpectedly in individuals who were quite normal before the episode began. The symptoms are just the opposite of the symptoms of depression. Instead of feeling sad, they feel joyous. Instead of suffering from a loss of self-esteem, they enjoy unlimited self-esteem and believe they can achieve anything. They suddenly feel brilliant, alert, creative, and euphoric, a fountain of energy and ideas. They feel *so good* that they cannot accept the idea that there may be something wrong or that they need treatment.

Manic patients often become quite delusional, but they have absolutely no insight about this. They behave in ways that are dangerous and foolish without any awareness of the consequences of their behavior. One of my manic patients, a young woman named Sarah, was walking past a government building in New York where she saw people picketing and television crews filming them. Apparently there was a complex labor disagreement between the municipal government and the employees' union. She stopped to talk to people in the crowd and developed a sudden "insight." She felt convinced she could negotiate a quick solution to the problem and demanded that the television cameramen interview her for the evening news. She also demanded an interview with Mayor Koch and said that she wanted to deliver a major address to the United Nations.

Another characteristic of mania is an extraordinary degree of physical and psychological energy. Manic patients talk constantly and excitedly, jumping from subject to subject. They may pace about or exercise vigorously for prolonged periods of time.

Some manic patients become extremely irritable if crossed or thwarted, and may be arrested or brought to emergency rooms after altercations with the police.

Although the symptoms of mania can be extremely dramatic, this disorder is not as rare as you might think. Many famous politicians and entertainers have suffered from manic-depressive illness. Current estimates indicate that approximately 0.5 to 1 percent of the adult population suffers from manic-depression. That means that between 1 and 2 million Americans have had or will have this affliction. Unlike unipolar depression, which is more common in women, bipolar disorder is equally common among men and women.

There is strong evidence that bipolar illness is inherited and caused by some, as yet unknown, chemical imbalance in the brain. Treatment with appropriate medications, such as lithium, can be extremely helpful to individuals with this affliction. (See Chapter 23 for a description of medications that can be used to treat depression, mania, and anxiety.) Psychotherapy is also crucial in the treatment of this illness. Between the episodes of mania, bipolar patients often suffer from low self-esteem and experience significant difficulties with their careers and personal relationships. A good therapeutic relationship can help to correct these problems and significantly improve the prognosis for this puzzling disorder.

CYCLOTHYMIC DISORDER

You may have known someone whose personality seems to run hot and cold. At times they are turned on by life—perhaps excessively so—and at times they are overly negative, pessimistic, and discouraged. They never seem to find the middle ground. If these oscillations between mild depression and mild elation have persisted for at least two years, the disorder is called cyclothymic disorder. This simply represents a combination of dysthymic disorder and hypomania. It isn't known whether cyclothymic disorder is a separate illness or a milder version of manic-depressive illness.

Suppose you feel that you fit into one or more of these diagnostic categories. What should you do? First, read the appropriate sections in this book. For example, if you have a social phobia, Chapter 14 should be of particular interest to you. If you suffer from public speaking anxiety, Chapter 15 may help.

When is professional therapy indicated? Any time a mood problem is chronic or severe or interferes with your normal functioning, you should seek a consultation with a qualified psychiatrist or psychologist. Many people do not have insight into the causes of their mood problems. If you suffer from anxiety or panic attacks, there's a good chance that you feel angry because of someone or something in your life that is bugging you. However, you may not be aware of this because you are avoiding the problem and pushing it out of your mind. It can sometimes be much easier to unearth and confront these difficulties with the help of a skillful and caring therapist.

If you qualify for one or more of the diagnoses in this chapter, it does not make you a weirdo or a neurotic, but a human being who's hurting. At my clinic we see large numbers of people with these problems. With a little persistence, compassion, and teamwork, these difficulties can be dealt with effectively, and the prognosis to *feel good* again is excellent!

4

•

Should *You Change the Way You Feel?*

Cognitive therapy is based on the idea that distorted thoughts, and not realistic ones, lead to unhealthy negative emotions like depression and anxiety. When you learn to think about your problems in a more positive and realistic way, you can change the way you feel. The effects are often dramatic.

This approach is exciting but quite controversial. Are your negative thoughts and feelings *always* unrealistic? Are you justified in changing the way you feel? In an article in the *New York Times* on June 17, 1981, entitled, "In Praise of Depression," David Ives wrote:

> Considering the state of the world, why does science still consider depression an aberration? . . . History, it would seem, is telling us that there is something compelling about the dark side of things. . . . For some of us, optimism is seen for what it is: a form of escapism. . . . Optimism is, in fact, a form of desperation that science would do well to investigate. . . . Depression, let it be said, is nothing more than realism.

There is clearly some truth in this. Life has many frustrations and disappointments. You make a trip to buy an appliance and when you get home and take it out of its box you discover that it doesn't work.

A friend is forty-five minutes late meeting you for lunch after promising to be on time. Your boss criticizes your work in front of other people and then pressures you to meet an impossible deadline. In addition to these day-by-day irritants, we are all confronted by real tragedies—the sudden death of a friend or family member, divorce or rejection by someone we love, or the loss of a job. You may work hard to make your dream come true and then your plans come crashing down. Isn't it appropriate to feel upset? Aren't these feelings inevitable?

I believe that the argument that stress and depression are always realistic is just as absurd as the suggestion that people should try to be happy and successful all the time. Sometimes negative feelings are healthy, and sometimes they are unhealthy. A young man hospitalized for depression told me how he once poured boiling coffee on his leg in an attempt to distract himself from his feelings of worthlessness and emptiness. The despair he felt was not the same as healthy sadness, and his actions were hardly an appropriate response to the problems in his life! By the same token, genuine remorse is not the same as neurotic guilt, realistic fear is not the same as an anxiety attack, and healthy anger is not the same as hostility and aggression.

If you feel that someone you care about is treating you badly, it's natural to feel hurt. You may feel angry and put down. Sharing these feelings openly can often help you understand each other and resolve the problem. When two people respect each other, the ability to be vulnerable and to reveal hurt feelings can create a powerful emotional connection that is the source of real intimacy and friendship.

Anger and irritability can also be unhealthy and destructive. I was recently working in my living room, attempting to write. I didn't feel very creative because it was the end of a long stressful day. My son, who was almost five, walked up to me and innocently asked if I could help him get an apple out of the refrigerator. Before I had even comprehended his question I snapped angrily, "Shut up! Can't you see that I'm busy? Go downstairs and stop bothering me!" He was stunned. Shock and grief swept across his face. In slow motion he turned and walked dutifully downstairs, weeping.

I suddenly realized the impact of what I'd said—crushing, totally without justification. By shouting at my son I had hurt someone I loved without any provocation—clearly a violation of my own moral code. I felt intense remorse. I rushed over to him, picked him up in my arms, and said, "Erik, please forgive me. What I did was wrong.

You didn't do anything wrong. Sometimes we do bad things without thinking when we're in a bad mood. I love you so much and I want you to forgive me." He gave me a wonderful hug and we got his apple and felt like pals again. It was a painful but tender moment that brought us closer together and made our love more vital.

From a practical point of view, how can you know when you should *accept* your feelings, when you should *express* your feelings, and when you should *change* them? The following questions can help you decide:

- How long have I been feeling this way?
- Am I doing something constructive about the problem, or am I simply brooding and avoiding it?
- Are my thoughts and feelings realistic?
- Will it be helpful or hurtful if I express my feelings?
- Am I making myself unhappy about a situation that's beyond my control?
- Am I avoiding a problem and denying that I'm really upset about it?
- Are my expectations for the world realistic?
- Are my expectations for myself realistic?
- Am I feeling hopeless?
- Am I experiencing a loss of self-esteem?

How long have I been feeling this way? Sometimes we hang on to feelings far beyond the time when they could serve any useful purpose. If you are still feeling guilty or angry about something that happened in the past, ask yourself, "Just how much longer do I intend to make myself miserable about this? What is the point of feeling so bad for so long?" A woman named Elaine obsessed constantly about a sexual affair she had nearly two decades earlier. All day long she berated herself. Even a convicted felon is usually set free long before that much time has expired!

Am I doing something constructive about the problem, or am I simply brooding and avoiding it? Sometimes a negative feeling becomes a way of life. You may feel sorry for yourself instead of doing something about the problem that's bothering you. You may be annoyed with someone and go around feeling sour and avoiding them so you won't have to tell them how you honestly feel.

It's natural to feel disappointed when you get rejected or when you fail to achieve a goal and things don't go as well as you hoped. It's important to grieve over the loss of a loved one and to surrender to the tears, to the feelings of loss, and to remember how much you cared about the one who died. You may feel remorse when you think of times you may have let that person down. I believe that these feelings, which seem so painful at the time, can be our greatest opportunities for growth and for experiencing our humanity, especially if we're not afraid to feel some pain and some despair. Most people bounce back and carry on with their lives after a period of time. We can only feel healed and whole if we will allow ourselves to feel broken.

On the other hand, when some people get depressed, they become cynical and hopeless and give up on life. They crawl into bed and avoid pleasurable activities, friends, and work because they're so convinced that life is pointless and that the future holds nothing but deprivation and misery. This is not healthy sadness but depression.

Are my thoughts and feelings realistic? Healthy negative feelings are based on a realistic appraisal of your circumstances. It is often best to express these feelings as constructively as possible, to confront problems squarely and honestly, and to take action to deal with things more effectively. But when your negative feelings are based on distorted and unrealistic thoughts, it is often better to change the way you think about the situation.

The list of cognitive distortions in Chapter 1, page 8, can help you see whether your negative thoughts are illogical. When you write them down, you will frequently discover that you're involved in "all-or-nothing thinking," "fortune-telling," "personalization," and so on. This means that you're viewing a situation in an unrealistic manner. When you modify these thoughts, your feelings will often change.

Will it be helpful or hurtful if I express my feelings? When you feel angry, you might tell yourself, "I have the right to feel this way!" Of course you have the right to feel any way you want, but the real question is whether or not you *want* to feel like that. Will it help you deal with the situation if you express your negative feelings? If the answer is yes, you should probably express them. If the answer is no, it may be better to change your feelings.

Suppose your five-year-old son runs out in the street to chase a ball. You may feel frightened and shout at him in an angry voice. This might make a more powerful and lasting impact than a calm and rational discussion about the dangers of getting killed in traffic.

Your anger would be healthy and it might someday save his life. On the other hand, if a police officer is giving you a ticket, shouting at him in an angry voice might have severe consequences. You might do better to count to ten and admit your error.

Many people are afraid to express their feelings, even when it's clearly indicated. I recently treated a young woman who was reluctant to break up with her boyfriend because she felt guilty about hurting his feelings. For six months she kept stringing him along. She wasn't really being kind to him, she was submitting him to slow torture. For months he'd been depressed and confused because he couldn't figure out where he stood with her. Once they talked things over honestly and she made it clear how she really felt, they broke up. Although he felt disappointed, he got over his disappointment in a couple of weeks and was able to get on with his life.

Am I making myself unhappy about a problem that's beyond my control? Sometimes we refuse to accept situations that are beyond our control, but it doesn't do much good. You may be caught in a traffic jam or stuck on an airplane that's delayed in taking off. If you tell yourself "This shouldn't have happened—how unfair!" or "I can't stand this," you'll have to cope with the stress and aggravation you feel as well as the inconvenience of the delay. You have plenty of other options if you're willing to be creative and to think about the situation more positively. Recently I was stuck on a commuter train for two hours. It was hot and muggy, and I was tired and eager to get home. I began talking with the man next to me and learned a great deal about the Iran-Iraq war from him. Although he didn't consider himself an expert, he knew far more about it than I did. The conversation was more enjoyable than sitting and fuming about the incompetence of the people running the railroad or the "injustice" of the delay!

Am I avoiding a problem and denying that I'm really upset about it? Sometimes one emotion can be a substitute for another. You may be angry with someone, but you don't admit it to yourself. You repress your feelings and get anxious and panicky instead. Your anxiety is simply a way of disguising a problem that you'd prefer to avoid.

I recently treated a 26-year-old interior decorator named Annie who had developed the obsession that she was going crazy. Annie had read my first book, *Feeling Good*, and had memorized the symptoms of schizophrenia described there. All day long she would review them over and over and would feel temporarily reassured that she wasn't crazy, since she didn't have any of them. However, the very act of compulsively reviewing the symptoms made her feel abnormal. This would get her even more upset, so she would review the list again.

If Annie is not really going crazy, what *is* going on? What's she really so anxious about? Six months ago Annie started living with her fiancé, Jim. Both of them have a "conflict phobia": they are afraid of anger and don't know how to talk about their problems, so they avoid anything that's upsetting.

When Annie was growing up, no one in her house ever fought or worked out problems. She grew up with the notion that nice people don't argue or get mad. When she feels annoyed, she doesn't know what to do with her feelings and she sweeps them under the carpet. She denies that she's upset with Jim. Then her feelings eat away at her, and her obsession about going crazy is the result. By worrying, Annie distracts herself from the real problem and doesn't have to admit that she's angry. I suspect that her anxiety and her fears about going crazy will be greatly improved once she and Jim have some couples communication training and learn to talk about their feelings more openly.

Are my expectations for the world realistic? After I finished a lecture to a group of mental health professionals in New York, a psychiatrist in the audience took issue with the idea that distorted thoughts and unrealistic expectations lead to negative emotions. She pointed out that life is filled with annoying experiences and argued that it's realistic to feel frustrated.

At first I thought she was right, but when I thought about it further, it dawned on me that frustration is rarely, if ever, "realistic," but it's eminently human. Frustration always results from a discrepancy between your expectations and reality. If you feel frustrated, it's because you expected something different from what really happened. You expected the subway to be on time, but it was late, so you got frustrated. This means that your expectations were, by definition, unrealistic. After all, the subway, *in reality*, was late. But it can be difficult to change these expectations because you may strongly believe that life *should* or *must* or *ought* to be the way you want it to be.

Frustration can be healthy when we take it as a signal for creativity and change. The irony is that for some people frustration becomes a way of life. Their theme is "Life stinks! Life should be different from the way it is," but they rarely do anything to make it better.

One evening I told my wife that I was frustrated with a particularly difficult patient who seemed determined not to give up her irrational self-criticism. No matter what this patient accomplished, she stubbornly insisted that it wasn't good enough and claimed that she was a totally worthless human being. I tried dozens of ways to help her turn this around, but she always found a way to be negative and defeat me. I told my wife that people *shouldn't* be so unreasonable!

My wife pointed out it wasn't particularly realistic to expect someone with a severe depression to be logical and optimistic. She also pointed out that if there weren't so many self-critical people in the world, I'd be out of business! She was right, so I thanked my lucky stars that there were so many "unreasonable" people who needed help!

I decided to view my work with this patient as a challenge instead of a burden. I became curious about *why* she was resisting me. Maybe she was mad at me but couldn't admit it openly. Or maybe she was afraid to change. As I became more supportive and less demanding, she began to let down her defenses. Soon we were working together productively. She couldn't change until I had accepted her as she was.

I call this the "acceptance paradox." If you try too hard to fight a problem within yourself or someone else, the very act of fighting will often create resistance. Sometimes when you accept the problem and stop trying so hard, things will suddenly begin to change.

Are my expectations for myself realistic? Some people beat on themselves because they think they're not as good or as happy or as successful as they should be. Do you ever have thoughts like these?

"I should always be able to help friends and family members solve their problems."

"I should always be able to please people and live up to everyone's expectations for me."

"I should always succeed at whatever I do and never fall short of any goal."

"I should always be in control of my feelings and never get overly anxious or upset or have any irrational feelings."

"I should always feel close to the people I care about and never fight or bicker."

"I should be able to get everybody's approval and make everybody like me."

"I should try to be perfect and never fail or make mistakes."

You may have difficulty accepting your imperfections and your limitations. You may harangue yourself whenever you fall short of a personal goal and tell yourself, "I *shouldn't* have made that mistake! I'm such a jerk. How could I screw up?" Although all this self-abuse creates guilt and depression, there may be a hidden payoff. Only a very special person could be expected to be so perfect. After all, most of us more average people make lots of mistakes! When we do, we try to learn from them and carry on again. But if you punish yourself and act as if your mistakes are unthinkable and unacceptable, it means you're superior to the rest of us!

Many people find it difficult to accept their feelings. If you have panic attacks, you may think that anxiety is abnormal and dangerous. You may fight your anxiety and insist that you should always be in control of your emotions. When you get any little twitch of nervousness, you may feel that something terrible is happening and think you're about to go crazy. As a result, normal feelings of anxiety mushroom into full-blown panic attacks.

Some people refuse to accept their anger. You may think you should never fight or argue or get mad. You may be afraid to express your negative feelings for fear you'll be rejected or will hurt the person you're mad at. Then your feelings may get bottled up and you may end up constantly bickering and feeling irritable. Because you are afraid of anger, you end up knee-deep in bitterness and conflict. In contrast, if you accept your anger as a normal part of any healthy, loving relationship, you'll discover that you can often resolve problems far more easily and your anger will more quickly disappear.

Am I feeling hopeless? Hopelessness is nearly always a sign of unhealthy emotions. People who are suffering from depression or anxiety frequently feel this way. You reason, "I *feel* so hopeless. Therefore I must really *be* hopeless." You give up, and nothing changes. Then you conclude that things really are hopeless. Many of my patients tell me, "I'm the one who will never get better. My problems are insurmountable. I'll feel this way forever. Why don't you just give up on me, Dr. Burns?" These feelings are nearly always based on a distorted assessment of yourself and your future. I tell my patients that I will *never* buy into their conviction that they are hopeless. Your chances of feeling joy and self-esteem again are extremely high, even if it doesn't seem so.

Am I experiencing a loss of self-esteem? Low self-esteem can lead to unhealthy anger, anxiety, guilt, and depression. If you feel good about yourself and someone has treated you badly, then expressing your feelings can show that you respect yourself. You can share your anger in a constructive way so that the problem can get resolved fairly. If you feel inferior, however, you may be defensive and constantly look for little signs of rejection and unfair treatment. You may lash out at people because you don't feel very worthwhile inside.

I recently had to reschedule a therapy session with a patient because of the death of a friend. Although I called her two days ahead of time and explained the circumstances, she got furious and wrote an angry letter terminating treatment. In the letter she stated that if I really cared about her I wouldn't have canceled the session. Fortunately she threw the letter away before mailing it and was able to work on her low self-esteem and fears of rejection during the next therapy session.

If you've ever been criticized or rejected or have failed to achieve an important goal, you know how natural it is to feel hurt and disappointed. But if you berate yourself as worthless and unlovable, you'll be giving yourself distorted messages and destroying your self-esteem. Being rejected and failing are universal human experiences. They don't make you "a reject" or "a failure"—they make you a human being.

Even if you behave badly, it won't do much good to write yourself off as a "bad person." You will simply waste time and energy ruminating about how lousy and terrible you are. This will only incapacitate you and make the problem worse. In addition, this is very self-centered because you're entirely caught up in yourself! Genuine self-esteem is based on humility and an acceptance of your shortcomings. This makes it possible to assume responsibility for your actions, to feel remorse, to apologize and make amends, and to get on with productive and joyous living.

PART TWO

Feeling Good About Yourself: How to Conquer Depression and Build Self-Esteem

How to Change the Way You Feel: The Four Steps to Happiness

Let's assume you want to change the way you feel. First you will need a pen or pencil. It's far better to confront your problems by writing them down than by simply thinking them through. I can't emphasize the importance of this enough, if you want positive changes in your life! You can jot down your negative thoughts whenever you feel upset—in your office, at home, on a plane or bus. Once you get in the habit, you will see in black and white just how unrealistic they are.

Many people will tell themselves, "I'll just read this book and try to think things through a little better and that will be enough." This is a real trap. When you're upset, your negative thoughts will chase each other around in your mind in endless circles. Once you get them down on paper, you develop a more objective perspective. As you read the following pages, try the techniques I describe, even if you're convinced they won't work for you. I think you'll be surprised to discover how helpful they can be.

There are four steps to becoming a happier person.

Step 1: Identify the Upsetting Event

The first thing I want you to do is to write a brief description of a specific problem that's bothering you at the top of the blank Daily Mood Log on page 75, where it says "STEP ONE: DESCRIBE THE UPSETTING EVENT." A completed example is illustrated on pages 78–79. As you can see, when Marge was baby-sitting her two grandchildren she inadvertently let her granddaughter use her grandson's toothbrush. Her grandson had a sore throat and Marge started worrying that her granddaughter might catch it from him. When she went to bed that night Marge obsessed about the incident. She was concerned that her daughter, who was often quite critical of Marge, would become angry when she found out. Marge described the situation this way: "I inadvertently let Luci use her brother's toothbrush. Now I feel tormented and I can't sleep."

Perhaps you feel annoyed because a friend made a rude remark. Or you're embarrassed because you wrote a check that bounced, or received an upsetting letter in today's mail. Some people even get upset when something good happens. A graduating law student heard that his roommate had just received a job offer from a prestigious law firm. He felt jealous because he hadn't yet received such an appealing offer.

Sometimes bad moods are triggered by a negative memory or fantasy that comes out of the blue. While editing this paragraph, I suddenly felt as if I'd been kicked in the stomach. I realized I had been thinking about a patient who was angry with me for being charged for a late cancellation of a therapy session—I was imagining being hauled into court for a malpractice suit.

The most important principle to keep in mind when you identify the upsetting event is to be *specific*. Don't write down "Life stinks." If you told me that you wanted help with this problem, I would ask you, "What time of day was it stinking? Where were you when you noticed the smell?" Obviously I wouldn't really know what your complaint meant. If you just had an argument with your spouse or your boss, that would be something specific we could work on.

An attractive but shy young woman named Rita with a mild chronic depression told me that the problem she wanted help with was that she didn't have enough fun in life. I think you can see the difficulty with this: it's a little too vague. I asked Rita *when* she

THE DAILY MOOD LOG*

STEP ONE: DESCRIBE THE UPSETTING EVENT_____

_____

STEP TWO: RECORD YOUR NEGATIVE FEELINGS—and rate each one from 0 (the least) to 100 (the most). Use words like sad, anxious, angry, guilty, lonely, hopeless, frustrated, etc.

Emotion	Rating	Emotion	Rating	Emotion	Rating
1.		3.		5.	
2.		4.		6.	

STEP THREE: THE TRIPLE-COLUMN TECHNIQUE—

Automatic Thoughts	Distortions	Rational Responses
Write your negative thoughts and estimate your belief in each one (0–100).	Identify the distortions in each Automatic Thought.	Substitute more realistic thoughts and estimate your belief in each one (0 and 100).

(Continue on next page)

Automatic Thoughts	Distortions	Rational Responses

(Continue on next page)

THE DAILY MOOD LOG (continued)

Automatic Thoughts	Distortions	Rational Responses

STEP FOUR: OUTCOME–Re-rate your belief in each Automatic Thought from 0 to 100 and put a check in the box that describes how you now feel:

☐ not at all better; ☐ somewhat better; ☐ quite a bit better; ☐ a lot better.

CHECKLIST OF COGNITIVE DISTORTIONS*

1. All-or-nothing thinking: You look at things in absolute, black-and-white categories.
2. Overgeneralization: You view a negative event as a never-ending pattern of defeat.
3. Mental filter: You dwell on the negatives and ignore the positives.
4. Discounting the positives: You insist that your accomplishments or positive qualities "don't count."
5. Jumping to conclusions: (A) Mind reading—you assume that people are reacting negatively to you when there's no definite evidence for this; (B) Fortune-telling—you arbitrarily predict that things will turn out badly.
6. Magnification or minimization: You blow things way up out of proportion or you shrink their importance inappropriately.
7. Emotional reasoning: You reason from how you feel: "I *feel* like an idiot, so I really must be one." Or "I don't *feel* like doing this, so I'll put it off."
8. "Should statements": You criticize yourself or other people with "shoulds" or "shouldn'ts." "Musts," "oughts," and "have tos" are similar offenders.
9. Labeling: You identify with your shortcomings. Instead of saying "I made a mistake," you tell yourself, "I'm a jerk," or "a fool," or "a loser."
10. Personalization and blame: You blame yourself for something you weren't entirely responsible for, or you blame other people and overlook ways that your own attitudes and behavior might contribute to a problem.

THE DAILY MOOD LOG*

STEP ONE: DESCRIBE THE UPSETTING EVENT <u>I inadvertently let Luci use</u>
<u>her brother's toothbrush. Now I feel tormented and can't sleep.</u>

STEP TWO: RECORD YOUR NEGATIVE FEELINGS—and rate each one
from 0 (the least) to 100 (the most). Use words like sad, anxious,
angry, guilty, lonely, hopeless, frustrated, etc.

Emotion	Rating	Emotion	Rating	Emotion	Rating
1. Anxious	90	3.		5.	
2. Guilty	90	4.		6.	

STEP THREE: THE TRIPLE-COLUMN TECHNIQUE—

Automatic Thoughts	Distortions	Rational Responses
Write your negative thoughts and estimate your belief in each one (0–100).	Identify the distortions in each Automatic Thought.	Substitute more realistic thoughts and estimate your belief in each one (0 and 100).
1. If Luci gets a sore throat it will be my fault. ~~(100%)~~ (20%)	1. personalization; fortune-telling.	1. I made an honest mistake. Luci probably won't get a sore throat. It won't be the end of the world if she does. I don't deserve to be punished like this. (100%)

(Continue on next page)

THE DAILY MOOD LOG (continued)

Automatic Thoughts	Distortions	Rational Responses
2. If Bess finds out, she will be angry with me. ~~(100%)~~ (20%)	2. fortune-telling; personalization.	2. I don't know for certain that she'll blame me. If she is critical, I can apologize for making a mistake. If she continues to be angry and upset with me, I can tell her that I made an innocent mistake and that I'm uncomfortable with the way she's treating me. (100%)

STEP FOUR: OUTCOME—Re-rate your belief in each Automatic Thought from 0 to 100 and put a check in the box that describes how you now feel:

☐ not at all better; ☐ somewhat better; ☐ quite a bit better; ☒ a lot better.

wanted to have more fun. At first she said "all the time." I pointed out that I didn't know *anybody* who had fun *all* the time! With some encouragement, Rita admitted that she wanted to have more fun on the train home to New York after her session. When I asked her to tell me what she had in mind, it turned out that she wanted to talk to other people instead of feeling left out. When I asked whom, she reluctantly admitted that she hoped to talk to a cute guy.

This seemed like an easy assignment, since Rita was as cute as a bug in a rug! I can imagine that practically any young man on the train would jump at the chance to meet her. However, Rita had many negative thoughts in social situations that made her feel inhibited, such as, "It would be embarrassing to get shot down or rejected" and "What if I make a fool of myself in front of the other passengers?" After we dealt with these fears, we talked about how she could be more outgoing so she could start conversations with attractive fellows on the train.

A high school senior told her therapist she wanted help with "an identity crisis." You could talk about that problem for years without getting anywhere. The expression doesn't really mean anything. Her therapist asked her if there were any specific problems in her life she needed help with. She answered that she couldn't decide whether to go to college at Vassar or Bryn Mawr. After two sessions reviewing the relative merits of each option, she decided on Vassar. She said she felt great. Then her therapist asked if she still wanted help with her "identity crisis." She said she didn't think she had one anymore, and she felt ready to terminate her therapy. Defining the specific problem was the key to success.

Remember: only *real* problems can be solved. To be real, a problem must occur at some place and at some time of day. Sometimes you may have a nagging feeling that something isn't quite right but you can't put your finger on it. When this happens to me, I review on an hour-by-hour basis the various things I've done in the past day or two. I often go through my appointment book to see what I've been doing. Usually this helps me figure out what's bothering me. If I still can't figure it out, I may ask my wife or an associate at work who will often know why I'm upset even when I don't!

If worse comes to worst and you can't think of the specific problem, just write a general description of what you were doing when you felt bad. Examples: "At home washing the dishes and feeling lousy" or "Reading this book and feeling discouraged."

Now I want you to write a brief description of a situation that is bothering you at the top of the blank Daily Mood Log on page 78. Once you've done this, you can proceed to the next step.

Step 2: Record Your Negative Feelings

Write down your negative emotions and rate each of them on a scale from 1 to 100. Use words like sad, frustrated, discouraged, angry, hurt, anxious, embarrassed, upset, or guilty. A score of 1 for any emotion would be the least you could feel and a score of 100 would be the most. You can put down several negative feelings, because you will usually have more than one. You can see in her Daily Mood Log that Marge rated her feelings as "anxious—90" and "guilty—90." This indicated she was quite upset about the toothbrush incident.

Some of you won't like to rate your emotions with numbers because it seems artificial or overly compulsive. However, it can be a surprisingly effective device because then you can estimate how much better you feel after you complete the Daily Mood Log. It can also help you break the habit of thinking about your emotions in an all-or-nothing manner. If your anxiety goes down from 100 to 50, you might still be feeling tense, but you're nevertheless feeling quite a bit better. Giving yourself credit for this improvement will boost your morale and keep it high until you've resolved the problem completely. By the same token, there may be times when you still feel upset after completing the Daily Mood Log. This is important information. You can review the Troubleshooting Guide on page 86 to find out why you're stuck. Once you know what the problem is, it will help you to turn your feelings around.

I want you to write down and rate each of your negative emotions about the upsetting event you described in your Daily Mood Log. Once you've done that, you will be ready for the next step.

Step 3: The Triple-Column Technique

Ask yourself, "What are the negative thoughts that are associated with my bad feelings? What am I saying to myself about the upsetting situation?" Tune in to your inner dialogue. Listen with your "third ear." For example, during an argument with your husband you may be telling yourself, "If he really loved me he would listen to what I have to say." If you didn't get the promotion you had your hopes pinned on, you might be telling yourself, "I'll be stuck at this crummy job forever" or "I'm not getting fair treatment" or "I just don't have what it takes." If you're on a diet and you overeat, you might tell yourself that you're a fat pig with no willpower. If you notice an ache or pain or a tightness in your chest, you might feel panicky because you think you're on the verge of a heart attack or are dying of some dreadful disease.

As you become aware of your negative thoughts, write them down and number them in the "Automatic Thoughts" column of your Daily Mood Log. They're called Automatic Thoughts because when you feel upset, they come into your mind automatically, without any effort on your part. Getting in the habit of recording these Automatic Thoughts is one of the most important things you will learn in this book!

Many of my patients resist doing this when they feel upset. They believe that the Daily Mood Log won't help them. Don't succumb to these feelings! These methods are much more likely to help if you will grab a pen and do some writing while you read! Turn to page 75 now, if you have not done so already, and write a brief description of any upsetting event. Then record your negative emotions and write down your Automatic Thoughts. Do it now!

Sometimes you might not be able to pinpoint your Automatic Thoughts. If so, there's a simple solution. Draw an unhappy stick figure with a bubble above its head, like the one on page 83. Make up some negative thoughts that are upsetting the stick figure and write them down in the bubble. Ask yourself, "Why is this stick figure so unhappy?" Just make something up—anything will do. What you write down will usually tip you off to what's bothering you. A woman who insisted she didn't know what she was feeling upset about wrote this in the bubble: "I'll never be able to finish my graduate studies and get my master's degree." This led to a productive discussion of her perfectionism and fears of failure. Psychologists call this a "projective" technique, because the thoughts you put in the cartoon figure's mind are ones that you are projecting from your own mind. So it's not so surprising that they turn out to be the same ones that are actually bugging you!

After you have written down your Automatic Thoughts, estimate how much you believe each of them from 0 (not at all) to 100 percent (completely), and write the figure down in parentheses. The first

When you can't figure out what your gloomy thoughts are, draw an unhappy stick figure. Make up some negative thoughts that are making the stick figure upset and write them down in the bubble over his or her head.

negative thought Marge wrote down was "If Luci gets a sore throat it will be my fault," and the second one was "If Bess finds out she will be very angry with me." She recorded her belief in each thought as 100 percent, because they both seemed absolutely true.

When these negative thoughts first cross your mind, you will nearly always believe that they are the gospel truth. After all, if you don't believe a negative thought, it can't affect the way you feel. For example, you probably don't believe the thought "The world is coming to an end today." Therefore this thought won't make you feel anxious or depressed. If you did believe it, you'd be *quite* agitated! You will eventually discover that the thoughts that upset you are nearly always quite unrealistic, although they seem completely valid when they are running through your mind. Your Automatic Thoughts are deceptive. They create the illusion of truth, even when they're extremely illogical. When you write them down, it will be easier to put the lie to them. The moment you see how unrealistic and pessimistic they are, you will feel better.

After you have written down and numbered each of your Automatic Thoughts, identify the distortion(s) in them in the middle column. You can refer to "The Checklist of Cognitive Distortions" on page 77 when you do this. What are the distortions in Marge's first negative thought, "If Luci gets a sore throat it will be my fault"? Put your ideas here:

1._____

2._____

Answer: One distortion is "personalization," because Marge is blaming herself for a negative event that is beyond her control. A second distortion is "fortune-telling," since she is predicting that Luci will catch her brother's sore throat.

You can see that her second negative thought contains the same two distortions. She's predicting that her daughter will be angry with her, and she's prepared to blame herself for her daughter's reaction. Many people with depression automatically blame themselves and get terribly self-critical whenever anyone is angry with them. Do you ever react this way? I know that I sometimes do, and it can really hurt! You just suddenly feel that you're "no good" inside.

After you identify the distortions in your Automatic Thoughts, substitute Rational Responses in the right-hand column, and indicate how strongly you believe each one from 0 percent to 100 percent. Marge's first Rational Response was: "I made an honest mistake. Luci probably won't get a sore throat. If she does it won't be the end of the world, and I don't deserve to be punished like this." In parentheses, she indicated that she believed this 100 percent. For the second Rational Response, Marge reminded herself that if her daughter did get hostile and critical—as she often did—she could calmly acknowledge that she made a mistake and apologize without getting defensive and without putting herself down. If her daughter continued to harangue her, she could indicate that she was uncomfortable with the way her daughter was treating her.

This illustrates that the solution to a mood problem frequently has both an *individual* and an *interpersonal* dimension. Marge needs to change the way she thinks. She needs to develop better self-esteem and to stop being so self-critical. That's the individual dimension. At the same time, she needs to change the way she relates to other people, including her daughter. That's the interpersonal dimension. This may require some communication training, because Marge is extremely unassertive and she's afraid to express her feelings. She is terribly insecure and afraid of anger or conflict, so she takes too much abuse from other people. She automatically blames herself whenever anyone is annoyed with her. She is like an animal that goes belly up when threatened, hoping the predator will lose interest and go away. In Part IV we will talk about how to solve personal relationship problems and communicate more effectively.

Now I want you to complete your Daily Mood Log. After you write down your Automatic Thoughts, write how much you believe each one on a scale from 0 to 100 percent. In the middle column, identify the distortions in each thought, using the list on page 77 as a guide. Then write down more positive and realistic thoughts in the Rational Response column. Indicate in parentheses how much you believe each of them.

It is not terribly important to do a good job, because this is your first effort. It's much like your first time on roller skates: all you have to do is go through the motions, even if your efforts don't seem terribly graceful or effective. Once you've completed your Rational Responses, you're ready for the next step.

Step 4: Outcome

After you've answered all of your Automatic Thoughts, re-rate your belief in each of them. Cross out the original percent you rate each one, and put a new estimate of how much you now believe it in light of your Rational Response. You can see that Marge crossed out 100% and put in 20%, indicating she no longer believed her two Automatic Thoughts nearly so strongly. You will feel better the moment you see that your Automatic Thoughts are not valid.

Finally, evaluate how much better you feel in the "Outcome"

TROUBLESHOOTING GUIDE*

If you still feel just as upset after you fill out a Daily Mood Log, ask yourself these questions:

1. **Have I correctly identified the upsetting event?** Sometimes you can't put your finger on the problem that's bothering you. You will often discover what it is if you review your activities for the past day or two. Make your description of the negative event specific: What happened? Where were you? What time was it? With whom were you involved?

2. **Do I want to change my negative feelings about this situation?** List the advantages and disadvantages of changing your feelings.

3. **Have I identified my Automatic Thoughts properly?** Remember not to put descriptions of upsetting events or feelings in the Automatic Thoughts column. If you have trouble figuring out what your negative thoughts are, use the stick figure technique.

4. **Are my Rational Responses convincing, valid statements that put the lie to my Automatic Thoughts?** Rationalizations won't make you feel any better. Your Rational Responses must not only be realistic and believable, but they must contradict your Automatic Thoughts. The moment you see that your Automatic Thoughts aren't valid, you'll feel better.

section at the bottom of the sheet. As you can see in her log, Marge indicated she felt considerably relieved. That's because her Rational Responses were more realistic and believable than her Automatic Thoughts.

If you don't feel better after you complete the exercise, review the Troubleshooting Guide on page 86. Ask yourself the following questions:

Have I identified the upsetting event correctly? Remember to make the event specific, not vague. If you feel overwhelmed because you have many problems, then just choose one to work on first. It usually won't make any difference which one it is. Overcoming one problem will give you some inspiration and make it a lot easier to deal with the others.

If you can't put your finger on precisely what's bothering you, then review what's been going on in your life. With whom have you been talking? What have you been doing recently? This is like retracing your steps when you've lost something. Usually it will suddenly dawn on you what the problem is.

Do I really want to feel better? Sometimes you will have mixed feelings about letting go of a negative emotion. In fact your negative feelings may be quite healthy and realistic. If so, it might be better to express them instead of trying to make them go away by using the Daily Mood Log. For example, if someone is mad at you, or you are angry with them, it may be better to talk the problem over with them instead of trying to change your feelings about the situation with cognitive techniques. The chapters in Part IV on communication could be especially helpful in this case.

In deciding whether or not you want to change your feelings, list the advantages and disadvantages of feeling upset. (See page 113 for this "cost-benefit" technique.) Maybe you want to pamper yourself and let the feelings pass, or maybe there's a realistic problem you need to deal with. If you discover that the disadvantages of feeling upset outweigh the advantages, then it will be much easier to modify your feelings using the Daily Mood Log.

Have I identified my Automatic Thoughts properly? When you fill out the Daily Mood Log, remember that the thoughts you write down in the Automatic Thoughts column are the *interpretations* of the upsetting situation, not descriptions of the actual event. If you feel annoyed because your husband is late coming home, it wouldn't be appropriate to put "George was late again" in the Automatic Thoughts column. This is the actual problem, so it goes in the space at the top of the sheet. The premise of cognitive therapy is that only your *thoughts*, and not actual events, upset you. In the Automatic Thoughts column you would put your negative thoughts about this event. You might be thinking, "This shows George doesn't love me" or "He's always late" or "He's probably having an affair with his secretary."

Another common mistake is to put descriptions of your feelings in the Automatic Thoughts column. Don't put "I feel hurt because my boss criticized me," because this is a situation ("My boss criticized me") and a feeling ("hurt"). Describe the situation at the top of the sheet and record your negative feelings. In the Automatic Thoughts column, put the thoughts that are associated with these feelings. Why do you feel hurt? Why was his criticism so upsetting to you? What are you telling yourself? You might be thinking, "He doesn't respect me" or "He's got no right to say that" or "I never do anything right" or "I'm about to get fired."

If you aren't sure what all your negative thoughts are, you can use the stick figure technique described earlier. When Jack was golfing with his friends, he suddenly felt very anxious and nervous. On the Daily Mood Log he recorded this Automatic Thought: "I shouldn't be feeling so nervous, since everything is going well for me." Jack is a stockbroker, and recently the market has been treating him well. He's been making lots of money and his clients are making lots of money. What is the main distortion in his Automatic Thought? Check the list of cognitive distortions on page 77 and put your ideas here:

_____

_____

Answer: Jack is making a "should statement," since he is telling himself he "shouldn't" feel anxious. He was able to come up with this Rational Response: "Human beings are not always perfectly rational. Some people do get nervous, even when things are going well."

This helped somewhat, because Jack was giving himself permission to feel nervous instead of condemning himself for being nervous.

However, Jack still hadn't identified all the thoughts that were making him feel nervous in the first place. Since he drew a blank, I asked him to draw a stick figure of a man very like himself, who was golfing and feeling nervous. I told him to make up some negative thoughts and to write them down in the bubble on top, to show what the stick figure was thinking. As you can see, the stick figure golfer was thinking, "This shot will probably go in the lake. . . .

Jack was upset while he was playing golf, but at first he didn't know why. When he wrote down the negative thoughts in the bubble over the stick figure's head, it became clear what he was worrying about.

I'm doing well at work but I can't keep it up. The stock market will probably go down and everyone will lose money and fire me." I asked Jack if his thoughts were at all similar to those, and he said, "Exactly!" I don't know why the stick figure technique is so effective, but it is! Use it any time you can't figure out what your Automatic Thoughts are.

Are my Rational Responses true and valid statements, or am I just rationalizing? Do they put the lie to my Automatic Thoughts? The purpose of the Daily Mood Log is to help you face reality. It won't be helpful if you deny your problems or try to cheer yourself up with phony rationalizations. After her boyfriend broke up with her, Linda felt guilty and depressed. She told herself she wasn't lovable and that everything was her fault. She felt there was something basically wrong with her personality, and she was terrified she'd never find a husband and end up a lonely old maid.

After talking about the problem with a friend, she decided that the fellow who rejected her was basically a jerk and that the problems in their relationship were actually his fault. This was simply a rationalization. Linda switched from "personalization" ("It's all my fault") to "blame" ("It's all his fault"). I don't think this is the most productive way to deal with the situation. I would prefer to see Linda pinpoint the specific problems in the relationship as fairly and objectively as possible so she can learn from the experience. Why did they break up? What did she do to contribute to the tension? What did he do? How could she deal with a similar problem differently in the future? If she confronts these issues without a loss of self-esteem, she won't get bitter or depressed and she can make her next relationship better.

In order to make you feel better, the statements in the Rational Response column must not only be valid, but they must also put the lie to your Automatic Thoughts. Suppose you meet an old school friend who is more attractive, more intelligent, more successful, and more popular than you. You might have the Automatic Thought, "Gee, I'm not as worthwhile as she is." This thought will make you feel insecure and inferior. You could come up with the Rational Response, "But I'm a better cook." While this might be absolutely true, it's not likely to give your self-esteem much of a boost! For example, your friend might be so successful that she flies to Paris in a Concorde jet and eats in five-star restaurants. Can you think of a Rational Response that would be more effective?

I don't want to create the impression that the solution to your problems will always be easy or magical. The successful application of these techniques can sometimes require persistent work over a period of time. If you want good results, I would recommend using the Daily Mood Log for ten to fifteen minutes per day, five days per week, for at least a month. This regular practice will help you get in shape emotionally, in much the same way that an athlete builds his strength and conditioning through daily workouts. Sometimes it will be easy to change your thoughts and feelings, but at other times it will be difficult because your negative thoughts will seem so powerful and convincing. It's a challenge for me sometimes, and I wrote the book! But if you work at it with determination, you'll get the job done.

Don't go to the other extreme of thinking that this will be too difficult for you. This method is within the reach of the average individual. In a study reported in the *British Journal of Psychiatry*, Dr. Ivy Blackburn and her associates at the University of Edinburgh found that these techniques were very effective for working-class people. This proves that you do not have to be psychologically sophisticated to make cognitive therapy work for you. In a recent study in the journal *Cognitive Therapy and Research*, Dr. Jacqueline Persons and I reported the results of our research, which showed that these methods work equally well for patients with different levels of education and with a wide variety of income levels and cultural backgrounds. We discovered that regardless of whether you're rich or poor, brilliant or of average intelligence, old or young, a change in your thoughts and attitudes will have an enormous impact on the way you feel.

The four steps to happiness are summarized on page 92. Part of the beauty of this approach is that you can apply it to all kinds of problems. You can use it to break out of virtually any kind of bad mood—worry, sadness, anxiety, stress, frustration, guilt, anger. You can use it when you're having problems in your personal relationships, in your career, or in your attempts to modify a bad habit like drinking too much. For your convenience, I've included an additional Daily Mood Log (pages 93 to 96).

Coming up with believable, effective Rational Responses that successfully disprove your Automatic Thoughts takes practice. In the next chapter, I will describe many techniques that will help you develop more positive attitudes and greater self-esteem.

THE FOUR STEPS TO HAPPINESS*

STEP ONE—Identify the upsetting situation. Describe the event or problem that's upsetting you. Who (or what) are you feeling unhappy about?

STEP TWO—Record your negative feelings. How do you feel about the upsetting situation? Use words like sad, angry, anxious, guilty, frustrated, hopeless. Rate each negative feeling on a scale from 1 (for the least) to 100 (for the most).

STEP THREE—Use the triple-column technique. Tune in to the negative thoughts that are associated with these feelings. What are you saying to yourself about the problem? Write these thoughts in the Automatic Thoughts column and record how much you believe each one between 0 (not at all) and 100 (completely). After you identify the distortions in these thoughts, substitute Rational Responses in the right-hand column and record how much you believe each one between 0 (not at all) and 100 (completely). Make sure that your Rational Responses are convincing, valid statements that put the lie to your Automatic Thoughts.

STEP FOUR—Outcome. Indicate how much you now believe each Automatic Thought between 0 and 100. Once your belief in these thoughts are greatly reduced, indicate how much better you feel.

THE DAILY MOOD LOG*

STEP ONE: DESCRIBE THE UPSETTING EVENT _____

_____

STEP TWO: RECORD YOUR NEGATIVE FEELINGS—and rate each one from 0 (the least) to 100 (the most). Use words like sad, anxious, angry, guilty, lonely, hopeless, frustrated, etc.

Emotion	Rating	Emotion	Rating	Emotion	Rating
1.		3.		5.	
2.		4.		6.	

STEP THREE: THE TRIPLE-COLUMN TECHNIQUE—

Automatic Thoughts	Distortions	Rational Responses
Write your negative thoughts and estimate your belief in each one (0–100).	Identify the distortions in each Automatic Thought.	Substitute more realistic thoughts and estimate your belief in each one (0 and 100).

(Continue on next page)

THE DAILY MOOD LOG (continued)

Automatic Thoughts	Distortions	Rational Responses

(Continue on next page)

THE DAILY MOOD LOG (continued)

Automatic Thoughts	Distortions	Rational Responses

(Continue on next page)

Automatic Thoughts	Distortions	Rational Responses

STEP FOUR: OUTCOME—Re-rate your belief in each Automatic Thought from 0 to 100 and put a check in the box that describes how you now feel:

☐ not at all better; ☐ somewhat better; ☐ quite a bit better; ☐ a lot better.

CHECKLIST OF COGNITIVE DISTORTIONS*

1. All-or-nothing thinking: You look at things in absolute, black-and-white categories.
2. Overgeneralization: You view a negative event as a never-ending pattern of defeat.
3. Mental filter: You dwell on the negatives and ignore the positives.
4. Discounting the positives: You insist that your accomplishments or positive qualities "don't count."
5. Jumping to conclusions: (A) Mind reading—you assume that people are reacting negatively to you when there's no definite evidence for this; (B) Fortune-telling—you arbitrarily predict that things will turn out badly.
6. Magnification or minimization: You blow things way up out of proportion or you shrink their importance inappropriately.
7. Emotional reasoning: You reason from how you feel: "I *feel* like an idiot, so I really must be one." Or "I don't *feel* like doing this, so I'll put it off."
8. "Should statements": You criticize yourself or other people with "shoulds" or "shouldn'ts." "Musts," "oughts," and "have tos" are similar offenders.
9. Labeling: You identify with your shortcomings. Instead of saying "I made a mistake," you tell yourself, "I'm a jerk," or "a fool," or "a loser."
10. Personalization and blame: You blame yourself for something you weren't entirely responsible for, or you blame other people and overlook ways that your own attitudes and behavior might contribute to a problem.

6

•

Ten Ways to
Untwist Your Thinking

When you feel bad, you are thinking about things in a negative way. These thoughts, and not what actually happens, are what make you feel upset. Dr. Albert Ellis has called this the "A-B-C" of emotion. "A" stands for the "actual event"—this is what actually happened. Let's assume that you got divorced. "B" stands for your "beliefs" about the event. You may be thinking, "It's all my fault. What will my family and friends think of me?" "C" stands for the "consequences" of your beliefs, including the way you feel and the way you behave. You might be feeling sad and ashamed, and you may crawl into a shell and avoid people because you feel so inadequate and unlovable. As the following diagram illustrates, your thoughts and beliefs make you feel the way you do:

"A" (Actual event = divorce)
↓
"B" (Belief = "I'm no good")
↓
"C" (Consequences = depression)

Your thoughts and beliefs about the event create your feelings. If you had thought, "It's all *his* fault—he's a self-centered jerk," you would feel angry and bitter rather than sad and ashamed.

Cognitive therapists have developed powerful techniques to help you change the way you think and feel. This chapter describes methods that I use every day in my office, and many additional methods will be described in later chapters. These techniques will provide you with a cognitive therapy tool kit that will help you overcome a huge variety of negative thoughts and feelings. Study these methods carefully!

1. Identify the Distortions

As we discussed in the last chapter, the first thing to do when you feel upset is to write down a brief description of the actual situation or problem that's bothering you. Next, identify and rate each of your negative emotions on a scale from 1 to 100. The third step is to write down and number each of your Automatic Thoughts in the left-hand column of the Daily Mood Log. Then identify the distortions in each negative thought, using the list on page 96 as a guide.

To give a simple example, a single man named Nick, who had a fear of intimate relationships, would frequent peep shows and prostitutes whenever he got anxious. Afterward, Nick had an extreme sense of self-loathing and sometimes felt suicidal, thinking, "I'm such a lowlife." What are the distortions in this thought? Review the "Checklist of Cognitive Distortions" on page 96 and put your ideas here:

1. _____

2. _____

Answer: It's an "overgeneralization," because Nick is generalizing from his behavior to his self. You could also call it "labeling," because he's attaching a negative label to himself.

Now you might think that Nick really is a "lowlife" and that he deserves to feel rotten. There are problems with this argument. When Nick thinks of himself as a "lowlife," he convinces himself that he's unworthy of love. Then he is even more likely to continue going to peep shows and prostitutes because that's what a "lowlife" does.

In addition, the shame and low self-esteem Nick feels will make it even harder for him to open up to a relationship with a woman he respects and cares about. He's afraid to risk being rejected, because Nick finds it inconceivable that anyone could ever love him. If he begins to accept himself, he may feel more lovable and find the courage to risk getting close to other people.

When you identify the distortions in any thought, you do not need to be overly precise. There's a lot of overlap between distortions, and the list you come up with may be a little different from mine. The important thing is to try to find at least one or more distortions in each Automatic Thought. That will make it easier to develop an effective Rational Response.

As an exercise, let's suppose someone criticizes you. You get upset and think, "I never do anything right. I'm such a loser." These thoughts make you feel inadequate and guilty. What are the distortions in these thoughts? Review the "Checklist of Cognitive Distortions" on page 96 and put your ideas here:

1. _____

2. _____

3. _____

4. _____

5. _____

6. _____

7. _____

8. _____

Answer: all-or-nothing thinking, overgeneralization, mental filter, discounting the positive, magnification, emotional reasoning, labeling, and personalization.

2. Examine the Evidence

After you write down a negative thought and you identify the distortions in it, ask yourself, "What is the evidence for this thought?" Because we *feel* so bad, we often believe things *are* bad without checking the facts. Once you examine the facts, things will frequently fall into a different perspective.

To continue with the previous example, how could you use the method of examining the evidence to talk back to your thought, "I never do anything right, I'm such a loser"? Put your ideas here:

_____

_____

_____

_____

Answer: You could ask yourself, "Is it true that I *never* do *anything* right? What are some things I do well? What are the things I'm not so good at?" If there's some truth in a criticism, you can try to learn from it in the spirit of self-respect. Focus on the specific problem instead of writing yourself off as a "a loser."

A single man named Eric told me that he could never find a wife because he was "only average-looking." How could Eric Examine the Evidence to find out if this belief was really valid? Put your ideas here:

_____

_____

_____

_____

Answer: I asked Eric to walk around the park on a Saturday and to rate how attractive (on a scale from 1 to 10) the couples were who were walking together. He discovered that some of them were very attractive (with ratings in the 7 to 10 range), some were only average (with ratings in the 4 to 6 range), and some were below average (with ratings in the 1 to 3 range). He also observed that the two partners' ratings were often quite different. Sometimes a very attractive woman was walking happily hand-in-hand with a man who was "only average," and vice versa. This made Eric aware that you don't have to be handsome or beautiful to develop a loving relationship with someone you care about. While it's true that very attractive people find it easier to meet others and to get dates, good looks are no guarantee that you will have a satisfying relationship. Eric's low self-esteem was the real problem. Once he learned to accept himself, he discovered that women were quite interested in him.

3. The Double-Standard Method

When you have a self-critical thought, ask yourself, "Would I say this to a close friend who was very much like me and had a similar problem?" We are frequently much harder on ourselves than on others. If you make a mistake or fail to achieve a goal, you might rip yourself to shreds and think, "I'm such a stupid jerk! I don't know what I'm doing. I'll never succeed at anything!" But if a friend made the same mistake, you'd probably be supportive. Why not be equally encouraging to yourself?

You may reply, "Because I have higher standards for myself." Let's investigate this argument. I would like to know why you have such high standards. You may say, "It's because I want to do my best." So essentially you rip yourself to shreds so you will try hard and do your best, right? I'm sure you'd also like your friend to do his or her best. Why not tell him, "You're such a stupid jerk! You'll never succeed at anything"?

The answer is obvious: because these harsh messages are utterly unrealistic and they won't help your friend do better. They'll just make him or her feel like giving up. These messages won't help you, either!

Why not treat all people, including yourself, with one standard that's both helpful and realistic? Give yourself the same encouraging messages you'd give a friend. This is the essence of the Double-Standard Method. It's an excellent way to answer Automatic Thoughts.

If you suffer from test anxiety, you may tell yourself, "When I take the test I'm going to blow it! I know I'll really screw up." You may give yourself this message hundreds of times while you're trying to study. These thoughts make you extremely nervous and you can hardly concentrate.

Can you imagine leaning over the shoulder of a friend who was trying to study and saying "You're going to blow it! You're really going to screw up"? But that's *precisely* what you do to yourself. That's why you feel so nervous and inadequate.

See if you can use the Double-Standard Method to talk back to those negative thoughts. Put your Rational Responses here:

_____

_____

_____

_____

Answer: Ask yourself what you'd say to a friend who was nervous and trying to study. I suspect you'd tell him or her something helpful and realistic. You might say, "You're doing a good job and all your studying will help you when you take the test." This would give your friend a needed boost of self-confidence. If you say this to yourself, you'll also begin to feel less nervous and more confident.

4. The Experimental Technique

When you have a negative thought, ask yourself if there's a way you could test it to find out if it's really true. Sometimes an experiment will help you get to the truth about things. To take a simple example, let's assume that you sometimes procrastinate. You may need to balance your checkbook, but you tell yourself, "It'll be such a drag," or "I just can't do it," or "It'll be too hard." These thoughts make you feel so upset that you can't stand to do it. The purpose of the Experimental Method is to test these thoughts. You can ask yourself, "Is it really true that it will be a 'drag' and that it will be 'too hard'?" Try to think of an experiment to test these ideas. Put your ideas here:

You could break the task down into small steps. First, locate your checkbook and your bank statement; second, see what checks have come in; third, add up the total amount of money for all the checks that come in; and so on. Then you could complete the first step—locating your checkbook. Ask yourself if it was "too hard" for you or if it was "a drag." You will probably discover that it wasn't nearly as difficult as you predicted. Then you can go on to the next step, and then the next, until the job is done.

The essence of this procedure is to test your negative thoughts by doing experiments. A depressed woman named Phyllis strongly believed that her husband didn't love her and that none of her friends liked her anymore. Consequently she stayed at home. She didn't even answer the phone. After a while people gave up and stopped calling. This convinced Phyllis even more that she was unlovable.

This often happens when you are depressed or annoyed with a friend or family member. Instead of dealing with the conflict, you avoid it. Then it eats away at you and the problem begins to feel far worse than it really is.

How could Phyllis test her belief that nobody liked her? I asked what she thought would happen if she called two or three friends and invited them out to lunch. She predicted they would all make excuses and say they were too busy. I urged her to call them so we could get some real data.

At our next session Phyllis told me that she was surprised: two friends had accepted her invitation, while the third took a rain check until after her vacation. All three seemed happy to hear from her and expressed concern that they hadn't gotten together sooner. This wasn't consistent with Phyllis's claim that nobody liked her anymore.

This doesn't mean that there was no truth whatsoever in Phyllis's negative thoughts. She did harbor resentment toward her husband and sometimes felt jealous of her friends. She may need to deal with these problems with the communication techniques described in Part IV. However, her belief that everybody had rejected her was simply not true.

5. Thinking in Shades of Gray

When you have a negative thought, ask yourself, "Am I looking at things in an either-or, black-or-white fashion? Am I thinking of myself as either a total success or a total failure?" If so, you are probably involved in "all-or-nothing thinking." This is one of the most common distortions. It can lead to anxiety and panic, depression, guilt, feelings of inferiority, hopelessness, perfectionism, and anger. Learning to modify "all-or-nothing thinking" has changed the lives of many of my patients.

One helpful technique is called Thinking in Shades of Gray. The basic principle is very simple: You remind yourself that things are usually somewhere between 0 and 100 percent instead of insisting that they're all one way or the other.

Linda is a spunky, petite 45-year-old woman from Chicago. After her husband died unexpectedly when she was 30, she began to manage his small construction company. Although it was a male-dominated industry, Linda valiantly persisted and eventually developed a booming business throughout Chicago. She constantly had to negotiate with union bosses, contractors, and city officials who could be tough and occasionally ruthless. During the late 1970s, a man who appeared to have mob connections coerced Linda into making several under-the-table payments of thousands of dollars. He threatened that if she refused, she might find that the construction workers would become suddenly uncooperative and unable to complete their jobs. He implied she would be blacklisted and bankrupted if she resisted.

Linda was torn. Out of panic—and greed—she made the payments and completed the project. Linda never again bid for contracts in this part of Chicago. She ran a clean shop and continued to do well and eventually forgot about the incident. Two months ago she received a subpoena from federal investigators. The man who had blackmailed her had been arrested, and a notebook listing payments from construction companies was seized. Linda's name showed up on the list. Linda's attorney was able to obtain immunity from prosecution in exchange for her testimony.

Linda feared for her life because of the possibility that the mob might retaliate if she testified. However, her greatest fear was the possibility of newspaper publicity during the trial. She had the thought, "My family and the people I do business with will find out that I was dishonest. They will think I have no integrity. They'll lose respect for me." She wept out of guilt and shame as she shared these feelings with me.

Can you identify any distortions in her thoughts? Check the list on page 96 and put your ideas here:

1. _____

2. _____

3. _____

Linda is "jumping to conclusions," including both "fortune-telling" and "mind reading." She's predicting not only that she will get negative publicity but also that everybody will look down on her. She really doesn't know this. There may be no publicity. If there is, people may be sympathetic and admire her courage in testifying against organized crime.

An even more profound distortion is the "all-or-nothing thinking." Linda tells herself that she has "no integrity." In the following dialogue, I encouraged Linda to "think in shades of gray."

DR. BURNS: They will see that you have no integrity? How much integrity have you had for the past fifteen years, on a scale from 0 to 100%? Zero? A hundred? How much?

LINDA: I'd have to say 95%. I return checks if people overpay. I try to run my business in a scrupulous way. This was a situation where I did have bad judgment, though.

DR. BURNS: So if you have 95 percent integrity, how do you reconcile this with the claim that you have no integrity? You haven't been perfect, but it sounds like you've done pretty darn well—better than most, I suspect.

LINDA: But what will other people think of me?

DR. BURNS: The most important thing is what *you* think of you. Only *your* thoughts will affect your self-esteem. You're upset because you aren't accepting yourself as an imperfect human being. Let's do some play-acting. I'll be Linda and you can be a business associate. You read about my testimony in the *Chicago Tribune* and you saw me on the network news. I want you to say the worst imaginable things to me. Tell me I have no integrity and that you won't do business with me anymore.

LINDA (*as Critic*): Gee, I read about you in the *Chicago Tribune*. Did you really make those payments to the mob?

DR. BURNS (*as Linda*): Yes, I did. It was bad judgment and I wish I hadn't done it.

LINDA (*as Critic*): So, you did something dishonest. You tried to bribe the unions! You did it out of greed!

DR. BURNS (*as Linda*): That's correct. Greed and fear motivated me. The mob threatened to destroy me if I didn't give in. I was frightened and confused, and what I did was not right.

LINDA (*as Critic*): Well, why should I ever give you any other contracts? You're a real wheeler-dealer!

DR. BURNS (*as Linda*): You might want to give me another contract because of the top-notch work I've been doing for you. I believe my company is one of the best in the city.

LINDA (*as Critic*): But you screwed up! Admit it! I look down on you. I've got no respect for you.

DR. BURNS (*as Linda*): I agree! I *did* screw up and I wish I hadn't. I paid for my mistake and I've learned a lot as a result of it. If you want to look down on me, you can certainly do that. Lots of times I feel exactly the same way. However, I believe I can still do outstanding work for you. If you want the best building at an honest, competitive cost, I'm available and eager to work with you. If you want someone who never screwed up, you may have to look elsewhere. But there are a lot of sharks in the ocean, so be careful!

Obviously people would never really say such insulting things to Linda. The point of the exercise was to show her how to accept herself and to talk back to her own self-critical thoughts. She did screw up, and it was a horrendously difficult situation. She could get defensive and stubbornly insist she was an innocent victim, but that would be defensive and unrealistic. Linda could also condemn herself as a rotten person and give up. Or she could acknowledge her mistake, forgive herself, and move forward with her life.

Linda said that the session caused profound relief because she discovered that she didn't have to be perfect or afraid of admitting her shortcomings. Instead of seeing herself as having either perfect integrity or none at all, she learned to accept reality. Her integrity had been quite high, but not perfect. This insight allowed her to admit her error without a loss of self-esteem, so she could learn from the situation instead of despising herself forever.

6. The Survey Method

One way to evaluate a negative attitude is to ask yourself, "Would other people agree that this thought is valid?" You can often perform a survey to find out.

A man named Richard became very upset whenever he and his wife had an argument, because he told himself, "People who really love each other shouldn't fight." What kind of survey could Richard conduct to find out how realistic this attitude is? Put your ideas here:

_____

_____

_____

Answer: I suggested he ask several happily married friends if they ever fought with their wives. He was surprised that nearly all of them reported that angry feelings and arguments were commonplace.

The head of a prestigious law firm was constantly tense and pressured because he would tell himself, "My associates will think less of me if I lose a case or make a mistake." How could he conduct a survey to find out whether this is true? Put your ideas here:

_____

_____

_____

Answer: The lawyer decided to ask his associates about this. Most of them said they would like him more, not less, if he lost a case because it would make him seem more human. This was a tremendous relief.

A year later he actually did lose a case—the first in over a decade. At a social function of a statewide law organization he told numerous friends and acquaintances that he'd just lost an important case. He was surprised that about half the people were extremely friendly and supportive. The other half were uninterested in the case *he* lost but seemed tremendously eager to talk about cases *they'd* recently lost! It turned out to be the most rewarding meeting he'd ever attended. This helped him discover that it's okay to be human, that sometimes his failures could help him get closer to other people. He also admitted that his many impressive achievements had never really made him feel accepted or close to anyone.

7. Define Terms

When you have a negative thought, ask yourself, "How am I defining terms? What do I mean by this? Am I using vague, pejorative labels that have no real meaning?" This method is especially helpful if you are putting yourself down as "a failure" or "a loser" or "a jerk" or "a fool." Once you try to define what you mean by "loser," "jerk," or "fool," you will usually see that your definition is meaningless or that it doesn't apply to you. Since there really is no such thing as "a loser" or "a jerk" or "a fool," then you cannot possibly be one!

Here's how it works. You feel embarrassed about something and you think, "I'm such a fool." Now, ask yourself: what's the definition of "a fool"? You might define "a fool" as "someone who does something foolish." But according to this definition we're all fools, because we all do something foolish at some time or other in our lives. Unless you concede that all human beings are fools, your definition can't be valid. And if you feel that all human beings are fools, then it can't be so terrible for you to be one, since you're no different from anyone else.

Try again. You might define "a fool" as "someone who does foolish things more often than other people." Now ask yourself what this means. More often than whom? More often than how many other people? You might say that a fool is one who does foolish things more often than half the human race. But now you're in the awkward position of claiming that half the human race—or two billion people—are "fools." In addition, you're now categorizing all people as either "fools" or "non-fools." Can you imagine walking down a crowded downtown sidewalk at the lunch hour and trying to figure out which of the people you see are the "fools" and which are the "non-fools"?

You can go on trying to define "a fool," but your definition will always turn into nonsense. That's because foolish behavior exists, but "fools" do not. Only human beings exist. Is this just semantics, a trick of words? No, it's not. Labels like "fool," "loser," "winner," "jerk," or "inferior person" are useless abstractions. It is far more productive to focus on what you *do*—and what you can do to learn and grow—than on what you *are*. If things don't work out well, ask yourself what you can do differently next time.

8. The Semantic Method

When you feel upset, ask yourself if you're telling yourself, "I *should* do this" or "I *shouldn't* do that." The Semantic Method is an effective way to combat "should statements." Substitute a phrase like "it would be nice" or "it would be preferable" in place of "I should." Instead of saying "I should go on a diet," you could tell yourself that "there would be some advantages in dieting." This change may seem subtle. We're trying to change the emotional coloring so a problem will seem less upsetting and less catastrophic. You stop making rigid, coercive demands on yourself and focus instead on your goals. This sounds less bossy and less judgmental.

You might be interested to know that the word "should" traces its origin to the Anglo-Saxon word "sceolde." The purpose of the Semantic Method is to help you stop scolding yourself. If you motivate yourself with a carrot rather than a stick, you won't feel so guilty and so coerced. When you punish yourself with "should statements," you will frequently just run into resistance because you feel rebellious.

If you feel anxious about public speaking or being at social gatherings, you may tell yourself, "I shouldn't feel this way." Can you see why this is self-defeating? It's self-defeating because it will make you feel worse. You'll feel guilty and anxious about feeling anxious.

What could you tell yourself instead of "I shouldn't feel anxious"? Use the Semantic Method and put your ideas here:

_____

_____

_____

_____

Answer: You could tell yourself that it would be *preferable* not to feel so anxious before a speech. You could also remind yourself that most people do have this problem. You will learn a great deal about how to cope with public speaking anxiety in Chapter 15.

So far we've talked about "self shoulds"—should statements directed against yourself. "Other shoulds" are directed against external events, like trains that arrive late or people who do something you don't like. "Other shoulds" lead to anger and frustration. If your train is late you may think, "It should be on time!" Then you will feel exasperated. Ask yourself if you want to feel this way. There are times when anger is healthy, but is this one of them? Will you do yourself any good if you work yourself into a stew? Will the train arrive any sooner?

How could you use the Semantic Method to talk back to this negative thought? Put your ideas here:

_____

_____

_____

_____

Answer: Instead of demanding perfection from the world, you could say, "It would be great if this train were on time, but it's late. That's inconvenient, but I'll survive. Next time I'll take an earlier train so I won't feel so pressured."

After giving a lecture on my book *Feeling Good*, I spoke with a woman who described her recent vacation to Hawaii with her family. When they arrived she discovered that the airline had lost all their luggage. She had spent so much time carefully buying and packing all the right clothes so they would have a perfect vacation! To make matters worse, their luggage wasn't even located until the last day of their vacation!

How would you have felt? You might have told yourself, "This shouldn't have happened!" Then you would feel miserable. Would you want to feel that way while you were in Hawaii?

She said they made the conscious decision not to get upset. Instead, they viewed the situation as a challenge. They made a game of it to see how much fun they could have without their luggage. She said they had more fun than on any vacation they'd ever had.

9. Re-attribution

One of the commonest cognitive distortions is called "personalization," or self-blame. You put yourself down and blame yourself for a problem you aren't entirely responsible for. One antidote to personalization is "re-attribution": you attribute the cause of a problem to something other than your "badness." Ask yourself, "What other factors may have contributed to this problem?" Then develop a list of possibilities. The aim of the procedure is not to deny any mistakes you might have made, but to assess the causes of a problem more objectively. If you contributed to the situation, accept this and try to learn from the experience instead of wallowing in self-loathing.

A man named Frank became depressed when his wife began to lose interest in sex. They had intercourse less frequently, and sometimes she just seemed to be staring at the ceiling waiting for Frank to finish. Frank's Automatic Thoughts were: "She doesn't love me. She's rejecting me. I must not be worth anything." What are the distortions in these thoughts? Check the list on page 96 and put your ideas here:

1. _____

2. _____

3. _____

Answer: One distortion is "personalization"—Frank is blaming himself entirely for his wife's sexual problem. A second is "mind reading"—he assumes that she doesn't love him. A third is "all-or-nothing thinking"—he tells himself he's "worthless."

To talk back to these thoughts, Frank can use the re-attribution method. He needs to explore other causes of his wife's loss of sexual interest. Are there any other possible reasons? Even if you're not a marriage therapist, I suspect you can come up with a few ideas. List them here:

1. _____

2. _____

3. _____

Answer: There are many possibilities. She might be angry with him about something. If they have trouble dealing openly with negative feelings, as so many couples do, then these feelings could easily get expressed as a lack of sexual interest. This would not mean that she didn't love Frank or that Frank was worthless. It would simply mean they needed to talk about their angry feelings.

There are other possibilities. Frank's wife could have an infection that causes pain during intercourse. She could have religious inhibitions that make it hard for her to enjoy sex. She could feel that Frank's lovemaking is too rushed but may be afraid to talk to him about what she likes and dislikes sexually because she doesn't want to hurt his feelings. She might also be depressed. A loss of interest in sex is a common symptom of depression.

Once Frank finds out what the cause of the problem is, he will be able to deal with it more effectively. Frank asked his wife to join us during his sessions and it turned out that she did have some pent-up anger that was making it hard for her to feel sexually excited. Frank also felt angry and rejected. After they shared those feelings they began to feel much better about each other, and her sexual interest returned.

10. Cost-Benefit Analysis

The Cost-Benefit Analysis is quite different from other cognitive techniques because it deals with your negative thoughts from the perspective of motivation rather than truth. Ask yourself, "How will it help me to believe this negative thought and how will it hurt me?" If it turns out the disadvantages are greater, you will find it easier to talk back to the thought. You can use the blank Cost-Benefit Analysis form on page 114 when you do this.

I recently treated a high school teacher named Chuck, who didn't get very high ratings from his students or from the principal. In addition to his career problems, Chuck had suffered from depression and feelings of inferiority since childhood. One of his recurring negative thoughts was "I'm an inadequate, defective human being." He had this thought many times every day, and whenever it crossed his mind he felt intense self-loathing. However, Chuck was unable to talk back to this negative thought. He believed that he really was an inadequate, defective human being because:

He'd been chronically depressed.

He had no self-esteem.

He was below par in his teaching skills.

He had few friends.

He didn't get along well with his family.

He felt shy and uncomfortable around women.

He'd never accomplished anything special that he could feel proud of.

I tried in vain to persuade Chuck that he was *not* "an inadequate, defective human being." Chuck insisted he was facing the bitter truth about himself and urged me to give up on him.

After months of being stuck on this issue, a light bulb went on in my head one evening when I was thinking about him. I called him the next morning and said that I wanted him to make one list of the advantages and disadvantages of calling himself "an inadequate, defective human being" and a second list of the advantages and disadvantages of thinking of himself as "a human being with defects." He agreed.

When I saw Chuck several days later, his depression had vanished. Chuck said that what I'd been driving at suddenly became clear to

COST-BENEFIT ANALYSIS*

The attitude or belief I want to change:_____

_____

_____

Advantages of Believing This	**Disadvantages of Believing This**

*Revised Attitude:*_____

_____

_____

him. The real problem, he explained, was not that he was defective at the core but that he had defects just like everyone else and that he could work on them. He said he could work on becoming a more effective teacher and he could learn to relate to people better. He said that although this difference in his thinking seemed small, the impact on his self-esteem was profound because he viewed himself more positively and realistically.

In the next few weeks, Chuck started dating and making all kinds of changes in his life. He was surprised to discover that the moment he felt better about himself, everyone else started liking him as well. Women were suddenly attracted to him, and his colleagues and students began to treat him with greater respect.

Although this seemed like a miracle, I see similar changes in my office every week. Self-esteem is one of the most powerful forces in the universe. Self-esteem leads to joy, to productivity, to intimacy. That's why I advocate a value system that promotes self-esteem. Self-esteem is like faith: it can move mountains!

The Cost-Benefit Analysis has many useful applications. You can use it to evaluate the advantages and disadvantages of negative emotions, negative thoughts and self-defeating beliefs.

- *Negative feelings:* When you feel angry, anxious or guilty, you can ask yourself, "How will it help me, and how will it hurt me, to feel this way?" When the disadvantages outweigh the advantages, it will be far easier to change your feelings with the Daily Mood Log.
- *Automatic Thoughts:* When you have a thought such as "I'm such a loser" or "I *shouldn't* be so upset," make a list of the advantages and disadvantages of giving yourself this message.
- *Self-Defeating Attitudes:* In the next chapter, you will learn that certain self-defeating attitudes can trigger painful mood swings. An example would be: "I must always try to be perfect" or "I must always try to get everybody's approval." You can ask yourself, "How will it help me, and how will it hurt me, to believe this," as in the example on page 116. When the disadvantages of an attitude are greater than the advantages, try to revise it with a belief that will be more realistic, as on page 116.

You may feel a little overwhelmed and wonder when and how to use each of these techniques. In fact, you can use almost any technichue for any Automatic Thought. By flexible and creative. Try a variety of methods until you find a way to put the lie to each

COST-BENEFIT ANALYSIS*

The attitude or belief I want to change: I must have everybody's approval to be happy and worthwhile.

Advantages of Believing This	Disadvantages of Believing This
1. It will feel good when people approve of me.	1. I'll feel lousy when people don't like me or approve of me.
2. I'll work hard to make people like me.	2. Other people will control my self-esteem.
3. I'll be very sensitive to other people's feelings.	3. People may not respect me in the long run if I don't stand up for what I believe in.
	4. I may be less sensitive to other people because I'll be so worried about criticism or conflict.

(35)————————(65)

Revised Attitude: It can be great to have people like me and approve of what I do. When people are critical of me, I can try to understand their point of view.

negative thought. Sometimes this will be easy, and sometimes it will require persistence. The summary on page 118 will help you identify the methods that are most likely to help.

You may be wondering when you should use each of the various techniques. I believe that you should always "identify the distortion" first. You will discover that certain techniques work especially well for particular kinds of distortions. For example, if the distortion in your negative thought is "all-or-nothing thinking," the method called "Thinking in Shades of Gray" is likely to help. If your negative thought is a "should statement," the "Semantic Method" will nearly always work well. If you're involved in "emotional reasoning," you may find it helpful to Examine the Evidence, or you could use the Experimental Technique.

Remember that any cognitive technique can usually be used with any negative thought, so don't be rigid in trying to match specific techniques to specific distortions. Also keep in mind that a method that works wonders for one negative thought may not be at all helpful for another. Determination and patience are crucial. If you keep at it, you will succeed!

I once treated a woman who had the thought "I deserve to suffer for the rest of my life because of my abortion." She had had an abortion two years earlier, and she felt enormously guilty. She told herself she was despicable and berated herself mercilessly all day long. I tried numerous methods to help her talk back to this thought, but none of them worked. She said she deserved to suffer and insisted that her problems were hopeless. We worked on her need to condemn herself for many months, with no success. Eventually, I asked her husband to join us for couples therapy sessions. Once they started to feel closer, she was able to forgive herself. After she let go of the guilt and the self-hatred, her depression disappeared. I still hear from her occasionally. She's had two more children and feels an immense joy in living.

I tell you this story because it illustrates the importance of patience and persistence. You may have to be creative and try many ways of challenging the negative thoughts that make you miserable. One of the great strengths of cognitive therapy is its enormous flexibility. Eventually you will learn to talk back to your self-criticisms. When you do, you will experience a profound transformation in your spirit and in your outlook on life.

TEN WAYS TO UNTWIST
YOUR THINKING*

1. **Identify the Distortion.** Write down your negative thoughts so you can see which of the ten cognitive distortions you're involved in. This will make it easier to think about the problem in a more positive and realistic way.

2. **Examine the Evidence.** Instead of assuming that your negative thought is true, examine the actual evidence for it. For example, if you feel that you never do anything right, you could list several things you have done successfully.

3. **The Double-Standard Method:** Instead of putting yourself down in a harsh, condemning way, talk to yourself in the same compassionate way you would talk to a friend with a similar problem.

4. **The Experimental Technique:** Do an experiment to test the validity of your negative thought. For example, if, during an episode of panic, you become terrified that you're about to die of a heart attack, you could jog or run up and down several flights of stairs. This will prove that your heart is healthy and strong.

5. **Thinking in Shades of Gray.** Although this method might sound drab, the effects can be illuminating. Instead of thinking about your problems in all-or-nothing extremes, evaluate things on a range from 0 to 100. When things don't work out as well as you hoped, think about the experience as a partial success rather than a complete failure. See what you can learn from the situation.

6. **The Survey Method.** Ask people questions to find out if your thoughts and attitudes are realistic. For example, if you believe that public speaking anxiety is abnormal and shameful, ask several friends if they ever felt nervous before they gave a talk.

7. **Define Terms.** When you label yourself "inferior" or "a fool" or "a loser," ask, "What is the definition of 'a fool'?" You will feel better when you see that there is no such thing as "a fool" or "a loser."

8. **The Semantic Method.** Simply substitute language that is less colorful and emotionally loaded. This method is helpful for "should statements." Instead of telling yourself "I *shouldn't* have made that mistake," you can say, "It would be better if I hadn't made that mistake."

*Copyright © 1989 by David D. Burns, M.D., from *The Feeling Good Handbook*

9. **Re-attribution.** Instead of automatically assuming that you are "bad" and blaming yourself entirely for a problem, think about the many factors that may have contributed to it. Focus on solving the problem instead of using up all your energy blaming yourself and feeling guilty.

10. **Cost-Benefit Analysis.** List the advantages and disadvantages of a feeling (like getting angry when your plane is late), a negative thought (like "No matter how hard I try, I always screw up"), or a behavior pattern (like overeating and lying around in bed when you're depressed). You can also use the Cost-Benefit Analysis to modify a self-defeating belief such as, "I must always try to be perfect."

7

•

How to Develop a Healthy Personal Value System

While the purpose of cognitive therapy is to help you solve specific problems in the here-and-now, it can also help you develop greater emotional strength and wisdom for the future. As you review your negative thoughts, you may discover certain recurring self-defeating attitudes. You may find that you're overly guilt-prone because you automatically blame yourself for everyone else's problems. You may discover that your anxiety and depression are usually triggered by criticism or arguments with people you care about. You may learn that you're a perfectionist, worrying excessively about failing at work or school or letting others down. You may discover that you are extremely vulnerable to stress because you think about things in an "all-or-nothing" manner and your performance never seems quite good enough.

Common attitudes that often lead to depression and anxiety are listed on page 121. As you review the list you may recognize the ones that are causing problems for you. These are sometimes called "silent assumptions." They make you vulnerable to painful mood swings. Once you identify them, you can work on them from a variety of angles and develop a healthier personal value system.

COMMON SELF-DEFEATING
ATTITUDES AND FEARS

1. "It would be terrible to be rejected, abandoned, or alone. I must have love and approval before I can feel good about myself."

2. "If someone criticizes me, it means there's something wrong with me."

3. "I must always please people and live up to everyone's expectations."

4. "I am basically defective and inferior to other people."

5. "Other people are to blame for my problems."

6. "The world should always be the way I want it to be."

7. "Other people should always meet my expectations."

8. "If I worry or feel bad about a situation, it will somehow make things better. It's not really safe to feel happy and optimistic."

9. "I'm hopeless and bound to feel depressed forever because the problems in my life are impossible to solve."

10. "I must always try to be perfect." There are several kinds of perfectionism that can make you unhappy.

   • Moralistic perfectionism: "I must not forgive myself if I have fallen short of any goal or personal standard."
   • Performance perfectionism: "To be a worthwhile person, I must be a great success at everything I do."
   • Identity perfectionism: "People will never accept me as a flawed and vulnerable human being."
   • Emotional perfectionism "I must always try to be happy. I must control my negative emotions and never feel anxious or depressed."
   • Romantic perfectionism: "I must find a perfect mate and always feel infatuated with him or her."
   • Relationship perfectionism: "People who love each other should never fight or feel angry with each other."
   • Sexual perfectionism: Men may believe "I should always have full and sustained erections. It's shameful and unmanly if I have an episode of impotence or come too quickly." Women may believe "I should always achieve orgasm or multiple orgasms."
   • Appearance perfectionism: "I look ugly because I'm slightly overweight [or have heavy thighs or a facial blemish]."

The Vertical Arrow Technique

The "Vertical Arrow Technique" can help you pinpoint your silent assumptions. The methods described in Chapter 6 involve putting the lie to your negative thoughts. You show that your negative thoughts aren't true by using logic, by examining the evidence, by doing experiments, and so on. The Vertical Arrow Technique involves precisely the opposite strategy. You *buy into* your negative thoughts and see where they lead you. This can help you understand the self-defeating beliefs that are creating unnecessary barriers to self-esteem, intimacy, and productivity.

Here's how you do it. First, identify a negative thought about a situation that's upsetting you. Suppose you're studying for an exam and you think, "If I don't study harder, I may blow it." This thought makes you tense and you have a hard time concentrating. Write this thought down and draw a small downward arrow underneath it, as illustrated on page 124. The arrow means "If this thought were true, why would it be upsetting to me? What would it mean to me?" You might think, "If I blow the test, I may fail the course." Then write this down as your second negative thought and put another arrow underneath it. Remember that the downward arrow always means "If that thought were true, why would it be upsetting to me? What would it mean to me?" These questions will lead to another negative thought, and then another, as illustrated.

After you've generated as many negative thoughts as you can, review what you've written. Ask yourself, "What do these negative thoughts tell me about my value system? What are my basic assumptions about the basis of happiness and self-esteem?" Now study the four Automatic Thoughts that are illustrated on page 124. Ask yourself what the silent assumptions are. Write your ideas here before you read on.

1. _____

2. _____

3. _____

Answer: The Automatic Thoughts contain several silent assumptions: (1) I must always be a success in life to be worthwhile and to be loved and respected by others. (2) I must get everybody's approval to be a worthwhile person. (3) If I fail to achieve any goal, it will be a catastrophe. Review the sample again and see if you agree.

One of the remarkable things about the Vertical Arrow Technique is that you can identify these self-defeating attitudes very rapidly. I often use the procedure in the first or second therapy session with a new patient. This allows me to pinpoint his or her underlying fears within five to ten minutes—considerably quicker than the years it might take to learn about yourself with psychoanalysis! The man whose thoughts are illustrated here in Figure 10 suffered from low self-esteem. He had a terrific fear of failure and abandonment and a desperate need for approval. These attitudes crippled him.

Once you have identified a silent assumption, you should ask yourself these three questions about it: (1) Is it to my advantage to believe this? What are the consequences, positive and negative, of this attitude? (2) Is it realistic to think this way? Is my silent assumption really valid? (3) What would happen if I confronted my worst fear? Would the world really come to an end if I changed this attitude?

The following three-step program will show you how you can develop healthier attitudes that will lead to better self-esteem and improved relationships with others.

STEP ONE: COST-BENEFIT ANALYSIS

You can evaluate the consequences of my silent assumption with the Cost-Benefit Analysis described in Chapter 6: you list the advantages and disadvantages of believing it. This helps you decide if a particular attitude is helping you or hurting you.

Let's work this out together, using the belief "I must always be a success in life to be worthwhile." Can you think of any advantages of thinking this way? Keep in mind that I'm not asking you about the advantages of being successful—I'm asking about the advantages of basing your self-esteem on your success. How will it help you to think you must earn your self-esteem through your achievements?

List the advantages of this attitude here:

1. _____

THE VERTICAL ARROW TECHNIQUE*

Automatic thoughts

1. **If I don't study harder, I may blow the exam.**

   If this were true, what would it mean to me? Why would it be upsetting to me?

2. **If I blow the exam, I may fail the course.**

   And if I failed, why would that be uspetting to me?

3. **That would mean I was a failure and people would think less of me.**

   And if I was "a failure" and if people thought less of me, what then? Why would this be upsetting?

4. **Then I'd feel terrible, because I need people's approval to feel happy and to be worthwhile.**

---

*Copyright © 1989 by David D. Burns, M.D., from *The Feeling Good Handbook*

2. _____

_____

3. _____

_____

4._____

_____

I can think of several: (1) You will work very hard to be successful. (2) Your value system will be similar to a lot of other people's. After all, many people believe that more successful people are inherently more worthwhile. This Calvinist work ethic has actually been around for over 200 years. (3) Life will seem simple and clear to you. You'll know exactly what you have to do to be worthwhile. (4) When you succeed at something, you'll feel good because you'll think, "I'm worthwhile now because I got an 'A' [or a promotion]."

Now, can you think of any disadvantages to this attitude? List them here:

1. _____

_____

2. _____

_____

3. _____

_____

4. _____

_____

Here are several that come to my mind: (1) You'll always be on a treadmill, having to *earn* your self-esteem. You'll never feel truly worthwhile inside, because you'll never know for sure whether you will continue to be successful. Even highly paid professional athletes can go into slumps. Sooner or later they age and lose their incredible athletic skills. Are they less worthwhile then? (2) You may feel lots of anxiety and avoid doing anything creative because of your fear of failure. (3) When you fail, you may get depressed because you will feel that you're not very worthwhile or lovable. (4) Even when you succeed, you may feel inferior to other people who are even more intelligent and successful—and there will always be someone who's doing better. (5) You may not pursue what *you* want in life because you're too busy figuring out how to be successful so you can get everyone's approval. As a result, you may end up being less happy and successful than if you believed in yourself and pursued the goals that made sense to you.

Once you've listed the advantages and disadvantages of a particular attitude, ask yourself which are greater. Does it help you or hurt you more to believe "I must be a success in life to be worthwhile"? If the disadvantages are greater, you will want to revise this attitude. What new attitude could you adopt instead? Put your suggestions here:

_____

_____

_____

_____

Answer: I like to think about it this way: "It's important to me to be productive and to do my best. Sometimes I'll do well and sometimes things won't turn out the way I hoped. I can enjoy my successes, but they won't make me any better than anyone else. My failures will be disappointing, but I can learn from them and they won't make me any less lovable or worthwhile."

For some readers, this new attitude will be obvious. For others it may be hard to grasp, hard to accept. There are strong influences in our culture that make us think that "winners" are more special and more lovable. I would suggest that the truth is the opposite: You can never be loved for your successes—only for your vulnerabilities. People may be attracted to you and may admire you if you are a great success. They may also resent and envy you. But they can never *love* you for your successes.

The attitude "My worth as a human being depends on my success" is neither true nor false. You are simply defining worthwhile human beings as those who achieve the most. This attitude could never be proven or disproven. Like any value system, it will have certain positive and negative consequences. The Cost-Benefit Analysis allows you to sort them out.

If you decide that you don't like this value system, you can decide to think of your self-esteem as unconditional, as something that doesn't have to be earned. This new attitude will also have certain consequences. One will be that you will always feel worthwhile, even when you fail. Another consequence is that you will never feel inferior to, or better than, any other human being. You will still take great pleasure in being productive, but your degree of success will not dominate your sense of self-esteem. You will never look down on people who are less successful and talented, and you will never feel less worthy than anyone else, no matter how successful or intelligent they are. So it really boils down to the consequences you choose for your life.

As an exercise, choose one of the silent assumptions from the list on page 121, and do a Cost-Benefit Analysis, using the blank form on page 128.

STEP TWO: TEST YOUR BELIEF

Let's assume that you have completed your Cost-Benefit Analysis and decided that an attitude of yours has more disadvantages than advantages. As the next step, you can ask yourself if that attitude is realistic. Sometimes you can do an experiment to test the validity of your silent assumption. I once treated a depressed perfectionistic physician who had complained of feeling frustrated and unrewarded for many years, despite substantial academic accomplishments. He desperately wanted to change because he could see that he was burning up way too much time on projects he couldn't complete because they were never quite good enough. He couldn't seem to let go of his compulsive perfectionism because he had the belief that he couldn't really enjoy anything in life unless he did it in an outstanding manner. He told me: "Dr. Burns, I struggle and struggle to

COST-BENEFIT ANALYSIS*

The attitude or belief I want to change:_____
_____
_____

Advantages of Believing This	Disadvantages of Believing This

*Revised Attitude:*_____
_____
_____

climb to the top of the mountain. But when I get there, I just see an even higher peak in the distance, and I feel tremendously let down. My parents always told me I should try to be number one. But where's the reward? Where's the payoff?"

Like many perfectionists, he believed he couldn't experience satisfaction from any activity unless he performed it perfectly. He found out differently—and thus won a degree of freedom from his perfectionism—after he tested this belief. First, he scheduled a series of activities with a potential for personal growth, satisfaction, or pleasure and predicted how satisfying each of them would be, using a scale between 0 and 100. After each activity was completed, he recorded how satisfying it actually was and estimated how well he performed.

The form he completed is illustrated on page 132. He was surprised to learn that he could experience greater personal satisfaction in doing a below-average job of fixing a broken pipe that had flooded his kitchen than in giving an outstanding lecture to a group of medical students. The discovery helped him realize that an excellent performance was neither necessary nor sufficient for satisfaction. In fact, he was shocked to observe that many activities he did in an "average" or "below-average" way were among the most rewarding. As a result, he began to think about activities in terms of their potential for making him feel rewarded. He reported that this helped him to feel more relaxed and gave him the courage to initiate a number of exciting professional projects about which he had procrastinated for years because he had feared an imperfect outcome.

Many people experience depression after a divorce or a romantic rejection. One reason is their belief that if they are alone, it means they are unlovable and bound to feel unhappy. What experiment could you do to test this belief? Put your ideas here:

_____

_____

_____

_____

Answer: You could use the Pleasure-Predicting Sheet on page 131. First, schedule a series of activities with the potential for pleasure (such as reading a good book) or personal growth (such as jogging) in the Activities column. In the Companion column, record whom you will do each activity with. Make sure you do some activities by yourself (put "self" in the Companion column) and some activities with friends or family (put their names in the Companion column). Before you do each activity, estimate how satisfying it will be on a scale from 0 percent to 100 percent in the Predicted Satisfaction column. After you have completed each activity, record how satisfying it turned out to be between 0 percent and 100 percent in the Actual Satisfaction column.

A woman who was separated from her husband did this experiment. She was surprised to discover that many of her most satisfying activities were the ones she did by herself, even though she anticipated feeling lonely and miserable. This was not consistent with her belief that if she was alone, she was bound to feel miserable. This gave her confidence a boost. Her mood brightened and his interest in her suddenly increased because she was no longer so needy and dependent on him.

STEP THREE: THE FEARED FANTASY TECHNIQUE

The Feared Fantasy Technique is another powerful cognitive method that can help you modify a self-defeating attitude. Essentially, you confront your worst fears in a dramatic way—and you discover that the monster you've been so afraid of is not real but just a hot air balloon.

The method should be of great interest to psychologists and psychiatrists because it represents a synthesis of cognitive therapy and behavior therapy. Behavior therapy is based on the notion that you must confront your fears before you can conquer them. If you have an elevator phobia, you must get on the elevator and stay there, no matter how frightened you feel, until your anxiety has vanished. This method usually does work. With the Feared Fantasy Technique, exactly the same thing happens except that the fear you confront results from a thought or an attitude, such as "I must be a success in life to be worthwhile."

I demonstrated the Feared Fantasy Technique at a recent meeting of the American Psychiatric Association. One of the participants, a psychologist named Manuel, agreed to play the role of a patient so I could show the audience how cognitive therapy actually works. As it turned out, the demonstration became quite real. Manuel had tears in

PLEASURE-PREDICTING SHEET*

| Activity | Companion | Satisfaction | |
		Predicted	Actual
Schedule activities with a potential for pleasure or personal growth	(If alone, specify "self")	(0–100%) Record this before each activity	(0–100%) Record this after each activity

THE PLEASURE-PERFECTION BALANCE SHEET			
Activity	Predict how satisfying the activity will be	Record how satisfying it actually was	Record how effectively you performed
Fix broken pipe in kitchen	20%	99% (I actually did it.)	20% (I took a long time and made a lot of mistakes.)
Give a lecture to medical school class	70%	50% (I didn't feel particularly gratified about my performance.)	98% (As usual, I got a standing ovation.)
Play squash with Joe	75%	90% (Even though I didn't play especially well, we had a hell of a good time.)	40% (I played subpar. So what?)
Jog to store and get ice cream cone	60%	90% (It was fun!)	50% (I did not improve my time for jogging this distance.)

his eyes once he began to talk about his belief that he had to be perfect to earn people's love. He said he felt ashamed because he cried and showed weakness in front of his professional peers. He was convinced they would look down on him.

I suggested we use the Feared Fantasy method to deal with this concern. I told him he could pretend to be a mean colleague named Jack and I would be Manuel. Jack would put me down and say the cruelest things he could possibly think of.

MANUEL (*as Jack*): Hi, Manuel! Didn't I see you doing that demonstration with Dr. Burns last week at our annual meeting?

DR. BURNS (*as Manuel*): Yes, that was me up in front. What did you think of the demonstration?

MANUEL (*as Jack*): Honestly, Manuel, I was embarrassed. You seemed to be on the verge of crying.

DR. BURNS (*as Manuel*): Actually, tears did come to my eyes during the demonstration. I found it very moving. Why was this embarrassing for you?

MANUEL (*as Jack*): Well, for a grown man, a psychologist no less, to be crying in front of a group of his associates is kind of inappropriate, don't you think?

DR. BURNS (*as Manuel*): You mean it's inappropriate to show my feelings? Or it's inappropriate to have strong feelings? Or what? I don't exactly get your drift.

MANUEL (*as Jack*): Well honestly, Manuel, crying in public like that isn't the most professional or put-together thing in the world.

DR. BURNS (*as Manuel*): I see. You think that a "put-together" person would not be moved to tears. Do you think less of me because I was moved to tears?

MANUEL (*as Jack*): As a matter of fact, I do. I don't intend to be cruel, but I feel you deserve to know the truth. I think you're a jerk.

DR. BURNS (*as Manuel*): Well, I could understand you might not approve of crying during a psychotherapy demonstration. I *do* think it's okay, and we could have a gentlemen's disagreement about that. The experience turned out to be extremely valuable for me because I learned to believe in myself and to stop being so afraid of criticism. You might not approve of being moved to tears or crying. You might think that it's more professional or manly to control your emotions in certain situations. For my part, I think we'd be better off if we were more natural and felt free to show our feelings. But I still can't grasp why you think I'm "a jerk." Am I "a jerk" because I cried? Or because I disagree with you? Or what?

MANUEL (*as Jack*): Touché. I give up!

We then reversed roles, and I became the ruthless critic. I tried to put Manuel down for crying, and he talked back to me. He did beautifully. He said the exercise gave him tremendous self-confidence. After the workshop was over, one of the participants said that the demonstration was one of the most moving experiences he'd had in many years. He said he was grateful that Manuel had dared to share his feelings with the group. It shows just how off-base we can sometimes be with our fears and self-doubt. Sometimes the vulnerabilities we try so hard to hide can be our greatest assets in terms of getting close to others!

You can do the Feared Fantasy exercise with a therapist or with a friend, or you can do it as a written exercise on your own. The following is an example that a patient of mine, Linda, completed as a homework assignment between sessions. Linda is attractive and personable and has a great career as a stockbroker, but she is afraid to flirt with men and to develop an intimate relationship because of her intense fears of becoming vulnerable and risking rejection. The Vertical Arrow Technique (see page 124) indicated that Linda's problems stemmed from "emotional perfectionism." She believed that she should never have or reveal negative feelings like anger, anxiety, or sadness. She thought that to be loved, she had to be a "perfectly mature" woman who was always completely poised and in control of her emotions. She felt that as soon as any man discovered her real self, she'd be rejected. Rather than risking this, she settled for loneliness.

I asked her to write out a dialogue with an imaginary man who was rejecting her after several dates because she was "too emotional." I told her to make him much worse than any real man would ever be, and to say the cruelest, most upsetting things she could think of. The purpose of the exercise was to get her to confront her worst fears so she wouldn't have to spend the rest of her life feeling afraid of intimacy. The following is a brief excerpt from the dialogue she wrote.

REJECTING MAN: Well, Linda, I've decided that I need a little "space," so I won't be seeing you for a while.
LINDA: I find that upsetting. Can you tell me what the problem is?
REJECTING MAN: Yes, I'll be happy to. You're emotionally retarded. You worry and you get upset about things. You're not strong. Now that I know you well, I'm disgusted, so I'm going to leave you.

LINDA: It sounds like your main complaint is that I get upset at times and I'm not strong and tough enough emotionally.

REJECTING MAN: Yes, that's just the problem. You always overreact. You're such a neurotic. When I met you, I thought you had it all together, but now I see you're an emotional invalid.

LINDA: Well, it's true that I do get upset about lots of things. I worry when the market goes down and my clients lose money. I also feel quite annoyed right now. These are just two things I have strong feelings about—there are many more. Do you think these strong feelings make me an "emotional invalid"? Are you looking for a woman with no feelings? Or am I misreading you? What exactly *is* your point?

The dialogue illustrates how Linda confronted her belief that a man could love her only if she met some ideal of how a perfectly mature woman feels and behaves. Writing out the dialogue helped Linda see that this ideal really represented an emotional straitjacket, and that if someone did reject her because she had feelings, it might be a blessing in disguise. Who would really want to be married to a man who didn't want his wife to have feelings? As obvious as it might seem, this insight helped her accept herself as a spontaneous and emotional woman. This gave her the courage to break out of her self-imposed isolation and to reach out to others.

Cognitive therapy has two goals: to help you feel better in the here-and-now, and to help you develop a more realistic personal value system so that you will not be so vulnerable to painful mood swings and conflicts with others in the future. The Vertical Arrow Technique can make you more aware of the beliefs and attitudes that may be causing problems for you. These silent assumptions are always operating in your mind, and they influence the way you react to the good and bad things that happen to you.

Once you identify one of your silent assumptions, you can evaluate it with a Cost-Benefit Analysis. This will help you sort out the advantages and disadvantages of believing it. You will see that these attitudes are always two-edged swords, with a healthy side and a hurtful, destructive side. When the disadvantages of an attitude outweigh the advantages, it can motivate you to think about things in a more self-enhancing way.

After you perform the Cost-Benefit Analysis, you should ask yourself if your silent assumption is realistic. Sometimes you can do an experiment to test the validity of your belief. When you see that an attitude is both self-defeating and unrealistic, you will be far more motivated to develop a new attitude that is more positive and helpful.

The Feared Fantasy Technique can help you transform your new attitude into an emotional conviction. This technique can be valuable because even when you have made an intellectual decision to change your attitude, you may still wilt in the face of adversity. But when you confront your own worst fears you will begin to realize that they're not nearly as terrifying as you thought. This experience can be liberating!

·

Cognitive Therapy in Action:
How to Break Out of
a Bad Mood

In the last two chapters you learned about a variety of methods that can help you develop more positive attitudes and greater self-esteem. These techniques are the basic tools you will need in order to talk back to the Automatic Thoughts that upset you. In this chapter, I'll show you how you can integrate these methods in a creative and effective way so you can deal with a variety of common mood problems, such as feelings of inferiority and insecurity, irritability and low self-esteem, frustration, guilt, stress, and depression.

Mood Problem #1: Feelings of Inferiority
and Insecurity in Social Situations

I recently treated a single man from Miami named Chuck. Chuck was concerned because he had a mild congenital chest abnormality in which the breastbone is curved inward, giving the chest a sunken appearance. Aside from this, Chuck is tall and good-looking. Whenever he thinks about going to the beach he feels so self-conscious that he decides to stay home instead. Chuck says he could never take his shirt off in front of other people because he tells himself: "I'm inferior to all these other men who have such better physiques. If I take off my shirt, everyone will stare at me and think I am abnormal."

For the moment, put yourself in Chuck's shoes. There may have been a time when you felt inferior to other people because you felt your figure wasn't good enough—you weren't tall enough, or thin enough, or smart enough. What are the distortions in Chuck's first negative thought: "I'm inferior to all these other men who have such better physiques"? Review the list on page 96 and list the distortions here:

1. _____

2. _____

3. _____

4. _____

Answer: It's clearly an "overgeneralization." Chuck is generalizing from his chest to his self. It may be that his *chest* is inferior, but does that make *him* an inferior person? You could also call this the "mental filter" plus "discounting the positive," since Chuck is thinking only about his one weak point, his chest, and he's ignoring his many good features. (He's tall, broad-shouldered, athletic, attractive, bright, warm and friendly, and he earns a good living.) Finally, he's involved in "emotional reasoning." He says, "I *feel* inferior and abnormal, therefore I must *be* inferior and abnormal."

As an exercise, see if you can identify the distortions in his second Automatic Thought: "If I take off my shirt, everyone will stare at me and think I am abnormal." Review the list on page 96 and list the distortions here:

1. _____

2. _____

3. _____

4. _____

5. _____

Answer: Chuck is involved in an "overgeneralization." Some people might stare at him, but not *everyone* will. He's also "jumping to conclusions," including "mind reading" and "fortune-telling." He doesn't know what other people will be thinking. Most people probably have better things to think about and won't dwell on the idea that he's abnormal. He's also "labeling" himself in a negative way: "abnormal" is a heavily loaded word. "Emotional reasoning" is a fourth distortion. He *feels* that he'll be the center of attention, so he concludes that he really will be. Finally, he's "magnifying" the importance of his chest to the people on the beach. He would probably be surprised to discover that most people just don't care very much about what he looks like.

How could Chuck talk back to these two negative thoughts, using the methods described in the last two chapters? One method would be to "examine the evidence." Chuck could go to the beach and see if it's true that all the men there have better physiques. He'd probably see a few muscle builders who did have magnificent bodies, but he'd also see lots of other men—and women—who weren't so fabulous looking. There would be fat people and skinny people and old people with wrinkles. You see *all kinds* of people at a public beach! This would not be consistent with Chuck's belief that everyone there has a better physique.

I recently stumbled across a nude beach while on vacation with my family at Lake Tahoe in California. I was floating along the water on my air mattress and suddenly, behind some rocks, I saw all these naked people! I noticed a man who looked like he might have been a Vietnam veteran because his left leg was missing below the knee. He seemed to be having just as much fun as anyone else. If I had been Chuck, I could have asked myself, "Is it true that everyone is staring at this man and thinking he's inferior or abnormal?" I noticed his missing leg, but I wasn't staring at him or looking down on him. Nobody else was either. In fact, he looked tough and was drinking beer and partying with a group of his buddies as well as with some attractive ladies. I don't think that anyone would have dared to cross any of them! I was happy that the one-legged man was there because he was accepting himself and having fun. This made me feel better about my own body, which is *far* from perfect.

Chuck could also use the Experimental Technique to test the validity of his negative thoughts. He could go to a beach and take his shirt off—something he'd never actually done!—and check out his prediction. He can find out if it's *true* that everyone will be staring at him. How many people are staring? How long will they stare? This method would have two advantages. First, Chuck would probably discover that his thoughts were exaggerated. Second, Chuck would have to confront his fears. When you confront your fears, you usually get over them; when you harbor them and hang on to them, they gain power over you. I'm sure Chuck would feel very self-conscious for the first few minutes after he took his shirt off. I also suspect that quite soon his anxiety would begin to fade away. Eventually he'd be swimming or playing volleyball and forget all about his chest.

Let's stop and do a little cognitive therapy quiz. Why does Chuck feel anxious and self-conscious at the beach?

a. Because of his chest.
b. Because of the way people would react to his chest.
c. Both a and b.
d. Neither a nor b.

If you answered a, b, or c, you haven't quite gotten the central idea of cognitive therapy yet—namely, that only your thoughts can upset you. Chuck feels uncomfortable because he tells himself that he's grotesque and inferior and that it would be awful to have everybody look down on him. Once he stops believing these thoughts, his feelings will change.

What are some additional strategies Chuck could use to talk back to his negative thoughts? We could list dozens of approaches, but here are just a few:

• *The Cost-Benefit Analysis.* Chuck could list the advantages and disadvantages of thinking of himself as an inferior person because of his chest. He could also list the advantages and disadvantages of being so hung up on his chest that he can't go and have fun at the beach. Maybe he feels just as happy never going to the beach. If so, he doesn't really have a problem. On the other hand, if he wants to feel free to go swimming, and wants to rid himself of his fears and inhibitions, then it would be worth it to confront his fears.
• *The Double-Standard Technique.* What would he say to a friend with the same problem? He certainly wouldn't say, "Gee, your chest looks like a satellite dish! People will be staring at you and squirming with discomfort all day."
• *Define Terms.* What is the definition of an "inferior" person?

- *Thinking in Shades of Gray.* How worthwhile does Chuck think he would be, in a range between 0 and 100, if he had a big muscular chest? How worthwhile does he think he is now, with the chest he has?
- *The Survey Technique.* He could ask people if they would like a friend any less if he or she had a physical imperfection, like fat thighs or a flat chest. He could ask people how frequently they think about other people's physical imperfections when they are at the beach.
- *The Vertical Arrow Technique.* Chuck could ask himself why it would be upsetting if someone thought he was inferior. He might say that people wouldn't like him or respect him. Then he could ask himself why that would be upsetting. He might discover that he has a fear of disapproval and learn that he's basing too much of his self-esteem on what other people think of him. If so, he can do another Cost-Benefit Analysis and list the advantages and disadvantages of believing that he always has to get everybody's approval. How will it help him, and how will it hurt him, to think this way?
- *The Feared Fantasy Technique.* Chuck could write out a dialogue with an imaginary group of strangers, the "hostile crowd," who were insulting him and saying cruel things about his chest. They should say far worse things than any real group of people would ever say to him. The dialogue might go like this:

HOSTILE CROWD: Gee, you really have a weird-looking chest. You should be in a freak show.

CHUCK: Yes, my chest is sort of hollow. I notice you all have massive, hairy chests.

HOSTILE CROWD: Yes, we lift weights and take hormones. Our chests are like the Rocky Mountains. Yours looks like a soup bowl.

CHUCK: I've always admired men with large chests. Mine does look like a soup bowl in comparison. You have some of the biggest chests on the beach!

HOSTILE CROWD: Yes, people all admire us because we're such handsome studs. But nobody admires you. In fact, everyone's staring at you and thinking that you're gross, deformed, and disgusting. Nobody wants to be seen with you.

CHUCK: It sounds like even being near me is making you real uncomfortable. Why is that? Perhaps you should go and see a psychiatrist I know, named Dr. Burns. They call him the Mood Doctor and he may be able to help you with your nervousness. Or if you feel so uncomfortable, perhaps you can hide your eyes while I walk past.

I find it helpful to think of a negative thought or a self-defeating attitude as a trap represented by the box in the illustration below. Each intervention, which is represented by an arrow, is a way of breaking out of the trap. The diagram shows that there are *numerous* ways to turn any negative thought around. If one technique doesn't work, try another, and then another. When you finally put the lie to a negative thought, you will experience a profound change in the way you feel at a gut level. If you feel stuck, just keep knocking until the door swings wide open and you feel good again!

You may be wondering when you should use each of the various techniques. I believe that you should always "identify the distortion" first. You will discover that certain techniques work especially well for particular kinds of distortions. For example, if the distortion in your negative thought is "all-or-nothing thinking," the method

THERE ARE NUMEROUS WAYS TO CHALLENGE
ANY AUTOMATIC THOUGHT

3. THE DOUBLE-STANDARD METHOD

2. EXAMINE THE EVIDENCE

4. THE EXPERIMENTAL TECHNIQUE

1. IDENTIFY THE DISTORTION

5. THINKING IN SHADES OF GRAY

Automatic Thoughts: "I'm inferior to all these other men who have such better physiques. If I took my shirt off, everyone would stare at me and think I was abnormal."

10. THE SURVEY METHOD

6. THE FEARED FANTASY TECHNIQUE

9. DEFINE TERMS

7. THE VERTICAL ARROW TECHNIQUE

8. COST-BENEFIT ANALYSIS

called "Thinking in Shades of Gray" is likely to help. If your negative thought is a "should statement," the "Semantic Method" will nearly always work well. If you're involved in "emotional reasoning," you may find it helpful to Examine the Evidence, or you could use the Experimental Technique.

Remember that any cognitive technique can usually be used with any negative thought, so don't be rigid in trying to match specific techniques to specific distortions. Also keep in mind that a method that works wonders for one negative thought may not be at all helpful for another. Determination and patience are crucial. If you keep at it, you will succeed!

Mood Problem #2: Irritability and Low Self-Esteem

Mary told me that she'd been feeling irritable toward her husband, Bob, and overreacting to things: "If Bob says something I don't like, I feel shocked. It's like I was stabbed by a knife and I get unglued. If we're at a church meeting and something happens that I don't like, I get suddenly angry and I feel like leaving. If we're even watching a movie on TV, I get annoyed with the program and I insist we should change to another one."

When you are feeling irritable, there's often something bothering you that you're not dealing with. When you find yourself flying off the handle, ask what's going on in your life. Think about the things that have happened recently. Usually you will come up with the problem that's bugging you.

Mary said that Bob, who is 61, had been advised by his accountant to sell his business within eighteen months to take advantage of favorable IRS regulations. (If he waited beyond that time, his taxes on the sale would be substantially higher.) When Bob told Mary about the accountant's recommendations, she said, "It just wiped me out. I felt devastated. I feel hot and upset just talking about it now."

It seemed we'd located the source of Mary's irritability, so I asked her to write this as the "Upsetting Event" at the top of a Daily Mood Log. She recorded her emotions as "Panic—99; Sad—99." It's interesting that she didn't feel angry. Apparently the sale of her husband's business was very threatening to Mary, since she felt panicky, and she also anticipated a loss, as indicated by her strong feelings of sadness. I was curious why Bob's retirement and the sale of the business were so upsetting to her. One of the great strengths of cognitive therapy is that the therapist doesn't have to rely on intuition to figure out what's going on. Any therapist's interpretations are frequently incorrect, and they sometimes say more about the therapist's feelings and beliefs than about what's actually going on in the patient's psyche! In contrast, a cognitive therapist will ask, "Why is this so upsetting to you? What are your negative thoughts?" These questions will usually reveal the essence of what's really bothering you.

Why don't you write down *your* theories about why Mary felt panicky and upset about the sale of Bob's business? Then you can compare your hunches with what was really going on in Mary's mind. Put your ideas here:

1. _____

_____

2. _____

_____

3. _____

_____

I asked Mary to write down her negative thoughts about the sale of the business. They were:

1. "How will it turn out?"

2. "What will happen to us?"

3. "We'll be 'has-beens.' "

4. "After Bob has worked so hard for thirty-five years to build his business, I hate to see him step down. He's finally doing well. He should have the chance to enjoy the fruits of his labor."

5. "It stinks."

I wanted to learn a bit more about this, so I used the Vertical Arrow Technique, described on page 122. I asked Mary to choose one of these thoughts that was particularly upsetting. She chose number 2, "What will happen to us?" I told her to draw a small downward arrow under it. This arrow means "Suppose this is true. Why is it upsetting to me? What am I really afraid of?" Using this technique, Mary generated several additional Automatic Thoughts:

6. "We won't be able to enjoy the same standard of living we've had in the past year."

    And why would that be upsetting to me?

7. "We'll have to go back to the more frugal life-style we had in the past."

    And why would that be upsetting?

8. "I won't be able to spend money for the things I love, such as jewelry, clothes, crystal, and so forth. We won't be able to get a larger boat."

    And why would that be a problem to me?

9. "I'm addicted to shopping and I'll have to break the addiction."

    And why would that be upsetting?

10. "Shopping is my escape from loneliness. If I can't go out and shop, I'll have to sit home and be depressed."

    And why would I be depressed if I couldn't go out shopping?

11. "I need to spend money to feel happy. Otherwise my life will be a bore."

Once we generated this list of negative thoughts, it became clear why Mary felt so threatened by Bob's imminent retirement. Mary was a shop-a-holic and thought she needed to spend money and buy attractive things to make life interesting. I asked Mary to review her negative thoughts to see if she could come up with any self-defeating beliefs that were causing this attitude. She said that her "silent assumption" appeared to be: "I'm lazy and I need to spend money to feel good." Although you might feel judgmental and think Mary is being selfish and childish, I admired her honesty in facing this. It's an attitude that many of us share. It *does* feel good to have extra money to buy things. We're a consumer society and we are constantly bombarded with advertising that implies that wealth confers status and happiness.

Mary said that this addiction to spending began after all her children had finished college and gotten married. Since her whole purpose in life had been to raise them, she suddenly felt lonely and her life seemed to have no focus. She felt frightened and bewildered. Bob was actively involved with his career and Mary felt resentful, lonely, and unfulfilled. Bob's business was finally beginning to pay off so they had plenty of extra money to enjoy the finer things in life. Mary naturally slipped into a pattern of spending money as a way of coping with the emptiness she felt inside. She said that she could see herself getting increasingly unhappy and more demanding, much like a drug addict who has to take more and more "stuff" to get high.

Mary sadly acknowledged that she also had a second self-defeating belief: "If I don't always get what I want, I'm bound to feel miserable." This attitude made her very irritable in her dealings with Bob. Any time they differed on where to go for dinner or what movie to see, she pouted. Since Bob felt terribly guilty whenever Mary was upset, she usually got her way.

In the last chapter you learned that one powerful way to deal with these "silent assumptions" is to do a Cost-Benefit Analysis. I asked Mary to make a list of the advantages and disadvantages of believing "I'm lazy and I need to spend money to feel good." The advantages included: "(1) There will be no effort required. I can just go and spend money if I'm in a bad mood. (2) I don't have to expose myself to the risk of failure." The disadvantages of her belief included: "(1) I won't grow and change. (2) Nothing in my life will get better. (3) I won't confront the problems in my life. I'll just get a quick fix at the shopping center instead. (4) We may run out of money if I spend it excessively. Then I'll feel, 'Ugh! I let Bob down.' (5) I don't believe in myself. (6) I'm a slave to another master. The money I possess will actually possess me. (7) Life has no real goals and no sense of accomplishment."

After weighing the two advantages against the many disadvantages, Mary clearly saw that her silent assumption was hurting her far more than it was helping her. I asked if she could think of another, more realistic belief she could substitute in its place. She suggested this one: "I can feel good as a result of doing things and getting creatively involved in life."

The advantages of this attitude were: "(1) I will make Bob happy.

(2) Our marriage will be less stormy. (3) My self-esteem won't be controlled by the amount of money we have." The disadvantages were: "(1) I will have to take more initiative. (2) I will have to face my fears." The advantages of this new belief outweighed the disadvantages.

The Cost-Benefit Analysis can help you with the *motivation* to change your thinking. Once you can see that your negative attitudes are hurting you more than they are helping you, you will be more likely to give them up. But you may still believe that these attitudes are *true*. Even though Mary can see that her preoccupation with spending money is unhealthy, she may still believe at the gut level that people with a lot of money to spend are inevitably happier than people on limited incomes. She may feel convinced that life will be more rewarding and exciting if she can go on these buying sprees. You may believe this at a gut level, too!

I suggested we take things one step further. I asked Mary to do an experiment to test her belief that spending money was the key to feeling happy and exhilarated (the Experimental Technique is described on page 102). I told Mary to write the following statement at the top of a Pleasure-Predicting Sheet: "Hypothesis: I need to buy things and spend lots of money to experience true pleasure and satisfaction in life." Then, in the Activity column, I asked Mary to write down a number of activities with a potential for pleasure, learning, or personal growth that might give her a feeling of satisfaction or a sense of accomplishment. Mary said that there were many things she might enjoy that she'd been putting off. These included sewing, doing psychotherapy self-help assignments between sessions, learning to use a computer, and getting more involved in church work. After listing each activity, she recorded whom she would do it with and estimated how much it would cost. This would allow her to compare the enjoyment she got doing things alone with the enjoyment she got from being with Bob and with friends. It would also allow her to see if spending money was always more satisfying than free or inexpensive activities.

In the Predicted Satisfaction column, Mary estimated *ahead of time* how rewarding each activity should be, between 0 (the least satisfying) and 100 percent (the most satisfying). The predictions she made reflect her belief that spending lots of money would make her happy, and that anything else would be a bore. She predicted the highest

PLEASURE-PREDICTING SHEET

Hypothesis: I need to buy things and spend lots of money to experience true pleasure and satisfaction in life.

Activity	Companion	Satisfaction	
		Predicted	Actual
Schedule activities with a potential for pleasure or personal growth	(If alone, specify "self")	(0–100%) (Record this before each activity)	(0–100%) (Record this after each activity)
Eat a dish of Häagen-Dazs Macadamia Nut ice cream at the train station	Self ($2.50 for the large dish)	75	75
Go window-shopping	Self ($0)	25	75
Shop for jewelry and buy something expensive	Self ($300)	90	10
Spend time sewing	Self ($0)	50	80
Rent a movie with Bob and watch it on the VCR	Bob ($2)	60	90
Fill out the Daily Mood Log between sessions	Self ($0)	20	90
Register for a class at the community college	Self ($200)	50	75
Play volleyball with the church group	Friends ($0)	60	85
Balance the checking account	Self ($0)	25	75

satisfaction for buying jewelry, and the lowest satisfaction for window-shopping.

In the Actual Satisfaction column, she was to record the outcome—how satisfying each activity actually turned out to be. As you can see, she felt so guilty after she purchased an attractive gold bracelet that her satisfaction turned out to be only 5 percent. In contrast, many of the activities that were free and that had frightened her, such as doing her psychotherapy homework between sessions, turned out to be very enjoyable. These experiences put the lie to Mary's hypothesis that spending lots of money was inherently more rewarding than less costly activities. This made it abundantly clear that her moods were not, in reality, connected to her pocketbook. She realized that some of life's greatest sources of satisfaction are absolutely free.

This is not exactly a revolutionary or new idea. Sometimes the rediscovery of an old truth can make a profound difference in your outlook and your self-esteem.

Mood Problem #3: Frustration, Guilt, and Stress at Work

Susan is a 32-year-old pediatric nurse at Children's Hospital in Philadelphia. She does direct patient care and also has some administrative and supervisory duties since she is the assistant head nurse on her ward. Susan came for treatment because she had felt mildly depressed, irritable, and burned-out at work for several years.

Sunday she was scheduled to work until 4:00 p.m. At 3:00 she was all caught up and was looking forward to going home on time when the lab called to say that a white blood cell transfusion was ready for one of her patients. This frustrated Susan because these transfusions require two hours of close supervision by one nurse and it meant she couldn't leave on time. White blood cells are supposed to be delivered at the beginning of the shift in the morning to prevent this problem. The cells had been sitting around in the blood bank and were about to expire, so Susan couldn't pass the job on to the next shift. To make matters worse, the attending physician, a woman doctor, arrived on the ward and started "swinging her weight around" when she learned the transfusion was behind schedule. She complained that the nurses were incompetent and that the patients were getting lousy care.

Susan described this in the Upsetting Event space at the top of a Daily Mood Log. She recorded her negative feelings as: "Angry—80; Frustrated—90; Guilty—95." The first thought she recorded in the Automatic Thoughts column was: "Here's a kid who's dying. I should be glad to give him his white blood cells."

This thought made her feel guilty. Can you identify the main distortions in it? Check the list of cognitive distortions on page 96 and put your ideas here:

1. _____

2. _____

Answer: It's a "should statement." Susan is telling herself she *shouldn't* get annoyed. Can you see why this is self-defeating? In addition to having to cope with a frustrating situation, she's turning her anger against herself and getting extremely self-critical. She's also involved in "personalization," because she's blaming herself for a problem she didn't cause.

What Rational Response would you suggest? Put your ideas here about how Susan could talk back to her negative thought:

_____

_____

_____

_____

Answer: In Chapter 6 we talked about two techniques that can help you deal with "should statements." One is the Semantic Method—you simply substitute an expression like "It would be nice if" or "It would be preferable if" in place of the "should." Another approach would be the Cost-Benefit Analysis. Susan could list the advantages and disadvantages of believing that she should be like Florence Nightingale and always feel happy when she encounters an annoying situation.

Susan's Rational Response was "It's natural to get annoyed when people foul up and you have to stay late." By giving herself permission to feel upset, she won't have to feel so guilty and self-blaming. This involves a substantial shift in Susan's attitudes. She is very perfectionistic and believes that she should *never* get angry and that she should *always* be pleasant and in control of her emotions.

Susan's second Automatic Thought was: "Why should I have to do this?" Susan recognized immediately that this was another "should statement." Just as she was expecting emotional perfection from herself, she was expecting perfection from the world.

What Rational Response would you suggest?_____

_____

_____

_____

_____

Answer: Susan couldn't come up with one. I suggested that one approach would be to use the Semantic Method. Instead of thinking "I shouldn't have to do this," she could tell herself, "It would be a lot better if I could go home on time and I didn't have to supervise this transfusion. I can let the blood bank know that I was uncomfortable because the late delivery caused problems for me. I can ask them to be sure to make their white cell deliveries in the morning."

When I proposed this Rational Response, Susan became extremely defensive. She insisted that calling the lab "wouldn't do any good." I was a little surprised by her reaction. I pointed out that I'd worked in the clinical laboratory at a hospital when I was a medical student and that we always tried to respond to the needs of the nurses and doctors who were involved in patient care. I wondered if she might be underestimating the extent of her influence as an assistant head nurse. I also pointed out that sometimes it helps to express your feelings—in a tactful but clear way—even if it doesn't bring about any real changes. I asked Susan if she wanted to work on learning how to express her feelings more effectively.

Susan got even more annoyed and insisted that I "didn't understand." She said she didn't want to pursue the matter any further. After the session, I felt somewhat put down. I felt I had missed the boat. However, it also seemed possible that I had hit the target and that Susan was very reluctant—for reasons that weren't yet clear—to change.

The next week Susan said she'd listened to the tape of our session twice and had reread the chapters on dealing with criticism and anger in *Feeling Good*. She had written some notes, which I have excerpted with her permission:

> I have come to the conclusion that I may be repressing anger . . . because I'm afraid of what may happen if I express hostile feelings. I have never learned to express angry feelings constructively. In the past, whenever I was angry or frustrated, I have reacted in one of three ways.
>
> The first way is to throw a fit. This usually involves ranting, raving, yelling, cursing, or crying. After these outbursts, I feel embarrassed, ashamed, guilty. I feel physically upset and may end up with a headache.
>
> The second way I react is to sulk. Instead of expressing my feelings, I mope and complain. I generally feel guilty because I know I've acted like a jerk.
>
> The third way is the martyr method. I have this one down pat. While other people are yelling at me or complaining, I maintain a calm exterior while they give me the business. Afterwards I feel bitter and disgusted. I accept all the blame for whatever it is that has upset that individual. I usually apologize and assure them that I will attend to the problem. This is my usual method of dealing with angry co-workers or parents of patients. Afterwards, I end up with jaw pain because I've been gritting my teeth.
>
> Lately, I have felt that I may lose control if I allow myself to feel anger. I'm afraid I may do physical harm to someone if I don't keep a tight rein on my emotions. I frequently feel like beating the hell out of someone. These impulses frighten me and I feel ashamed of them. I feel like I deserve to be punished.
>
> I agree with you that I allow things to happen to me and I make no effort to change things. I have an almost fatalistic outlook. When I am treated badly by someone, it reinforces my belief that I deserve no better.

I was thrilled with this analysis. It seemed accurate and it showed me that Susan had the capacity for some pretty honest introspection. Anyone who can look at herself with that degree of openness and honesty has a great opportunity for growth. Some people are so fearful of change and so committed to maintaining the *status quo*—in spite of how miserable they feel—that they resist therapy. They sometimes deny their problems, or they may insist that everyone else is to blame. Others, like Susan, say, "This is where I'm at. I admit it and I'm hurting." Then some exciting personal changes become a very real possibility.

As we discussed her analysis, it seemed clear that Susan had a "conflict phobia." She has an intense fear of disagreements or angry interactions and tries very hard to avoid them. This is like trying to run away from a monster in a nightmare. It seems as if you're running through molasses and you just can't get away. Although Susan tells herself repeatedly that she should always try to be happy and loving, she just can't avoid feeling irritated. Then she doesn't know what to do. Blowing up, sulking, and acting like a martyr all make her feel even more miserable. Blaming herself is equally unsatisfactory.

Susan agreed that learning to deal with people in a more direct way would be an important goal of her therapy, one that would have important ramifications in her professional life and in her personal life as well. After this discussion, we decided to complete the analysis of her negative thoughts about the blood bank.

Susan's third Automatic Thought was: "I probably was incompetent and should have called the blood bank earlier."

What are the distortions in this thought?

1. _____

2. _____

3. _____

Answer: You can see that this is another "should statement." It is also an example of "fortune-telling," because Susan expects herself to foresee other people's errors. The third distortion is "personalization," because she is automatically blaming herself for the blood bank's error. It seems that Susan either directs the "shoulds" inwardly and blames herself, or else she directs "shoulds" outwardly and blames the world. When she blames herself, she hates herself and feels guilty and inadequate. When she blames the world, she feels frustrated and furious. Either way, life becomes extremely unrewarding and exhausting. Since her work as a nurse is filled with numerous unexpected irritations and disappointments, it's little wonder that she feels so burned out! What Rational Response would you suggest?

_____

_____

_____

_____

Answer: The Rational Response Susan came up with was quite simple: "I had no way of anticipating this problem."

Susan's fourth Automatic Thought was: "Dr. Jones thinks I'm incompetent and no good. She acts as if the kid wouldn't get his cells if she didn't take over and 'save the day.' "

This thought angered Susan. She felt *furious* with Dr. Jones. What are the distortions in Susan's Fourth Automatic Thought?

1. _____

2. _____

3. _____

The most obvious distortion is "mind reading," since Susan's jumping to conclusions about what Dr. Jones is thinking. It may also be a hidden "should statement," since she thinks Dr. Jones shouldn't act bossy and insensitive. The third distortion is "blame"—Susan thinks Dr. Jones is making her feel guilty and inadequate. What Rational Response would you suggest?

_____

_____

_____

_____

Answer: Susan's Rational Response wasn't very good. It was: "I don't know what Dr. Jones is thinking, but she has the right to think whatever she wants." The difficulty is that this sounds defensive and hostile. Furthermore, Susan hasn't challenged her Automatic Thought—she's simply buying into it. She still seems convinced that Dr. Jones doesn't respect her.

I used the methods of Re-attribution (see page 111) and Examine the Evidence (see page 100) to help Susan come up with a better Rational Response. I asked, "Is there any evidence that Dr. Jones thinks you are 'incompetent' and 'no good'?" Susan told me that she and Dr. Jones were actually good friends. She said that Dr. Jones had frequently expressed admiration for her professionalism and compassion for her patients. This was clearly inconsistent with Susan's Automatic Thought. I asked if there might be any other explanation for why Dr. Jones was acting irritable and throwing her weight around. Susan mentioned that she was recently widowed; her husband had unexpectedly died of a heart attack several months earlier. This, along with the daily stresses of caring for seriously ill children, was an equally plausible explanation for why Dr. Jones might be feeling on edge. Susan was able to come up with a better Rational Response: "Dr. Jones probably feels tense and frustrated with the situation, as I do, and she's just letting off a little steam. Maybe we need to talk it over and try to clear the air."

Changing her Automatic Thoughts by using the Daily Mood Log reduced a good deal of the guilt and frustration Susan was feeling. We then worked on how she might communicate more effectively in situations like this. Certainly some annoyance is natural. It's not realistic to expect that cognitive therapy—or *any* form of therapy— can eliminate all your negative feelings. Sometimes it's appropriate to tell people how you feel. The five principles of effective communication will be described in detail in Chapter 19, but we can discuss the issue briefly here. What could Susan say to the people at the blood bank and to Dr. Jones? Put your ideas here:

_____

_____

_____

_____

Answer: She could tell the people at the blood bank something like this: "I was uncomfortable that we were notified about the white blood cells at 3:00 on Sunday. This means that someone on the day shift has to stay late to administer them. This is demoralizing because the staff is always eager to leave on time. Would it be possible to alert us in the morning whenever a white cell transfusion has been ordered?" This statement has the following characteristics: (1) She expresses her negative feelings in a direct, honest way. However, she does this tactfully when she says, "I was uncomfortable. . . ." (2) She tells the people at the blood bank specifically what she wants them to do differently so she won't come off a complainer. Although there are no guarantees that she will get a friendly, cooperative response, at least she will feel she's standing up for herself in a dignified, professional way instead of acting like a wounded and resentful victim.

What could Susan say when Dr. Jones complains and "throws her weight around"? Put your ideas here:

_____

_____

_____

_____

Answer: There are, of course, many ways Susan might respond. Here's just one idea. She could say, "I'm also frustrated that we were notified so late about the white blood cells, and I share your concern that this patient should get the best possible care. I'm a little uncomfortable because you may think I'm not doing a good job for your patients. Is this true? I respect you a lot and I want to hear about any problems you've noticed on the ward. Do you have any ideas on how I could deal with the blood bank more effectively? I'm planning to call them to remind them that we need these white cells delivered in the morning." Notice that she shows some appreciation of how Dr. Jones is feeling, and she also expresses her own feelings in a tactful way. Instead of getting defensive or ignoring Dr. Jones's irritation, she asks Dr. Jones to say exactly what's on her mind. She compliments Dr. Jones, so Dr. Jones will not view this as some kind of battle or put-down. Dr. Jones will probably calm down and stop acting so frazzled and will communicate in a friendlier way.

However, it's possible that Dr. Jones might continue to gripe and complain. If she's in a really bad mood, Dr. Jones could say, "I *can't believe* you haven't already taken care of this transfusion! Don't you know that timing is essential? If the patient doesn't get these cells right away, they won't be fresh anymore. Then we'll have to order a new batch." What could Susan say next?

_____

_____

_____

_____

Answer: Susan could say, "You're absolutely right about that, and I feel every bit as annoyed as you do. I'm going to have to stay late to supervise the transfusion. I'm feeling blamed for this problem and I'd like your help in finding a solution. You may have more clout with the blood bank. Could you back me up and stress the importance of delivering these white cells in the morning? Then we wouldn't be under so much pressure at the end of the shift." Notice that Susan finds truth in Dr. Jones's criticism, but at the same time she expresses her feelings so she doesn't appear to be a doormat. She asks for Dr. Jones's help in solving the problem instead of allowing feelings of antagonism to develop.

This brief excerpt from Susan's treatment illustrates an important aspect of cognitive therapy. Part of the treatment is individualistic—we will work hard on changing Susan's distorted negative thoughts and self-defeating attitudes. At the same time, we will work on developing the skill necessary to communicate more effectively with others, so Susan can build more rewarding relationships at work and in her personal life. The goal of the therapy is to reduce the rage, the guilt, and the loneliness Susan feels so that she can develop greater self-esteem and feel closer to others.

Mood Problem #4: Irritability, Frustration, and Marital Conflict

Let's look at another example of how cognitive therapy can help deal with feelings of irritability and frustration. Frank is a 34-year-old dentist who recently married a 36-year-old woman named Fran, after enjoying many years of happy bachelorhood. Several weeks after the wedding Frank told me, "I feel irritable all the time. I feel like Fran's intruding on my territory. I feel trapped. When I come home from work I feel exhausted. I want to have a beer and unwind for a while. But I feel I have to talk to Fran, make love to Fran, and be interested in her day. I try to watch TV and Fran climbs all over me. She does this erotic dance and tries to turn me on. She thinks I should be constantly making love to her. All I want is to be alone."

Frank explained that his feelings of annoyance weren't just limited to coming home from work: "I get irritated when I see her things in the medicine cabinet. We've moved into a small apartment and we've got no space at all. This morning I couldn't find the toothpaste and I said, 'Where the hell did she put it!' Then I saw it right in front of me on the sink.

"When we're out with friends I have a lot of escape fantasies about having sex with other women. I feel trapped. I feel like my independence has been taken away from me. It's been five years since I was living with someone. I feel like I want to make love with another woman just to prove I can be free."

Frank said that when he comes home from work, he has these feelings: "Angry—75; Trapped—75; Anxious—80; Frustrated—80." I asked Frank to write down the Automatic Thoughts that were associated with these feelings. They were:

1. "Fran shouldn't intrude on me."

2. "I should want her sexually right now. If I don't want her sexually *all the time*, then there must be something wrong with this marriage and I should find someone I'm more attracted to."

3. "She doesn't respect my feelings or my need to be by myself and unwind."

4. "I should never allow anyone to control me. I should get angry."

5. "Things will get worse. I made a mistake getting married."

One of the things I like the most about cognitive therapy is that it shows so clearly and accurately where a person is coming from. It's as if all your secret inner thoughts and negative attitudes come spilling right out of your head, so they can be understood and dealt with.

Frank's negative thoughts tell us a great deal about why he feels so upset, and they also point the way to the cure. You can see that it's not Fran who makes Frank feel trapped and dissatisfied—it's Frank. He has very perfectionistic expectations about what marriage should be like. He thinks he and Fran should *always* want to be together and that he should *always* feel romantic and sexual and excited by her.

He also expects Fran to read his mind. He wants her to respect his need to be alone, but he stubbornly refuses to tell her that he feels this way! Of course, he cannot tell her that he needs a little time by himself when he comes home at night because that would be an admission of defeat and failure. He would have to admit his marriage is more "ordinary" and less "special." It's amazing to me how our desires for perfection so often condemn us to misery and loneliness!

Frank found it relatively easy to talk back to his negative thoughts. Let's work on his first one. When Fran approaches him, he tells himself, "She shouldn't intrude on me." What are the distortions in this thought?

1. _____

2. _____

3. _____

4. _____

Answer: First, it's an obvious "should statement," since he's telling himself she should automatically be just the way he wants her to be. Second, it's an example of "mind reading," since Frank thinks about her motives in a negative way. She probably doesn't feel like an "intruder," but like a wife who misses her husband. Finally, it's an example of "discounting the positive," since he turns something positive—Fran's love—into something negative when he labels her enthusiasm as an "intrusion."

What Rational Response would you suggest? Put your ideas here:

_____

_____

_____

_____

Frank came up with this one: "Fran doesn't intend to be intrusive but to be affectionate because she misses me. She loves me and her motivations are positive. She may feel insecure and want some affection. That's a normal reaction."

What's the distortion in Frank's second thought: "I should want her sexually right now . . . and *all the time*"? Put your ideas here:

1. _____

2. _____

Answer: This is another obvious "should statement." Frank's first "should statement" was directed toward Fran, and this one is directed toward himself. He seems to be very demanding and has exceedingly high expectations for himself and for other people. In addition, like most perfectionists, he's trapped by "all-or-nothing thinking." He thinks that if he isn't always wildly turned on by Fran, it means his marriage is a failure. If you were Frank, what Rational Response could you come up with?

_____

_____

_____

_____

Answer: Frank's was quite simple: "It's not realistic to assume I should be sexually excited and active all the time." This thought made him considerably less tense.

In the last chapter you learned about the Vertical Arrow Technique. This method can help you discover certain self-defeating attitudes, called "silent assumptions," that are lurking underneath your negative thoughts. Once you identify these assumptions, you can modify them and grow as a person. When you refute your negative thoughts you will feel better at the moment, but when you modify a silent assumption, you will be developing a healthier value system that can pave the way for greater joy and intimacy and personal meaning throughout your life.

In order to unearth Frank's silent assumptions, I asked him this question: "Suppose you're not sexually turned on by Fran all the time. Why would that be upsetting to you? What would that mean to you?"

FRANK: That would mean I was getting old and my life was becoming boring. I feel like I should always seek out excitement.

DR. BURNS: And suppose your life was becoming boring and you weren't always seeking out excitement. Why would that be upsetting to you?

FRANK: Then I would be just like everyone else.

DR. BURNS: And then what?

FRANK: Then my life would be empty.

DR. BURNS: And suppose your life was empty. What then? Would that be a problem for you?

FRANK: Then I couldn't be happy. I feel I should strive to be happy *all the time*. I think I shouldn't have negative emotions.

This brief dialogue revealed the "emotional perfectionism" lurking underneath Frank's annoyance. He has a rule in his mind which states that he should try to be a very "special" kind of person who's constantly filled with passion and zest for life and who never feels bored or unhappy. You could also say that Frank suffers from "emotophobia," which literally means "phobia about negative emotions." Frank appears to be afraid of feelings such as boredom, sadness, or anger.

One of the elusive things about these silent assumptions that get us into so much trouble is that they're not completely irrational—they're often a subtle mixture of good and bad. Certainly there's nothing wrong with Frank's desire to make his life meaningful and exciting and fulfilling. His enthusiasm and zest for living are among his strengths. But these very strengths can also become weaknesses when he lets them dominate his life. As Frank put it, "This fear of negative emotions has made me leave *every* job and *every* woman I've ever had. This belief that I'm entitled to be happy all the time has caused endless frustration and anger, because I can't tolerate any negative feelings. I'm demanding and impatient, and I panic when I get any unpleasant emotion. This makes me terribly lonely because I can't share my feelings with Fran."

One of the advantages of giving up the expectation that he should always be happy and have a constantly thrilling marriage is that he will be free to communicate more openly with Fran. He can tell her how he feels when he comes home at night, and they can talk about how much time they want to spend doing things together. Too much togetherness can ruin any marriage. Frank's trapped feelings are simply his way of reminding himself that he needs some time to be alone and that he and Fran need to talk things over. Fran may think that it's perfectly okay for Frank to unwind alone for a while when he gets home after a hard day at the office. She may agree that they don't have to spend every single minute of their lives together. They may decide to spend a night or two each week doing things separately. They may want to spend an occasional weekend apart. It's a matter of negotiating a balance that will make sense to both of them. Frank will have to compromise with some of his grandiose expectations for his marriage. He will have to swallow some of his pride and give up the idea that his relationship with Fran will be perfect and thrilling at every moment. As he gives up his goal of an ideal relationship, he may discover the rewards of a real one.

Frank and Fran may benefit from some communication training along the lines described in Part IV. He needs to learn to share his negative feelings more openly with Fran. The capacity to reveal hurt and vulnerable feelings is hardly a sign of marital failure; it is the very meaning of true intimacy. Comprehending this may require a transformation in Frank's basic values, because he will no longer view his negative emotions as a bad thing. He will begin to see them as a pathway to a more profound appreciation of his uniqueness as well as what he shares with the rest of humanity.

Mood Problem #5: Depression

George, who is 36 years old, recently experienced his second serious depression. The first episode, which lasted six months, occurred around the time he got married, ten years ago. Up to the time of his most recent depression, George felt happy. He opened a successful restaurant, and he and his wife started a family. Their two lovable boys are now 5 and 7 years old.

Prior to seeking treatment at my clinic, George had been treated unsuccessfully with medications and psychotherapy by a psychiatrist near his home. Because this wasn't helpful, George was hospitalized for three weeks. A nurse on the ward gave him a copy of *Feeling Good*. George experienced a strong mood lift when he read it and worked on some of the exercises in the book. He called my office after he was discharged, because he was still depressed.

Testing at my clinic indicated that George had a severe "biological depression," since his serum cortisol level was markedly abnormal. His treatment was particularly interesting since it indicates that irrational negative thoughts do occur in these so-called "chemical depressions." Helping George talk back to these negative thoughts relieved his feelings of hopelessness and despair. This can be crucial early in the treatment when you are trying to find an effective antidepressant medication.

During a recent session, George showed me twenty upsetting thoughts that he had written down for homework between sessions. The list included:

1. "I'm a failure. I never succeed at anything."

2. "I'm a rotten father because I don't love my children. My boys are afraid of me."

3. "I'm hopeless and I will never get well. My state of mind will go on forever."

4. "This depression means I don't love my wife. If I really loved her, I wouldn't feel this way."

5. "Everyone, including Dr. Burns, is getting disgusted with me."

6. "I'm letting everyone down."

7. "I shouldn't be feeling this way."

These thoughts made George feel hopeless, ashamed, and worthless.

I asked George to identify the distortions in the first thought: "I'm a failure. I never succeed at anything." Review the list on page 96 and see what distortions you can identify in this thought:

1. _____

2. _____

3. _____

4. _____

Answer: It's certainly an example of "emotional reasoning." George is thinking, "I *feel* worthless. I *feel* like a failure. Therefore I must really *be* a failure." It's also an example of "discounting the positive," since he is overlooking the many things he's succeeded at. (He's hardworking, he's managed to build a successful business, he's gone to work every day in spite of intense feelings of depression, and he has a loving family.) It's also an example of "all-or-nothing thinking," since he thinks of himself as a total failure just because he's depressed. Finally, it's an example of "personalization," since George is blaming himself for his depression. He really did nothing to deserve it or to bring it on.

It was relatively easy to help George turn this thought around. I used the method called Examine the Evidence. I simply asked George to list a number of the many things he'd accomplished, and then asked how he reconciled this with the claim that he was "a failure." I also used the Double-Standard Method, and asked if he would say "You're a failure" to a friend with a similar level of depression who was struggling so hard to overcome it. This helped George see that he was being unreasonably hard on himself.

I used a similar strategy on his second Automatic Thought: "I'm a rotten father because I don't love my children. My sons are afraid of me." He had come to this conclusion for two reasons. First, there were times when he felt anxious and irritable around his children. In the past week he'd snapped at his son for misbehaving, and he concluded he must be a cruel ogre. In addition, because of his depression George didn't have strong feelings of love for his children or for his wife—or for anyone. George concluded that he must not love them anymore. Interestingly, George wept constantly when he told me about this.

What are the distortions in George's second Automatic Thought?

1. _____

2. _____

3. _____

Answer: First, he's "discounting the positive," since there was abundant evidence he *did* love his children and there was no evidence that they were afraid of him. For example, after the previous session, when he joined his wife and sons in the waiting room, his two boys ran up to him. One hugged his leg and the other jumped into his arms and started talking to him excitedly. Then he picked up the son who was hugging his leg and stood with one child in each arm with tears in his eyes. It was clear that his boys were absolutely delighted to be with him. This hardly supported his belief that they were afraid of him or that he hated them! In addition, why would a man who didn't love his children be sobbing about them? George's tears were evidence that he did care a great deal—probably more than 99 percent of the fathers in Philadelphia that day!

Another distortion in his thoughts was "emotional reasoning." George was saying, "If I don't *feel* love at every minute, then I must not love them." But it's extremely difficult to feel *any* positive emotion, such as love or happiness, when you are severely depressed. Fortunately those positive feelings return when the depression disappears.

Finally, George was involved in a "should statement." He's telling himself that he should always want to be with his children and should never feel irritable or annoyed with them. Although an ideal imaginary father might be like that, real fathers are not.

The same two methods—Examine the Evidence and the Double-Standard Technique—helped George turn his second negative thought around. He was able to see that he was a loving and committed father even though he didn't always *feel* that way when he was depressed. Although this insight may seem obvious to you, it was a tremendous relief for George.

As an exercise, see if you can identify the distortions in one of George's five other Automatic Thoughts. Then see if you can substitute an effective Rational Response, using one or more of the methods described in the list on page 118. George's responses can be found in his Daily Mood Log on page 167. You can see that he initially believed all his Automatic Thoughts 100%. After we came up with convincing Rational Responses, his belief in each Automatic Thought went down considerably, and he felt much better. That's the essence of cognitive therapy.

THE DAILY MOOD LOG

Automatic Thoughts	Distortions	Rational responses
1. I'm hopeless and I will never get well. My state of mind will go on forever. ~~(100%)~~ (30%)	Fortune-telling; emotional reasoning; all-or-nothing thinking; discounting the positive	1. I may *feel* hopeless but that doesn't mean I *am* hopeless. My first depression ten years ago eventually disappeared, so this depression probably will too. The therapy has already been helpful to me, so I can't be completely "hopeless." (100%)
2. The depression means I don't love my wife. If I really loved her, I wouldn't feel this way. ~~(100%)~~ 30%	Emotional reasoning	2. Men who love their wives can get depressed. I don't *feel* a lot of love, but that's probably just a symptom of my depression. If we have some problems, we can talk them out. I don't have any desire for any other women. (75%)
3. Everyone, including Dr. Burns, is getting disgusted with me. ~~(100%)~~ 25%	Overgeneralization; mind-reading; magnification	3. I may think that everyone is disgusted with me because I'm disgusted with myself. Is there any evidence that Dr. Burns is disgusted? I can ask him about this and see. If he is feeling frustrated with me, I can find out why. (100%)

(Continue on next page)

Automatic Thoughts	Distortions	Rational responses
4. I'm letting every- one down. (100%) 0%	Overgeneralization; mind reading	4. I can't be letting *everyone* down be- cause I don't know everyone. Further- more, there's no evidence that I'm letting anyone down. I'm putting tremendous pres- sure on myself to get well, but no one else is pressur- ing me. Dr. Burns says I may be trying too hard and that it's okay to be pa- tient and to give myself a little time to recover. (100%)
5. I shouldn't be feeling this way. (100%) 25%	Should statement	5. I should feel this way because I'm depressed. It will eventually pass. (75%)

9

•

Why People Procrastinate

In the previous chapters, we've talked about changing your thoughts and attitudes when you feel upset. You can also do a great deal to brighten your moods by becoming more productive and involved with life. However, many people procrastinate and become immobilized when they feel anxious or depressed. In this chapter you will discover why you procrastinate. In the next chapter, I provide a unique program that has helped many people put an end to their procrastination and unleash their full potential for productivity and creativity.

To start, take the Procrastination Test on page 171. Each statement on the test describes a mind-set that I often see in patients who have difficulties being productive. You'll notice that some of the causes of procrastination are internal—they have to do with your own thoughts and attitudes. Other causes have to do with your relationships with others. There's considerable overlap between the various categories, so don't be surprised if you recognize yourself in several of them!

1. **Putting the cart before the horse.** In your opinion, which comes first—motivation or productive action? If you said "motivation,"

don't feel bad. You made a good guess. That's the way a lot of procrastinators think. But it's not the correct answer.

Procrastinators tell themselves, "I don't feel like it. I'll wait until I'm in the mood." The problem is that if you wait until you're "in the mood," you may be waiting forever. Did you really think you were going to feel like mowing the lawn, cleaning the garage, or balancing your checkbook? You're never going to "feel like it"! These are boring, unpleasant tasks!

People who are extremely successful know that motivation doesn't come first—productive action does. You have to prime the pump by getting started whether you feel like it or not. Once you begin to accomplish something, it will often spur you on to do even more.

When I give lectures or workshops, I find that as the time of the presentation approaches, I begin to dread it. I wish I didn't have to go through with it. The night before, I feel petrified, and I want to get sick so I can bow out gracefully. I tell myself that I don't have anything interesting to say. The idea of standing up in front of hundreds of psychologists and psychiatrists and talking for several hours seems terrifying.

Shortly after I begin speaking, my feelings begin to change. I notice warm smiles and receptive faces. Many of the people seem intrigued by what I'm saying. As they begin to ask questions, my enthusiasm builds. By the end of the presentation I feel exhausted, but I can't wait to have the chance to do it again.

The same principle can apply to any job you're putting off. Once you get started, it usually turns out to be far less horrible than you had imagined, and you feel more like doing it.

The diagram below illustrates how action can lead to motivation and then to further action:

The message is simple: the more you do, the more you'll feel like doing; but *doing something* comes first!

2. **The mastery model.** People who procrastinate often have an unrealistic view of how a productive person really functions. You may

THE PROCRASTINATION TEST*

This test describes attitudes that some people have when they procrastinate. Put a check (√) in the box that best describes your feelings:	0–NOT AT ALL	1–SOMEWHAT	2–MODERATELY	3–A LOT
1. I often put things off because I don't feel like doing them or because I'm not in the mood.				
2. I sometimes give up on tasks because they turn out to be more frustrating and difficult than I anticipated.				
3. I sometimes procrastinate because I'm afraid of failure.				
4. I don't like to start something if I feel I won't be able to do it perfectly.				
5. I often feel that I haven't accomplished anything worthwhile because I'm so critical of my work.				
6. When I procrastinate, I feel guilty and I tell myself I really *should* get started.				
7. I sometimes put things off when I feel annoyed or upset with people.				
8. I often agree to do things I don't really want to do because it's so hard for me to say no.				
9. I sometimes put things off because I feel that people are acting bossy and making unreasonable demands on me.				
10. I often feel like I have lots of things to do that I'm not very committed to or enthusiastic about.				

assume that successful people always feel confident and easily achieve their goals without having to endure frustration, self-doubt, and failure. This "mastery model" of success is quite unrealistic. Achieving personal goals is stressful. You will usually have to overcome numerous obstacles and setbacks along the way. If you think that life should be easy and that other people don't have to struggle, you will conclude that something is "wrong" and give up when things get tough. You'll have such a low tolerance for frustration that any disappointment will be unbearable.

Highly productive people are more likely to have a "coping model" of success. They assume that life will be frustrating and that there will be numerous rejections and failures on the road to success. When they encounter these obstacles, they simply assume that things are as they should be, and they persist. They rise to the occasion with renewed determination and commitment.

My daughter was not studying her chemistry book very ambitiously during her sophomore year of high school, and she was barely getting C's on the tests. Although she read each chapter once, she wasn't persisting and putting in the long hours necessary to master the material. Every time she studied she got frustrated, because a lot of what she was reading didn't make sense to her. As a result, she put off studying until the night before her exam.

The "mastery model" was the problem. She had never challenged the notion that the material should be easy. I explained that I often had difficulty learning things and that I simply put in lots of extra time and effort. At first she did not accept this. She thought I was just saying it to be nice. Then I showed her a chapter of a statistics book I'd been studying for over a year but still didn't understand very well. She could see for herself how worn and underlined the pages were. I told her that my slow progress didn't frustrate me because I understood a little more each time I read the chapter, and I was proud of what I had been able to learn on my own. Once she accepted this, she began to think about chemistry as a challenge instead of an enemy. Her moods and her study habits improved enormously.

3. **The fear of failure.** Although we often think of people who procrastinate as "lazy" and "irresponsible," the real problem is sometimes just the opposite—success may be overly important to you. Rather than risk failure, you may do nothing at all.

People with the fear of failure often base their self-esteem on their

WHY PEOPLE PROCRASTINATE 173

accomplishments. If you fail at your work, you may feel that you are a failure as a human being. This makes it too dangerous to try. The stakes are simply too high.

Ted had purchased a small established chocolate manufacturing company near Chicago that had been run as a family business. Although the company was only breaking even, it seemed that with effort it could grow and prosper. However, Ted was neglecting the business. Instead of going to the office in the morning, he would dawdle at home or run errands that weren't really important.

Ted told me that he was terribly afraid of failure. This was the first time in his life he'd ever owned his own company—previously he'd always worked for large corporations. I explored Ted's fear of failure during a session.

DAVID: And suppose you did try and failed? What would that mean to you?

TED: The last corporation I worked for had a serious financial setback, but it never upset me because I was working for someone else. I always felt I could be helpful to the company. But if my own company failed, I'd feel like it was a personal failure.

DAVID: And why would that be upsetting to you?

TED: It would mean I was a failure.

DAVID: And suppose you were a failure. What would that mean to you?

TED: Well, people would find out I was a failure.

DAVID: And then what?

TED: Then they wouldn't love me anymore.

DAVID: Who wouldn't love you?

TED: My wife and kids . . . my son. My son is working with me. Maybe he'd lose respect for me.

This brief conversation made us both aware that Ted felt he had to *earn* the love of the people he cared about. I suggested that he could confront this attitude head on, if he was willing, using the Feared Fantasy Technique (see page 130). I told him that we would do some role-playing and pretend that his business had failed. I would play the role of his son, but I would be more hostile than any real son would ever be. I instructed Ted to play himself. Here's how the dialogue evolved:

SON: Gee, Dad, how's the business doing?

DAD: Not well, son. I'm afraid we'll have to file for bankruptcy. There just isn't any way we can pay all the bills.

SON: Bankruptcy! You mean the business is going under? Will we lose our house? How could you do this to us?

DAD: The business is going under and there's a chance we may have to move.

SON: Wow, you really blew it! Here I am ready to start college, and when I need your financial help the most, you let me down.

DAD: Well, you'll have to work and help out, too. We can make it, but we'll have to pull together as a family.

SON: Come on, Dad! This is terrible!

DAD: I can appreciate how you feel. But why is this so terrible?

SON: No one else's father has these problems. Everyone else is doing well. Why can't you? What are people going to think of us?

DAD: I'd be more interested in what *you* think of me. You sound pretty angry.

SON: Well I am! What do you expect when your father's a loser?

DAD: It sounds like I have to be successful and make a lot of money for you to love and respect me. Do I read you right?

Now Ted was confronted—in fantasy—with his worst fear. He'd dreaded failure and rejection since he was a little boy, but he'd never really faced it head on. Instead of feeling shocked or overwhelmed, he started giggling—and so did I—because his worst fear seemed so ludicrous! It dawned on him that his worries were based on several distortions. First, he was "magnifying" (or "catastrophizing") the financial consequences of a business reversal. He actually had other assets, so even if the company failed, his family wouldn't end up penniless. Second, he was involved in "mind reading." His wife and son wouldn't really be so crass and rejecting if he failed, and the family would probably feel closer in the face of adversity. Finally, and most important, he saw that he was "personalizing" his son's rejection. If someone did reject him because of a failure, it would be a reflection on that person and not on Ted. This insight was illuminating to Ted.

He felt immediate relief. One week later he reported that his depression had vanished and he was working happily in his new business.

4. **Perfectionism.** Finding a publisher for my first book, *Feeling Good,* was a tremendous chore. I was an unknown author, and a self-help book on depression seemed unappealing to most publishers. In addition, the first draft of the book was rather dull and long-winded. Ultimately I found a publishing house and an editor, Maria

Guarnaschelli, whom I really liked. When I went to New York to meet with her and sign the contract, we discussed how I should revise the book. Maria showed me how to rewrite it so it would sound more lively and appealing. She said she loved the book and told me it was sure to be a best-seller.

I went home with a check for the advance in my pocket. It was more money than I'd ever seen at one time, and Maria's accolades were ringing in my ears. I should have felt on top of the world, but for some reason I was discouraged.

After I got home, I sat at my desk, staring into space, for ten days. I just couldn't get started on the revision. In fact, I couldn't come up with one good sentence! I also felt physically exhausted and couldn't run more than half a mile without getting winded, in spite of the fact that I was in perfect health. I knew I was upset, but I couldn't figure out what was bothering me.

Finally I reached for a sheet of paper and wrote down my negative thoughts. The first one was: "This book has to be a best-seller. But I'm a psychiatrist, not an author, and I don't know how to write a best-seller. Maria will be disappointed in me."

The moment I got the thought on paper, I felt a flood of relief, because I decided to think about it like this instead: "It's not my job to write a 'best-seller.' However, I can write a helpful book if I write it in exactly the same personal style that I use with my patients. That will be easy for me, and that's all I'm really responsible for. How well the book sells is the publisher's responsibility." My energy suddenly returned and I went out and ran over seven miles without getting tired. I felt like an antelope! I came back and revised *Feeling Good* over the next several months without any stress at all.

Many of us were raised with the belief that we should always try to do things perfectly and that there would be some special reward for being "the best." Unfortunately, we perfectionists sometimes reach for the stars and end up clutching air. When I try too hard and put too much pressure on myself, I may feel so stressed that I procrastinate and do nothing at all. In contrast, when I lower my standards just a tad, I sometimes feel more relaxed and become far more productive and creative.

I don't want to give you the impression that it's wrong to have high standards. Without a concern for quality and excellence, great achievements in science and in the arts would be a rarity. However,

PERFECTIONISM VS. THE HEALTHY PURSUIT OF EXCELLENCE*

Perfectionism	The healthy pursuit of excellence
1. You are motivated by the fear of failure or by a sense of duty.	1. You are motivated by enthusiasm and you find the creative process exhilarating.
2. You feel driven to be number one, but your accomplishments, however great, never seem to satisfy you.	2. Your efforts give you feelings of satisfaction and a sense of accomplishment, even if you aren't always "the greatest."
3. You feel you must earn your self-esteem. You think you must be very "special" or intelligent or successful to be loved and accepted by others.	3. You enjoy a sense of unconditional self-esteem. You do not feel you have to earn love and friendship by impressing people with your intelligence or your success.
4. You are terrified by failure. If you do not achieve an important goal, you feel like a failure as a human being.	4. You are not afraid to fail because you realize that no one can be successful all the time. Although failure is disappointing, you see it as an opportunity for growth and learning.
5. You think you must always be strong and in control of your emotions. You are reluctant to share vulnerable feelings like sadness, insecurity, or anger with others. You believe they would think less of you.	5. You're not afraid of being vulnerable or sharing your feelings with people you care about. This makes you feel closer to them.

*Copyright © 1989 by David D. Burns, M.D., from *The Feeling Good Handbook*

compulsive perfectionism is not the same as the healthy pursuit of excellence, as you can see in the comparisons on page 176.

5. **Lack of rewards.** The greatest motivating force in the world is a feeling of excitement and satisfaction in what you do. If you feel rewarded for your efforts, it will motivate you to work harder. But if nothing you do is ever good enough, life will become an exhausting, joyless treadmill.

People who are highly successful and productive usually give themselves credit for what they do. Because they think about their work in a positive way, they feel excited and involved.

Procrastinators sometimes do just the opposite. They constantly put themselves down. If you clean the house, you may tell yourself that what you did "wasn't good enough" or "didn't count" or "wasn't very special." Then at the end of the day you feel drained and you don't think you've accomplished anything worthwhile.

In fact, some procrastinators display a brilliant ability to discount the value of anything they do. A woman who worked for a computer company told me that for over two years she had been hiding in her office, doing virtually nothing aside from clipping her nails, making personal phone calls, and reading magazines. She was afraid her boss might discover how little she was doing and fire her. She wanted me to help her become more productive.

I wanted to find out what her idea of "becoming more productive" would be. Notice how unwilling she is to give herself credit for anything positive:

DAVID: Let me see if I can understand what you have in mind when you say you want me to help you become more productive. Suppose you made a plan for yourself and you were able to work four hours a day for the next week. Would you consider that a step in the right direction?

SUSAN: That wouldn't count because I'm supposed to put in seven hours a day. [Notice how she discounts the positive.]

DAVID: Okay. Let's suppose you then continued to improve and during the second week you put in seven hours a day. What would you think about that?

SUSAN: I'd say it wouldn't count at all. You see, I was supposed to start working on this project last February. Even if I put in seven hours a day, I'd still be way behind. [Notice that she discounts the positive again.]

DAVID: And suppose you started putting in ten hours a day, seven days a week, and eventually you got all caught up. Would you give yourself credit? Would you feel you were becoming a little more productive?

SUSAN: Well, if I did . . . then I'd think that I was still behind everybody else and worry about all the time I've wasted in the past two years.

DAVID: Okay. Suppose you continued working ambitiously and your efficiency went up to some incredibly high level and they started raving about you as one of their most productive, efficient employees. Let's say they even promoted you. What would you think then?

SUSAN: That would be spooky. I'd say I must have made a pact with the devil and it had nothing to do with me.

DAVID: I see. So I take it then that regardless of whatever you do at work, whatever effort you put in and whatever degree of success you achieve, you'll continue to believe that you're incapable of being productive and undeserving of any praise or credit?

SUSAN: Yeah.

I've included this dialogue to illustrate Susan's enormously persistent tendency to put herself down. Do you ever do this yourself? Do you tell yourself that your efforts and accomplishments aren't any good? If so, you'll feel beaten down no matter how hard you try, and you'll feel unappreciated and unmotivated.

We usually think of rewards as coming from the outside. A compliment for a job well done feels good. Getting a high grade on a test or making a sale to a difficult customer can be highly motivating. But ultimately all rewards must come from within. Only your thoughts can make you feel good or bad. If you never give yourself credit, you will feel that you can never do anything well enough to satisfy yourself, so it will become pointless to try. Why keep banging your head against a wall?

6. **"Should statements."** Procrastinators often tell themselves: "I really *should* write those letters. I *ought to* get started." These "should statements" usually aren't very effective, because they make you feel guilty and resentful, so you avoid the task. The moment you tell yourself "I really *should* do it," you will probably have the thought ". . . but I don't really have to right now. I'll wait until later."

Sometimes, the more you tell yourself that you *should* do something, the harder it is to do it!

You may have difficulty with this idea. You may insist that there's nothing wrong with using the word "should." You may think that it's your duty to clean your desk or to study hard. You may feel it's something you really *should* do!

There are actually three valid uses of the word "should" in the English language. One is the "moral should." You "should" not intentionally take advantage of someone, because this violates your moral code. The second is the "legal should." You "should" not drive at 90 mph because it's dangerous and you'll probably get a ticket. The third is the "laws of the universe should." Things "should" happen because the forces of nature make them happen. For example, if you drop your pen, it "should" fall because of the force of gravity.

When you say "I should straighten up my desk," is this a "moral should"? Obviously not, unless one of the Ten Commandments says "Thou shalt not have a messy desk." Is it a "legal should"? Obviously not, unless there are laws that prohibit messy desks. Is it a "law of the universe should"? Obviously not, since there's no law of nature that says that people with messy desks will always straighten them up right away.

Since it's not a "moral should," a "legal should," or a "law of the universe should," the word "should" really isn't appropriate here. When you say "I should straighten up my desk," I suspect what you really mean is "It would be to my advantage to straighten up my desk." But then why not simply think about it like that instead? Keep the word "should" out of the picture. Every time you tell yourself "I really *should* do X or Y," change it to "It would be desirable for me to do X or Y." Since this doesn't sound so moralistic, it won't make you feel rebellious and guilty.

Of course, this is based on the assumption that you've thought the matter through and have decided that it really is important to you to clear up your desk. You may discover that there is no compelling reason to have an organized desk. One of my friends at college prided himself on having one of the messiest rooms of anyone on campus. Papers and clothes were strewn several inches deep all over the room in what looked like total chaos. He said that people were always telling him to straighten it up, but that it *was* organized and he liked it just the way it was. He said he knew where everything was, even though it looked messy to other people. In fact he was a superb student, and he was the most organized person I ever knew. His messy room was not a real problem for him.

Maybe procrastination isn't a problem for you, either. The fact is, you've probably been getting along okay for a long time with your desk the way it is. Cleaning it up will be time-consuming and anxiety provoking and you probably have better things to do. And if you do straighten up your desk, it will just get messy again. Remember that there's a certain amount of status in having a messy desk. And if you do clean it up, people may begin to expect more of you. This will put you under tremendous pressure. With a messy desk they'll be reminded that you're a rather disorganized person and you may be able to get away with a lot more.

In addition, there may be someone you're annoyed with who gets upset every time they see your desk. By leaving it messy, you can let them know indirectly that you're upset without being too obvious about it. This way, you won't have to confront them directly with how you feel. You can avoid an argument or a fight, which could be very upsetting for both of you.

Do you still want to clean up your desk, in light of all those reasons not to? If so, you will need some compelling reasons to do it. What are they? Keep these reasons in mind so you will know why you're cleaning it up. Then you will be doing it because you want to and not because you think you "should."

7. **Passive aggressiveness.** People who procrastinate are often afraid to express negative feelings openly and directly. You may avoid conflicts and deny that you're upset because you think it's not "nice" to be angry. Your true feelings may come oozing out indirectly. You may fail to return an RSVP for a party you don't really want to go to, or you may "forget" to repay a debt because you're annoyed with the person who lent you the money. You may chronically show up late for appointments because you're annoyed with your boss. You may "forget" to take out the trash because you feel upset with your spouse for nagging you about it.

You may not be completely aware that your procrastination is provocative or frustrating to others. You may push your negative feelings out of your mind and say "I just forgot." That way you can deny how you really feel.

You can develop some insight about this if you ask yourself if a family member, a teacher, or someone you work with feels frustrated or annoyed because of your procrastination. If so, ask yourself if you feel upset or annoyed with them. This could be the cause of your procrastination.

8. **Unassertiveness.** Many people procrastinate because they are unassertive and agree to do things they don't really want to do. You may give in to unreasonable demands from others because you think you should be nice. You may think you should meet everybody else's expectations and base too much of your self-esteem on what other people think of you. You may be terrified of disapproval or criticism. You may be afraid to say no and run the risk that someone would get annoyed with you. Then you may put something off and get anxious every time you think about doing it. You could think of your procrastination as a way of being on strike.

Of course, there are times when we all do things we don't want to do to help others, but this niceness can go too far if you feel that you always have to say yes and please everybody. You may get overcommitted and procrastinate instead of being honest and direct with people about how you feel.

9. **Coercion sensitivity.** You may procrastinate because you feel that people are acting bossy and making unreasonable demands on you. You may be stubborn and refuse to do what they ask as a way of rebelling. Other people may find this behavior annoying and act even pushier. This leads to a power struggle, because no one wants to give in.

Your procrastination may be an indirect way of expressing your annoyance with the person who's nagging you. Even if it is to your advantage to go along with them, you may feel the need to resist so you can show that you won't let them control you. One morning a woman named Sarah made a decision to start her diet. She did well all day. That evening her husband, who was unaware of her decision, reminded her that she shouldn't eat so many sweets. She felt hurt and told him, "I can eat anything I darn well please!" She ate a giant hot fudge sundae in front of him to prove her point!

10. **The lack of desire.** This last cause of procrastination may sound ridiculously obvious, but it's the commonest cause of all. When you procrastinate, it's often because you simply don't want to do whatever it is that you're putting off. Most procrastinators aren't in touch with this. All you know is that there's some task you vaguely feel you should do, but you get really uncomfortable when it's time to do it,

so you do something else. Instead of telling yourself that you didn't want to do it and admitting that you made a conscious choice not to, you act as if the whole process is mysterious. You think, "Gee, I really am a procrastinator. I must really be lazy. That must be why I didn't balance my checkbook [or study or clean my desk or mow the lawn]." But this is just a lot of fancy talk. The real reason you didn't do it was because you didn't want to!

Now you might say, "So what? Everyone knows that!" However, admitting that you don't want to do something can be a useful insight. Once you become aware of why you're procrastinating, it may put the problem into a different perspective. If you're procrastinating, ask yourself why. You may have good reasons.

You may put something off because it's not a high priority. You may feel that it wouldn't be wise for you to do it, and in your heart of hearts you may not really want to do it or need to do it. Perhaps your family, friends, or boss has encouraged you to pursue a goal that you don't really feel committed to or ready for. Maybe it isn't quite right for you, but you haven't admitted this to yourself. Instead of owning up to the fact that the task may not be right for you, you may postpone it while you tell yourself that you "should" do it or that you "need" to do it. Then you may berate yourself and get anxious. Your procrastination may really be a healthy response that you need to listen to.

Soon after *Feeling Good* was published, I obtained a contract for *The Feeling Good Handbook*. However, I didn't feel ready to write the book. I forced out a number of chapters, but my writing was wooden and the material seemed boring. I wasn't convinced that I had anything new or important to say because it seemed I had already said nearly everything in *Feeling Good*. Furthermore, I couldn't think of a format for the *Handbook* that excited me. This state of affairs dragged on for years. Every now and then my editor would call or write to tell me how well *Feeling Good* was doing and would ask about the new *Handbook*.

One evening it suddenly occurred to me that I was ready to write the *Handbook*—for years I had been teaching and treating patients and doing research, and I had learned a great deal that I wanted to share. It also dawned on me that there were probably a lot of people who would appreciate learning more about how to break out of bad moods. I felt full of new ideas and rapidly produced a draft of the *Handbook*. The experience of writing it was exhilarating, and I was glad that I had put the project off until I felt ready.

10

•

A Prescription for Procrastinators

The following five-step program can help you become more productive and successful. What is one thing you've been putting off? It might be calling the doctor or dentist for a checkup, paying your bills, writing an overdue letter, calling on a customer, balancing your checkbook, organizing your desk, outlining a proposal, asking someone for a date—it can be anything. Choose one thing. Make sure it's specific and not vague. Think about this for a moment and see if you can come up with one thing you're putting off before you read on.

Some people might tell me, "Dr. Burns, I'm procrastinating about everything." This problem is too abstract. It's overwhelming. The best way to get your life together is to get started on one specific task. This will often give you the momentum to do other things you've been putting off. Select something concrete and real that you'd like to do, like cleaning the garage. Describe the task you've chosen:

_____

_____

Have you thought about something and written it down? If not, I really want you to do this before you read on. I want you to interact with me and to do the written exercises as you read this. Are you willing to? If so, that's great! You will be rewarded for your efforts!

Step 1: Cost-Benefit Analysis

First, ask yourself *why* you should stop procrastinating. Make a list of the advantages of putting this task off:

1. _____

_____

2. _____

_____

3. _____

_____

4. _____

_____

5. _____

_____

When you make your list, remember that procrastination has many advantages: it's easy; you can do something else that would be more relaxing; you can put the problem out of your mind so you won't feel so upset; you can avoid hard work; you don't have to face the possibility of failure; you can frustrate the people who are unfairly nagging you to get it done; and you can prevent people from pressuring you and making so many demands on you. If you put the task off long enough, they may begin to accept the fact that you're not going to do it and they'll expect less of you.

Procrastination may also give you some status. After all, it's only very lucky or very wealthy people who don't have to work hard at things. If you procrastinate and take it easy, you may be saying, "I'm a special kind of person—I'm one cut above the rest. I shouldn't have to work hard and hustle. I deserve to play and have fun."

It's crucial to be aware of these advantages of procrastination because they may be too good to give up. You'll need some pretty powerful reasons to change. Developing some insight into the rewards of procrastinating will make you more aware of why you put things off. You wake up and tell yourself "I'm really going to get started on X today." "X" could be dieting or cleaning your desk or any chore you've been putting off. At the end of the day, you realize that you haven't followed through on your plan. Instead of dieting, you binged. Your desk is even more littered. You still haven't studied or gone out on a job interview. You get frustrated and mad at yourself, and you wonder why you're being so irrational. Maybe you're *not* being so irrational. You undoubtedly have a lot of powerful reasons why you procrastinate.

You may decide that you don't want to change. Remember the discussion in the last chapter—that procrastination is sometimes healthy? You may be doing something, like going to college or selling life insurance, because you think it's what you *should* be doing. Everyone pressures you to do it, but in your heart of hearts it's not what you really want to be doing. Maybe you cut classes and avoid studying because you don't want to be in school right now. Maybe you want to take a year off and bum around and think about what you really want to do with your life. I took a year off from medical school on two different occasions because I wasn't sure I wanted to be a doctor. I was not a pre-med student in college, and I only went to medical school so I could become a psychiatrist. I didn't enjoy medical school, and on many occasions it just didn't seem worth all the hassle. Those years off helped me get in touch with what I really wanted to do with my life, and I discovered a far greater degree of commitment than was there when I left.

Can you think of any disadvantages in procrastinating about the task you chose? You may feel guilty; you may get tired of people nagging you; you won't enjoy the satisfaction of completing the job. List the disadvantages of procrastinating here:

1. _____

_____

2. _____

_____

3. _____

_____

4. _____

_____

5. _____

_____

Now weigh the advantages of procrastinating against the disadvantages. Ask yourself whether the costs or the benefits of putting it off are greater. The man whose Cost-Benefit Analysis is illustrated on the next page was procrastinating about cleaning his desk. He decided that the disadvantages of procrastinating outweighed the advantages by a 60–40 margin.

Now make a similar list of the advantages and disadvantages of getting started on the task *today*. Notice that I did not say "sometime." Also notice that I've asked you to list the advantages and disadvantages of *getting started*, and not of completing the task. This is important, because the task may seem overwhelming. While I've been writing this book, lots of papers have piled up in my office. I haven't taken the time to keep up with all the filing that needs to be done. I would estimate that I have at least five hours of organizing and straightening up to do. When I decide to get started, I'll only do a little bit at first. Then I'll chip away at it over a period of a couple of weeks. That way it won't seem overwhelming. If I told myself I had to do it all at once, I might never get started.

PROCRASTINATION
COST-BENEFIT ANALYSIS

What are you procrastinating about? Describe the task here:

Straightening my desk

List the advantages and disadvantages of procrastinating:

Advantages	Disadvantages
1. I can do something else I want to do.	1. I feel guilty every time I look at it.
2. It seems like a hideous chore.	2. I feel disorganized and I lose respect for myself.
3. If I put it out of my mind, I won't have to think about it.	3. I can't find the things I need.
	4. It looks like a mess and my wife is annoyed about it.
	5. I don't enjoy the satisfaction of getting it done.
40	60

Outcome: Weigh the advantages of procrastinating against the disadvantages on a 100-point scale, and put the score in the circles.

List the advantages and disadvantages of getting started today:	
Advantages	**Disadvantages**
1. I'll probably feel better about myself if I at least get started.	1. It will make me uncomfortable to face the mess.
2. I'll be more organized and able to find the things I need.	2. There are other things I'd rather be doing.
3. The room will look better.	3. It may take a long time.
4. My wife will be pleasantly surprised.	

$$\boxed{55} — \boxed{45}$$

OUTCOME: Weigh the advantages of getting started today against the disadvantages, and put that score in the circles.

Think about the advantages of getting started today on the task you've been putting off: you may feel greater self-esteem; other people may get off your back and respect you more; you may experience a mood lift; you might feel more motivated once you get started. List the advantages of getting started today:

1. _____

_____

2. _____

_____

3. _____

_____

4. _____

_____

5. _____

_____

The disadvantages of getting started could include: the task may be difficult; you may feel frustrated and nervous; you may feel obligated to do even more once you get started; you may fail; people may get ticked off at you if you don't do a good job; you won't be able to use the time to do something that's more enjoyable. List the disadvantages of getting started here:

1. _____

_____

2. _____

_____

3. _____

_____

4. _____

_____

5. _____

_____

After you've completed these lists, weigh the advantages of getting started today against the disadvantages. Which seem greater to you? You can see that the man who completed the form on page 188 decided that the advantages slightly outweighed the disadvantages, by a 55–45 margin.

Once you've compared the costs and benefits of getting started today with the costs and benefits of procrastinating, you can decide which option is the best. I've included a blank Cost-Benefit Analysis for your use at the end of this chapter.

Your analysis may indicate that even though you don't want to do a particular task and you don't "feel like it," it may still be in your best interest to get started. This insight can help you break the habit of thinking you always have to feel motivated or "in the mood" before you do something.

The Cost-Benefit Analysis can be especially helpful if someone is putting pressure on you to do something and you feel the urge to resist them. Maybe your spouse or a parent or a teacher is nagging you to lose weight, to jog, to study, to apply for a job, or to clean up your room. You may feel stubborn and dig in your heels. You need to decide what *you* want to do. Sometimes it turns out to be better to do something in spite of the fact that someone's being obnoxious and nagging you about it!

By the same token, after you review your Cost-Benefit Analysis, you might discover that you really don't want to get started at this time. You may discover that you may *never* want to do the thing you've been putting off. That's perfectly okay, because you've made a free choice. Once you make this decision, you're no longer procrastinating. Procrastination, by definition, is avoiding a task that you've chosen to do. If you decide not to do it, your problem has been solved. There's really no reason to read any further! On the other hand, if your Cost-Benefit Analysis indicates that you do want to get started, then you're ready for the next step.

Step 2: Make a Plan

Have you decided that the advantages of getting started today outweigh the disadvantages? If so, I want to know exactly what time you will start. Write the time down here:

_____

Have you written the time down? If the answer is no, I'm puzzled. This indicates that you do not plan to get started on the task today. Either you're reading this chapter out of curiosity, or else you have decided not to get started on the task. This is okay, but we should be perfectly clear with each other that you do not have any intention of overcoming your procrastination at this time.

On the other hand, if you *have* written the time down, congratulations! You are beginning to change your life one step at a time. You've already taken the biggest step. If you keep filling out the blanks as you read, I believe that you'll be able to lick this problem. Keep it up! If you haven't written the time down, you can still do it. Grab your pen and fill in the blank now!

Many patients complain that they want help with their procrastinating. They express a vague commitment to doing something to solve the problem. They may say they'll go home and start jogging or they'll apply for a job or do whatever it was they've been putting off. In the early days of my practice, I would get my hopes up, only to discover when they came back the next week that they hadn't followed through. The typical story was "I forgot" or "Gee, I didn't get around to it."

After feeling puzzled and frustrated by this for several years, I finally found a good way to combat it. If you were my patient and you told me you planned to do something you had been putting off, I would ask, "At what specific time today do you plan to do it?" After squirming, you might name a time. Then I would say, "Can you think of any distractions or problems that would conceivably prevent you from following through?" We would list these together. Then I would say, "Now, I want you to tell me how you will combat each of these obstacles so you can guarantee that nothing can prevent you from following through." Once I felt convinced that you meant business, I would ask you to call my office at an agreed-upon time and report either that you had completed the job or that you "stubbornly refused."

This may seem insulting and heavy-handed, but I have found that once you make a commitment to getting started at a specific time, the likelihood of success is enhanced.

Since you may not have put down a specific time when I asked you to several paragraphs back, let me give you the chance again here:

Have you done this? If so, the chances are high that you're about to change your life in a very fundamental and important way.

Now make a list of any problems or obstacles that could prevent you from following through. Fred, a perfectionistic professor, kept procrastinating about writing the outline for his book because he was afraid that it wouldn't be good enough. After completing the Cost-Benefit Analysis in my office one morning, he agreed to work on it from 3:00 to 4:00 that afternoon. I asked him to list any problems that could conceivably prevent him from carrying out this plan. These were:

1. "I won't feel like it when 3:00 rolls around."

2. "I'll get distracted by other things. I'll decide that I should straighten up my office first."

3. "A student might want an appointment."

4. "Once I try to write the outline, I'll feel inadequate. I'll tell myself that I don't have anything important to say."

I asked Fred how he would solve each of these problems. This was his "solution" list:

1. "I can tell myself I've made a decision to work on the book between 3:00 and 4:00 whether I feel like it or not."
2. "I can work on it at the library instead of my office. Then I won't feel so tempted by the distractions in my office."
3. "If a student wants an appointment, I can say that I have a commitment from 3:00 until 4:00 p.m."
4. "I can decide to jot down some ideas for one hour, whether or not it seems like I have anything worthwhile to say. Then I will give myself credit for that."

Fred called my office at 4:15 and left the message that he'd written steadily during the entire hour and felt great about it.

This simple method can be effective for you too. Think about the task you've decided to get started on today. In the left-hand column below, list any problems or obstacles that could sabotage your good intentions. Then put solutions to these problems in the right-hand column.

Problems	Solutions
1. _____ _____	1. _____ _____
2. _____ _____	2. _____ _____
3. _____ _____	3. _____ _____

Once you've decided when you will get started and have thought of ways to deal with any problems that might sabotage your good intentions, you're ready for the next step.

Step 3: Make the Job Easy

You can make a difficult job easy if you have modest, realistic goals instead of grandiose, perfectionistic ones. You might think that if the first sentence of your report isn't a masterpiece of modern prose, it won't be any good at all. This expectation will put enormous pressure on you and you may end up doing nothing. Why not try to write an "adequate" first sentence instead? That would be far easier, and at least you could get started. Once you have one "adequate" sentence on the paper you can add another and another, until you complete an "adequate" paragraph or a page. Then you can do some "adequate" editing the next day and make this material even better. Often things turn out the best for me when I'm not trying so hard. The same may be true for you.

Another way to make a tough job easy is to do a little bit at a time. You may feel overwhelmed because you tell yourself you have to do things all at once. Instead, break the job down into its smallest component parts and concentrate on one part at a time.

The secret involves getting into the here-and-now instead of worrying about everything you have to do in the future. Life exists one minute at a time, so all you'll ever have to do at any time is one minute's worth of work. That's not so hard, is it?

There are two ways to break a big job down into small parts. One is to tackle the job in a step-by-step fashion. If you have to paint your porch, the first step might be to select a color. The second step would be to go to the hardware store to buy the paint. The third step would be to carry the ladder out to the porch. And so forth. Make sure each step of the task is reasonably easy.

The second way to break a task down is to work in short spurts. Would you be willing to work at a big job you've been putting off for only fifteen to thirty minutes today? You may resist this suggestion. Nearly every procrastinator tells me, "That would be useless. I'm not going to study [or work at my taxes] for only fifteen to thirty minutes! That would be only a drop in the bucket compared to all I have to do!"

Remember that no one could possibly do any more than fifteen to thirty minutes of productive work in any fifteen- to thirty-minute period. So telling yourself you have to do more than that is pointless! Of course, once you've put in fifteen or thirty minutes, there's nothing to prevent you from deciding to put in another fifteen to thirty minutes. Once I get rolling on a difficult job I often feel so good about it that before I know it several hours have passed. But I rarely tell myself to do more than fifteen minutes worth of work at any one time. I tell myself that everything beyond fifteen minutes is gravy. This is, admittedly, a way of fooling myself, but I'm quite gullible and the method is enormously effective. Give it a try!

Here are the advantages of working in short spurts:

- You'll break big jobs down into small parts that can be completed in short periods of time. This will make your task seem less overwhelming.
- You can accomplish your goal of doing fifteen minutes worth of work soon after you begin. The sense of accomplishment will often reduce the feelings of tension and motivate you to do more. You'll begin to feel more relaxed and productive.
- You won't be so tempted to procrastinate and put things off, because you'll never be obligated to do more than fifteen minutes worth of work at any one time. It's really not so hard to sit down and work at an unpleasant task if you feel you have to stick with it for only a little while.

- Trying to cram everything in at once is usually not the best way to master a difficult assignment. You can often work more creatively and efficiently by doing things in short bursts. If you're studying or writing a report, your mind will digest ideas between these short work periods. You will produce a higher-quality product than you thought you were capable of, with far less effort and stress.

Once you've made a plan to make the task easier and less of a hassle, you can move on to the next step.

Step 4: Think Positively

When you think about a task you've been avoiding, you may feel upset and want to do something else instead. This is because you give yourself negative messages that make you feel guilty and over-whelmed. Suppose you're procrastinating about writing thank-you letters. You may tell yourself: "Oh, I have all those letters to write. I can put them off until later when I'm more in the mood. I really should write them now, but I don't feel like it. It'll be so unpleasant. I think I'll watch television for a while instead."

You can learn how to deal with these negative thoughts so they won't undermine your efforts. Ask yourself, "When I procrastinate, what am I telling myself? What negative thoughts are running through my mind?" Write these thoughts down. This is crucial—you cannot change the way you think and feel if you refuse to write your thoughts down. Write down any negative thoughts you may have about the task you're putting off:

1. _____

_____

2. _____

_____

3. _____

_____

Once you write them down, you may see that you engage in a subtle process of self-deception when you procrastinate. It's not the actual task, but the unrealistic way you think about it that makes you want to put it off. Let me repeat that: You procrastinate because you think about the job in an unrealistic, illogical way. When you avoid a task, you are always fooling yourself about something!

Dr. Aaron Beck has called these distorted negative thoughts "TICs," for "Task-Interfering Cognitions," because they interfere with your ability to get started. You can replace them with "TOCs," for "Task-Oriented Cognitions," with the help of the "TIC-TOC Technique." TOCs are positive and realistic thoughts that will make you feel more productive and motivated.

For example, the first negative thought, or TIC, illustrated on the next page is "I have all those letters to write." The distortion in this thought, which you would write down in the middle column, is "all-or-nothing thinking." You're telling yourself you have to write all those letters today. This will make you feel overwhelmed, and you'll give up before you even begin. You could substitute this TOC in the right-hand column: "I don't have to do them all tonight, but I'd probably feel a whole lot better if I finished at least one of them." You could even decide that all you have to do tonight is locate some stationery and address one or two envelopes. That would be a good first step.

The second TIC is "I can put them off until later when I'm more in the mood." Can you identify the distortion in this thought? Review the list on page 206 and put your ideas here:

_____

_____

The distortion is "emotional reasoning," because you're waiting until you feel like writing the letters. This is putting the cart before the horse. Usually action comes first and motivation comes second.

What could you tell yourself instead? Put your TOC here:

_____

_____

_____

THE TIC-TOC TECHNIQUE

What are you procrastinating about? Describe it here:
Writing thank-you letters

What negative feelings do you have when you think about doing it? Use words like "anxious," "guilty," "frustrated," or "overwhelmed" and indicate how strong each one is between 0 and 100.

	Emotion	Rating		Emotion	Rating
1.	Guilty	80	3.	Unmotivated	90
2.	Bored	90			

TICs (Task-Interfering Cognitions)	Distortions	TOCs (Task-Oriented Cognitions)
1. I have all those letters to write.	1. All-or-nothing thinking	1. I don't have to do them all tonight, but I'd probably feel a whole lot better if I did at least one of them.
2. I can put them off until later when I'm more in the mood.	2. Emotional reasoning	2. I don't have to be "in the mood" to get started. Once I get started I'll probably feel more like doing it.
3. I really should write them now, but I don't feel like it.	3. "Should statement"; emotional reasoning	3. It would be to my advantage to start them now.

TICs (Task-Interfering Cognitions)	Distortions	TOCs (Task-Oriented Cognitions)
4. It'll be such a drag. I think I'll watch TV for a while instead.	4. Fortune-telling	4. How do I know it will be a drag? Maybe it won't! I can write one letter and find out. Watching TV may not be so great, because I'll feel guilty about not doing the letters.

You could think about it this way instead: "I don't have to be 'in the mood.' Once I get started, I'll probably feel more like doing it."

As an exercise, cover up the middle and right-hand columns in the following examples. The TICs in the left-hand column are upsetting thoughts that patients of mine have had about tasks they were putting off. Try to identify the distortions in these TICs and see if you can substitute TOCs. Then compare your answers to the ones I've suggested. Don't be concerned if your responses are different from mine. Part of the beauty of this technique is that there's a lot of room for your own unique approach.

You may have the thought: "This TIC-TOC technique is just a silly gimmick that wouldn't work for me. How dumb!" This is another TIC that will make you procrastinate. Can you see what distortions it contains? Check the list on page 206 and put your ideas here:

1. _____

2. _____

3. _____

The thought is an example of "fortune-telling," because you're predicting that this technique won't help you. We don't have any real evidence for that. It's also an example of "emotional reasoning," because you feel that these methods won't help, so you conclude they really won't. Finally, you're "labeling" the technique a "gimmick." This is pejorative. If you think of it as a "method," you will be more open-minded and willing to give it a try.

TICs	Distortions	TOCs
1. I'll never get the garage cleaned. The junk's been piling up for years.	1. Fortune-telling; all-or-nothing thinking	1. I can do a little bit. I don't have to do it all today.
2. I don't want to study for the exam!	2. Emotional reasoning	2. I don't have to *want* to study, but it would be advisable to do it anyway.
3. I have so much to study. It's overwhelming!	3. All-or-nothing thinking	3. The sooner I get started, the sooner I'll get done. I can think of what I need to do in the next hour instead of worrying about all I have to do.
4. I have no confidence. I don't know how to work some of the problems in the book.	4. Emotional reasoning; "should statement"	4. I'm not supposed to feel confident yet. That's why I need to study.

TICs	Distortions	TOCs
1. I should ask my boss for a raise—but I really don't feel like it.	1. "Should statement"; emotional reasoning	1. It would be to my advantage to ask my boss for a raise because I've been working hard and it's time for a salary review. Asking him for a raise is scary, but I can do it even if I don't feel like it.

Can you think of a way to talk back to this negative thought? Put your ideas here:

_____

_____

_____

_____

You could substitute this TOC: "It seems as if writing down my negative thoughts wouldn't help, but I can't know this until I try. Maybe the method will work, and it will only take a few minutes to find out!"

Now write down your negative thoughts about the job you've been avoiding in the left-hand column of the blank form at the end of this chapter. Identify the distortions in these thoughts, and substitute more positive and realistic thoughts in the right-hand column. You will be surprised by how helpful this can be!

Step 5: Give Yourself Credit

Once you've begun a job you've been avoiding, it's important to give yourself credit instead of discounting your efforts. A mental reward will boost your motivation. A housewife told me that she worked like a hornet all day long. At the end of the day she'd obsess about all the things she hadn't had time to squeeze into her crowded schedule. This made her feel as if she hadn't accomplished anything at all! She felt burned out and unrewarded. I suggested that she could make a list of everything she accomplished each day. Simply reviewing this list at the end of the day made her feel better, because she could see that she had done a great deal.

Let's assume that she still continued to feel inadequate and miserable in spite of the fact that she was doing a great deal every day. What would you think the real problem is? You be the psychiatrist, and put your diagnosis here. Why does she feel burned out each day?

_____

_____

_____

_____

I would speculate that doing housework and errands all day long may not be what she really wants to do. Her negative feelings may be her way of telling herself that she would like to go back to school or pursue a career. She may be pushing herself to do what she thinks she *should* do, rather than doing what she *wants* to do.

There can be some advantages to this. It may protect her from taking a chance of doing something new and risking failure. Being an unhappy but dutiful, perfectionistic housewife may be less threatening. But by the same token, life becomes a joyless treadmill, and the chronic resentment and unhappiness she feels may poison her marriage.

You may wonder how you can tell if your goals are appropriate for you. I would say that if you feel a sense of commitment and excitement about what you're doing, you're in good shape. This doesn't mean that you constantly have to feel high and exhilarated.

Pursuing any goal involves lots of hard work and frustration along the way. But if you have a sense of meaning and purpose, all the hard work falls into a different perspective. This is what is meant by the expression "a labor of love." Your discomfort becomes like the pain of labor, because you're giving birth to your own destiny.

Let's summarize the five steps to greater productivity. First, pinpoint one specific task that you've been putting off and do a Cost-Benefit Analysis. This will help you decide if you really do want to get started on the task. Many people have a knee-jerk reaction and tell themselves "I should do this" and "I ought to do that" when they don't really feel committed. You may discover that your procrastination is not a bad habit but simply your way of telling yourself—and the world—that a particular activity is not right for you. You may want to rethink your priorities instead of feeling guilty.

The second step is to decide on a specific time to get started today and to anticipate ways you might sabotage yourself. Make a plan to handle these distractions. The third step is to make the job easy, either by breaking it down into parts or by working at it for short periods of time. Then it won't seem so overwhelming. Next, use the TIC-TOC technique to change the negative thoughts that create emotional barriers, such as guilt, frustration, and anxiety.

Finally, give yourself credit for the things you accomplish instead of insisting that your efforts are never good enough. When things don't turn out as well as you had hoped, you can learn from the experience and move forward instead of giving up and deciding that you're "a failure."

PROCRASTINATION
COST-BENEFIT ANALYSIS*

What are you procrastinating about? Describe it here:

_____

List the advantages and disadvantages of putting it off:

Advantages	Disadvantages

OUTCOME: Weigh the advantages of procrastinating against the disadvantages on a 100-point scale, and record the score in the circles.

(Continue on next page)

List the advantages and disadvantages of getting started today:

Advantages	Disadvantages

Outcome: Now weigh the advantages of getting started today against the disadvantages on a 100-point scale, and record the score in the circles.

THE TIC-TOC TECHNIQUE*

What are you procrastinating about? Describe it here:

_____

What negative feelings do you have when you think about doing it? Use words like "anxious," "guilty," "frustrated," or "overwhelmed" and indicate in parentheses how strong each one is between 0 percent and 100 percent.

Emotion	Rating	Emotion	Rating
1. _____		3. _____	
2. _____		4. _____	

TICs (Task-Interfering Cognitions)	Distortions (See list on page 206)	TOCs (Task-Oriented Cognitions)

(Continue on next page)

*Copyright © 1989 by David D. Burns, M.D., from *The Feeling Good Handbook*

TICs (Task-Interfering Cognitions)	Distortions	TOCs (Task-Oriented Cognitions)

CHECKLIST OF COGNITIVE DISTORTIONS*

1. All-or-nothing thinking: You look at things in absolute, black-and-white categories.
2. Overgeneralization: You view a negative event as a never-ending pattern of defeat.
3. Mental filter: You dwell on the negatives and ignore the positives.
4. Discounting the positives: You insist that your accomplishments or positive qualities "don't count."
5. Jumping to conclusions: (A) Mind reading—you assume that people are reacting negatively to you when there's no definite evidence for this; (B) Fortune-telling—you arbitrarily predict that things will turn out badly.
6. Magnification or minimization: You blow things way up out of proportion or you shrink their importance inappropriately.
7. Emotional reasoning: You reason from how you feel: "I *feel* like an idiot, so I really must be one." Or "I don't *feel* like doing this, so I'll put it off."
8. "Should statements": You criticize yourself or other people with "shoulds" or "shouldn'ts." "Musts," "oughts," and "have tos" are similar offenders.
9. Labeling: You identify with your shortcomings. Instead of saying "I made a mistake," you tell yourself, "I'm a jerk," or "a fool," or "a loser."
10. Personalization and blame: You blame yourself for something you weren't entirely responsible for, or you blame other people and overlook ways that your own attitudes and behavior might contribute to a problem.

Feeling Confident: How to Conquer Anxiety, Fears, and Phobias

11

♦

Understanding Anxiety

There are three competing theories about the causes of anxiety. A cognitive therapist would claim that negative thoughts and irrational attitudes cause anxiety. For example, if you believe that you must always get everyone's approval, you might feel very nervous if your boss was criticizing you or if you had to give a speech before a large audience.

A psychoanalyst would argue that repressed conflicts make you anxious. When you were growing up, you may have gotten the idea that children should be seen but not heard. You might have been afraid of sharing any negative feelings with your parents. As an adult, you may still be afraid of expressing anger or telling people how you really feel. When you have a conflict with your boss, you may clam up because you feel he will put you down, just as your parents did. The effort to avoid the conflict makes you repress your feelings, and you get terribly nervous and panicky.

Some psychiatrists think that an imbalance in your body chemistry causes feelings of fear and panic. These therapists might tell you that all you need is the right drug to correct the problem. Many patients are equally convinced that their nervous problems are medical. Some think their anxieties are caused by food allergies or low blood sugar.

Others fear they have a brain tumor or a heart condition. They go from doctor to doctor looking for a diagnosis and cure that never seem to materialize.

Which of these three ideas is correct? In this chapter, we will examine the merits of each.

How Your Thoughts Can Frighten You

Cognitive therapy is based on the premise that your thoughts, not external events, make you upset. This is just as true for anxiety and panic as for any other negative emotion. You have to interpret a situation and give it a meaning before you can feel worried or nervous about it. This idea has tremendous practical importance, because when you change the way you think, you can change the way you feel. You can overcome fear, worry, anxiety, nervousness, and panic.

Many people find this idea exciting. Others react with irritation. They insist that it can't be so. They tell me that if you're about to be hit by a train, it's the event, and not your thoughts, that makes you frightened. What do you think about this?

One evening recently I was going home from the airport in a taxi. As we crossed the railroad track about a mile from my house, I noticed a train coming in the distance. I was alarmed to see that a man was slowly driving his car down the railroad tracks—not crossing them, but actually driving down the tracks! I had no idea why anyone would be doing that, but I could see that he was on the same set of tracks as the oncoming train. If he didn't immediately back up, turn, and get off, it was clear that his car would be crushed.

I told the driver to stop and jumped out of the taxi. I shouted, "Get off the tracks!" The man simply pulled to a stop and waited. I rushed up to the window and urged him to back up, to get his car off the tracks immediately. He smiled at me in a leisurely, friendly way and asked if I knew the way to City Line Avenue. I couldn't comprehend why he would ask such a dumb question! The train was approaching at high speed and City Line Avenue is about ten miles away. He had less than thirty seconds to back up his car and get to safety. I exclaimed, "Back up! Back up!" He slowly backed up his car and then turned and positioned it so the hood was directly in the path of the oncoming train.

I ran and stood directly in front of his car, waving my arms wildly.

I screamed, "Back up! Back up!" He only had to back up five or ten feet to save himself.

Instead, he did the opposite! He slowly crept forward, inch by inch. By now the train was just a hundred yards away, coming fast with the horn blowing. I shouted "Faster! Faster!" Instead of speeding up, he smiled again and pulled to a stop. A crash seemed inevitable. The moment before the impact, I ran to avoid the collision. The train hit his car at high speed and crushed it.

The train was over a mile long and it was nearly a minute before it came to a full stop. I rushed up to the demolished car. The point of impact was directly behind the driver's head. The back half of the car was smashed to bits, but the front half was relatively intact, except for lots of broken glass. My heart was pounding as I peered through the mangled window. I saw that the driver was a frail, skinny, elderly gentleman. Miraculously, he appeared uninjured. He slowly turned to me, still smiling. Then he asked me in a lazy, relaxed voice if I could direct him to City Line Avenue. He explained that he'd been looking for City Line Avenue for some time—he thought he might be lost and asked if I'd kindly point him in the right direction. He said that all he needed was a few directions. I was flabbergasted.

"Direct you to City Line?" I asked incredulously. "That's over ten miles from here and your car is smashed!"

"Smashed?" he asked. He sounded surprised and skeptical.

"Look at it," I replied. "You've just been hit by a train! I'm astonished that you weren't killed."

"What train?" he asked in a disbelieving voice.

"*That* one!" I said, pointing at the train. He slowly turned and looked at the smashed rear half of his auto and at the train a few feet behind him.

He finally became animated. He seemed filled with enthusiasm and exclaimed: "Oh! Hit by a train? Can I sue?" I told him, "You'll be lucky if they don't sue *you*! You've been driving down the railroad tracks."

It suddenly dawned on me what had happened. This elderly man was apparently getting senile and he was confused by the dark. This experience underscored a simple concept at the heart of cognitive therapy. You cannot have *any* emotional reaction to an event until you have a *thought* about it and have given it meaning. He had no anxiety whatsoever because he did not perceive that he was in danger.

He did not have the thought "I'm about to be hit by a train," so he had no emotional response to the event.

The railroad engineers soon appeared on the scene. When the police and the ambulance arrived, I gave them my story and went home. The next day when I was jogging I noticed a man inspecting the scene of the accident. I learned that he was the elderly man's son. When I described what had happened, he explained that his father was getting old and confused and had lots of difficulties driving at night.

The story also illustrates a second principle of cognitive therapy: There is a difference between healthy fear and neurotic anxiety. The thoughts that lead to healthy fear are realistic; they alert us to a danger that we need to deal with. My fear probably saved the old man's life. In contrast, neurotic anxiety results from distorted thoughts that have little or no basis in reality. If you are having a panic attack, you may believe that something terrible will happen if you let your anxiety get out of hand. You might think you'll pass out from a stroke or have a heart attack or go crazy. Although these fears seem legitimate, they're quite unrealistic because: (1) Anxiety *never* causes strokes or heart attacks. (2) Most people who are afraid of passing out during a panic attack have never once passed out when in a state of panic. In fact, you *cannot* pass out during a panic attack because your heart is beating rapidly and pumping extra blood to the brain. (3) Panic attacks never lead to insanity or a loss of control. You are worrying about something that's blatantly unrealistic.

And why do you believe these distorted thoughts? Because of the way you *feel*. You feel as if you're in danger, so you think you really must *be* in danger. You say, "I feel so frightened and out of control that I must be on the verge of losing control." Or "I'm dizzy and confused. I feel like I'm about to pass out, so I must be on the verge of fainting."

Although you may easily see that other people who feel depressed or anxious are being irrational and illogical, it is not so easy to accept the fact that your own negative thoughts are equally unrealistic. You may feel convinced that your fears and insecurities are absolutely valid. Changing them may require hard, persistent effort. Many powerful techniques to help you get rid of these frightening thoughts will be illustrated in the following chapters.

How Repressed Feelings Can Make You Anxious

Freud said that repressed anger causes depression. He thought that people get depressed because they're afraid to express their angry feelings, for fear of being rejected or abandoned by the people they care about. Then they turn these feelings inward and direct their anger against themselves. Depression, Freud thought, is a form of self-hatred which results from this bottled-up anger.

I have seen few, if any, patients whose depression resulted from repressed anger. I do not believe Freud's theory has a great deal of merit, although large numbers of people still believe it. However, my clinical experience has led me to the overwhelming conviction that anxiety and panic—and not depression—do result from repressed anger. People who suffer from anxiety and panic attacks nearly always have unexpressed negative feelings about some problem in their lives. You may not be completely aware of these feelings because you push them out of your mind. When you deny your feelings and avoid the conflicts that are bothering you, you will start to feel nervous and panicky. When you confront these problems, your anxiety will frequently diminish or disappear.

There are two kinds of feelings that people with anxiety are likely to deny: anger and unexpressed wishes or desires. Let me give you an obvious example. Ted is a businessman from San Francisco who was very unhappy when he was growing up. He had a variety of allergies that caused him to miss a lot of school. He often had to go to the doctor. He was sickly and had few friends. He was often teased because he couldn't participate in sports. The allergies caused severe skin problems, and Ted felt ugly and unpopular. He told himself, "If I'm really successful when I grow up, everything will be okay. People will like me."

So that's exactly what Ted did. He got an MBA, and although he wasn't a top student, he was determined to succeed. Following graduation, Ted took over his uncle's business which was on the verge of bankruptcy. He took out a second mortgage on his house and invested every penny in the company. It was a highly speculative gamble, and Ted worked his tail off from early morning till late at night seven days a week to make it work. In a few years the business recovered and started to prosper. Then the business boomed. Profits began pouring in. The company went public and was listed on the

New York Stock Exchange. The stock soared in value, and soon Ted's company was worth millions of dollars. He started new business ventures that turned into bonanzas. Soon he was featured in national magazines such as *Time* and *People*. Ted had become the "golden boy," married to a beautiful woman and considered handsome and debonair himself.

But there was one problem. Ted was still unhappy. He was constantly anxious. He worried all day long about his health, his business, and his popularity. He was a bundle of fears and phobias. He looked me up one day after reading *Feeling Good*, and told me sadly that in spite of all his money, the only happy days he could recall were when he'd been nearly penniless, working as a lifeguard during the summers when he was in college at U.C.L.A. He felt free then, working in the day and having fun with friends at night.

The cognitive techniques were helpful to Ted. He was able to see how irrational his fears were. He began to have days and then weeks when he felt relaxed and free of anxiety. Life began to seem like fun again. But every now and then, Ted's fears would return. Sometimes his airplane phobia would come back. This was especially inconvenient because his business required him to travel extensively. On other occasions, Ted would worry that he was about to have a heart attack. Then he'd worry that he was about to go broke. In spite of his rational awareness that these fears were unfounded, they would come back over and over to plague him.

One day it occurred to me that every time Ted got anxious, there was some problem that he was avoiding. During a session when we were dealing with his airplane phobia and his fears of bankruptcy, I asked him in passing how things had been going at work and at home. He told me they were going great except for his irrational worries. I asked again if anything was bothering him or upsetting him. He insisted there was not. He explained that he and his wife had been staying at their spacious new home overlooking the Pacific Ocean and that there were several relatives staying with them. He said that everyone was having a great time.

When I asked how long these relatives had been there, Ted said "Several weeks." My eyebrows went up. I asked if he was feeling at all uncomfortable with relatives camping out at his house and whether he knew when they planned to leave. At first Ted insisted that this wasn't a problem. He reasoned that since it was such a large house, it was only fair that he should share it with everybody! He said it would be selfish to live there with just the servants and his family. He said he was worried that the relatives might get mad at him if he tactfully asked how long they planned to stay.

Well, I suspect you get the drift. The theme in Ted's life was "I need everybody's approval. I must make sure that everybody likes me, even if I have to ignore my own needs and feelings." After we talked about this, Ted admitted that he felt very uncomfortable with all those people living in his house. In spite of his generous desire to share his wealth and good fortune, he felt trapped and missed his privacy. He talked this over with his wife, and the relatives moved out. His anxieties about going broke or dying in an airline crash suddenly vanished.

This pattern is common. You may deny your feelings and ignore certain problems in your life because you don't want to upset anyone or hurt their feelings. Suddenly you're worrying and having panic attacks and you have no idea why! It becomes so important to be nice that you get distracted from what's really bothering you. It's as if you think you don't have permission to feel the way you do. When you ignore these feelings of resentment and frustration, they may get converted into anxiety. You may dwell on your anxiety and your feelings of panic instead of dealing with the problems that are bothering you. When you confront them, you will often feel relief.

Will Ted's dramatic improvement last forever? Of course not. He will probably get upset and deny his feelings again on many occasions, just as you and I do. When he does, he'll have to have a little chat with himself and ask, "What am I *really* upset about?" Then he'll have to do something about the situation that's bothering him.

All of this may seem obvious to you. I hope it does. But I have been to professional symposia on the treatment of anxiety and panic by some of the world's leading experts, where the idea that patients may have family or career problems that need to be addressed is usually not even mentioned as a possible cause of anxiety. Instead, patients may be told that they have a "chemical imbalance" needing treatment—possibly indefinitely—with drugs. Although medications can be helpful for some patients, this is rarely, if ever, the whole story.

Medical Causes of Anxiety and Panic

So far we've talked about the two common psychological causes for anxiety: negative thoughts and repressed negative feelings. Many patients and many doctors think that the origin of anxiety and panic is not psychological but medical. In one study, over 90 percent of the patients with panic attacks had consulted at least one physician because they believed that they had some disease or chemical imbalance. Over 70 percent of these patients had seen ten or more physicians in the search for some medical illness that would account for their symptoms of anxiety!

This is not so surprising. Most patients with anxiety or panic attacks are convinced that something is physically or mentally wrong with them. In fact, the distorted belief that something is wrong with you is one of the most common symptoms of anxiety and panic. When you feel depressed you may reason, "I feel hopeless, therefore I must really be hopeless." When you feel anxious you may reason, "I feel like there's something terribly wrong with me, therefore there must really be something wrong."

Another reason for the preoccupation with medical illness is that many of the symptoms of anxiety are physical, as described in Chapters 2 and 3. When you feel nervous you may get lightheaded and develop a headache and worry that you have a brain tumor. Your chest may feel tight and you may think you have a heart condition. You may feel short of breath or feel a lump in your throat and think that your windpipe is closing down.

A third reason that people with anxiety go to physicians is because they would feel so much better if they had a real illness rather than an emotional or psychological problem. I first became aware of this when I was a medical student working in the outpatient medical clinic at Stanford University Medical Center. Patients came to this clinic from all over the western United States, with thick medical charts and long histories of aches and pains no one could diagnose. The majority of them had nothing medically wrong with them.

I can vividly recall the day when an ambulance pulled up and a woman was rushed in on a gurney for "emergency surgery." This was slightly unusual because emergencies were generally sent to the emergency room, but for one reason or another she ended up in the clinic. She was screaming and complained of excruciating abdominal pain. I wondered if she had a ruptured appendix, but I became a little suspicious when I examined her stomach. It was soft, not hard and rigid as it should have been with a ruptured internal organ. As I reviewed her medical chart, which was two inches thick, I discovered that she'd had seven previous operations on her abdomen for unexplained stomach pain! The biopsy reports of tissue samples obtained during these operations were always perfectly normal.

I asked her husband to wait in the waiting room while I spoke to her. She told me that he had shot her in the stomach during an argument seven years earlier. Since that time, she'd been working in his factory, packing sardines into cans fourteen hours a day. She admitted that she hated the job and was very unhappy with her marriage. As we talked, her pain disappeared. Then she told me that the mysterious stomach pain always got worse when her husband was around and usually disappeared completely when she wasn't with him.

Well, I guess you can make the proper diagnosis. She didn't need X-rays or surgery, but she did need marital counseling. The couple made the decision that day to separate for several weeks, to reduce the pressure they both felt so they could decide either to deal with the anger that was eating her alive or to get divorced.

You may think, "That's so obvious. How could any doctor miss it?" Physicians are trained to think about medical problems rather than human ones. Once your doctor has done a physical exam and ordered the proper tests, he or she feels the job is done. Talking to you about personal problems is time-consuming and costly. And many patients often strenuously resist a psychological interpretation. They pressure their physicians to do medical tests and to prescribe drugs. When physicians inquire about personal problems or suggest a referral to a psychiatrist or psychologist, many people feel deeply offended.

You may think that the woman with abdominal pain was very different from you. You may think her situation is dramatic and unusual and believe there really is something wrong with you. Certainly if you have headaches or pains or if you feel dizzy, it's reasonable to have a consultation with your doctor. He or she will listen to your symptoms and perform a physical examination, possibly ordering a blood test or an electrocardiogram. In the vast majority of cases, there will be no abnormalities to account for your symptoms. If so, you should suspect that a problem in your life, not in your body, is at the root of your difficulties.

However, there are several medical problems that can occasionally cause the symptoms of anxiety. Stimulants such as amphetamines or even coffee, as well as sedatives such as alcohol or marijuana, can make some people feel panicky and out of control. Many people with panic attacks report that the first episode occurred when they were high on a drug. Afterward the panic attacks can occur spontaneously.

In addition, if you abruptly stop taking any sedative drug—including alcohol, sleeping pills, tranquilizers, and most antidepressants—you may have feelings of anxiety and panic as well as other withdrawal symptoms. Research indicates that treating anxiety with large doses of tranquilizers or sleeping pills for more than a few weeks can be hazardous (see Chapter 23). The potential for addiction is great. I saw a woman recently who told me that after she stopped taking an average dose of Dalmane—a commonly prescribed sleeping pill—which she'd used nightly for several years, she was completely unable to sleep for two months!

Patients with panic, anxiety, or depression may rarely have abnormalities of the thyroid gland. "Hyperthyroidism" means an abnormal increase in thyroid output. This stimulates the body's metabolism. In addition to anxiety, people with this disorder may feel speeded up, experience increased appetite, weight loss, and an inability to tolerate heat, and have bulging eyes. The disease is uncommon and can easily be diagnosed with appropriate blood test. The opposite disorder, hypothyroidism, is caused by insufficient thyroid output. This leads to a slowing of the metabolism along with mood changes, including psychosis and depression. This disorder, too, is rare.

It has been known for decades that extraordinarily low levels of blood sugar can cause symptoms of anxiety, including sweating, trembling, racing heart, lightheadedness, and hunger. However, this syndrome, called hypoglycemia, is rare in the general population and it is almost never the cause of panic disorder. Although 25 percent of the normal adult population appear to have low blood sugar levels during testing, this usually does not cause the feelings of panic or anxiety that afflict so many people. One obvious exception would be a diabetic who made a mistake and injected too much insulin. This would cause a temporary severe fall in blood sugar with the symptoms of hypoglycemia. However, the cause of the symptoms is obvious, and this problem is not ordinarily confused with panic disorder. The only time that hypoglycemia would be suspected as a cause of panic attacks would be if your symptoms only occur one to two hours after eating and are always quickly eliminated by eating something sweet like candy or drinking orange juice or soda. (This is because the sugar goes into your blood and corrects the problem.)

Another extremely rare medical problem, a tumor of the adrenal gland called a pheochromocytoma, can cause a sudden dramatic increase in blood pressure along with headache, palpitations, flushing, sweating, and nausea. These tumors are exceedingly rare, and most people who have them do not experience typical panic or anxiety attacks.

In recent years, there has been a great deal of publicity about the relationship between panic attacks and a cardiac disorder called mitral valve prolapse. The mitral valve closes when the heart contracts to pump blood into the aorta. In some people, the leaflets of the mitral valve may bulge excessively during the heartbeat. Your doctor might pick this up when he hears an extra "click" while he listens to your heart with his stethoscope. The finding can be confirmed with an echocardiogram.

A number of studies have suggested that mitral valve prolapse is somewhat more common in patients with panic attacks than in the general population. However, estimates of how many panic attack patients have mitral valve prolapse are controversial, because of wide differences in the precise criteria that physicians use to diagnose mitral valve prolapse. The meaning of the association between mitral valve prolapse and panic attacks is unclear. There is no evidence that mitral valve prolapse causes panic, and there is no evidence that panic attacks cause mitral valve prolapse. In addition, mitral valve prolapse tends to be benign and does not need to be treated, whether or not you also have panic attacks. The treatment of the panic attacks will be the same regardless of whether or not you have this condition.

In summary, medical problems only rarely cause symptoms of anxiety and panic. The pursuit of a nonexistent disease is costly and time-consuming and often distracts people from dealing with the problems in their lives.

Psychiatrists are just as likely as internists to reinforce this notion that the causes of your anxiety are chemical or physical. Even in the absence of any medical problem, patients are frequently told that a "chemical imbalance" is responsible for their anxiety, and that their symptoms must be treated with drugs that will correct this "imbalance." Let me make one thing abundantly clear: We do not know of any physical or chemical imbalance that causes anxiety or panic.

Psychiatrists who tell you that you have a "chemical imbalance" are confusing theory with fact. Although psychiatrists strongly believe that there may be some physical tendency that makes some people more likely to develop anxiety or panic attacks, there is as yet no proof of this theory. And although much interesting research is being done, we still do not have the answer.

I do not mean to imply that your anxiety is "all in your head." Anxiety is a total body reaction. Your heart may speed up, your fingers may tingle, and you may perspire. However, most of these bodily changes are not causes but simply the effects of anxiety. And when you feel better as a result of treatment, these physical sensations will diminish or disappear entirely.

I do not mean to argue that medications should never be used in the treatment of anxiety and panic. Although the majority of patients with milder forms of anxiety and panic can be treated without drugs, many with more severe problems can be helped with medications. However, these drugs should never be used as a substitute for counselling or psychotherapy. With a little courage and some compassion, you can conquer your fears and resolve the problems that gave birth to the feelings of fear and panic in the first place.

12

•

How to Fight Your Fears and Win

A 32-year-old man was lying on his bathroom floor, writhing in agony from a sharp stomach pain. He felt as if he was about to explode. He pleaded with his wife to call an ambulance. Terrifying images of emergency rooms and intravenous tubes raced through his mind. By the time the ambulance arrived, twenty-five minutes later, the "attack" had mysteriously vanished. A careful medical examination by his doctor the following week revealed no organic cause for the pain.

Four weeks later the man was walking with his wife through a department store when he suddenly felt overwhelmed and confused. He developed tunnel vision and felt as if he was floating across the ceiling. He was consumed by an irresistible urge to flee from the building, so he told his wife that it was time to go and rushed her outside. As he stood in terror waiting for a taxi, sweat rolled down his forehead. He was ashamed of his feelings and fought desperately to appear calm. By the time the cab arrived his symptoms had disappeared.

Do you get the idea that this man is an oddball? In fact he is a relaxed, articulate young professional with a lovely wife and family and an impeccable reputation. The dreaded disease he suffers from is simply a common panic attack.

A panic attack is usually triggered by a negative thought or a frightening daydream. Once a panic attack develops, your thoughts, feelings, and physical symptoms feed each other in a vicious cycle, as illustrated on pages 223–224. You can see in these diagrams that your panic is triggered by your negative thoughts. Your heart pounds and your thoughts race as adrenaline pours into your blood. These sensations alarm you and you think, "Gee, something must really be wrong." This thought creates even more fear and frightening physical symptoms.

At the same time, your negative thoughts and feelings feed each other. You feel so anxious and tense that it seems that something dreadful must be wrong. After all, why would you feel so frightened if you weren't in real danger? This is called "emotional reasoning," because you take your emotions as evidence for the way things really are.

Finally, your actions also make things worse. If you think you're dying or cracking up, you may crawl into bed with the lights off and try to hang on for dear life. This is like a sensory deprivation experiment, and it lets your fantasies run wild! You feel abnormal and impaired. This convinces you that there must be something terribly wrong.

These fears can feel absolutely terrifying and absolutely realistic, but there is usually no real danger. That's because distorted thoughts, not realistic ones, cause anxiety. If there's one message I want you to understand as you read this book, that's it!

The problem, of course, is that you won't know how unrealistic your fears are during a panic attack. Between attacks you may realize that it's absurd to think you're on the verge of a heart attack or going crazy, but when you feel anxious you will need some concrete evidence to show you how irrational these fears are.

Margaret is a 32-year-old mother of two children who took up jogging in an effort to lose weight. While jogging, Margaret would become obsessed with the idea that she might be putting too much strain on her heart. When she was done, she'd sit down in a particular living room chair and wait to see if she was okay. Her heart would pound, since she'd just been exercising strenuously, and she would notice a certain tightness in her chest. This made her suspect she might be in the beginning stages of a heart attack. She would develop fantasies of being in a coronary care unit with intravenous needles in her arms and tubes in her chest. The images would send waves of panic through her body. Her fears would build to such

THE PANIC CYCLE: THE FEAR OF A HEART ATTACK

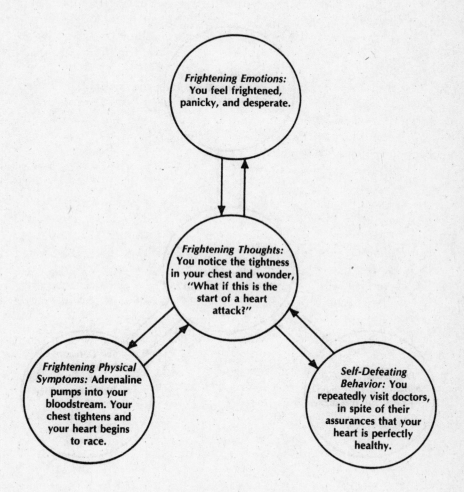

THE PANIC CYCLE: THE FEAR OF GOING CRAZY

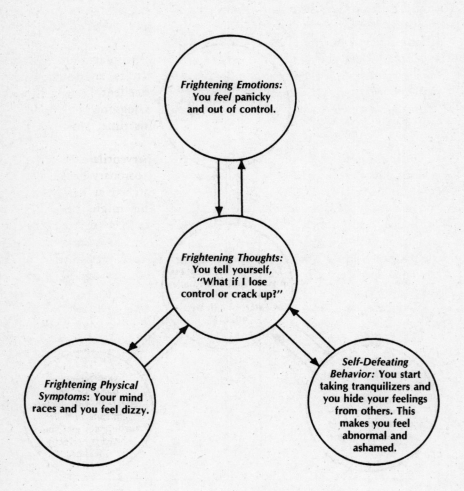

a crescendo that she couldn't stand the suspense, so she would walk outside and stand in front of the medical building next door. Her rationale was that if she did suddenly have a heart attack, the doctors and nurses in the building would see her collapse on the grass and would rush out and save her. After standing there for ten to fifteen minutes, Margaret's symptoms would subside and she'd go home, feeling relieved but humiliated.

Margaret had gone to several cardiologists for elaborate studies of her heart including electrocardiograms, treadmill tests, and so on. In spite of repeated assurances that she was in excellent health, her neurotic behavior persisted. Each time she went jogging she would ask herself, "Maybe it really is a heart attack this time. How can I know for sure?"

During a session, I asked Margaret to hyperventilate (breathe rapidly and deeply) and to picture herself in a coronary care unit. Within thirty seconds she became pale and clutched at her chest. She got lightheaded and said she was afraid this might bring on an actual heart attack. I asked her to estimate how nervous she felt on a scale from 0 to 99. She blurted out "Ninety-nine— the worst—I can't stand it!" Her intense reaction proves what a powerful impact your negative thoughts and fantasies can have on your feelings.

Now before we go on, I'd like to ask a very simple question: What was the cause of Margaret's intense, overwhelming fear? Why was she having this panic attack in my office? I'm asking because I want to see if you understand the basic principle of cognitive therapy. Write your answer here:

_____

_____

_____

_____

When I pose this question to audiences during lectures or workshops, I get a variety of answers. Some people say it's a hormonal reaction. Others say her anxiety must be due to subconscious conflicts. My experience leads to a very different answer: She feels anxious because of her thoughts. She believes she's about to have a heart attack. This irrational thought is the cause of her panic.

Now let me ask a second simple question. What would have to happen to make Margaret's fear disappear? What would make her feel immediately calm and happy as a lark? Put your ideas here:

_____

_____

_____

_____

When I ask professionals or lay people these questions, again I get a variety of answers. Some people say she needs years of psychoanalysis. In fact, Margaret had eight years of unsuccessful psychoanalytic treatment. Some people say she needs large doses of tranquilizers to suppress her panic attacks. This would probably only cover up her symptoms, and she could become addicted. She may still be vulnerable to these panic attacks when she tries to go off the medication. Others say she should go to a cardiologist for testing and reassurance, but she's already been to many.

I believe that Margaret can eliminate her anxiety if she eliminates the cause. Doesn't that make good sense? Her negative thoughts make her anxious. She believes something that isn't true—namely, that she's on the verge of a heart attack. If she became convinced that this thought wasn't true, her symptoms would vanish. How could Margaret put the lie to the thought that she's about to have a heart attack? Think about this for a moment before you read the next section.

THE EXPERIMENTAL METHOD

In Chapter 6, you saw that there are many ways to untwist distorted thoughts. I have developed a number of techniques that are especially effective for anxiety and panic attacks. One of these is called the Experimental Method. It can help you prove beyond the shadow of a doubt that your fears are just a figment of your imagination. The calming effects can be dramatic and immediate.

I asked Margaret if she could think of a way to test her belief that she was on the verge of a heart attack. Could she think of an experiment that would prove with absolute certainty whether or not she was having a heart attack? She suggested "I could get an electrocardiogram." I replied, "But I don't have one in my office and you don't have one at home. Can you think of any other test?" She replied, "I could take my pulse and see if it's racing." I replied, "But it could be racing because of your anxiety, so that won't prove anything one way or the other. If you were having a heart attack right now, what would be something you could not do?" She thought about this for several moments and replied, "I'd be weak and in terrible pain. My heart would be failing, so I could barely move." I replied, "Exactly. So what experiment could you do to find out right now whether or not you're having a heart attack?" Her face lit up and she said, "I could see if I could stand up. Then I could see if I could walk. Then I could see if I could jog. If I could do those things, it would show I wasn't having a heart attack!"

I suggested that she do just that. She stood up—no problem. She walked across the office—no problem. Then I suggested we jog together down the hall outside my office. She did this with no problem. Then I suggested we jog up and down several flights of stairs together. In the process, her symptoms vanished. Margaret tried the method at home the next time she developed the fear of a heart attack, with equally dramatic results. She terminated treatment after several sessions and wrote to me the next Christmas to report that she was still doing well.

The results of the Experimental Technique aren't always so dramatic, but this method is frequently extremely helpful. The instant that you see with absolute certainty that your fears are groundless, you'll have no reason to feel upset.

You may have the thought: "I will never get well that fast. I'm hopeless." In fact, most people *don't* get well that fast. Successful treatment with a difficult mood problem can often require trust and persistent hard work over a period of time. Remember, too, that Margaret had struggled unsuccessfully for eight years before she came to me and we quickly found the intervention that "clicked." This often happens with my own patients—we work and work and work, seemingly making no progress. The patient feels hopeless and wants to give up, but I urge them on, saying, "Keep trying! We'll eventually get it." Then one day, long after they've given up believing there's any chance, the clouds suddenly lift and they experience the joy and relief that Margaret did. This can happen for you as well.

Some people are afraid to put their fears to the test. A businessman named Jack had symptoms similar to Margaret's. Whenever he felt upset, he'd obsess about some ache or pain, notice a tightness in his chest, and become convinced he was dying of heart failure. In the six months prior to our first session, Jack had spent over $10,000 getting physical examinations, X-rays, electrocardiograms, and laboratory tests from numerous physicians. The results of these tests always proved to be entirely normal. I demonstrated the Experimental Technique in my office and asked Jack to jog down the hall. Like Margaret, he experienced instantaneous relief and agreed to try this at home instead of running to a doctor the next time he felt he was having a heart attack.

Several days later, Jack got anxious and felt some chest pain, but he was so petrified that he refused to get out of his chair for two hours. He was afraid that the slightest movement might trigger a heart attack! Jack's resistance to testing his fears illustrates how enormously convincing your negative thoughts can seem, even when they're absolutely unrealistic.

As a way of getting around Jack's resistance, I suggested that he begin with very minimal exercise the next time he felt he was having a heart attack, and then he could try exercise that was increasingly demanding. He devised the following plan:

1. I will see if I can take five deep breaths. That will show I can still breathe properly.

2. I will raise my right arm five times.

3. If that works, I will raise both arms five times.

4. Then I will stand up and sit down.

5. If this goes okay, I will walk back and forth across the room.

6. Then I will touch my knees, toes, and floor.

7. Then I will try five sit-ups.

8. Then I will try five push-ups.

9. Then I will see if I can walk around the block slowly.

10. Then I will run around the block rapidly.

He concluded that if he could do all ten things, it would prove that he was not really having a heart attack.

The next time I saw Jack he was pleased but embarrassed. Between sessions he had gotten anxious and felt convinced he was having a heart attack. By the time he'd completed five of the ten tests, it became crystal clear that he wasn't having a heart attack. His chest pain and his anxiety vanished.

The Experimental Technique can be an effective way to put the lie to your irrational fears. Here's how you do it: First, identify the negative thoughts that upset you during a panic attack. The commonest ones are: "I may be cracking up," "I may be having a heart attack," "I may be losing control," "I may be about to faint," and "Maybe I'm about to die." Second, devise an experiment to test this fear. Ask yourself, "If I *were* losing control and cracking up, how would I know this for sure? Do I have any symptoms of schizophrenia now?" List the symptoms on a piece of paper and see if you have any of them. When you prove that your fears aren't valid, you will feel better.

If you would like to learn how to use the Experimental Technique to deal with your feelings of panic, turn to the four examples at the end of this chapter (page 254). When you have worked through these practice exercises, you will have a much better feeling for how to use this powerful technique.

PARADOXICAL TECHNIQUES

There's another method that can show you that your fears of insanity are irrational. It works like this: If a patient becomes anxious during a therapy session and tells me he's afraid he's about to crack up, I may reply, "I know you've been afraid of cracking up for many years. This would be as good a time as any to go ahead and get it over with. After all, you are with a psychiatrist. Why don't you go ahead and do it? Please try your hardest to lose control and crack up."

The patient usually looks shocked and protests that he doesn't understand what I am asking him to do. I tell him that he could stand up and flail his arms and legs about or babble gibberish and try his best to go crazy. In order to help inhibited clients, I sometimes demonstrate this myself. One time I did a somersault on the floor of the office, another time I stood on my desk and sang the "Battle Hymn of the Republic."

After I have demonstrated this bizarre behavior, I invite the patient to try to go insane. They usually laugh and feel relieved once it dawns on them that they can't crack up, even if they try with all their might.

If you would like to try this, when you're in a good mood, act crazy or eccentric for several minutes in the privacy of your home. You can talk in tongues, flail your arms about, dance, make baby sounds, or do whatever you like. After you've practiced this and you're comfortable with it, you can try it again during an anxiety attack when you feel convinced you're cracking up. It can be reassuring to discover that you cannot go crazy, no matter how hard you try.

This type of intervention has been called "paradoxical treatment" by psychologists and psychiatrists, because you do the opposite of what you are inclined to do. Instead of desperately clinging to your sanity, you try your hardest to go insane. However, because this technique could conceivably backfire and upset you, it might be best to try it under the supervision of a professional therapist if you have any doubt about it.

SHAME-ATTACKING EXERCISES

People with panic attacks often suffer from the fear of losing control and looking foolish in front of others. In a recent session a woman told me about her fear of being in situations she can't easily escape from—like being at the hairdresser's or in the dentist's chair or attending a church service. She said she feels trapped and gets a panic attack. She imagines becoming hysterical and running out of the room and making a fool of herself in front of other people.

Like many anxiety-ridden people, she believes she should be in complete control of her emotions at all times, and she thinks that people would look down on her for feeling nervous or insecure. These attitudes make her so tense that she loses all her spontaneity in social situations.

One antidote to this fear involves purposely doing something foolish in public. I believe that this "Shame-Attacking" method was originally developed by Dr. Albert Ellis, a noted psychologist. The idea is to do what you're most afraid of so you can learn that the world doesn't come to an end after all.

Because I don't like to recommend any self-help method that I haven't tried myself, I performed a "Shame-Attacking" Exercise one summer, while on vacation with my family at a casino resort on Lake Tahoe. I put on a cowboy hat and dark glasses and got on a crowded hotel elevator with my two children. Then, at every floor, from the twelfth floor down, I called out the numbers. I had to force myself to blurt out, "This is floor number eleven," because I told myself, "My gosh! What will all these people think of me?" It was much like the feeling just before you jump off a high dive for the first time. People began to chuckle more and more at each floor as I continued to announce, "Tenth floor . . . ninth floor. . . ." By the time we reached the main floor, everybody was laughing and giggling. As we walked off the elevator and the passengers merged with the crowd, I realized that nothing terrible had happened. It turned out to be a lot of fun to make "a fool" of myself. This helped me feel more relaxed and willing to be spontaneous around other people.

Other Shame-Attacking Exercises could include:

- Go into a crowded store and announce the time of day. You can say, "It is now 3:42 p.m." Wait for a moment until people have turned to stare at you. Then repeat the time loudly and clearly.
- Announce the street stops on a crowded bus.
- During a serious conversation with a friend, stick your pencil in your nose and let it hang there (insert the eraser end!)

CONFRONT YOUR FEARS

The reason the Experimental Method, the Paradoxical Technique, and the Shame-Attacking Exercises can be so effective is that you confront your fears instead of running away from them. People with fears and phobias usually do just the opposite—they avoid situations they're afraid of. When you avoid frightening situations, you simply make your problems worse. This is a guarantee! It's like running away from a bully—he will just continue to chase you and frighten you. And the opposite is just as true: Facing your fears will help you conquer them. You learn that the catastrophe you fear will not really happen.

The best way to confront your fears is to stop avoiding the situation you're most afraid of. Instead of trying to control your anxiety, surrender to your symptoms. Let them run their course. Do not fight them. Let the worst occur, if there is a worst. If you stick it out, you will discover that there are no terrible consequences after all.

Flora had agoraphobia—the fear of being away from home alone. Whenever she left her house, her mind was flooded with images of being arrested by the police for a crime she didn't commit. If she was walking down the street she would reason, "Just suppose I accidentally dropped my wedding ring here, and then coincidentally a murder was committed on this very spot. The police might find the ring and link me to the crime. Then I'd have no way to prove I didn't commit it. I'd be arrested and thrown in jail. Then I'd be separated from my son and daughter and they'd have to be raised by someone else."

In my office she realized that this chain of events was extremely unlikely, but she nevertheless believed it was at least remotely possible. Whenever she was out and feeling frightened, these ruminations seemed perfectly realistic and were so frightening that she would rush home. As a result, Flora would never leave her house unless she was accompanied by a friend. Her rationale was that a friend could testify to her innocence in the event she was brought to trial for murder.

Flora is not insane. She's attractive, bright, and friendly. She's from a prominent New York family, and she's considered a pillar of the community. You would never suspect that she had such irrational fears. Yet anxieties like hers are very common.

After Flora and I talked about how important it was to confront her fears, she agreed to walk alone to a nearby park on a Saturday around noon. She promised to sit down on a park bench and to stubbornly refuse to give in to the compulsion to go home, no matter how frightened she got.

When Flora left her home, her anxiety began to increase. She sat on the bench and every two minutes recorded how anxious she felt, on a scale from 0 to 99. Terrifying thoughts and feelings began to flood her mind. She didn't budge. She was determined to sit there no matter how nervous she got. Her anxiety shot up to 99—sheer panic. A policeman walked by and she felt certain he was about to arrest her. Her heart pounded and a voice inside screamed, "Go home!" But she bravely stayed glued to the bench in sheer terror for ten or fifteen minutes. The policeman didn't arrest her but smiled and said hello. Her anxiety started to melt away. After twenty minutes, the anxiety disappeared entirely. Freedom! She had called the bluff on her fears and won! This gave her the courage to get up and do some shopping. As she entered the grocery store she began to feel ecstatic—it dawned on her that she had surrendered to the anxiety and nothing terrible had happened!

During the experiment, Flora found it helpful to repeat the following statements to herself: "This attack can't go on forever. No matter how bad it gets, it will eventually go away, and I can take it. It will not destroy me. I am not on the edge of a nervous breakdown, even though it feels that way. I will sit here and confront my worst fears. I will defeat them and become stronger." She also found it helpful to talk to her symptoms in this way: "Go ahead and do your worst. This is your big chance. I am not going to run away from you any longer. I have not committed any crime, and I have the right to sit here as long as I want."

The technique of surrendering to your symptoms has been called "flooding" or "exposure" by psychiatrists and psychologists. Essentially, you "expose" yourself to your fears and you allow yourself to become "flooded" with uncomfortable symptoms. After a time, they reach their crest and fade away. As they disappear you will often experience exhilaration instead of the shame and humiliation you felt when you let your fears get the better of you.

Example: If you're afraid of elevators, you could get on an elevator and ride it up and down as long as necessary until your anxiety goes away. No matter how terrified you get, stay on the elevator! Do not get off until your fears have vanished.

Some readers may think, "But what if my phobias really *are* dangerous? What if I'm afraid of snakes or insects or dogs? These animals actually *can* kill you!" Again, I want to remind you that phobias, by definition, are irrational fears that get in the way of productive living. The fear of a rattlesnake about to strike is no phobia. But people with snake, insect, or dog phobias are afraid of *all* snakes, insects, and dogs, even the ones that are not dangerous. For example, tarantula spiders are not poisonous to humans, and they can be quite friendly. In my high school biology class in Arizona, all the students were required to let tarantulas crawl across their hands so we could overcome our fear of spiders. You could do this at home by letting a daddy longlegs crawl across your hands. If you have a dog phobia, you could force yourself to pet and play with a neighbor's friendly dog.

When you expose yourself to something you fear, you can keep an ongoing record of your feelings. Divide a sheet of paper into three columns. In the left-hand column, record the time every two minutes. In the middle column, record how anxious you are, between 0 and 99. In the right-hand column, jot down any frightening thoughts or daydreams you may be having. This written log will make you more aware that your anxiety will not go on forever. After a while, your fears will begin to fade away.

I recently treated a 26-year-old systems analyst named Steve, who had been troubled by severe anxiety, panic attacks, and depression since he graduated from college several years earlier. These feelings were the worst when he was at work or when he was on airplanes or away from home. The constant anxiety, stress, and tension had worn him to a frazzle. Steve was feeling pretty beaten down and hopeless when he first sought treatment.

Steve's problems stemmed from an intense fear of being alone. Although we could have spent years trying to analyze the childhood origins of this fear, I doubt this would have helped him. And to be quite honest, I don't believe that psychiatrists or psychologists really know where these deeper fears come from. They may come from traumatic experiences when we were small, from our genes, or from cultural influences like school, television, and advertising. Regardless of the cause, Steve was afraid of being alone and in need of a cure.

The intervention that was the most helpful to Steve was spending a week alone in Washington, D.C., staying in the apartment of a friend who was away on vacation. This was terrifying to him at first. He was afraid he'd crack up or have a nervous breakdown and be unable to take care of himself. But he did survive, and as the hours passed, his self-confidence began to grow. This put the lie to his belief that he was inadequate and unable to survive on his own. His fears continued to fade until they were gone. This experience gave him a tremendous boost. He experienced a sense of triumph and completed his therapy shortly after this. I have heard from him on many occasions since then, and he has continued to do well.

Some people don't like to face their fears so dramatically. They prefer to expose themselves to anxiety-provoking situations more gradually, so they can back off whenever their anxiety becomes too intense. This approach can also be helpful. The most important thing is to confront your fears persistently and courageously until they disappear. Confronting the fear can be terrifying, but the beneficial effects are often dramatic.

Dr. Stanley Rachman of the University of British Columbia has capitalized on this idea to devise a slightly different approach to treating agoraphobia. His technique is to move through your fears toward the person you feel safe with. Suppose you feel safe with your spouse but are afraid of going on a bus alone or waiting alone at a bus stop. You could walk to a bus stop together. Your spouse boards the bus and gets off at the next stop. Then you can wait alone for the next bus, take the bus, and get off at the first stop, where your spouse will be waiting for you.

Next, ask your spouse to go to the second or third stop and wait for you. Each time you can go a little farther on the bus alone. The advantage of this technique is that you're going *toward* safety instead of thinking you have to bite the bullet and confront your fears all at once, without any moral support. Another advantage is that you and your spouse will be able to work together as a team. Many friends and family members of agoraphobics want to help, but they feel frustrated because they don't know what to do. I like to think of Dr. Rachman's technique as the "partnership method" because someone who wants to help can be a partner in your treatment.

Let's see if you can think of an application of this method. Suppose you are afraid of walking away from home alone. How could you work with your spouse to overcome this fear? One approach would be for him to go outdoors with you and walk ahead one block and wait for you to meet him. Then he could walk two blocks ahead and wait while you walk toward him. You could gradually build up your distance until you walk a mile or even more alone.

THE DAILY MOOD LOG

The Daily Mood Log, described in Chapter 5, is another useful method for fighting anxiety and panic attacks. When you feel anxious, write down the negative thoughts that make you feel so frightened. Then identify the distortions in these thoughts, using the list on page 260. When you substitute more positive and realistic thoughts, it will often turn your fears around.

A 45-year-old woman named Victoria avoided going on trains because she would get anxious and have fantasies of fainting in the aisle. The first Automatic Thought Victoria wrote down was: "What if I get so uptight that I pass out?" She identified the distortion in this thought as "fortune-telling," since she was making an unrealistic prediction. She substituted this Rational Response: "It is unlikely that I will pass out on the train since I haven't actually passed out once in my entire life."

Then she wrote down a second Automatic Thought: "But what if I did pass out? That would be terrible! And who can say I won't?" See if you can identify the distortion(s) in this thought.

1._____

2._____

Victoria noted that she was again involved in "fortune-telling," because she was predicting a disaster. She was also "magnifying" how terrible it would be if she did faint. She countered it with a new Rational Response: "Why would it be so terrible if I did pass out? I would simply fall on the floor and wake up a moment or two later. I would then probably notice a circle of people around me who would offer to help. I could stand up and thank them for their concern and tell them I was okay. I would sit down in my seat and get off at my destination."

Then a third Automatic Thought crossed her mind: "But they'll look down on me. They'll think I'm a fool because I caused a commotion." What are the distortions in this thought?

1._____

2._____

3._____

Victoria noted that this involved "mind reading" and "fortune-telling," because she was assuming that people would look down on her if she did faint. She was also "labeling" herself as "a fool." What Rational Response would you suggest?

_____

_____

_____

_____

Victoria's Rational Response was: "There's no evidence they'll be looking down on me. Would I look down on someone or call them a fool simply because they fainted? That would be absurd!"

Her final Automatic Thought was: "But what if someone did look down on me? I couldn't stand it! That would be terrible!" She noted that this was "fortune-telling" and "magnification" again. Her Rational Response was: "Why would that be so terrible? What can they do to me? Shout at me? Frown? Call up my friends and tattle? Put a headline in the paper? If someone looked down on me for fainting, it would mean that they had an immature attitude and it wouldn't reflect on me."

The next time I saw Victoria she announced with a sense of triumph that she had taken a commuter train to the therapy session. It hadn't been easy, but she'd done it! This was a major victory.

I've included an extra Daily Mood Log for you at the end of this chapter on page 258. When you use it, you will see that your Automatic Thoughts are nearly always predictions that something bad is about to happen. To illustrate this, write down the kinds of negative thoughts you might have in each of the following anxiety provoking situations:

You have an airplane phobia. As you're boarding the plane at the beginning of your vacation you're drenched with sweat and your heart is pounding. What are you thinking?

———————————————————————————

———————————————————————————

———————————————————————————

———————————————————————————

You have a big test coming up in school. You're really nervous about it. What are you thinking?

———————————————————————————

———————————————————————————

———————————————————————————

———————————————————————————

In each situation you're undoubtedly making dire predictions about all the terrible things that are going to happen. As you board the airplane you may be thinking, "What if it crashes?" Then you picture the plane going down in flames. These thoughts scare the living daylights out of you. Before an examination you may tell yourself, "It's going to be so tough." Then you imagine getting an "F" on the test. These thoughts make you so nervous that you can't concentrate on what you have to study.

In all of these situations, you're involved in the cognitive distortion called "fortune-telling." *All* anxiety results from this distortion. Do you know why these negative predictions are distortions? It's because the catastrophes you predict are *not* realistic. The fact is, the plane you are boarding *won't* crash. And if you prepare diligently for the test, it's very unlikely that you'll fail.

One way to deal with fortune-telling is to make positive, realistic predictions instead of unlikely, negative ones. If you feel nervous about an airplane flight, you can tell yourself that it's going to be a pleasant flight. Imagine landing safely at your destination and having a good time on vacation. When studying for a test, tell yourself that you *are* learning the material and that the more you study, the higher your score will be.

Many people seem taken aback by this advice. They tell me: "That's silly! It sounds like The Power of Positive Thinking. I don't want to be Pollyanna and look on the bright side all the time. It's not realistic. It is possible that I might do lousy on the test. What if I get petrified and my mind goes blank? So why tell myself I can study effectively and do well? That's just plain stupid!"

If this is how you think, you may be caught up in a self-fulfilling prophecy. You may use up all your energy worrying and telling yourself how awful you'll do instead of preparing systematically to do the best you can. When I feel confident and I anticipate doing well, I usually perform much better than when I worry and catastrophize about failure.

Some people defend their worrying with this argument: "It's safer to worry. I may protect myself against danger if I'm nervous. Maybe I can keep the airplane up if I worry about a crash. Maybe I'll study harder if I worry about flunking the test. If I relax and think about things positively, something bad may happen." Can you see any loopholes in these arguments? A small amount of anxiety may boost your performance by helping you "psych up," but too much anxiety will only make you miserable.

THE COST-BENEFIT ANALYSIS

If you have a fear or a phobia, you will need to decide whether or not you really *want* to get over it. One part of you may want to stop worrying and start feeling better, while another part may resist changing because you believe your fears are helping you or protecting you.

One way to deal with this problem is with the Cost-Benefit Analysis. Ask yourself, "How will it help me to worry and predict catastrophes, and how will it hurt me?" List the advantages and disadvantages and weigh them against each other. Then make a second list of the advantages and disadvantages of thinking positively and imagining that things will turn out well. Again, balance the costs against the benefits of being optimistic. This may make it easier for you to let go of your worrying and to start believing in yourself.

An elderly woman who sought treatment for agoraphobia stubbornly resisted her therapist's suggestions to go out of the house alone. She explained that she was afraid that she might get mugged or murdered. She pointed out that there were newspaper reports of mugging almost every day.

There are two issues here. First, does she want to be so preoccupied with this fear that she loses the freedom to leave her house? The Cost-Benefit Analysis can help her sort this out. What are the advantages and disadvantages of being housebound? The big advantage of staying in is feeling safe. The disadvantage is a loss of freedom. She needs to think this through and make a choice. Otherwise she will be at odds with herself and with her therapist.

If she decides to confront her fears and leave her house, she may need to perform a second Cost-Benefit Analysis. What are the advantages and disadvantages of worrying constantly when she's away from home? She has to ask herself if panic and worry will prevent something terrible from happening. Certainly there are commonsense precautions that every citizen should consider: you should always walk with a friend if your neighborhood isn't safe; you shouldn't go out alone at night; you shouldn't carry large amounts of cash with you; you should keep a list of your credit card numbers at home in the event they're lost or stolen; and you should not attempt to fight or argue with a robber.

Once you've taken these precautions, further worrying won't help much. I suppose she could argue that if she's in a constant state of panic she'll be especially careful and suspicious of every stranger, but the cost of such excessive vigilance is emotional misery. There's a point at which you have to say: "Okay, I've taken every rational precaution to protect myself. Beyond this, absolute safety is impossible, so I might as well assume that I'll be safe and relax and enjoy myself."

If you have a phobia, you should pay careful attention to this issue. You may have a vague desire to feel better, but you may resist my suggestion to confront your fears. Sometimes there are hidden advantages in your fears that you're unaware of. Some agoraphobics get a lot of attention from others and this can be hard to give up. We all like attention—it's just a fact of human nature. At the same time, change involves pain and hard work. And that may not sound like much fun! You will need a pretty strong reason to change if that's what you want to do.

The Cost-Benefit Analysis can help you develop the motivation you need to change. You might be anxious about going on planes or elevators, being in crowds, or leaving home alone. In the left-hand column list the advantages of worrying: it makes you cautious, so you don't take reckless chances; you don't risk making a fool of yourself; you may get extra attention from other people; and so on. In the right-hand column, list the disadvantages of worrying: it's uncomfortable; it restricts your freedom; other people get frustrated with you; and so on.

Once you've completed these lists, balance the advantages against the disadvantages. Ask yourself: "Do my fears help me more? Or do they hurt me more?" If you decide that the disadvantages of your fears outweigh the advantages, you'll be more motivated to change. The Cost-Benefit Analysis may not cure you, but your determination and commitment will be the key to getting better.

POSITIVE IMAGING

People with panic attacks or phobias are often preoccupied with frightening fantasies and daydreams. A 22-year-old musician would imagine losing control and screaming whenever she was in a crowd.

This fantasy was so upsetting that she avoided groups or social situations. Hypochondriacal individuals worry constantly about getting diseases; they picture themselves in hospitals whenever they notice a slight ache or pain.

These images are not hallucinations but simply daydreams. Most of us have daydreams throughout the day, but we usually don't pay much attention to them. To understand this better, try to picture something vivid and harmless, like a red apple in a brown basket. Can you see it? These are the kinds of pictures that pass through your mind when you daydream. If you daydream about something pleasurable, like sex or hitting a good shot while playing tennis, you'll feel good. When you daydream about the things you fear, you will frighten yourself.

You may not be aware of these frightening daydreams and fantasies unless you look for them when you feel nervous. Once you notice them, you can trace the obvious connection to your fears. It's important to realize that since you create these frightening fantasies, you can learn to control them. If you modify them in a creative way, you will feel less anxious.

You might want to choose to substitute a peaceful image of a place you love, like being on vacation at the shore or in a cabin in the mountains. Breathe slowly and deeply when you picture it. One anxious patient found it helpful to imagine herself walking along the beach in the evening, since she loved the ocean. She would visualize the moon and waves. Her imagination was such that she could even feel the cool ocean breeze across her skin and faintly smell the salty ocean air. She said she could almost feel the sand under her feet.

I suggested that she repeat this message to herself while she visualized the scene: "I have no cares in the world. Everything is taken care of. My husband and children are well. The bills are all paid. I have many people to be close to and many happy activities to look forward to. It is so peaceful here." As she imagined this scene, she was flooded with a wave of inner peace, and her anxiety disappeared within moments.

Another patient with strong religious feelings found it helpful to recite the words of the Twenty-third Psalm during the visualization exercise: "He makes me lie down in green pastures. He leads me beside still waters. He restores my soul."

Why can this simple exercise reduce your anxiety? It's because you change the pictures in your mind, just as a movie director prepares for a totally different scene. And the effect of the peaceful scene can be quite profound.

Try the technique to see how it works for you. Sit down in a comfortable chair. Begin by putting a frightening image or daydream in your mind. Choose the one that ordinarily upsets you. You could imagine dying, cracking up, or saying something foolish at a social gathering. You can intensify the effect by breathing rapidly and telling yourself things like "This is terrible. I can't stand it." You may notice how your tension builds up.

Now erase those images and project some peaceful ones in your mind. Breathe slowly and deeply and select a scene that appeals to you: fishing in a quiet lake, receiving your diploma the day you graduated from high school or college. The scene can be a happy memory or a pleasant fantasy. Give yourself positive reassuring messages. You will notice how your mood improves.

DISTRACTION

Some people find it helpful to distract themselves from the frightening thoughts and images that become so intense during a panic attack. If you concentrate on something else, it will frequently take the edge off the uncomfortable symptoms.

Several types of distractions can be helpful. The first is mental distraction. You could purchase an inexpensive puzzle that requires concentration and manipulation. It should be small enough to fit in your wallet or handbag. One woman used one of those little square puzzles where you have to rearrange the numbers or letters to conform to a certain pattern. Another woman found a small plastic dome in which you flip tiny plastic doughnuts onto a hoop. The puzzle should be one that requires several minutes of concentrated activity to solve. A Rubik's Cube would be ideal.

During an anxiety attack, take the toy out and concentrate on it, focusing all of your mental energy on every detail of the game. This can interrupt the flow of frightening images in your mind. Other people have distracted themselves by performing calculations in their heads, balancing their checkbooks, or engaging in some other mentally demanding task.

The second form of distraction is physical. When you feel anxious or stressed, strenuous exercise like swimming, jogging, aerobics, or speed walking might be helpful. You might prefer a competitive sport like squash or tennis. Long, slow runs have been reported to be especially helpful for people who feel down and depressed. Shorter, more intense exercise seems to be helpful for anxiety and panic. It isn't known for sure whether the exercise creates an actual chemical change in your brain or simply serves to break the flow of negative thoughts. Exercise does give you a sense of accomplishment and self-control when you feel helpless and terrified. As a result, you calm down and feel more relaxed.

A third type of distraction is to get involved in productive work or a hobby. You might read your favorite novel, work on your coin collection, or work in the garden. You might find it helpful to do something you've been putting off, like straightening up the house or writing thank-you letters.

When you feel anxious, you may resist doing this. You may give yourself endless excuses: "I just can't concentrate now" or "I don't feel like it." Don't give in to this urge—that will only make the anxiety worse, because you will flood your mind with frightening thoughts and fantasies. Instead, do something productive. You'll be surprised to find that you *can* get involved. As you do, you'll begin to feel better.

THE ACCEPTANCE PARADOX

Many of the techniques in this chapter will help you reduce your anxiety. However, that's only half the battle. Although one purpose of the therapy is to help you *change* your negative feelings, a second and somewhat contradictory goal is to help you *accept* your negative feelings. I call this the "Acceptance Paradox," and grasping it is a crucial part of the cure. The essential message is that you cannot overcome your negative feelings until you have first learned to accept them.

But that's just the rub. You may have a great deal of difficulty accepting your negative feelings because of attitudes like these:

1) Emotional Perfectionism: You may feel that you should always be happy and in control of all your feelings. You may think that "normal" people don't get anxious and label yourself as "weirdo" or a "neurotic" whenever you feel nervous, frightened, insecure, or panicky. Do you ever think this way?

———yes   ———no

2) Castastrophizing: You may think that anxious feelings are very dangerous and will lead to insanity if you let them get out of control. This makes you fight your anxiety and it mushrooms into sheer panic. Do you ever think this way?

 _____yes   _____no

3) Fear of Disapproval: You may be convinced that others would look down on you if they found out how nervous, shy, lonely, or insecure you feel in certain situations. You may think you have to impress people as a "winner" who is always poised and confident. Do you ever feel this way?

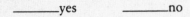 _____yes   _____no

4) Conflict Phobia: You may feel that "nice" people with good relationships don't ever feel upset or annoyed with each other. This makes it hard to express your anger as well as other vulnerable feelings such as loneliness, insecurity, or jealousy. This attitude makes it difficult to resolve conflicts or to achieve genuine intimacy. Do you ever feel this way?

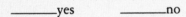 _____yes   _____no

5) Emotophobia: Emotophobia is the fear of negative emotions. You may believe that you should not have to endure any negative feelings like anxiety, panic, frustration, anger or sadness. When you feel upset, you may overreact and harangue yourself, thinking that something is terribly wrong. This mind-set doubles your troubles, because you not only get upset, but you get upset about being upset. Do you ever feel this way?

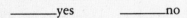 _____yes   _____no

If you think you *must not* feel anxious or upset and you believe you should be happy and in control all the time, you may be creating extra grief for yourself because no one really can feel happy, loving, and confident all the time. When you feel nervous or annoyed with someone, you will get self-critical and feel like a failure. This robs you of self-esteem and makes it far more difficult to get close to others. We are lovable because of our flaws and imperfections; it is our vulnerability that makes us human.

You may see this intellectually, without really believing it at the gut level. Like so many of my patients, you may embark on a crusade of self-abuse whenever you feel anxious, or angry, scolding yourself and insisting you *shouldn't* feel that way.

Helen is a 32-year-old woman I treated for panic attacks with the methods described in this chapter. She improved rapidly, but feared that the panic attacks might return. I pointed out that this was quite likely and asked what her negative thoughts would be the next time she did feel panicky. They included, among others:

1. "I'm a hopeless case."

2. "These anxiety attacks are a sign of weakness."

3. "I'm inferior. There must be something wrong with me."

4. "This is shameful. People will look down on me."

The fear of exposure and disapproval is extremely common among people who suffer from anxiety. Helen feels as if her panic is a dreadful, shameful secret. I suggested that we could deal with this with the "Feared Fantasy Technique" which is described on page 130. I told Helen to pretend to be a really mean person who was looking down on her, and I would be Helen. I told her to be as ruthless as she could possibly be and to say cruel things that she imagines people would be thinking about her if they knew she had panic attacks.

As you will recall, in this exercise Helen is not playing the role of a real person, but simply a frightening fantasy that represents the projection of her own worst fears. I am asking her to verbalize all her own self-criticisms, so that I can show her how to deal with them more effectively and develop greater self-acceptance.

HELEN *(as the Feared Fantasy)*: Helen, I understand that you suffer from depression and panic attacks. Is this true?

DAVID *(as Helen)*: Oh, I do! I have *tremendous* panic attacks!

HELEN *(as the Feared Fantasy)*: Well, it doesn't make any sense. What could possibly be going on in your life to upset you or make you anxious? You have a beautiful family and you have loads of money. What's wrong with you?

DAVID *(as Helen)*: Probably a lot more than what meets the eye. You're right that my anxiety and depression don't make a lot of sense. That's one of the funny things about these feelings. They don't always make a lot of sense. It's one of the most interesting aspects of it.

HELEN (*as the Feared Fantasy*): Well, this is all very irrational and disturbing. I don't think I like you, now that I know all this about you.

DAVID (*as Helen*): Oh? Why's that?

HELEN (*as the Feared Fantasy*): Because I just can't understand how someone in your position can be so weak and give in to these irrational feelings. You're just making a mountain out of a molehill. I mean, come on! Get off it!

DAVID (*as Helen*): I'm probably even weaker than you think I am. I have all kinds of weaknesses that you don't even know about, yet. So if you like real strong people, I may not be your cup of tea.

HELEN (*as the Feared Fantasy*): What's wrong with you? I've never had panic attacks. I've never been depressed like you. I am rational and sane and in control of my feelings.

DAVID (*as Helen*): You're a pillar of strength. I think of you as the Rock of Gibraltar.

HELEN (*as the Feared Fantasy*): I love your sarcasm. It's great. But I find people like you so pathetic.

DAVID (*as Helen*): You sound annoyed with me. Are you?

HELEN (*as the Feared Fantasy*): Yes, I *am* annoyed with you. I really despise you because I'm so strong and I know that everyone can be this way. If I can do it, everyone can do it. I really look down on pathetic people like you. I'm going to tell people that you are such a basket case. They'll know how emotionally unstable you are.

DAVID (*as Helen*): I can let you borrow the phone if you'd like to call them all now. Or, if you prefer, you could just drive up and down the streets shouting out my name out on a megaphone and telling people how sick I am.

HELEN (*as the Feared Fantasy*): Touché.

DAVID (*as self*): What's the point of this? What are we driving at here?

HELEN (*as self*): Actually, I'm not sure, but it's funny. I can see some humor in it, so at least that's something.

DAVID (*as self*): I'm glad humor is helpful. But aside from the humor, there's a point to this.

HELEN *(as self)*: I'm not sure what the point is. Am I blowing out of proportion what other people would think?

DAVID *(as self)*: Well, I guess that's probably true, but I'm driving at something deeper. The point is this: If someone wants to look down on you for being an imperfect human being, it's more of a reflection on them. You suffer from depression and anxiety so we could say that you're emotionally imperfect. Some people get divorced and they may be imperfect in their ability to resolve conflicts and to get close to others. Some people have very limited incomes and they could be imperfect in their ability to earn money. You may not be a genius, so we could say that your intelligence is imperfect or you may be overweight and out of shape so your figure is imperfect. If people want to throw rocks at you for *any* imperfection you might have, they can. But the question is, who is being irrational? Is this anything you really need to be concerned about? If you accept yourself as a human being with flaws, then you don't need to be afraid of anybody's put-downs. That's the point I'm trying to illustrate in a dramatic way.

Throughout the session, Helen and I continued to work on her belief that her anxiety made her a "weak" person. She was convinced that other people would never accept her the way she was, but the real problem was her inability to accept herself. This "emotional perfectionism" and fear of disapproval are extremely common among people who suffer from anxiety and depression. Sometimes you cannot deal with your feelings effectively until you surrender and accept them. This accomplishes two things: First, you learn that you *can* handle negative emotions, and the world doesn't come to an end simply because you're feeling angry or anxious or discouraged. Second, once you accept your emotions, they will frequently diminish and become a positive force in your life. But if you try to avoid or deny your feelings, insisting that you *shouldn't* feel that way, they will often intensify and mushroom way out of proportion.

If you still believe that you *shouldn't* get so upset, do a Cost-Benefit Analysis, as described on pages 113 and 123. List the advantages and disadvantages of always trying to be happy and in control of your emotions. Ask yourself, "How will this attitude help me, and how will it hurt me?"

It can also be helpful to ask yourself if this attitude is realistic.

I find life very stressful at times, and I frequently get annoyed or anxious or sad. This seems pretty normal, and I don't know many people who are dramatically different from me in this regard. I often tell my patients that if they could aim for five happy days per week, on the average, and two miserable days, that would be a pretty good deal. How would you feel about a goal like that? One advantage would be that when you felt upset, you could use your energy to deal with the problem that's bothering you instead of catastrophizing about feeling bad.

The secret of successful treatment is not to become a perfect, shining star or to learn to be in complete control of your feelings. These strategies are doomed to failure. In contrast, when you accept yourself as an imperfect but eminently lovable human being, and you stop fighting your emotions so strenuously, your fear will often lose its grip over you.

Helen improved rapidly. One key to her rapid recovery was her willingness to listen to the tapes of therapy sessions and to do the homework exercises between sessions. However, I don't want to create the impression that therapy is always easy and magical. If you have long-standing or severe difficulties, it may require more time and patience before you get better. I believe that you will be successful if you persist, and I have always felt that the sweetest victories are the battles that were the hardest fought!

GETTING IN TOUCH

In the last chapter you learned that if you are anxious, you may be avoiding certain problems and conflicts in your life that you feel angry or upset about. Getting in touch with what's really upsetting you can often be very liberating.

When you were growing up, you may have learned that you weren't supposed to express your feelings. When you tried, you got punished. Your family may have operated on the philosophy that people should try to be happy and loving all the time, and that if you've got something bad to say you shouldn't say it. As a result, you may have no models for how people can deal with problems successfully and share vulnerable feelings openly.

One consequence of this mind-set may be that you get anxious and obsess about something completely unrelated to the real problem when you feel upset, and you may not even be aware that you're doing this. Like many of my patients, you may become hypochondri-acal and go from doctor to doctor in search of a disease when in reality you're upset with your spouse. You may fear you have cancer or heart disease because you feel so convinced that something is wrong. You are right—something *is* wrong! But it has to do with your life—the people you care about or perhaps your career. You're pushing the problem out of your mind because you don't know how to deal with it or because you think you've got no right to feel angry or upset in the first place.

Anxiety is like living a dream. The real problems in your life are disguised symbolically so that you don't recognize them. The solu-tion, of course, is to confront the problem you've been avoiding. This usually involves expressing your feelings more openly.

A medical student named Mickey became upset when his fiancée, Gail, decided to go home for the weekend to attend her high school class reunion. Mickey and Gail had talked things over and the plan made good sense to Mickey. He had to spend the entire weekend studying for his final exams, so there was no reason for Gail to hang around.

However, soon after Gail left, Mickey began to feel tense and uncomfortable. He sensed that something was wrong. He noticed a bruise on his arm and developed a mild cough. For no apparent reason, he started to worry that he might be coming down with AIDS. This wasn't especially likely, since he'd had sex with only one other woman in his life. Nevertheless, Mickey began to obsess about dying from AIDS. He asked himself, "How can I be absolutely sure? People are dying of AIDS right and left." He became so overwhelmed with anxiety that he went to the emergency room of the hospital where he worked and got a blood test. The results several days later confirmed the obvious: he was in perfect health.

This pattern of obsessing about medical illnesses is extremely common with people who are anxious. There's generally no logical reason to suspect they have a disease. I have seen many people with an AIDS phobia, and none of them were at risk. They were not intrave-nous drug users and they had not had many sexual partners. Their fears were completely irrational and developed whenever they were upset about something.

What was really going on? Inside, Mickey felt bad about spending the weekend alone, even though he'd made the rational decision that it was a good idea for Gail to attend the reunion. Mickey felt lonely and jealous and insecure, but he felt he shouldn't express these feelings. He told himself that his feelings weren't reasonable, and that it made perfect sense for her to go. He was afraid that if he told her he felt hurt about spending the weekend alone, she might think he was weak and unmanly. He thought a man was supposed to be strong and rational and not have feelings like these. Finally, Mickey was concerned that he might appear manipulative or controlling. He told himself he had no right to tell Gail what to do.

People nearly always have lots of good reasons not to express their feelings! I have a hunch that there may be times when you don't tell people how you feel, either. Am I right?

What could Mickey have said to her? He could have told her, "I'll be feeling lonely and a little jealous when you're gone, because I really love you. I know it's a good idea for you to go, but part of me wishes you could stay." This would show Gail how he felt without demanding that she stay. Sharing his inner feelings—even if they didn't seem completely rational—probably would have made Gail feel a lot closer to him. The tenderness would have reassured him and prevented his anxiety attack.

I suggested that Mickey and Gail come in together for a few sessions. When they sat down, he was still agitated. He told me he was still worrying that he'd contracted AIDS, in spite of the fact that his blood test was normal. He said he'd read dozens of articles about the symptoms and was worried that they'd confused his lab test with someone else's. He wondered if he should perhaps have a second test just to be sure.

I told Mickey that checking out his symptoms in that way was unacceptable, and urged him to share his feelings with Gail. At first they both admitted that they were afraid of being open with each other. They were worried about hurting each other's feelings. But once they got started, they did beautifully. At the end of the session, Mickey said that his depression and worry about AIDS had suddenly and mysteriously vanished and he felt much closer to Gail.

Does this mean that Mickey was miraculously "cured" because of this experience? Obviously not. The tendency to repress your feelings can be deeply entrenched. In the future when Mickey is upset, he may begin to obsess again about AIDS or some other dreadful catastrophe. When this happens, he can ask himself "Am I upset with someone?" Instead of using his energy worrying about his obsessions, he can try to pinpoint what's really bothering him. His obsessions are really a reminder that something's bugging him that he's trying to ignore. Dealing with his feelings more openly and directly will require ongoing effort to reinforce the communication skills he is beginning to learn.

Sharing angry and vulnerable feelings in an atmosphere of trust can often have profound mood-elevating effects. If you cannot tell someone how you feel, true intimacy is impossible. Although anger can drive people apart, it can also draw people closer together when there's no threat to anyone's self-esteem, when the feelings are expressed honestly and listened to nondefensively, when there's no threat of rejection or retaliation, and when the underlying attitude is one of caring, trust, and respect.

The anti-anxiety techniques described in this chapter are summarized on page 252. It isn't necessary to master all of them, but it should be encouraging for you to know that there are numerous ways to overcome fears and phobias. You may find that you can apply these techniques on your own and get gratifying results. Or if you feel overwhelmed, you may want the help of a professional therapist. Once you call the bluff on your fears, you will win. Sometimes this takes time and effort. If you're determined, I believe you will eventually discover the inner peace and confidence you so richly deserve!

HOW TO OVERCOME
FEARS, PHOBIAS, AND PANIC ATTACKS*

1. **The Experimental Method:** Do an experiment to test your belief that you're "cracking up" or "having a heart attack" or "losing control."

2. **Paradoxical Techniques:** Exaggerate your fears instead of running away from them. If you have the fear of cracking up or having a stroke, you try your hardest to crack up or have a stroke.

3. **Shame-Attacking Exercises:** Purposely do something silly in public, in order to overcome your fear of appearing foolish.

4. **Confront Your Fears:** Expose yourself to whatever you're afraid of instead of running away and letting your fears cripple you. There are three ways of doing this:

   • **Sudden exposure or "flooding."** You allow yourself to experience all your symptoms, no matter how bad they get. You endure your fears until they run their course and wear out.
   • **Gradual exposure.** You gradually expose yourself to whatever you're afraid of (like being away from home alone, going into grocery stores, or taking buses or elevators). You back off when your anxiety becomes too great.
   • **The partnership method.** If you're afraid of being alone, you can ask someone you feel safe with to walk a certain distance ahead of you and wait for you. Then you walk and meet them there. The next time you ask them to go a little farther, so you can gradually increase the distance you can walk alone.

5. **Daily Mood Log:** Write down the negative thoughts that make you feel anxious or frightened. Identify the distortions in these thoughts and replace them with more realistic, positive thoughts. Instead of worrying yourself sick by constantly predicting failure and catastrophes, tell yourself that things will turn out reasonably well.

*Copyright © 1989 by David D. Burns, M.D., from *The Feeling Good Handbook*

6. **The Cost-Benefit Analysis:** Make a list of the advantages and disadvantages of worrying and avoiding whatever you fear. Weigh the advantages against the disadvantages. Make a second list of the advantages and disadvantages of confronting your fears. Weigh the advantages against the disadvantages.

7. **Positive Imaging:** Substitute reassuring and peaceful images for the frightening daydreams and fantasies that make you feel so anxious.

8. **Distraction:** Distract yourself with intense mental activity (like working on a Rubik's Cube), strenuous exercise, or by getting involved in your work or a hobby.

9. **The Acceptance Paradox:** When you feel anxious or panicky, you may make matters worse by insisting that you *shouldn't* feel this way. This is like throwing gasoline on a fire, and your anxiety gets worse. One way to develop greater self-acceptance is to write out a dialogue with an imaginary hostile stranger who puts you down for feeling anxious. The hostile stranger is simply a projection of your own self-criticisms. When you talk back to them, you will develop greater self-acceptance, and your anxiety will usually diminish or disappear.

10. **Getting in Touch:** When you feel anxious or panicky, you are probably ignoring certain problems that need to be dealt with. Review your life and try to get in touch with the situation that's making you feel so upset. When you find the courage to deal with the problem more openly and directly, it can be very liberating!

Practice Exercises for the Experimental Technique

Each of the following patients used the Experimental Technique successfully. See if you can figure out how they tested their fears. Don't look at the solutions until you've thought about each problem first.

PROBLEM #1. THE FEAR OF LOSING CONTROL WHILE DRIVING

Emily had a freeway phobia. When driving on a busy highway she would become nervous and tell herself, "What if I lose control of the car?" Then she would panic and pull off to the side of the road to avoid a wreck. She would wait there until a policeman would come along to help her. These experiences were so frightening and humiliating that she stopped driving on freeways entirely. How could Emily test her belief that she's "losing control" when she's driving? Put your suggestions here:

_____

_____

_____

Solution: While she is driving, Emily can test her belief that she is "losing control" by (1) turning the radio on and off, (2) looking in the rearview mirror, (3) using the turn signal and changing lanes, (4) speeding up and slowing down, (5) keeping the speed at 50 mph.

These maneuvers convinced Emily that she was in control. Her anxiety went away almost immediately and she was able to continue driving without having to pull off to the side of the road. Her self-confidence increased and she began to use freeways more and more frequently.

PROBLEM #2. THE FEAR OF LOSING CONTROL AT WORK

Jane is a secretary who sometimes feels as if she's "losing control" at work. Her heart suddenly begins to pound and her mind races wildly. Then she goes to the women's lounge and lies down on the couch in a cold sweat, trying to hang on to her sanity. This is about as helpful as throwing gasoline on a fire. How can Jane test her belief that she's "losing control" when she suddenly feels anxious and panicky at work? Put your ideas here:

_____

_____

_____

Solution: Jane developed these tests to see if she was really losing control: "(1) I can see if I can stand up and walk around the room. This will prove I can control my arms and legs. Then I can try to walk to the drinking fountain. (2) I can try to read a sentence from the newspaper and see if I can summarize what it says. This will prove that I can control my thinking. (3) I can try to perform calculations by adding up numbers in my head. This will prove that I can concentrate. (4) I can call up Information and ask for the telephone number of a friend. This will prove that I can communicate properly. Then I can call up the friend and talk for a few minutes. This will prove I can carry on a normal conversation."

Jane performed these tests the next time she was anxious, and she was able to complete each of them successfully. This convinced her that she was in control in spite of her anxiety, and she felt better.

PROBLEM #3. THE FEAR OF BEING UNABLE TO BREATHE

People with panic attacks often develop a mistrust of their bodies. When they get nervous they may breathe too rapidly, and this makes them feel dizzy. This is a perfectly normal physiological reaction, because your body takes in too much oxygen and blows off too much carbon dioxide. If you breathe extremely rapidly for several minutes right now, you'll see what I mean.

Whenever she's alone, Cindy breathes too rapidly and gets very frightened. She thinks she might suffocate and lose control of her breathing and imagines that her windpipe will suddenly "close up." Because of this intense fear, Cindy spends nearly twenty-four hours a day with her husband. They work together, they play together, they sleep together. I asked Cindy how it would help to be with her husband if her windpipe "closed." She hadn't thought this through very clearly, but felt he might in some way be able to "open it up" for her or at least to call for emergency medical help. This excessive togetherness has put a strain on their marriage because they both feel trapped and resentful at times.

How can Cindy test her belief that she's about to lose control of her breathing and suffocate whenever she's alone and feeling anxious? Put your ideas here:

Solution: Whenever Cindy felt she was losing control of her breathing she performed this test: "(1) Can I inhale slowly? (2) Can I hold my breath? (3) Can I exhale smoothly and slowly?" She agreed that if she could do all three things, it was proof that she could breathe properly.

This put the lie to her belief that she was suffocating or that her windpipe was closing off, and she was able to tolerate being alone for longer and longer periods. She also began a jogging and exercise program. The intense breathing and exertion helped her gain greater self-confidence because she learned that rapidly breathing is not dangerous.

PROBLEM #4. THE FEAR OF CRACKING UP

While he's studying, Jerry gets anxious and his thoughts race. This makes it difficult to concentrate. He tells himself, "I must be cracking up." Then he gets fantasies of being a catatonic schizophrenic in a mental hospital. This terrifies him and he paces about for hours, trying to hang on to his sanity. Fears of "cracking up" or having a nervous breakdown are extremely widespread among anxiety-prone individuals. While anxiety attacks can be intensely uncomfortable, they do not represent the onset of insanity.

How can Jerry test his belief that he's "cracking up"? Put your ideas here:

Solution: Jerry agreed that the following are the symptoms of schizophrenia: visual hallucinations; hearing imaginary voices; feeling that you are like God; the belief that some important group like the FBI or the KGB is plotting against you; the conviction that your thoughts are being broadcast on radio and television programs. He developed this "insanity test":

Yes	No	
_____	_____	1. Am I hallucinating? Do I see things that aren't there?
_____	_____	2. Do I hear voices coming from outside my head?
_____	_____	3. Do I feel that I am a god or a great genius?
_____	_____	4. Do I feel the FBI is conspiring against me?
_____	_____	5. Do I feel that people are reading my mind or that my thoughts are being broadcast on loudspeakers?

The next time Jerry felt he was "losing his mind," he took his "insanity test." Since the answer to all these questions was no, he realized there was not one shred of evidence that he was going insane. This was not consistent with his belief he was "cracking up," and it took the edge off his fear.

THE DAILY MOOD LOG*

STEP ONE: DESCRIBE THE UPSETTING EVENT _____

_____

STEP TWO: RECORD YOUR NEGATIVE FEELINGS—and rate each one from 0 (the least) to 100 (the most). Use words like sad, anxious, angry, guilty, lonely, hopeless, frustrated, etc.

Emotion	Rating	Emotion	Rating	Emotion	Rating
1.		3.		5.	
2.		4.		6.	

STEP THREE: THE TRIPLE-COLUMN TECHNIQUE—

Automatic Thoughts	Distortions	Rational Responses
Write your negative thoughts and estimate your belief in each one (0–100).	Identify the distortions in each Automatic Thought.	Substitute more realistic thoughts and estimate your belief in each one (0 and 100).

(Continue on next page)

THE DAILY MOOD LOG (continued)

Automatic Thoughts	Distortions	Rational Responses

(Continue on next page)

Automatic Thoughts	Distortions	Rational Responses

STEP FOUR: OUTCOME—Re-rate your belief in each Automatic Thought from 0 to 100 and put a check in the box that describes how you now feel:

☐ not at all better; ☐ somewhat better; ☐ quite a bit better; ☐ a lot better.

CHECKLIST OF COGNITIVE DISTORTIONS*

1. All-or-nothing thinking: You look at things in absolute, black-and-white categories.
2. Overgeneralization: You view a negative event as a never-ending pattern of defeat.
3. Mental filter: You dwell on the negatives and ignore the positives.
4. Discounting the positives: You insist that your accomplishments or positive qualities "don't count."
5. Jumping to conclusions: (A) Mind reading—you assume that people are reacting negatively to you when there's no definite evidence for this; (B) Fortune-telling—you arbitrarily predict that things will turn out badly.
6. Magnification or minimization: You blow things way up out of proportion or you shrink their importance inappropriately.
7. Emotional reasoning: You reason from how you feel: "I *feel* like an idiot, so I really must be one." Or "I don't *feel* like doing this, so I'll put it off."
8. "Should statements": You criticize yourself or other people with "shoulds" or "shouldn'ts." "Musts," "oughts," and "have tos" are similar offenders.
9. Labeling: You identify with your shortcomings. Instead of saying "I made a mistake," you tell yourself, "I'm a jerk," or "a fool," or "a loser."
10. Personalization and blame: You blame yourself for something you weren't entirely responsible for, or you blame other people and overlook ways that your own attitudes and behavior might contribute to a problem.

13

•

Dealing with the Fear of Death

Since death represents the ultimate confrontation with the unknown, it's not surprising that people who suffer from anxiety and panic are often afraid of death. Many people think that the fear of death is inevitable, but nothing could be further from the truth. The fear of death is one of the easiest fears to overcome if you apply some simple techniques.

One disclaimer is necessary here: The methods described in this chapter were not developed for people with serious illnesses, although they may also find these concepts helpful. Those who will benefit the most are people who are in good health but who become terrified by fears of death during panic attacks.

The first step is to examine specifically what you're afraid of. It can be helpful to conceptualize death in terms of three stages. Stage One is the dying process, up to the point when you pass into unconsciousness. Stage Two is the instant that you slip into unconsciousness, the actual moment of death. Stage Three is the period of time after you have died. Let's look at each of these stages and find out what you're afraid of.

If you are concerned about Stage One, the process of dying, then what you're really afraid of is life, not death. While you are in the process of dying you are still alive. What is it that you're afraid of? Is it the pain? The discomfort? Ask yourself, "Have I ever been sick or uncomfortable before? Was I able to cope with it then?" If you were able to cope with an illness at other times in your life, then there's no reason to think you won't be able to cope with the process of dying. Have you ever had a fever of 102°? Were you able to cope with that? Have you ever had a broken arm? Were you able to cope with that? What did you do for the discomfort? Did you take medication? Painkillers are generally available to individuals suffering from terminal illnesses, and the pain can usually be managed in a humane manner.

Perhaps you have experienced great pain in the past and you dread the thought of having to endure such suffering again. It's important to realize once again that it's not death, but life, that you fear. If someone with a terminal illness is in great agony, they are usually not at all afraid of death. Death, to them, is frequently a blessing and a welcome escape.

Your concerns might be different. You might have negative thoughts like "If I'm dying I will know I didn't fulfill all my dreams for my life. There are so many things I wanted to do, and I'll realize I only had a chance to do some of them." Once you've identified a negative thought like this, write it down. Then try to identify the distortions in it. Can you? Review the list on page 260 and see if you can find it.

One distortion is "all-or-nothing thinking," since you're telling yourself you didn't fulfill *all* your dreams and you didn't do *everything* you wanted during your life. It's also an example of the "mental filter," since you are thinking about all the things you *didn't* do rather than the many things you *did* do during your life.

Can you think of a more realistic way to look at it? One patient came up with this response:

No one can fulfill all of their dreams, but there are many things that I have been able to do. I always wanted to be a schoolteacher, and I have spent many years as a schoolteacher. I wanted to raise a family, and I have raised a family. I haven't done everything I wanted, but very few people could make that claim. When I die I will have to make a compromise between the dreams I had as a child and the reality of what I accomplished as an adult. I can think about all the things that I have done and feel a sense of satisfaction, or I can think about the many things I haven't done and make myself unhappy. The latter would be arbitrary and cruel.

Once she thought about it this way, she began to feel better because she no longer felt that death represented the ultimate defeat. Her perfectionism, and not the fear of death, was the real culprit.

The second stage of death involves the actual moment of dying, the instant when you slip into unconsciousness. Many patients tell me this would be terribly frightening because it represents the ultimate loss of control. But is this such a terrifying or unknown experience? Not really. You've actually had this experience every day of your life. The experience of slipping into unconsciousness is just like the experience of going to sleep. If you're not afraid of falling asleep, why be afraid of the moment of dying? You have also had this sensation if you were anesthetized. One moment you're conscious, and at the next instant you're asleep. There's literally nothing to it.

The third stage of death is the period after you have died. Again, ask yourself, "What is it that I am afraid of?" Try to pinpoint the negative thoughts that cross your mind when you think of being dead. One patient had the thought, "What if I wake up and I'm buried alive?" If this is your concern, then once again it's life, not death, that you're afraid of, because you'd be alive. But instead of getting upset about the situation, you could thank your lucky stars you are still alive! That's about the best thing that could happen to someone who thought they were dead! Concentrate on digging your way out so you can plan a big celebration! You could also put a provision in your will that you have to be buried with a small garden spade just in case this unlikely but wonderful event should happen.

Most people aren't so afraid of being buried alive, but they worry about being in an unconscious state and unaware of what's going on. In fact, there's no unpleasantness involved in this. Why do surgeons anesthetize people before they operate on them? It's to make sure that they will not experience any discomfort.

One patient was terrified by the thought "After I die there will be nothingness. I couldn't stand that!" After he wrote it down on his Daily Mood Log, he was able to substitute this Rational Response: "Then there will be 'nothing' to be upset about!" This helped him feel better, because he'd never really tried to think about it logically before.

The Daily Mood Log below lists several negative thoughts another patient had about being dead. You may recognize some of the fears that you have had at times. Notice how he refuted each of his negative thoughts.

THE DAILY MOOD LOG*

STEP ONE: DESCRIBE THE UPSETTING EVENT
<u>Thoughts of being dead.</u>

STEP TWO: RECORD YOUR NEGATIVE FEELINGS—and rate each one from 0 (the least) to 100 (the most). Use words like sad, anxious, angry, guilty, lonely, hopeless, frustrated, etc.

Emotion	Rating	Emotion	Rating	Emotion	Rating
1. Fear	99	3.		5.	
2.		4.		6.	

STEP THREE: THE TRIPLE-COLUMN TECHNIQUE—

Automatic Thoughts	Distortions	Rational Responses
Write your negative thoughts and estimate your belief in each one (0–100).	Identify the distortions in each Automatic Thought.	Substitute more realistic thoughts and estimate your belief in each one (0 and 100).
1. After I die, there will be many things that I won't be able to enjoy anymore. I won't be able to play tennis. I won't be able to go to work. I'll have to give up all these activities. ~~(100%)~~ 20%	Mental filter	1. There are many times when I'm not playing tennis now, and that isn't so terrible. I'm not playing tennis at this moment, for example. If it's not necessary for me to be playing tennis now, it certainly won't be necessary for me to play tennis after I die. Furthermore, I'll be unconscious and unaware of the fact that I am not playing tennis, so I won't feel disappointed! (80%)
2. There will be no one to care for my wife and children. They may face hardships without me, and my children may not grow up successfully	Fortune-telling	2. There are many times when I have been away from my family on weekends and on other occasions, and nothing terrible has happened. Other in-

(Continue on next page)

Automatic Thoughts	Distortions	Rational Responses
without my guidance. ~~(75%)~~ (10%)		dividuals cope with the loss of a loved one. There's no reason to feel that my family wouldn't be able to cope. They would undoubtedly feel a sense of loss if I died, and that's natural. It would show they loved me. Eventually they will find happiness again, just as other people do. (100%)
3. But I'm afraid of the unknown, and I have no idea what death would be like. ~~(100%)~~ (25%)	Fortune-telling	3. Death will either be "something" or "nothing." If it's "something" it won't be "un-known," and if it's "nothing," there will be "nothing" to worry about! Since I don't know what will happen one minute from now, that also represents the unknown. Tomorrow is the unknown, and the day after that is unknown. I have been living with the unknown since the time I went down the birth canal. I have been coping with it so far, so there's no reason to think I won't be able to cope with it in the future. (100%)

STEP FOUR: OUTCOME–Re-rate your belief in each Automatic Thought from 0 to 100 and put a check in the box that describes how you now feel:

☐ not at all better; ☐ somewhat better; ☐ quite a bit better; ☒ a lot better.

I'd like you to identify the stage of death you're concerned about. Is it the period just before you die (Stage One), the actual moment of death (Stage Two), or the time after you're dead (Stage Three)? Write it down here:

_____.

Now record your negative thoughts about it on a Daily Mood Log (a blank form is included on pages 269–271). Identify the distortions in your thoughts, and substitute Rational Responses in the right-hand column. Once you record your negative thoughts, you may discover that your fears about death aren't particularly realistic. This can help you feel a lot better about life.

You may feel the way many of my patients do when I first describe these techniques. They tell me, "Dr. Burns, I can see that these methods are extremely logical, but they won't really help me get over my feelings. You see, I know my fear is irrational, but it's very real and I've felt this way all my life." I tell them to go ahead and write down their negative thoughts about death on the Daily Mood Log anyway, even though they feel convinced that this "logical" approach won't help. The next session they nearly always report that their fear of death "spontaneously" disappeared, and I usually never hear about the problem again. I hope the method proves to be as helpful to you!

You might even want to go one step further and think about death in a positive way. Although that might seem ludicrous at first, it really isn't.

The other day I discovered the mutilated corpse of a rabbit in our garden. Apparently our cat had captured and killed it. This rabbit used to come to feed in a certain section of our lawn, so I had a hunch it would only be a matter of time until our cat captured it.

Its moment of death must have been unbearably painful and terrifying. Death was a blessing, an escape. Just think how horrible it would have been if the rabbit had been unable to die!

If you have trouble identifying with a rabbit, then think about yourself or someone you love. Suppose your body was riddled with cancer and you couldn't die. Imagine that you were smashed to bits in a plane crash and you couldn't die. Now are you so sure that death is such a bad thing?

Can you imagine what it would be like to grow old if there were no such thing as death? Consider how feeble and sickly people in their eighties and nineties can become. Now try to imagine how decrepit you'd be if you lived to be 180! Or 580!

If you think that life without death would be a good thing, think the scenario through to its ultimate conclusion. I think you'll discover that the consequences are more grotesque and terrifying than anything you have ever imagined.

Suppose, for example, that everybody stopped growing old at the age of 21 and we all lived forever. You might add that there would be no illness and no violence in the world. To make the fantasy even more appealing, let's assume that everyone is attractive, healthy, and intelligent. You might think this would be wonderful. But would it be?

What would happen is that we'd have a population explosion of unparalleled proportions. People would reproduce like bacteria—after all, there would be an endless abundance of young, attractive, healthy people to mate with. Soon there would be not billions, but trillions and trillions of people competing for space on the planet. Eventually there wouldn't even be one square inch of soil left and people would be stacked five feet deep over the entire surface of the earth. There'd be absolutely no way of getting rid of anyone since people couldn't die. Just imagine how uncomfortable it would be if you had claustrophobia, with all those attractive people lying on top of you and no way to get out!

The existentialist philosophers like Sartre, Camus, and others claim that when you face the ultimate inevitability of death, life becomes meaningless. I believe the truth is exactly the opposite. Accepting death can make life more meaningful, more rewarding.

When I was a child, time crawled at a snail's pace. I can remember long summer days that seemed like an eternity. The week I drafted this chapter, I turned forty-two. It could be a few years or it could be thirty years before I die, but either way, it won't seem all that long. These days, the days fly by like minutes and weeks can seem like hours. Today I saw a patient whom I hadn't seen in over six months, and yet it seemed as if I'd just seen him yesterday.

Noticing how short life is may seem morbid. But the knowledge that time is running out can help us understand how precious life is and make us more aware of the importance of sorting out our priorities. My eight-year-old son won't be a little boy much longer. Soon he'll be a grown man. But he's still a little boy today, and if I want to love him and spend time with him, I can do that. So this evening we played some badminton and hit the birdie over the net fourteen times without missing. That's our new record. While we were playing I told him that I was writing a chapter about the fear of death. I reminded him that someday, I would die, and so would he. I was curious how he felt about it. He told me he loved me and said that people wouldn't worry so much about death if they were having fun. Then he asked me to serve.

THE DAILY MOOD LOG*

STEP ONE: DESCRIBE THE UPSETTING EVENT _____

_____

STEP TWO: RECORD YOUR NEGATIVE FEELINGS—and rate each one from 0 (the least) to 100 (the most). Use words like sad, anxious, angry, guilty, lonely, hopeless, frustrated, etc.

Emotion	Rating	Emotion	Rating	Emotion	Rating
1.		3.		5.	
2.		4.		6.	

STEP THREE: THE TRIPLE-COLUMN TECHNIQUE—

Automatic Thoughts	Distortions	Rational Responses
Write your negative thoughts and estimate your belief in each one (0–100).	Identify the distortions in each Automatic Thought.	Substitute more realistic thoughts and estimate your belief in each one (0 and 100).

(Continue on next page)

THE DAILY MOOD LOG (continued)

Automatic Thoughts	Distortions	Rational Responses

(Continue on next page)

Automatic Thoughts	Distortions	Rational Responses

STEP FOUR: OUTCOME—Re-rate your belief in each Automatic Thought from 0 to 100 and put a check in the box that describes how you now feel:

☐ not at all better; ☐ somewhat better; ☐ quite a bit better; ☐ a lot better.

CHECKLIST OF COGNITIVE DISTORTIONS*

1. All-or-nothing thinking: You look at things in absolute, black-and-white categories.
2. Overgeneralization: You view a negative event as a never-ending pattern of defeat.
3. Mental filter: You dwell on the negatives and ignore the positives.
4. Discounting the positives: You insist that your accomplishments or positive qualities "don't count."
5. Jumping to conclusions: (A) Mind reading—you assume that people are reacting negatively to you when there's no definite evidence for this; (B) Fortune-telling—you arbitrarily predict that things will turn out badly.
6. Magnification or minimization: You blow things way up out of proportion or you shrink their importance inappropriately.
7. Emotional reasoning: You reason from how you feel: "I *feel* like an idiot, so I really must be one." Or "I don't *feel* like doing this, so I'll put it off."
8. "Should statements": You criticize yourself or other people with "shoulds" or "shouldn'ts." "Musts," "oughts," and "have tos" are similar offenders.
9. Labeling: You identify with your shortcomings. Instead of saying "I made a mistake," you tell yourself, "I'm a jerk," or "a fool," or "a loser."
10. Personalization and blame: You blame yourself for something you weren't entirely responsible for, or you blame other people and overlook ways that your own attitudes and behavior might contribute to a problem.

*Copyright © 1980 by David D. Burns, M.D. Adapted from *Feeling Good: The New Mood Therapy* (New York: William Morrow & Company, 1980; Signet, 1981).

14

•

Social Anxiety:
The Fear of People

The *Diagnostic and Statistical Manual* of the American Psychiatric Association defines a social phobia as "a persistent fear of . . . [social] situations in which the person is exposed to possible scrutiny by others and fears that he or she may do something . . . that will be humiliating or embarrassing." These situations might be dating, attending social functions and parties, or being introduced to strangers. Common fears include saying foolish things or being unable to answer questions when making conversation in a group, choking on food while eating in front of others, being unable to urinate in a public bathroom, having your hand tremble when signing your name in public, or having your mind go blank when giving a talk in public.

Dr. Aaron Beck has pointed out an interesting contrast between social phobias and agoraphobia. The agoraphobic fears that something terrible will happen if he or she is lost or alone. In contrast people with social anxiety fear the opposite—being around others and being the center of attention. Agoraphobics have been compared to children who are afraid of being lost and abandoned by their parents in a strange place, whereas people with social phobias feel more like children who are afraid of being under the critical scrutiny of a group of adults. Unlike agoraphobia, which is far more common in women, social phobias are more common in men. Perhaps this is because men experience greater pressures to perform, to assume leadership, to be emotionally "strong," and to initiate social contacts with the opposite sex.

Here are some common attitudes of individuals with social anxiety. Do you recognize these feelings?

- You feel that you're in the limelight, being judged by others. You believe that people are cold and would readily hurt or humiliate you.
- You believe you have to impress people to get them to like and respect you. However, you don't think you have anything interesting or worthwhile to say that will impress them. You are more preoccupied with pleasing people and acting the way they expect you to act than in being yourself.
- You don't believe that people will like the "real" you. You fear that if people found out about the "real" you, they would brand you as a fraud or look down on you. You feel inferior and defective in comparison with others.
- You believe that people have X-ray eyes and can always see how you are feeling inside, and that feelings of shyness or anxiety will be noticed and judged as foolish and unacceptable. This makes you avoid social situations. You would rather die than let anyone know how nervous you feel.
- You think that people are very judgmental and expect you to be polished, poised, and perfect. You have stereotyped ideas of appropriate social behavior. You have rigid standards of how you should feel, how you are supposed to act, and so on.
- You are terrified that you will make a fool of yourself in front of others. You feel convinced that if you do, the word will spread like wildfire and soon everyone will look down on you.
- You have extreme difficulty expressing negative feelings like anger. You are very unassertive and you avoid conflicts or disagreements with others.

Although we often think of people with social phobias as timid and shy wallflowers, they are sometimes highly successful and prominent individuals whom you would never suspect of having this problem. Gregory is the executive vice-president of a prestigious New York corporation. He confided to me that in the past thirty years he has rarely, if ever, said anything during staff meetings. He lives in constant terror that someone might ask for his opinion or ideas. I asked Gregory why this was so frightening. He confessed, "I

probably wouldn't have anything very intelligent or creative to say."
I was curious about why this was so threatening to him:

DAVID: And suppose you didn't have anything intelligent or creative to say. What then?

GREG: I'm a professional man and I'm expected to have something significant to say.

DAVID: And what if you didn't?

GREG: People would think I'm not a very capable person.

DAVID: And then what?

GREG: It would hurt my professional career.

DAVID: What would that mean to you?

GREG: Then I'd be a failure.

DAVID: And then?

GREG: I'd have no money. I couldn't pay the bills or the children's college tuition.

DAVID: What would that mean to you?

GREG: That would be a catastrophe because my style of living would collapse. I wouldn't be able to have the things I want. I'd be miserable.

This dialogue revealed the self-defeating attitudes at the root of Gregory's fears: he feels he must always appear competent, and he thinks he should never make mistakes. He believes that his colleagues are extremely judgmental and won't accept him unless he's perfect.

It's easy to see that these attitudes would make Gregory awfully uneasy, but there are also hidden benefits. As long as Gregory thinks he should be perfect, he'll put a tremendous effort into his work. He won't have to take risks and he'll always play it safe. Furthermore, he can secretly think of himself as a very "special" person. After all, only someone very "special" would be expected to be so perfect.

At the same time, Gregory pays a price for thinking this way. He feels constantly stressed; he rarely dares to express his own creative ideas; he's terrified of mistakes and criticism; and he often feels lonely, because he can't open up and share his feelings.

SELF-DISCLOSURE

Gregory feels insecure only in groups where he is expected to speak up. In one-to-one interactions, he feels fine. Some people with social phobias are a little different. They experience great anxiety even when talking to a friend when no one else is present. A college freshman at the University of Arizona named Jed told me that he felt especially anxious around a friend named Terry. He admired Terry because Terry seemed like a "cool dude." Terry was polished and good-looking and self-confident, and all the girls liked him. At the same time, Terry seemed a little too slick and glib, and Jed felt intimidated.

Jed's difficulties began one night when he and a bunch of friends, including Terry, were out drinking. Jed became intoxicated and started clowning around. He became the "life of the party," and all his friends seemed to be impressed by him. Jed said he felt he was being "cool."

The next day, Jed ran into Terry. Terry tried to strike up a conversation and said he had a lot of fun the night before. Without the benefit of a couple of drinks, Jed no longer felt loose and flippant. Instead, he felt nervous and self-conscious. He stared at the ground, hoping Terry wouldn't notice how anxious he felt, and mumbled brief replies.

After that, whenever he ran into Terry, Jed's heart started racing and he panicked. He tried to avoid Terry and acted uninterested whenever they spoke. Terry made overtures of friendship on several occasions and suggested they should get together, but Jed never followed up. Eventually they drifted further and further apart. Terry joined one of the "snobby" fraternities and they saw each other less frequently.

Jed said that this was not an isolated example but was typical of his relationships with friends. He said he put Terry on a pedestal and saw him as better than he was. Then he felt terribly pressured to compete and to impress Terry to prove he was Terry's equal. This made Jed extremely anxious and insecure.

Jed exemplifies many of the self-defeating attitudes described earlier that lead to social anxiety. He feels he must impress people and put on a show to be likable; he has stereotyped ideas of proper, acceptable behavior; he feels that his anxiety is shameful and unacceptable; and he is convinced that his "true self" would not be acceptable to his buddies. Jed constantly wears a mask, a manufactured "social self," that he presents to the world in hopes of being liked. This creates constant tension. Jed always has the terrible fear that someone will find him out and see his real, unacceptable self hiding behind the mask.

I suggested that Jed might want to tell Terry how he felt as a way of breaking the ice and making Terry more aware of why he had been acting aloof. I explained that he could let Terry know that he liked him but that he also felt a little nervous around him. I suggested he could point out that while he admired Terry, he felt that Terry was so smooth and polished that he sometimes felt uncomfortable when he was with him.

Jed replied, "No way, José!" He explained emphatically that students don't say stupid things like that and that if he did, which he never would, Terry would think he was a "real wimp." Jed's greatest fear was letting Terry know he felt nervous and anxious.

Jed's reaction is typical of nearly every socially anxious individual I've ever treated. He has rigid ideas of "right" and "wrong" social behavior. He is dogmatically convinced that sharing his feelings openly would not be socially acceptable. This was *not* the kind of help Jed had in mind! What he hoped was that I could teach him to *eliminate* his anxious feelings so he'd feel bold and relaxed and confident, as he did when he was intoxicated.

Notice the contradiction in what Jed is asking for. On the one hand he says, "Help me develop better self-esteem." But at the same time he says, "P.S. Make me into a very different person. Help me become the mask I wear. Don't ask me to accept myself the way I am! The real me is no darn good. A real stud doesn't feel nervous!"

Jed wants to believe that his real self is that joking, charming, totally self-confident guy who was impressing everyone when he was drunk. He feels that the nervous, insecure guy who usually inhabits his body isn't his real self, but an alien. He thinks that the shy, insecure Jed is a shameful, sick aberration, a mentally defective twin, who must be hidden behind locked doors.

Jed might outgrow some of his social anxiety through greater personal disclosure. Instead of feeling anxious and nervous and holding all his feelings inside, he could tell people how he feels. This can be remarkably helpful. If you suffer from social anxiety you may dig in your heels and hesitate to use this technique, just as Jed did, because of your "emotional perfectionism." You may think it's shameful to feel nervous and insecure. This attitude intensifies your anxiety, because you carry a double burden: you feel anxious and you feel that you have to hide your anxiety.

Jed and I became increasingly frustrated with each other because we seemed to have different agendas. It seemed that he was determined to become Mr. Cool. All he wanted was for me to teach him how to impress guys and score with women. In contrast, I wanted him to accept himself as a real human being, so he could admit his feelings of insecurity and nervousness without shame or a loss of self-esteem. I encouraged him to tell his friends that he sometimes felt nervous, but he wouldn't budge. He said he'd rather die than do that. I didn't disagree with his goal of feeling more comfortable and self-confident, but I felt certain he was using the wrong approach.

One day in a staff meeting my assistant, Retta Jo Bender, told me that whenever Jed was waiting for his appointment he came on "real strong" and talked a lot. She said Jed seemed like a nice person but he always seemed to be trying to impress her. She said this made her uncomfortable.

I realized that this was probably what he did with classmates at school, which would explain why he didn't have anyone he felt close to. The next time I saw Jed I told him what Retta Jo had shared with me. I said, "You know, Jed, I think she's fond of you but she's real turned off by you. You're trying to be so great, so special. The fact is that most of us don't feel so high and mighty. You seem determined to be better than everybody else. I want you to know that I resent it and I'm sick of it and it just won't wash. I bet that most of the people you know are real turned off by you, just the way I am!"

After I said this there was a long silence, and I felt very awkward. I was concerned that I'd overstepped my bounds and that I'd been unprofessional and too aggressive. But Jed's whole attitude suddenly seemed to change. He appeared humbled and said he understood what I'd been trying to tell him. He said that I was honestly expressing my feelings to him, and he could see why it was so important for him to express his feelings. He said it was the best session we'd ever had, and asked why I had waited so long to tell him how I felt!

After the session he began to feel much more relaxed and open with people. He even told his girlfriend that he'd been bothered by anxiety in social situations for several years. He was surprised that she said she felt the closest to him that she'd ever felt.

We often make the mistake of thinking that people will accept and admire only our strengths and will reject us if they know of our vulnerabilities and weaknesses. Because of this belief, we are afraid to tell people that we feel uncomfortable or that we have negative feelings about them. This is the mistake that I had been making with

Jed. I noticed how annoying and inappropriate his behavior was, and yet I was afraid of hurting his feelings or portraying myself as anything other than kind and helpful. As a result, I had been just as dishonest with him as he was being with the rest of the world. Once I opened up, our relationship became much more genuine, and he was able to experience real trust and closeness.

Personal disclosure is a powerful antidote to social anxiety, if you are willing to muster the courage. Tell people that you feel anxious in certain situations. Ask them if they ever feel nervous or worried. If you're afraid they might think less of you, ask them.

Like Jed, you may be thinking, "I couldn't tell people I feel anxious! It's a ridiculous idea. I'd make a fool of myself." Let's look at each of these objections carefully. When you say, "I *couldn't* do that," what you really mean is, "I don't *want* to tell anyone how anxious I feel." That's your prerogative, but you could if you chose to. If you insist on hiding your feelings, you'll continue to believe that you're somehow "different" or "defective." If you share your feelings, you might learn that other people are also quite human and willing to accept you.

Shortly after I opened my psychiatric practice, my wife and I bought a home in a nice neighborhood. Our daughter began playing with a girl who lived in a nearby house that looked like a mansion. One night, dressed in Levi's and an old T-shirt, I stopped by to pick up my daughter. Janice, the mother of the girl, met me at the door. She was dressed to the hilt and looked like a model in *Vogue* magazine. Janice invited me in and I found myself in a large hallway filled with expensive antiques. The walls were covered with oil paintings that looked several hundred years old—it was like a museum.

I felt quite awkward. Janice noticed how nervous I seemed and asked if I was feeling uncomfortable. I had the urge to deny how I felt in a defensive tone of voice, but instead I confessed that I did feel tense because I wasn't used to being in such a fancy house. She said she was quite surprised that a "shrink" would ever feel insecure! I felt even more embarrassed and teasingly reassured her that this was the only time since 1955 that I had felt any small tinge of nervousness! Janice laughed and we became good friends.

I believe that being open about my insecurities disarmed her, and we both felt more comfortable. Denying how I felt would have added to the tension and made me appear phony. Although some people do appear very glamorous and successful, most of us feel pretty human underneath. Sharing your vulnerabilities can be one of the best ways to overcome social anxiety and to develop close relationships with others.

THE FEARED FANTASY TECHNIQUE

Let's look at the worst possibility. Suppose you told someone you felt anxious and they *did* conclude you were a basket case. Would this be so terrible? How would you handle it?

A young woman named Joan, who works as an administrative assistant for a sportswear manufacturer, always felt very anxious around good-looking men. One of Joan's duties was to take sales representatives on tours of the plant facilities. Because many of these salesmen were attractive young men, she'd often get tense and the muscles of her neck would tighten up. Then her head would start to shake. She'd become preoccupied with the fear that one of the men would notice her head bobbing and look down on her. This thought made her anxiety unbearable, and the more she tried to hide her feelings the worse she felt. When I suggested that she might relieve some of the pressure by simply telling the group she felt a little nervous, she seemed as shocked as if I'd asked her to take her clothes off and run naked through the plant!

I proposed we examine her concerns with the Feared Fantasy Technique (see page 130). I suggested that she pretend to be a handsome man and insult me because I was nervous and my head was shaking. I told her to try to make me feel as foolish and humiliated as she could, by saying the things that a person would never really say but might be thinking. The purpose of the role-playing was to show her that even if the worst happened, it wouldn't be nearly as terrible as she imagined.

JOAN (*as the hostile handsome young man*): I noticed that your head is shaking. Why is that?

DAVID (*as Joan*): My head is shaking because I feel nervous.

JOAN (*as the hostile man*): Gee, that looks funny to have your head shaking like that.

DAVID (*as Joan*): It probably does look funny. It does that when I'm nervous.

JOAN (*as the hostile man*): Only a nut would let their head shake in public!

DAVID (*as Joan, smiling*): I've suspected that I was a little bit nutty for some time now. As a matter of fact, I think that might even become one of my better qualities.

JOAN (*as the hostile man*): Well, I don't think it's such a great quality. You've got to be some kind of a weirdo to have your head shaking like that in public. You must be ready for the loony bin!

DAVID (*as Joan*): Oh, absolutely! In fact, I'm probably much loonier than you think. I'm actually on my best behavior now. Tell me, do you find crazy ladies interesting?

JOAN (*as the hostile man*): This is ridiculous. I don't know what's wrong with you, except that you seem awfully nervous. I think you're a mental case and I don't want to have anything to do with you!

DAVID (*as Joan*): Well, I have learned something new. I always thought that being nervous made people human. Now I've discovered that it makes them "mental cases." I think you're quite wise in not getting involved with any "mental cases" like me. That could be quite dangerous! You would have no idea what crazy thing I might do next!

Joan was able to see that I was unperturbed by her attempt to humiliate me. She saw that the foolish behavior belonged to the hostile man. Although a real person would never be so critical, the imaginary stranger represented Joan's own self-critical thoughts. We then did a role reversal so she could learn to talk back to the imaginary put-downs.

You might want to try the Feared Fantasy Technique by role-playing with your therapist or with a friend or by writing out a script. When you talk back to the worst criticisms you can think up, you will begin to see how unrealistic they are. This can liberate you from your deepest fears and help you accept yourself as an imperfect but lovable human being.

THE SHAME-ATTACKING EXERCISE

Another way to squelch this fear is with a powerful technique called the Shame-Attacking Exercise (see page 230). The essence of the exercise is to confront your fears head-on, in a shameless, bold manner.

A handsome New York television anchorman named Steve was recently helped a great deal by a Shame-Attacking Exercise when he participated in the "intensive" program at my institute. Steve seems to have it all together, and you'd never suspect that he suffered from shyness and severe social anxiety. Steve has a mild, inherited tremor, so that his hands shake whenever he tries to hold a cup of coffee or write his name. He'd been to numerous neurologists in the hope of finding a cure, but they all said it was essentially untreatable and he'd just have to learn to live with it.

One of Steve's most terrifying fears was that someone would notice his tremor and look down on him. The tremor became noticeably worse whenever he was around people, and he constantly worried that they would discover his secret. He had developed all kinds of mannerisms to try to hide the tremor—for example, he never drank any fluid in front of other people. He was afraid that his producers would notice the tremor and decide he was defective and abnormal. He felt this would end his television career.

Steve had never actually challenged any of these beliefs. He had no real evidence that anyone would look down on him because of his tremor. He was so good at hiding it that no one had ever found out about it. I suggested that his problem was not his tremor, but his negative thoughts and feelings about it. These were his negative thoughts: "(1) It would be awful if anyone saw my hand shaking. (2) They would think there was something wrong with me. (3) This would be humiliating."

I wanted Steve to test these thoughts and confront his fears. I instructed him to go to a fashionable boutique where there were attractively dressed men and women shopping for expensive clothes. I suggested he could buy something inexpensive, like a tie or a handkerchief, and charge it on his credit card. Then, when the sales clerk asked him to sign his name—which terrified him—he could say in a loud, clear voice that everyone could hear, "Oh, there goes my shaky, trembling hand. My, oh my! Look at that tremor!" While he spoke, he could let his hand shake as much as possible so everyone could see it.

I told Steve that once he'd done this, he should tear up the charge slip and ask for a new one, explaining that his signature was too shaky. When he signed the second charge slip, he could call attention to his tremor again. Finally, before he left the boutique, he could ask for a drink of water. When he received the cup, he could hold it so that everyone could see the cup shaking and the water splashing about. Then he could say, "There goes my shaky hand again!"

Steve was not at all enthusiastic about this assignment! In fact, he stubbornly refused to do it for several days. Finally he gave in. I assigned a psychology graduate student to go along and observe him so we could be sure that he did the exercise completely.

With great misgivings, Steve entered a boutique in a fashionable area and purchased a tie. While he was signing his name as planned, he experienced sheer panic. However, nobody seemed terribly preoccupied with his shaky hands. One of the saleswomen started flirting with him when he was filling out the charge slip. By the time he left, his anxiety had diminished substantially. He felt encouraged and went into several additional stores and repeated the exercise. Each time, people seemed interested in him and no one seemed put off by his shaky hands. These experiences put the lie to his belief that it would be unbearable to let someone see his hands shaking.

Although he was partially relieved, Steve still thought that people were just acting polite. He believed that most people would secretly think he was abnormal, that something was terribly wrong with him, because of his tremor. To test this, he began telling people he met at my clinic—as well as strangers he met on the street—that he was in Philadelphia to get treatment for his "shaky hands." He was surprised that people were warm and friendly and didn't seem at all turned off by him.

The Shame-Attacking Method is similar to a method many therapists call "flooding" or "exposure." Essentially, you expose yourself to your fears and you allow yourself to be flooded with anxiety. It's like confronting a bully and saying, "Take your best shot." Usually your fears will peak, and then plateau, and then subside. Often they will disappear entirely! The effects can be profound. I strongly recommend this method for people with social anxiety.

Let's see if you understand how to use the Shame-Attacking Exercise. Imagine that you're a good-looking 26-year-old carpenter man who feels intensely shy and nervous in any social situation. When you go to singles' bars, you tell yourself, "These people are all so much more poised and self-confident than I am. If they knew how nervous I felt, they'd all think there was really something wrong with me." These thoughts make you so tense you can barely stand being in social situations for more than a few minutes. How could you attack these fears with the Shame-Attacking Exercise? Put your ideas here:

_____

_____

_____

_____

Answer: You could go to a singles' bar and strike up a conversation with someone. While you're getting to know them, you could tell them that you get very nervous in crowds and ask them if they ever feel that way. A man named Frank who received intensive treatment for a social phobia actually did this, with good results. He reported that the candid disclosure of how nervous he felt actually put other people at ease and made it easier for him to get to know them. This was not consistent with his belief that people would think his anxiety was shameful, and he felt much more relaxed.

THE EXPERIMENTAL TECHNIQUE

We often assume that our negative thoughts and beliefs are true without really questioning them. A young man from England named Martin worked in New York as a chemist. Martin had severe social anxiety and felt extremely awkward around groups of people. Standing in grocery store lines was a nightmare. He thought that all the people in the line were chitchatting with each other in a friendly, charming way. He imagined that they expected him to be equally witty and charming. He would stare anxiously at the floor, hoping no one would notice how inappropriate and klutzy he felt. He berated himself and told himself he wasn't supposed to stare at the floor. He told himself he should move his head and eyes around in a relaxed, spontaneous fashion. Needless to say, all the pressure he put on himself made him feel exceedingly awkward.

The moment it was time to pay for the groceries was terrifying. Martin felt that everyone was watching him and expecting him to say something clever and lighthearted to the cashier. Since he could never think of anything at all to say, the experience was sheer hell. He would leave the store feeling ashamed, embarrassed, and humiliated.

A student therapist at my unit suggested that he could test his belief that all the people in grocery lines were chitchatting amicably. She told Martin to forcibly lift his eyes from the floor and look at the other people in line. Since Martin was a scientist, she told him to calculate what percent of the people were actually socializing with one another. She also asked him to study and analyze what the other people in line did with their eyes. Did they always gaze into each other's faces in an animated manner, or did they sometimes stare off into space, just as he did?

Martin was extremely reluctant to perform this experiment. He felt that all the people would notice him staring at them. He was convinced that they would scowl at him in a judgmental way. It seemed much safer just to keep staring at the floor. Nevertheless, she twisted Martin's arm and he finally agreed to do it.

The next session, Martin reported with relief and surprise that most of the people in line were not chatting with each other. Many of them were daydreaming or looking at the candy or the magazines next to the check-out line. When they paid the cashier, they didn't act particularly charming, but simply paid their bills and left with their groceries. This discovery was an enormous relief.

In another session Martin told me that when he was walking down the street or standing in line at fast-food restaurants, he often felt that people were glaring at him in a disapproving way because they didn't like his looks. This made Martin feel intensely anxious and angry. He had thoughts like "He's got no right to look down on me! I'd like to punch him in the mouth." Then he would glance at people in a defiant way. Although Martin is a pleasant-looking fellow, he did tend to dress plainly due to his low self-esteem, and he sometimes needed a haircut. However, it did not seem at all likely to me that people were put off by his looks. Nevertheless, the defensive hostility he projected put people on edge, and when he saw the discomfort in their faces he thought, "I was right. They really *don't* like my looks!"

Can you think of an experiment Martin could do to test his belief that people glared at him because they didn't like his looks? Put your ideas here:

_____

_____

_____

_____

Answer: I suggested that he might smile and say hello to twenty strangers when he was walking down the street or standing in line at fast-food restaurants. Then he could keep track of the number of people who smiled back in a friendly way and the number who ignored him or said something rude.

Martin found this assignment difficult at first. In fact, he refused to do it for two months. He said he was so angry and anxious that he didn't feel like smiling. I told him he could just force out a smile and a hello, regardless of how uncomfortable he felt. Finally he agreed to practice smiling in front of a mirror for a few days before he began the experiment.

At the next session, Martin was euphoric. Although a few people did seem sour and ignored him, the majority smiled back and were exceedingly friendly. He got into conversations with several people, and ended up talking for over three hours to a fellow he knew from work. This was very unusual because he'd barely spoken to a fellow employee in over two years. He said he suddenly started to feel confident and charming and he loved meeting people. Not bad for someone who had felt tense, hostile, and lonely for much of his life!

THE SEMANTIC METHOD

Like Martin, most people with social anxiety feel intensely uncomfortable and fearful of saying or doing something foolish in front of others. This is a particularly painful and humiliating form of suffering. In spite of your intense desire to feel close to others, your fears of making a social blunder and making yourself the object of ridicule may prevent you from taking the necessary steps to initiate relationships.

Some of this anguish results from the cognitive distortion called "magnification." When you feel nervous in social situations, you may be using overly colorful language and blowing things out of proportion in your mind. For example:

- You spill a drink on yourself at a party and you tell yourself, "My gosh! This is terrible!"
- You're afraid to say hello or flirt with an attractive person you'd love to have a date with. You think, "If she [or he] gives me a hard time I'll look like an idiot. I couldn't stand that! It would be awful!"

The Semantic Method can be an extremely helpful antidote to this "magnification." You simply use more modest and less colorful language when you think about the problem. For example, when you spill a drink on yourself, you could tell yourself that it's a little embarrassing or inconvenient rather than dramatizing it as "terrible."

Some people may resist this. There may be several hidden payoffs when you catastrophize your shortcomings and magnify your mistakes. First, you may enjoy attracting attention to yourself by carrying on about your problems in a dramatic fashion. Second, when you act helpless and overwhelmed, the hidden message you project is, "I'm really such a remarkably superior person, it's practically inconceivable that I would do something as clumsy as spilling a drink on myself at a cocktail party. I will act terribly upset so you will know this is highly unusual!" Third, you may have the belief that if you blow your problems out of proportion and berate yourself sufficiently, you will improve. Perfectionists often think this way. They beat on themselves endlessly, thinking that somehow they will achieve salvation.

If you stop magnifying your mistakes and overreacting to them, you'll have to give up this kind of self-importance. This means you will have to accept your mistakes in a low-key way instead of viewing them as a federal offense. See if you can do this. Let's suppose that you flirt with someone and they give you the brush-off. What could you tell yourself instead of, "Gee! I really looked like a total idiot"? Put your Rational Response here:

_____

_____

_____

_____

Answer: Some people might tell themselves: "If he doesn't like me, it's his problem! He's probably a snob anyway." I don't like this approach because now you're putting the other person down. This has a hostile, insecure sound to it. I would suggest that you maintain a friendly, lighthearted attitude. Tell yourself that you looked like a human being, and not a "total idiot," and you get credit for trying. Remind yourself that you can flirt with other people and that eventually you will find someone who's fun to talk to.

THE "WHAT-IF?" TECHNIQUE

When you are blowing things out of proportion and predicting social catastrophes, try the "What-If?" Technique. This variation of the Vertical Arrow Technique can be especially helpful for the thoughts that lead to anxiety (see page 122). When you insist that some social foible would be "terrible," ask yourself, "What are the worst possible consequences of this? What if they really did happen?" When you face them squarely, you will frequently discover that your worst fears aren't nearly as terrible as you imagined.

To continue with the previous example, suppose you smile and say hello to an attractive woman who's picking out apples in the grocery store. She tells you to get lost. Several people are watching. You may think, "This is awful!" Ask yourself, "Why is this so awful?" You might say, "All those people will think I'm a jerk." Now ask yourself again: "And what if they do? Suppose they all think I'm a jerk. Why is that so awful?" You might say, "They'll look down on me and tell other people what a klutz I was." Now ask yourself: "And what if this happened? Why would that be so awful? How many people would they tell? What's the worst possible thing that could happen?"

Let's imagine that they'd each told several other people how lame you were. Now ask yourself: "Is that the very worst that could happen? Could I live with that? Why would that be so awful?"

You might not give up so easily. Let's imagine that each of those people told several more people, and so on, until eventually there were several hundred people who knew that you had made a fool of yourself. And they might all agree that you were a loser and decide that they didn't like you.

Once you've pushed your fears to their worst imaginable extreme, ask yourself these two questions: "How likely is this? Could I live with this if it did happen?" You could remind yourself that there are

200 million people in the United States. If several hundred people thought you were a jerk, so what? Could you still survive and find happiness? Do you want to let these people—assuming that this incredibly unlikely chain of events actually happened—have so much power over your life? What could they do to you anyway? Could they arrest you? Would they get together in groups and snicker about you?

If you decide you *could* live with these unlikely consequences, then you're free. You're free to flirt with anybody you want, and you can stop letting your insecurities spoil your life. Certainly not everybody will find you attractive or interesting. Some people *will* think you're a jerk. I can assure you there are hundreds of people who think I'm a jerk! I would be inclined to agree with them, too! I've often felt that being a jerk was actually one of my better qualities.

When you believe in yourself, your supporters will far outnumber your critics. Many people will respond to you positively, and this can lead to rewarding relationships and opportunities. Are you willing to take the risk?

THE DAILY MOOD LOG

So far we've talked about a number of causes and cures for social anxiety. The "Daily Mood Log" should be added to the tools you use because it will show you precisely why you are afraid of people and how you can deal with these feelings more effectively. You may recall the specific steps, which are described in detail in Chapter 5:

Step One: Write a brief description of a social situation that made you feel anxious.

Step Two: Record your negative feelings and rate how intense each one was between 0 (not at all) and 100 (the worst).

Step Three: The Triple-Column Technique: Write down the Automatic Thoughts that made you feel nervous and insecure in the Automatic Thoughts column. Indicate how strongly you believed each one between 0 and 100. Then identify the cognitive distortions in each negative thought, using the list on page 296, and substitute more positive and realistic thoughts in the Rational Response Column. Indicate how much you believe each of them between 0 and 100.

Step Four: Outcome: Re-rate your belief in each Automatic Thought on the scale of 0 to 100. Once your belief in each negative thought is reduced, indicate how much better you now feel.

Let's assume that you usually feel insecure and self-conscious around groups of people. This is so painful to you that you go to great lengths to avoid social situations. Imagine that your boyfriend recently asked you to go shopping with some friends who were visiting from California. You felt panicky and wanted to back out. You recorded your negative emotions as: "Nervous—100; Frustrated—100; Hopeless—100."

Next, you wrote down the following "Automatic Thoughts" on the Daily Mood Log:

1. I will not know what to talk about.

2. I will feel so stupid.

3. His friends will think I'm not very interesting.

4. When I speak they will stare at me and think that what I have to say doesn't count.

5. I will feel so tense that I won't be able to walk and talk freely.

6. I *shouldn't* feel this way! What's wrong with me?

7. I'll never change.

I'm sure you can see the connection between your negative thoughts and your anxious feelings. Let's see how you might deal with some of them. Your first thought was "I will not know what to talk about." What are the distortions in this thought? Review this list of cognitive distortions on page 296 and put your ideas here:

1. _____

2. _____

3. _____

4. _____

5. _____

Answer: first, this is a prime example of "fortune-telling." These negative predictions often function as self-fulfilling prophecies. If you keep telling yourself that you have nothing to say, you may get so nervous that you will have difficulties thinking of things to talk about.

You are also making a "should statement." You are pressuring yourself that you must come up with things that are witty and entertaining in order to be liked by others.

A third distortion would be "discounting the positive." If you went shopping with these people, you probably would have things to talk about, and you could ask questions to get to know the other people a little better. But you may censor all your ideas and feelings because they seem too ordinary to impress people.

A fourth distortion is "emotional reasoning"—you *feel* like you'll have nothing to say, so you assume that you really won't. But you have no evidence for this. A fifth distortion would be "all-or-nothing thinking." You may not be a geyser of conversation and wit, but you'll certainly have *some* things to say.

The Ten Ways to Untwist Your Thinking on page 118 lists many ways of talking back to negative thoughts. What could you tell yourself instead of, "I will not know what to talk about"? Put your ideas here.

_____

_____

_____

_____

Answer: One approach would be to use the "Double Standard Method." If you had a friend who felt nervous before shopping with friends, would you tell her, "Hey, you won't have *anything* to talk about?" You wouldn't say this because it would be mean. Instead, you'd be supportive and you'd encourage her. Would you be willing to talk to yourself in the same supportive way you would talk to a friend? If so, you could tell yourself something like this: "I will have something to say, and I can ask these women about themselves. I can be a good listener, and they might appreciate the fact that I'm interested in them."

A second approach would be the "Cost-Benefit Analysis." You could list the advantages and disadvantages of telling yourself, "I won't be able to think of anything to say." One obvious advantage would be that you'll feel so discouraged that you'll stay home, so you won't have to confront your fears. The main disadvantage would be that you'll spend the day in anguish, hating yourself. Weighing the advantages against the disadvantages can sometimes motivate you to say, "Hey, I'm tired of this. I think I'll take a chance and do things differently for once."

A third approach would be the "What-If?" technique. Suppose you *did* go shopping and couldn't think of much to say. What's the worst that could happen? Conceivably, one or more of these people might decide they didn't like you because you were so shy and quiet. If so, what's the worst thing that could possibly happen? Would they start telling other people about what a nervous and undesirable person you were? How many people would they tell? Would they put an article about you in the newspaper and polarize the entire city against you so you'd never again have the chance of making any friends?

Once you push your fears to their most exaggerated conclusions with the "What-If" technique, ask yourself, "how likely is this? And even more important, could I still accept myself if this unlikely chain of events did occur?" In evaluating this, you might need to do another "Cost-Benefit Analysis." You could list the advantages and disadvantages of believing, "I must have everyone's approval to be a worthwhile human being."

It's important to realize there are numerous ways to change your negative thinking patterns. When one method's not helpful, you can try another, and then another, until you finally find a Rational Response that makes good sense to you.

Now I want you to see if you can talk back to your second negative thought, "I will feel so stupid." Identify the distortions in this thought, using the list on page 296:

1. _____

2. _____

3. _____

4. _____

5. _____

6. _____

Now, substitute your Rational Response here:

_____

_____

_____

_____

A blank Daily Mood Log is located at the end of this chapter on page 294 for your convenience. Remember that to make you feel better at the gut level, any Rational Response must have these two characteristics:

1. It must be absolutely true and realistic. Phony rationalizations will never help you. Ask yourself how much you believe your Rational Response between 0% and 100%. Your belief in it should be close to 100% if it's going to do you any good.

2. The Rational Response must put the lie to your negative thought. The moment you stop believing your Automatic Thoughts, you will feel better.

How much better? The aim is not to reduce your anxiety from 100% (the worst) to 0% (no anxiety at all). That would be unrealistic. If you can reduce your anxiety by about half before a social function, you will be more likely to mix with other people and open up. This *will* be anxiety-provoking at first. But once you do, you'll see that the world doesn't really come to an end, and your self-confidence will increase.

Social anxiety is caused by double-barreled mistrust. First, you don't believe that you can be accepted as a vulnerable and imperfect human being. You imagine that people are extremely vindictive, hostile, and judgmental and will not accept you as you really are. In addition, you do not accept yourself. You may despise yourself for your vulnerabilities and think you must be better than you really are to be lovable and worthwhile. The solution to this dilemma cannot exist in your head but can only be worked out in your relationships with others. Much like someone with an elevator phobia, you've got to get on the elevator and discover firsthand that you won't get trapped or fall after all. This means mixing with other people in social situations and being more open about your feelings. This will be anxiety-provoking at first. If you stubbornly persist and expose yourself to social situations over and over, you will slowly begin to gain greater and greater self-confidence. As you stop running away and begin to connect with other people, you will gain freedom from the fears that have plagued you.

THE DAILY MOOD LOG*

STEP ONE: DESCRIBE THE UPSETTING EVENT _____

_____

STEP TWO: RECORD YOUR NEGATIVE FEELINGS—and rate each one
from 0 (the least) to 100 (the most). Use words like sad, anxious,
angry, guilty, lonely, hopeless, frustrated, etc.

Emotion	Rating	Emotion	Rating	Emotion	Rating
1.		3.		5.	
2.		4.		6.	

STEP THREE: THE TRIPLE-COLUMN TECHNIQUE—

Automatic Thoughts	Distortions	Rational Responses
Write your negative thoughts and estimate your belief in each one (0–100).	Identify the distortions in each Automatic Thought.	Substitute more realistic thoughts and estimate your belief in each one (0 and 100).

(Continue on next page)

*Copyright © 1984 by David D. Burns, M.D., from *The Feeling Good Handbook*, copyright © 1989

THE DAILY MOOD LOG (continued)

Automatic Thoughts	Distortions	Rational Responses

(Continue on next page)

Automatic Thoughts	Distortions	Rational Responses

STEP FOUR: OUTCOME–Re-rate your belief in each Automatic Thought from 0 to 100 and put a check in the box that describes how you now feel:

☐ not at all better; ☐ somewhat better; ☐ quite a bit better; ☐ a lot better.

CHECKLIST OF COGNITIVE DISTORTIONS*

1. All-or-nothing thinking: You look at things in absolute, black-and-white categories.
2. Overgeneralization: You view a negative event as a never-ending pattern of defeat.
3. Mental filter: You dwell on the negatives and ignore the positives.
4. Discounting the positives: You insist that your accomplishments or positive qualities "don't count."
5. Jumping to conclusions: (A) Mind reading—you assume that people are reacting negatively to you when there's no definite evidence for this; (B) Fortune-telling—you arbitrarily predict that things will turn out badly.
6. Magnification or minimization: You blow things way up out of proportion or you shrink their importance inappropriately.
7. Emotional reasoning: You reason from how you feel: "I *feel* like an idiot, so I really must be one." Or "I don't *feel* like doing this, so I'll put it off."
8. "Should statements": You criticize yourself or other people with "shoulds" or "shouldn'ts." "Musts," "oughts," and "have tos" are similar offenders.
9. Labeling: You identify with your shortcomings. Instead of saying "I made a mistake," you tell yourself, "I'm a jerk," or "a fool," or "a loser."
10. Personalization and blame: You blame yourself for something you weren't entirely responsible for, or you blame other people and overlook ways that your own attitudes and behavior might contribute to a problem.

15

·

Public Speaking Anxiety

Imagine that in five minutes you will have to speak or give a talk in front of a group of people. It might be a church group, a class or an important business meeting. How worried or nervous would you be feeling?

_____ Not at all
_____ A little bit
_____ A moderate amount
_____ An extreme amount

If you indicated that you would feel at least a little anxious, I want you to tell me how you would be thinking. Write down any negative thoughts you might have just before you give your talk:

_____

_____

_____

_____

Although everyone is different, you might be telling yourself something like this: "What if they think I'm a bore? What if my mind goes blank? I'll probably look nervous and my voice will tremble and shake. Everyone will see what a dodo I am." You may imagine yourself fumbling awkwardly as you begin to speak. You may anticipate that people in the audience will quietly chuckle or yawn in boredom and slip out the back door before you're done. Or you may be afraid that people will interrupt you and ask embarrassing questions that will make you look foolish.

These fears are extremely common. However, many people with public speaking anxiety think their problems are very unusual.

If you're willing to work at it, you can conquer your fears of public speaking. You'll feel better about yourself and others will respect you more. The ability to speak in front of groups can mean getting better grades in school, getting a promotion at work, or possibly finding a new and more rewarding career.

The crucial first step is to recognize the connection between your negative thoughts and the way you feel. You feel worried and uptight because you give yourself negative messages. When you write these negative thoughts down, it becomes easier to see how distorted and self-defeating they are. Since you put these frightening thoughts and fantasies in your mind, it's within your power to get rid of them.

A businessman named Frank wanted to expand his business by offering a series of seminars to potential clients in his community. He had procrastinated about arranging these seminars for years because he was afraid he would appear nervous and do a bad job. He thought this would damage his professional reputation.

Frank's intense anxiety about speaking in front of a group resulted from these negative thoughts: "If I'm nervous I won't be able to present my ideas very clearly. I shouldn't feel so anxious! People will notice my voice trembling and they'll think, 'Gee! That guy sure is nervous.' Then they'll think I'm not a very worthwhile person and they won't want to do business with me."

Once you write down your negative thoughts, you can identify the distortions in each of them using the list on page 308. Frank's first negative thought was: "If I'm nervous I won't be able to present my ideas very clearly." Can you identify the distortions in this thought? Put your ideas here before you read on:

1. _____

2. _____

It involves "all-or-nothing thinking" because he's telling himself that he will either feel completely relaxed and present his thoughts articulately, or that he will feel extremely nervous and make a totally garbled presentation. In reality, he will probably be able to present his ideas reasonably well even if he does feel nervous. And if he gives a series of seminars, he'll get better and better at it each time.

Frank is also involved in "fortune-telling" (also known as "jumping to conclusions") because he's predicting a bad outcome. You may argue that this prediction is realistic, since he *will* be nervous and he may have some trouble with the presentation. That may be partially true, but it's quite destructive for Frank to give himself this message. If he had a friend who planned to give a seminar, would Frank tell him, "you're going to be nervous and confused" over and over in the days before the presentation? Of course he wouldn't! And yet that's exactly the kind of negative message Frank gives himself!

Once you identify the distortions in a negative thought, you can substitute a Rational Response. What Rational Response would you suggest? What could Frank tell himself in place of, "If I'm nervous I won't be able to present my ideas very clearly"? Write your ideas here:

_____

_____

_____

_____

_____

Frank and I came up with this Rational Response: "I may feel nervous at first, but that's natural. I'll probably feel more relaxed once I get started. I will be able to get my ideas across even if I'm not the world's greatest orator."

Now let's repeat the process with his second negative thought, "I *shouldn't* feel so anxious!" Check the list of cognitive distortions on page 308 and see which ones this thought contains. Write your ideas here:

1. _____

2. _____

This is a classic "should statement," since Frank's insisting he *shouldn't* be nervous. Why shouldn't he be nervous? He may have an imaginary ideal of himself as an invulnerable superman who has total mastery of every situation. This emotional perfectionism is very common among anxious individuals. You *condemn* yourself for having normal feelings of anxiety. Frank's thought also involves "personalization," since Frank is blaming himself for feeling nervous.

What Rational Response would you suggest?

_____

_____

_____

_____

Frank probably wouldn't impose such rigid demands on a friend. If a friend felt nervous before giving a speech, Frank would be more encouraging. He'd say, "It's okay to feel nervous. We *all* feel that way." He can extend the same compassion toward himself by giving himself that same message. This could be Frank's Rational Response.

You may object to this approach. You may argue, "But I have higher standards for myself than for other people. I don't want to tell myself that it's okay to be nervous. That's like giving up!" These high standards may be unrealistic and self-defeating. You apparently do feel nervous about public speaking, like most human beings, or else you wouldn't be reading this! You might feel more relaxed if you would lower your standards just a tad and *accept* the fact that you feel anxious.

Some readers might continue to object: "A normal person may feel a *little* anxious, but I feel *petrified* and that's not normal!" You may feel petrified because you label these nervous feelings as "abnormal." If instead, you tell yourself that nervousness is normal, you won't feel so intimidated by these reactions. This is the "Acceptance Paradox." If you resist your anxiety, and you insist that you shouldn't feel anxious, your anxiety will get worse. If, in contrast, you accept your anxiety, it loses its power over you.

Now look at Frank's third negative thought: "People will notice my voice trembling and they'll think, 'Gee! That guy sure is nervous!'" What distortions can you identify in this thought?

1. _____

2. _____

This is an example of fortune-telling and mind reading, since Frank is predicting that everyone will notice how nervous he is and look down on him. It might also be the "mental filter" since he imagines people will only think about his nervousness and overlook everything else he has to say. What Rational Response would you suggest?

_____

_____

_____

_____

Frank's fourth negative thought was: "Then they'll think I'm not a very worthwhile person and they won't want to do business with me." What distortions does this thought contain?

1. _____

2. _____

3. _____

Once again, it involves fortune-telling and mind reading. These distortions are *extremely* common in nearly all forms of anxiety. Frank's thought is also an overgeneralization, since Frank assumes that if *some* people don't like him, then nobody will. He thinks that everyone will react in exactly the same manner, like sheep. Is this likely, given how different and how unpredictable people are?

Frank is also generalizing from his *performance* to his *self*. If he fails to give an outstanding presentation, he will feel like a failure *as a person*. This means that his ego and self-esteem are always on the line. Even if it turns out that Frank is not a charismatic lecturer, does it follow that he's not a worthwhile *person*? Or a savvy businessman? I have personally given many talks in my life. Some have gone well, but I can remember a few that were real bombs! On those occasions, was I a less worthwhile *person*? Or simply a less effective lecturer? This may seem like a subtle distinction, but the impact on the way you feel about yourself is about as subtle as the Grand Canyon!

Instead of telling himself that people will despise him and not want to do business with him if he appears anxious, how could Frank think about it? Put your Rational Response here:

_____

_____

_____

_____

Here's the Rational Response that Frank came up with after we discussed it: "Getting nervous makes me very human, not less worthwhile. Most of the people who attend the seminar will be more interested in what they can learn about making money than in judging how 'worthwhile' I am as a person."

This exercise gave Frank the courage to take a risk and give one seminar. He did feel nervous at first, but it went well and he got a good response from the participants. Following the seminar he began to feel the best he'd felt in years. As you confront and conquer a fear it often turns into its opposite—exhilaration. This payoff makes it all the more important not to run away from the things you fear.

Before we go on, let's summarize what you've learned about public speaking anxiety so far. What is the cause of your public speaking anxiety? Put your answer here:

_____

_____

_____

_____

_____

Answer: Anxiety results from your negative thoughts. Although they may seem realistic, they are often quite distorted and illogical. Some of the commonest distortions that are associated with public speaking anxiety include:

- Fortune-telling: "I'm going to blow it!"
- Mind reading: "Everyone will notice how nervous I am and look down on me."
- All-or-nothing thinking: "My presentation will be a complete fiasco."
- Overgeneralization: "This will show what a lousy, inferior human being I am."
- Should statements: "I *shouldn't* feel so nervous. I *should* be in total control of my emotions at all times."

When you substitute more positive and realistic thoughts for the ones that are negative and distorted, you will often feel better. John is a television announcer in Boston who lost his job after eight years of broadcasting when the station was sold. This job was a blow to his self-esteem, and he felt angry and depressed. At times John felt old and over the hill.

After several months he landed a job with another television

THE DAILY MOOD LOG*

STEP ONE: DESCRIBE THE UPSETTING EVENT _____
Feeling nervous before television broadcasts.

STEP TWO: RECORD YOUR NEGATIVE FEELINGS—and rate each one from 0 (the least) to 100 (the most). Use words like sad, anxious, angry, guilty, lonely, hopeless, frustrated, etc.

Emotion	Rating	Emotion	Rating	Emotion	Rating
1. Anxiety	80	3.		5.	
2. Shame	80	4.		6.	

STEP THREE: THE TRIPLE-COLUMN TECHNIQUE—

Automatic Thoughts	Distortions	Rational Responses
Write your negative thoughts and estimate your belief in each one (0–100).	Identify the distortions in each Automatic Thought.	Substitute more realistic thoughts and estimate your belief in each one (0 and 100).
1. I'll probably blow it when I get on the air. ~~(100%)~~ 0%	1. Fortune-telling, discounting the positive	1. I usually do quite well once I get started. (100%)
2. I still feel anxious after twenty years in broadcasting. A "true professional" wouldn't feel so nervous. I should feel poised and confident. ~~(100%)~~ 10%	2. "Should statement," labeling	2. There are many times when I do feel poised and confident. Who says I have to feel that way all the time? There's no such thing as a "true professional." I'm a human being, and regardless of my skill or experience, there will be times when I feel nervous. (90%)

STEP FOUR: OUTCOME—Re-rate your belief in each Automatic Thought from 0 to 100 and put a check in the box that describes how you now feel:

☐ not at all better; ☐ somewhat better; ☒ quite a bit better; ☐ a lot better.

station but felt insecure and nervous before broadcasts. His self-confidence was shot because he told himself, "I'll probably blow it when I get on the air. How can I still feel anxious after eight years in broadcasting? A 'true professional' wouldn't be so nervous. I should feel poised and confident."

You can see on page 304 how he identified the distortions in each automatic thought and substituted Rational Responses in the right-hand column. Your Rational Responses might have been different, but this is not a problem. There's tremendous room for your own unique approach.

Now I'd like you to work on some of your own negative thoughts using the blank Daily Mood Log on page 306. In the "Upsetting Event" space at the top describe the type of public speaking situation that you might be confronted with. Next, record your negative feelings—like anxious, ashamed, or nervous—in the appropriate spaces and rate how strong each feeling is between 0 (for the least) and 100 (for the worst). Then record your Automatic Thoughts and number each of them in the left-hand column. See if you can identify the distortions in each thought, using the list on page 308. Finally, substitute Rational Responses in the right-hand column. When you've completed the exercise, indicate how much it helped by checking one of the four "Outcome" boxes at the bottom. You'll be surprised how effective this simple procedure can be. *Don't try to do it in your head!* Doing the exercise on paper is far more effective.

When you write down your negative thoughts and you substitute Rational Responses, you will put things in a more positive and realistic perspective. This will help reduce some of the anxiety. Remember, though, that a certain amount of anxiety is perfectly natural. The goal is not to achieve complete tranquility or total control of your emotions. If you remind yourself that you are not the same as what you do, you can maintain a sense of self-esteem regardless of how well you do when you give your talk.

Your anxiety can make you uncomfortable, but it won't stop you from doing a good job if you don't let it. One way to prove this to yourself is to make a list of all the ways you think your nervousness could louse you up if you were giving a talk. Once you pinpoint the specific problems, it's usually fairly easy to solve them.

Suppose you're afraid that you'll get so nervous that your mind

THE DAILY MOOD LOG*

STEP ONE: DESCRIBE THE UPSETTING EVENT _____

_____

STEP TWO: RECORD YOUR NEGATIVE FEELINGS—and rate each one from 0 (the least) to 100 (the most). Use words like sad, anxious, angry, guilty, lonely, hopeless, frustrated, etc.

Emotion	Rating	Emotion	Rating	Emotion	Rating
1.		3.		5.	
2.		4.		6.	

STEP THREE: THE TRIPLE-COLUMN TECHNIQUE—

Automatic Thoughts	Distortions	Rational Responses
Write your negative thoughts and estimate your belief in each one (0–100).	Identify the distortions in each Automatic Thought.	Substitute more realistic thoughts and estimate your belief in each one (0 and 100).

(Continue on next page)

*Copyright © 1984 by David D. Burns, M.D., from *The Feeling Good Handbook*, copyright © 1989

Automatic Thoughts	Distortions	Rational Responses

(Continue on next page)

THE DAILY MOOD LOG (continued)

Automatic Thoughts	Distortions	Rational Responses

STEP FOUR: OUTCOME—Re-rate your belief in each Automatic Thought from 0 to 100 and put a check in the box that describes how you now feel:

☐ not at all better; ☐ somewhat better; ☐ quite a bit better; ☐ a lot better.

CHECKLIST OF COGNITIVE DISTORTIONS*

1. All-or-nothing thinking: You look at things in absolute, black-and-white categories.
2. Overgeneralization: You view a negative event as a never-ending pattern of defeat.
3. Mental filter: You dwell on the negatives and ignore the positives.
4. Discounting the positives: You insist that your accomplishments or positive qualities "don't count."
5. Jumping to conclusions: (A) Mind reading—you assume that people are reacting negatively to you when there's no definite evidence for this; (B) Fortune-telling—you arbitrarily predict that things will turn out badly.
6. Magnification or minimization: You blow things way up out of proportion or you shrink their importance inappropriately.
7. Emotional reasoning: You reason from how you feel: "I *feel* like an idiot, so I really must be one." Or "I don't *feel* like doing this, so I'll put it off."
8. "Should statements": You criticize yourself or other people with "shoulds" or "shouldn'ts." "Musts," "oughts," and "have tos" are similar offenders.
9. Labeling: You identify with your shortcomings. Instead of saying "I made a mistake," you tell yourself, "I'm a jerk," or "a fool," or "a loser."
10. Personalization and blame: You blame yourself for something you weren't entirely responsible for, or you blame other people and overlook ways that your own attitudes and behavior might contribute to a problem.

---

*Copyright © 1980 by David D. Burns, M.D. Adapted from *Feeling Good: The New Mood Therapy* (New York: William Morrow & Company, 1980; Signet, 1981).

will go blank. Can you think of any solutions to this? Write your solution to this problem here:

_____

_____

_____

   One good solution would be to put a brief outline of your talk on a 3" × 5" card and hold it in your hand or place it on the podium so you can refer to it if you get lost. This is far more effective than reading your speech. Reading your speech will make you sound unbearably boring and will guarantee a poor result. Just glance at the outline on the 3" × 5" card from time to time and talk to people just as if you were sharing your ideas with a friend. This will make you come across in a more personable and spontaneous way.

   Even if you don't have an outline you can easily solve the problem of having your mind going blank. I was giving my "Feeling Good" lecture to a women's group in Virginia, and there were some temporary problems with the sound system. As I was speaking, I noticed that people in the audience began to snicker, but I couldn't figure out what they were laughing about. Then I noticed that a spare microphone on a stand behind me was slowly and magically "walking" across the stage all by itself! Apparently a stagehand was pulling it by its cord to try to get it off the stage. It looked ridiculous and I started laughing, too.

   After the problem got straightened out I discovered I had completely forgotten what I'd been talking about. I looked out at a sea of 600 ladies staring at me. They were patiently waiting for me to say something wonderful. I drew a total blank! After a long, dramatic silence I asked them, "Have any of you ever had the fear that you'd be in front of a large audience and your mind would suddenly go blank? If so, raise your hands." A few hands went up gingerly and then huge numbers of hands went up. Then I said: "Well, that just happened to me! I don't have the vaguest notion what I was talking about! Where was I?" This evoked further laughter and won the audience over to my side. Many hands went up and the women told me where I'd left off. They saw that I was vulnerable and became very relaxed and friendly. As a result, the presentation went unusually well.

Here are some other public speaking problems and suggestions about how you could solve each of them.

Problems	Solutions
1. Someone in the audience might ask a question I can't answer.	1. I could tell them it's an excellent question and I don't know the answer.
2. My heart will pound and I'll feel terribly tense before I have to speak.	2. I could walk or jog or do some calisthenics to work off the excess energy.
3. I might say something stupid.	3. I could acknowledge my error and correct it.
4. I might do a lousy job. People would be bored.	4. I could ask several friends to critique me afterward. I could take a night-school course in public speaking so I could learn how to make my presentations more interesting and useful.

Now I'd like you to try this. Write down problems that you might have if you were to give a presentation in the left-hand column. In the right-hand column, write down solutions to these problems. If you have difficulty, ask a friend who has more experience in public speaking.

Problems	Solutions
1. _____	1. _____
_____	_____
_____	_____
_____	_____
2. _____	2. _____
_____	_____
_____	_____
_____	_____
3. _____	3. _____
_____	_____
_____	_____
_____	_____

Probably the most important key to public speaking success is to make contact with your audience in a friendly way. You may be afraid that someone in the audience will ask a hostile question or make a critical remark during the question and answer session at the end of your talk. This is one of the easiest problems in the world to solve—*if* you follow several simple suggestions. What you must *not* do is argue with them or defend yourself. That *never* works. Instead, find a way to compliment them (called "stroking") and to agree with them (called "disarming"). This nearly always works like a charm.

1. *Stroke them:* Give them a genuine compliment. Say something positive about their ideas. Remember that people who come on

in an aggressive, critical way are frequently insecure and looking for recognition. They want to feel important and they may be jealous because you're in the limelight. If somebody asks an intimidating, hostile question you could simply say, "That's a very important question. Thank you for asking it." If you say this in a genuine way it will immediately make them feel flattered and you will appear cooperative and friendly. You won't end up in an awkward debate that will make everyone tense. There's another big benefit. When you compliment people who ask questions, the others in the audience will feel like it's safe for them to share their ideas and ask questions, too. Pretty soon lots of hands will go up and you'll reap the benefits of a lively audience response instead of a long, dull silence at the end of your talk.

2. *Disarm them:* In addition to stroking them, find some grain of truth in what they have to say. This is the exact opposite of your normal impulse to defend yourself and argue. It's amazingly effective because you'll appear flexible and open-minded and not rigidly stuck to one narrow point of view.

During a radio show last week I was talking about how negative thoughts can lead to depression and anxiety. The host of the show said, "Dr. Burns, can't we go too far with this philosophy of optimism and positive thinking? Isn't negative thinking more realistic?" I replied: "Absolutely (disarming). Some of the latest research shows that too much optimism can be just as destructive as low self-esteem (disarming). For example, Hitler was extremely optimistic. Compulsive gamblers can be overly optimistic. This is an exciting area for new research (disarming)." This response won the host over to my side because he saw me as an ally and not as a competitor. We had a fabulous interview.

You can learn the stroking and disarming techniques if you write down imaginary questions or criticisms that people in the audience might raise during your talk. Then write down how you might respond, as in this example:

AUDIENCE MEMBER: Your ideas about the economy are a lot of bunk. We need higher taxes and a lower defense budget.

YOU: Those are important issues, for sure (stroking). If we can lower the federal deficit, it will mean a stronger economy and less inflation (disarming). This is important, and it deserves serious consideration (disarming).

Now try some script writing yourself. Write down the difficult questions or critical comments that might come up during the question-and-answer period at the end of your talk. Then write down how you might respond, using the stroking and disarming techniques.

Audience member (write out a critical remark that someone might make here):

_____

_____

_____

You (write out how you could respond here):_____

_____

_____

_____

_____

Use additional paper to write responses to other questions or criticisms from audience members. With practice, you'll get the knack of it. If you have difficulty coming up with good answers, ask a friend for help. After you've come up with some good answers on paper, try role-playing with a friend. Let them pretend to ask threatening questions and you can disarm and stroke them. If your response sounds phony or defensive, do a role reversal and let them give it a try. After a while you'll discover that there's really *nothing* that people could ever say or ask that you couldn't turn to your advantage if you use these techniques. This will reduce your fears and your friendly style of fielding questions will make your presentations more effective.

I used this method once to prepare for a Mike Wallace interview on national television. During the early 1980s the staff of "60 Minutes" developed a daytime show called "Up to the Minute." They were interested in new treatments for depression and made an eight-minute documentary film which illustrated excerpts from actual cognitive-therapy sessions with patients in my office. After the film was shown, Mike Wallace was to interview me for twenty minutes on live television.

One of my patients warned me that Mike Wallace could be a tough, hard-hitting interviewer and asked if I knew what I was getting into. This put me into a panic because when I agreed to do the show I wasn't really clear who Mike Wallace was. I had imagined that he was a kindly gentleman who was interested in depression. Then I watched him on "60 Minutes" and got terrified! I began to imagine all kinds of embarrassing and intimidating questions he might ask in order to discredit me. I wrote them down and thought of how I might answer them. I practiced by talking to myself. First I would imagine I was Mike Wallace, and I would say something terribly insinuating: "Dr. Burns, is it true that you make a living on other people's suffering?" The question seemed silly, but there was something terribly guilt-provoking about it.

I decided I could answer Mike Wallace like this: "As a matter of fact, you've raised an important question [stroking]. I do make money by treating illnesses, as does any physician [disarming]. Sometimes it really doesn't really seem right to me—it seems crass [disarming]. I feel bad about it, and I wish we had a better way to deliver medical care [disarming]."

Of course the actual show wasn't at all the way I had imagined it. Mike Wallace turned out to be a very friendly person. He came to my dressing room before the show and said he'd seen the film of the therapy and was impressed with the method. Then he asked if I would teach him how to talk back to *his* Automatic Thoughts!

The show went well and the experience gave me tremendous confidence. You may never be under intense pressure from someone who's trying to discredit you, but it's nice to know there's such a simple and effective way to handle hostile questions and accusations.

Let's suppose you follow all these suggestions and you give a talk. How will you feel if it doesn't go as well as you had hoped? If you flub, you can thank your lucky stars, because this will give you the golden opportunity to discover that the world doesn't come to an end after all. Life goes on even if you're not successful all the time.

You can prepare for this now by writing down all the negative thoughts you'd have if you gave a speech that turned out to be a complete flop. You might be telling yourself, "Those people must really think I'm a jerk. What a loser I am! I made such a fool of myself. I can't stand it!" Study the list on page 308 and try to identify the distortions in these thoughts. One distortion would be "magnification," since you're telling yourself that you "can't stand it." It may be uncomfortable, but you can stand it. It's not nearly as bad as being boiled in oil, for example. Another distortion would be "labeling," since you are calling yourself "a jerk," "a loser," and "a fool." We all behave foolishly at times, but this makes us human beings, not "fools" or "jerks." A third distortion would be "mind reading." You're assuming that everyone in the audience will be as unforgiving and critical as you are.

If you have trouble talking back to your negative thoughts, ask yourself what you would say to a dear friend who didn't do a very good job giving a talk. Would you say, "Gee, you're such a jerk"? Of course you wouldn't! You'd probably be more supportive and helpful and say, "There's a lot you can do to improve your presentation, but you deserve credit for trying." Then you'd help him pinpoint the specific problems so he could do a better job the next time.

Now let me ask you this question: If you would treat a friend in a helpful way, why are you so hard on yourself? Would you be willing to treat yourself the same way you would treat a friend?

What do you do when you fail? Do you mope and tell yourself what a loser you are? Would you treat someone you loved that way? When you fail, why not take yourself out to dinner at a fancy restaurant instead? Anybody can celebrate when they succeed. Why not treat yourself in a special way when you fail? That's when you need the support the most!

Some people not only fear failure, they also fear being average. Several years ago an associate and I gave a workshop in Chicago. The presentation was adequate but not one of our best. He'd been up half the night with the flu and I was in a bad mood as well. I got defensive during the question-and-answer period, and while our workshop was informative, it didn't sparkle. Several days later I told my associate how disappointed I felt. He asked why. I said I thought our presentation was below average. He said, "Remember, Dave, we can only be above average half the time. The other half the time we'll be below average. It's impossible to beat these odds, because 'average' is, by definition, the halfway point. We can look forward to being above average next time!" I felt immediate relief. How great not to have to shine all the time!

The methods described in this chapter can help you cope with your anxiety more effectively. Try not to get too perfectionistic about it. Your goal is not to achieve complete control of your feelings—this would be impossible. A certain amount of nervousness before any performance is inevitable, even for professional entertainers. When you stop fighting your anxiety and accept the idea that it is natural, you can sometimes use it as a positive force that will make your presentation more effective and exciting. This idea has been quite helpful to me.

I used to get very nervous about appearing on television. If I felt tense, I found it difficult to come across in a personable, animated way. A patient once told me how different I was in the office, where I was lively and full of spark, than on a television show she'd seen— I had seemed stiff and awkward. The problem was that I'd freeze up and feel intimidated and lose all my spontaneity. Then I'd tell myself I should relax, and that made things even worse! The harder I tried to relax, the more nervous I got!

People gave me all kinds of advice about ways to beat this problem, but their suggestions weren't terribly helpful. The worst advice was "Just be yourself." That didn't work because I *was* being myself! The "real me" simply felt tense and self-conscious the moment the cameras started rolling.

Eventually I stumbled across a solution. I decided it was okay to feel nervous, but I decided to view the nervousness differently, not as a bad thing but as a form of energy that I could use to come on strong and "sock it to 'em." After all, I have a number of controversial and powerful convictions about the causes and cures for emotional problems. Why worry about coming across in a warm, charming way on television? Why not be strong and exciting instead?

Recently I tried this on the *A.M. Philadelphia* show. They'd arranged a debate between another psychiatrist and me on the relative merits of drugs and psychotherapy in the treatment of mood problems. On the opening segment I felt he hit below the belt by implying that I was "just an author" and not a researcher. I felt angry, because I do a fair amount of research that I'm quite proud of. I decided to fight back and to present my ideas with the conviction they deserved during the next segment. Instead of being polite and courteous and meek, I felt energized and presented myself in the best possible light. I made a conscious effort to win the viewers over to my side and to cast him in a negative light. I shouldn't admit this, but that's the truth! And what's even worse—I loved every minute of the show! I got lots of positive feedback about it.

Giving up on the idea that I should relax paradoxically helped me feel more confident and relaxed. I was able to use my anxiety as a source of energy, because I wasn't fighting it. The key was the decision to believe in myself and to be forceful rather than trying to please everyone and worrying about how other people would judge me.

Therapists call this concept "reframing." You view a problem in a different light so that you think about it as something positive and good. Many people think that public speaking anxiety is "bad." They tell themselves that their nervousness makes them "abnormal" and "inferior." You can reframe your thinking about public speaking anxiety if you think of the anxiety as something good that can lead to a superior performance. View it as a source of energy, and use the anxiety to put extra zest into your performance. Believe in yourself and concentrate on what you have to say, rather than criticizing yourself for feeling nervous. Instead of fighting the anxiety, come on strong and deliver your message with conviction and charisma.

Let's review the methods described in this chapter:

1. *Daily Mood Log:* Write down the negative thoughts that made you anxious, such as: "I'm really going to blow it." Then identify the distortions in these thoughts, such as "fortune-telling" and "all-or-nothing thinking," and substitute more positive, realistic thoughts.

2. *Problem solving:* If you think your anxiety will cause problems for you (like making your mind go blank), list these problems and think of specific solutions to them (such as having a brief outline of your talk available on the podium).

3. *Script writing:* Write out difficult or critical questions that people in the audience might ask. Instead of getting frazzled or defensive, "stroke" them by saying something positive about their ideas and "disarm" them by finding some truth in what they have to say. This will make them feel good, and you'll win them over to your side.

4. *Unconditional self-esteem:* If you base your self-esteem on being a success, you'll be plagued by constant anxiety and stress, because you'll always be afraid of failure. If you have uncondi-

tional self-esteem, you can learn from your failures with a spirit of compassion and self-respect.

5. *Positive reframing:* Instead of worrying about your anxiety or thinking of it as "bad," think of it as a source of energy. Use the anxiety to put extra zest into your performance. Instead of fighting the anxiety, use the energy to come on strong and deliver your message with conviction and charisma.

16

·

How to Give a Dynamic Interview When You're Scared Stiff

It's natural to get nervous before an interview for a new job or for a school admission. It seems like you're in a spotlight and every shortcoming will be examined. You feel as if all the people you're competing with are enormously more talented and poised. You may think you'll look klutzy when they ask you embarrassing questions about your qualifications and experience.

I'd like to show you how to deal with these feelings so you can give a dynamic interview and present yourself in a positive and appealing way. In addition, I want you to have enough self-confidence to really listen during interviews, so you can ask yourself, "How impressed do I feel with the person who's interviewing me? Is this the job [or school] that will really be the best for me?"

In order to learn more about how people react to job interviews, I recently asked sixty individuals how they would be feeling and thinking if they were in the following situation: "You are interviewing for a job. You are presenting yourself in your best light. You can't tell how the prospective employer is reacting to you." Some people said they would feel annoyed with the interviewer. Typical responses were:

"It is not fair to leave you in limbo."

"This person is being very impersonal."

"Why doesn't he act more open and straightforward?"

"I don't like game-playing or power trips."

Other people imagined that the interviewer didn't like them. Typical responses were:

"He is bored."

"Did he notice my short fingernails?"

"I am making a fool of myself. I will probably never get the job."

"I'm thinking he doesn't like me and I'm wasting his time."

"He's probably interviewed other people for the job and I don't compare with them."

"I must try to hide and control the nervousness."

A third group reported more positive thoughts and feelings. These responses were characteristic:

"I'd feel calm. I'm being honest with my presentation."

"I hope this guy likes me. If he does, maybe he'll give me the job."

"I will just keep being myself. I'm happy with the way I present myself, and if it's not what the company is looking for, then the job isn't for me."

I also asked people how they would be thinking and feeling if, during a job interview, the prospective employer said: "Based on the interview and a review of your application, you're by far the most promising candidate I've seen so far."

There was still a wide variation in the way people reacted. One woman wrote that she would feel ecstatic: "Fantastic. I love it. Who should I go out and celebrate with? Maybe I'll make president of the company, maybe even the U.S.A." Most were more cautious in their enthusiasm, and some people even sounded annoyed and self-doubting, because they interpreted the interviewer's compliment as a put-down. One woman wrote: "I'll probably blow it anyway. He's just handing me a line."

The study showed that there can be a tremendous variation in the way people react to interviews and that these reactions depend on how they think about the situation. What kinds of thoughts would you have if you were being interviewed? Would you tell yourself you're doing a lousy job? Would you get defensive? Would you feel panicky and tongue-tied? When you identify the distortions in the thoughts that upset you, you can substitute more positive and realistic ones, and you will often feel better.

Although I obviously can't know precisely how you might be thinking during a stressful interview, many people tell themselves, "I shouldn't be so nervous." Do you recognize the distortion in this thought? Stop for a moment and see if you can find it in the list on page 308. Write down your ideas here:

It's a "should statement." You're telling yourself you shouldn't be so nervous. This is unrealistic, because you're telling yourself you ought to be different from the way you really are. It sounds judgmental and it will make you feel worse.

Instead, you could think about it this way: "It would be nice to feel more confident, but most people do feel nervous about job interviews. It's understandable that I would feel this way." Notice that you accept the fact that you feel nervous instead of demanding complete poise and self-confidence. This involves a shift from self-condemnation to self-acceptance. This is an important key to self-esteem.

A second negative thought you might have would be, "All the other candidates are probably so much better than I am." Can you identify the distortions in this one? Put your ideas here:

1._____

2._____

3._____

It's an example of "jumping to conclusions," since you have no real evidence that all the other candidates are more qualified than you are. In addition, you are using the "mental filter" and are "discounting the positives," because you're thinking about all your shortcomings and overlooking your strengths. Can you imagine saying something like that to a friend: "Hey, Joan, when you apply for that job, just remember that all the other candidates are so much better than you"? Since you wouldn't put someone else down, why be so hard on yourself?

A third negative thought about an interview might be, "I'll stammer and my mind will go blank. I'll look like a jerk." There are several distortions in this one. Can you identify them? One is "fortune-telling"—you're predicting negative results ahead of time. This is like self-hypnosis. If you give yourself negative messages over and over, you'll begin to believe them and they may become self-fulfilling prophecies. Can you imagine saying "You're going to blow it, you're going to blow it!" over and over to your friend before an interview? What could you tell yourself instead? Can you think of a more positive thought? Put your ideas here:

_____

_____

_____

_____

You could tell yourself that you're going to go out on many interviews and that each one will be a learning experience. You could also tell yourself that you'll get better and better at it and that eventually you will find the job you're looking for.

Now see if you can do it. First, indicate how strongly you would feel each of the following kinds of emotions during a job interview. Put a check (√) in one of the boxes to the right of each of the eight kinds of emotions.

TYPE OF NEGATIVE EMOTION	How strongly would you feel this way during an interview?			
	0–NOT AT ALL	1–SOMEWHAT	2–MODERATELY	3–A LOT
1. Nervous, worried, uptight, anxious, tense, panicky, scared, frightened				
2. Inferior, inadequate, second-rate				
3. Angry, annoyed, irritated, ticked off				
4. Frustrated				
5. Guilty, ashamed				
6. Embarrassed, foolish				
7. Sad, unhappy				
8. Hopeless, discouraged				

In the left-hand column on page 324, write down some of the Automatic Thoughts you might have during a job interview. Remember not to just record your emotions, because you've already indicated how you might feel. "I feel nervous" is not an Automatic Thought; it's a description of how you feel. Instead, put the thought that makes you feel nervous. It might be "I'll make a fool of myself." Once you've recorded your Automatic Thoughts, see if you can find the distortions in them, using the list on page 308. Record the distortions in the middle column. Finally, substitute more positive and realistic thoughts in the right-hand column.

If you have trouble with this step, ask someone you respect how they would think about the situation. It can also be helpful to ask yourself what you'd say to a close friend who was about to be interviewed. Would you put them down and tell them they were going to look like a fool? Or would you be upbeat and encouraging? Then why not talk to yourself in the same supportive way?

Automatic Thoughts	Distortions	Rational Responses

What can you expect when you change your thoughts? After you begin to think more positively, you still will feel some anxiety. That's natural—you don't have to gain perfect control over your emotions. Just try to put things into a more positive and realistic perspective so your self-doubts don't get out of hand. Your mind is like a powerful beacon. If you constantly focus that light on dangers and catastrophes, you'll feel frightened. But if you focus on a positive outcome, you'll be more likely to feel good and end up with the job you want.

The Five Principles of Dynamic Interviewing

So far, we've talked about changing your attitudes and feelings. Now let's discuss what you're going to say during the interview.

PRINCIPLE #1: BE PERSONAL AND FRIENDLY

During an interview, you'll probably feel that you're in the spotlight. You may put pressure on yourself to impress the person who is interviewing you. But since you feel so tense and awkward, this seems impossible.

Instead of trying to impress the interviewer, try to get to know him or her. There's no rule that says you have to sit back and answer questions the entire time. You can also ask questions. Express an interest in what he or she has to say. Remember—you're there to learn about the company. How long has the interviewer worked there? What type of work does he or she do? How did he or she get involved in this type of work? What does he or she like and dislike about the firm?

These questions will often lead to informal, friendly conversations that will set you more at ease. Remember that the people who interview you may also feel somewhat nervous. Most people are eager for attention, and if you express a genuine interest in them, they will feel better about you and you'll be more likely to get a job offer.

One of the greatest headaches that administrators have is the sour apple on the staff who demoralizes others with a bad attitude. If you come across in an enthusiastic and friendly way, you'll be a much more attractive candidate. In addition, when you express an interest in the person who interviews you, you'll feel less self-conscious yourself. It's far easier to get excited about someone else's accomplishments than to try to impress them with your own. When you don't try so hard, you often end up making the best possible impression.

I used to do consulting for the University of Pennsylvania Law School. Law students typically get nervous during their first and last semesters. During the first semester, they worry because of doubts about performing adequately under the intense competition from so many bright classmates. During the last semester, they feel anxious because of fears that they won't get any good job offers. Many of the senior students I treated told me they had had as many as ten or fifteen job interviews without a single offer. They felt panicky and depressed.

When I asked them to describe a typical job interview, it was always the same. They would sit down with some intimidating attorney in a pin-striped suit who would let them know there was a huge number of extraordinarily talented applicants for one opening at the firm. Then the attorney would ask the law student to describe his or her qualifications. They would lamely describe themselves as bright, loyal, hardworking, and so on, just as every other applicant did. The interviews were incredibly boring. Needless to say, job offers never materialized.

I discovered a method that dramatically changed this. I told the students that people are almost never hired on merit alone, no matter how talented they are, but also on the basis of a personal relationship. People offer jobs to people they like and whom they consider friends. I said, "Don't bother talking about your qualifications. It just sounds immature and self-centered, and it won't do you a bit of good. They already know you're bright, or you couldn't have made it through law school. They want someone they'll enjoy having in their firm, someone the other attorneys and the clients will like. If the clients like you, they will refer other clients and the firm's reputation will grow. This is as important as a doctor's bedside manner."

I told them to try to get to know the attorneys who interviewed them by asking questions such as these: what do they like and dislike about the practice of law? How did they get the assignment of interviewing new candidates? What type of law do they practice? Why? How do they reconcile the long hours of a law practice with family life?

The students seemed dubious but agreed to try. Their success shot up tremendously. One student who hadn't received a single nibble got seven job offers out of his next ten interviews! He said that what was bizarre about it was that these thirty-minute interviews often went on for an hour or more, and he almost never said anything whatsoever about himself. He just expressed a genuine, friendly interest in the men and women who were interviewing him. He said he sometimes asked if they found the interviews interesting or boring. You can imagine that it might get tiresome having to interview ten or twenty nervous law students in a day! He said they seemed overjoyed to have the chance to talk about themselves. They would talk and talk, and eventually they would say, "My goodness! We went an hour over the time limit and there are all these other students waiting. And I forgot to ask you about yourself. Oh well, we'll have plenty of time to get to that later—when you join our firm!"

PRINCIPLE #2: MAKE THEM SELL THEMSELVES TO YOU!

Don't try too hard to sell yourself during interviews. Instead, make them sell themselves to you. This can work like a charm. Suppose the person interviewing you says, "We have many outstanding candidates for this position. Why should we consider you?"

Instead of getting defensive and trying to recite a list of your best qualities—a strategy that is doomed to failure—use a little reverse psychology. You can say, "You obviously have a top firm [or university] and you deserve someone outstanding for this position. Could you tell me a little bit about the kind of person you really want? Then I'll tell you about myself so we can see whether or not I might fill the bill."

Once you learn about the kind of person the firm is looking for—someone who's honest, hardworking, creative, or whatever—it will be infinitely easier for you to portray yourself in a way that will specifically appeal to the interviewer. Then you can say, "I'd like to hear more about your company [or university]. I've heard some great things but I'd like your point of view. What are some of the potential benefits of working for this firm? What do you like about the company? What are some of the negative aspects of working here?"

Now you've challenged them to sell themselves to you! Instead of acting desperate and reciting a long and boring list of your good points, you're making it clear that you're there to evaluate them in just the same way they are learning about you. It's a two-way street, because the interviewer will have to persuade you to join his or her company. You can afford to pick and choose. When you ask about the positive *and negative* aspects of the company, you make it clear that you have self-esteem, and that you deserve a job that will be good for you. They will try harder to win you over.

Ask specific questions about the job you're interested in. Whom will you be working with? Has the morale of the group been high? What hours will you be expected to work? What are the possibilities for promotion? Why did the last person leave the position?

These questions will give you useful information and make you appear self-confident. Instead of trying to sell yourself, you become the shopper. This has an enormous impact on the balance of power. If you're even vaguely suitable for the job, your value will instantly escalate!

In life there are the pursued and the pursuers. You must choose one role or the other. This is true whether you're looking for a mate or for a job. The pursued usually get what they want, and the pursuers usually get rejected. If you give in to the urge to answer every question and try too hard to sell yourself, you will become the pursuer and you probably won't get the job. Instead, invite the interviewer in a friendly way to sell himself or herself to you, and you will be much more likely to get the job you want.

I don't mean to imply that a job interview is just a game or that you should try to get the better of the other person. However, power is an important issue that you do need to take into account. If you simply answer questions without asking any of your own, it will make you look desperate. It will appear that you don't care what kind of outfit you work for. It may also look as if you're not really interested in the person who interviews you. In contrast, when you ask questions and express an interest in the company, you will project intelligence and self-respect. You'll be far more likely to get the job.

PRINCIPLE #3: BE HONEST—BUT PRESENT YOURSELF IN A POSITIVE LIGHT

Let's assume there's something that makes you a less desirable candidate. Maybe you're inexperienced, you've never worked before, or you didn't get along with your last boss. When you're applying for a new job, you may be asked about these problems. Perhaps you took a year off from school because you were depressed and flunking three subjects. The interviewer may say, "I see you have a year that's not accounted for on your resume. Can you explain this to me?" How can you, without sounding like a liability?

It's simple. Just say that you took a year off to think about your goals in life. Emphasize that it was a valuable experience that made you more aware of your priorities. This is an honest and positive statement. Most interviewers would respect you more for it.

Let's suppose that you're a 34-year-old woman and you're looking for a job for the first time in your life. The man who interviews you says, "I notice that you don't have any previous work experiences listed on your resume." How can you respond without seeming totally inept?

Put your ideas here:_____

_____

_____

_____

_____

You could say, "As a matter of fact, this is the first job I've applied for. I've raised three happy kids and I've completed college in my spare time. I can't offer you a lot of professional experience, but I can offer a lot of human experience along with plenty of persistence and enthusiasm. Can you tell me more about what the job involves so I can see if I could make a contribution to your firm?"

This response is honest and upbeat. I would be impressed if I were interviewing you. Notice that you're asking the interviewer to do some of the talking. This will give you a better idea of what he or she is looking for. If you do have the skills for the job, then point this out. If you don't, just be frank and ask them to keep you in mind for a more suitable opening later on.

PRINCIPLE #4: DON'T GET DEFENSIVE ABOUT YOUR SHORTCOMINGS

Many people are afraid of being asked about something really embarrassing. To take an extreme example, suppose the interviewer says: "I notice that you were asked to leave your position with the XYZ

Corporation because of insubordination. Is it true that you were fired because of a personality conflict with your supervisor?" Let's assume this did happen. It's probably about the worst thing you could hear! How would you respond? Put your ideas here:

_____

_____

_____

_____

Many people would get tense and defensive, but this will make you look bad. You could blame your old boss or deny the accusation, but then your chances of being hired are nil. The interviewer won't believe you. Do you have any winning options? Yes! Disarm the interviewer. Agree, don't argue.

You could say: "As a matter of fact, I think that's pretty accurate. I was inexperienced and I was too dogmatic and inflexible. My supervisor was difficult for many staff members to get along with, but I made the mistake of being too argumentative and I foolishly locked horns with him instead of trying to understand his point of view. I could have handled the situation much better than I did. I learned a lot from the experience. I learned that I can't always expect people to be tactful, reasonable, and pleasant. I think I've gotten a little more tolerant and flexible because of that experience."

The advantage of this response is that you display yourself as a reasonable and open-minded person. There's no way you can erase what happened. If you insist that it was unfair and argue that it was all your supervisor's fault, you'll simply confirm that you're still hard to get along with. You'll be arguing with the person who's interviewing you, just as you argued with your former boss! I guarantee that someone else will get the job. But if you assume responsibility for the problem and genuinely agree that you screwed up, the interviewer might just admire your courage and decide that you're the kind of person they want on their team! (See page 376 for more about "disarming.")

PRINCIPLE #5: WHEN YOU DON'T KNOW WHAT TO SAY, PARAPHRASE THE QUESTION OR PUNT

Some people get rattled during interviews. Their minds go blank and they can't think of anything to say. There's a simple solution to this: Paraphrase the question before you attempt to answer it. Let's say the interviewer asks you, "What are your strengths and weaknesses?" Before you try to answer the question, repeat it like this: "Let's see. You'd like me to tell you about my strong points and weak points? Is that right?"

"Yes."

"I'd be glad to do that."

When you paraphrase a question, you get a few moments to gather your thoughts, and it becomes easier to respond in a meaningful way.

You can also use the "punting" technique, described on page 434, when people try to put you on the spot to gain an advantage in a negotiation. A patient of mine was visiting a law firm in New York to see if he might be interested in working for them. Jerry already had a good position with a firm in Philadelphia, and he hadn't clearly decided that he wanted to move to New York. He was just exploring the possibilities and wanted to learn more about the firm.

The man who interviewed Jerry seemed impressed and invited an associate to join the interview. He told Jerry that he would work with this woman if he joined the firm. She began to ask Jerry pointed questions. She asked how much salary he was asking for and why he thought his skills were good enough to merit a position in their firm. She pointed out that their work was of a highly technical nature and said she was skeptical that Jerry had enough experience and expertise.

Jerry was on the spot. He felt defensive and was squirming with anxiety. In reality, he really didn't have all the technical expertise she required and he hadn't even thought about his salary requirements. He mumbled something about not wanting to take any less than he was getting at his current job in Philadelphia and tried to present his skills in the best possible light. This came across rather lamely. He felt annoyed with the woman and sensed, quite rightly, that the man who had interviewed him was quickly losing interest. Needless to say, Jerry was never asked back for a second interview.

What should Jerry have said instead? How could he have handled the situation differently? This woman wanted to know his salary requirements and precisely how he would fit into their firm, but Jerry hadn't even thought about these issues. If you were Jerry, what would you have said?

_____

_____

_____

_____

_____

He could say, "I haven't really thought about my salary requirements yet. I think that discussion might be premature, because I don't even know how I might fit into your firm. Today I'd like to learn more about what you're doing and to tell you a little about my work. Then if it seems useful, we can meet again to explore the specifics of working together. I wouldn't dream of talking about my salary requirements unless I was convinced I had a real contribution to make. I hope I will, but I don't think either of us knows that yet."

The key technique is "punting." He simply drops back and punts. Jerry isn't obligated to answer all her questions. She has the perfect right to ask him anything she wants, but there's no rule that says he has to answer. The fact is, he doesn't know how much money he wants, and he doesn't even know if he should work for this firm. He can simply say this in a polite way. He will avoid letting her run the show and he won't end up in a fourth-down position.

There's a second benefit to punting: Jerry will reveal himself to be a skillful negotiator. If he doesn't pursue them, then they will have to pursue him. They will have to convince him that he should join their firm. Their interest in him will instantly and dramatically increase.

Script Writing

So far I've given you some insights about successful job interview strategies. You can probably see that some of these ideas have merit and might help you. However, you will need to be able to do it when you're actually having a job or school interview. This is where the "script-writing" method can be helpful. Think of several questions you might be asked during an interview. Imagine one or two routine questions ("What are your qualifications?") along with one or two of the most anxiety-provoking questions you can imagine ("Is it true that you were arrested for assault at your last job?"). Write down several interview questions here:

1._____

_____

2._____

_____

3._____

_____

Have you written the questions down yet? It's very important for you to do this instead of just reading this chapter. If you want to sharpen up your interview skills, these written exercises will be invaluable. We'll come back to the questions shortly.

I recently treated an executive named Tim, who had moved to the United States from Australia to head up a candy company that a friend of his had purchased. After several months it began to dawn on Tim that their product simply wasn't going to be competitive in the American market. The candy was good, but the product didn't have eye appeal. It was packaged in a rather ordinary wrapper that didn't grab the eye. In addition, they were underfinanced and didn't have the millions of dollars they would need to advertise the candy nationally and get it placed on the shelves of grocery stores and drugstores.

After a year and a half of frustrating attempts to boost distribution, the company lost $500,000 and Tim was stuck with a warehouse filled with stale candy. It was clear that he had to start looking for a new job, but he felt depressed and thought of himself as a "loser." He was convinced that his career was over and felt he could never get another decent job. He was in a panic about job interviews because he was afraid he'd be asked about his depression and grilled about why the candy venture had failed.

I asked Tim to list the most intimidating and personally embarrassing questions he could imagine being asked during an interview. Here's the first one he wrote down: "I notice that the candy company lost half a million dollars soon after you took over as president. Is this true? And if so, why should we want you to assume the leadership of our company?" How would you handle this question? Put your response here:

_____

_____

_____

_____

Here's what Tim and I came up with: "It's true that we did lose half a million dollars due to several crucial marketing errors. We were vastly undercapitalized and didn't have a sufficient advertising budget. We also overestimated the American demand for a product that was quite popular in Australia." Notice that this honestly acknowledges the mistakes that were made, but without a sense of shame or humiliation. Business errors of this type are not unusual.

I asked Tim to write the script of a tough interview and helped him edit his responses to the questions. Keep in mind that these are imaginary questions, not ones that would be asked during an actual interview. They represent Tim's worst fears. Learning how to handle these gave Tim a great boost in self-confidence, because he realized that any real interview would be far easier by comparison. It went like this:

INTERVIEWER: Why should we want you? How can we know you won't make the same mistakes with us?

TIM: It depends on how valuable you think a degree in the school of hard knocks is. If you look at my work record during the past twenty years, you'll see many successes along with this failure. I've learned a lot from my successes and a lot from my mistakes. I think I have more to offer because of it.

INTERVIEWER: But I understand that you went into a severe depression and you even had to go to a psychiatrist. Is this true?

TIM: Yes. At first I blamed myself entirely for the failure of the company, and life looked pretty bleak. Now I can see that I made a valiant effort in a tremendously difficult situation, and I feel proud of that, even though the results were disappointing.

INTERVIEWER: How could we be sure you wouldn't get depressed again if you were working for us? Isn't depression a sign of a weak character? We want a strong leader as the head of our group.

TIM: I think almost anyone would feel discouraged by a business reversal, especially when they had worked as hard as I had. I don't think that means I have a "weak character," but simply that I'm human and that I care a great deal about the work I do. Can you tell me a little more about your company and your needs so I can see if I can be of help to you?

We practiced role-playing so Tim could learn to field these insulting questions. He enjoyed the exercise and listened to the tape of the session several times. He said it was a relief to discover that he could even turn hostile questions to his advantage. Then he went out on several job interviews, which went smoothly. He was offered the presidency of two of the three companies that interviewed him, and he was the second choice at the third company. Not bad for a "loser"!

Now it's your turn. You have written down several difficult or embarrassing questions that you might be asked during an interview. Select one of those questions and think about how you might answer it. Keep in mind the six principles of effective interviewing:

- Be personal and friendly.
- Express an interest in the person who interviews you.
- Don't try too hard to impress the interviewer; make the interviewer sell him- or herself to you.
- Be honest, but present yourself in a positive light.
- Don't get defensive about your shortcomings.
- If the question is confusing and you don't know how to answer it, repeat the question and ask for a clarification, or punt.

Write your response to the question here:_____

_____

_____

_____

_____

If you have trouble coming up with a good response, think about it for a day or two, or ask a friend for suggestions. Sometimes you will need several days before an effective answer will suddenly pop into your mind. Practice is the key. After you've worked at this for a while, you'll get the knack of it. It's well worth the time and effort. Once you see that you can handle any question that's thrown your way, you feel more self-confident in an actual interview.

Turning Failure Into Success

When you go out on interviews, some people will like you and some people won't. Sometimes you'll do well, and sometimes you won't. You can turn your failures into successes if you keep several ideas in mind.

Don't put all your eggs in one basket. You may need to go out on many interviews before you find the right job. Pinning all your hopes on one job is foolish. You'll pressure yourself too much, and it will feel like a catastrophe if you don't get the job.

Your "batting average" in a competitive job market may be only one offer in every ten interviews. That means you'll have to endure an average of nine rejections for every offer you get. But every rejection will take you one step closer to your goal. The more rejections you get, the quicker you'll find a job. In fact, you need all the rejections you can possibly get!

Don't base your self-esteem on how well you do. Job interviewing, like golf or cooking, is a skill you can develop—you can get better and better at it over a period of time. Your success at it has nothing to do with what kind of a person you are. People who do well on interviews are often poised and skillful, but they're not more worthwhile human beings.

Don't blame yourself for a rejection. You may be tempted to tell yourself that you're no good, and you may feel as if you'll never get a job. Instead of putting yourself down like this, try to learn from the situation. What are the specific reasons you didn't get the job? Sometimes the person who interviewed you will give you some feedback if you ask in a friendly way. Maybe you were inexperienced; maybe you had good qualifications but they had to pick from many qualified people; maybe you didn't interview well; maybe your skills didn't match their needs; maybe it was politics and the daughter of the company president got the job. If you can find out why you didn't get the job, it usually takes the sting out of it because you won't feel so worthless and defeated. If there's a specific reason, make a plan for what to do next instead of giving up.

Don't blame someone else for a rejection. Instead of blaming themselves, many people go to the opposite extreme. They insist that life is unfair and blame the world. Cynthia lost a public relations job at a New York hospital because she was inexperienced and somewhat disorganized. After she interviewed unsuccessfully for a new position with another hospital, she discovered she had been the second choice among the candidates. Cynthia was furious because she had her heart set on this job. She told me they hadn't given her a fair shake and insisted they didn't understand her full potential. When she later learned that the man they hired had ten years of successful experience in public relations, she understood that being the second choice was a compliment and a basis for optimism. She persisted in her job search and ultimately landed an equally desirable position.

Think about rejections as opportunities. When someone turns you down, don't get defensive or annoyed. Instead, thank them for their time and ask them to keep you in mind if something more suitable comes up in the future. Most successful people have learned that rejections will often turn into successes later on. It's not wise to burn bridges or to view rejections as "the end." Often a rejection is just the first awkward step in what later turns into a productive, successful relationship.

Remember that an offer you don't really want is worth its weight in gold. This is the "Burns Rule": People only want what they can't get, and they never want what they can get. What it boils down to is this:

trying to get the first offer can be tough. Since you're what people can get, you're not in demand. But once you get an offer, even if it's not the one you want, you can easily get many more offers. Since you're what people can't get, you're in demand. Everyone will want you.

Let me give an example of how this works. A divorced woman with two children applied for admission to graduate school in psychology. Her options were limited to programs in Chicago, where she lived, because she didn't want her kids to have to change schools. She had her heart set on a highly competitive program at the University of Chicago, but knew her chances for admission were only marginal because of the large number of applicants. After her interview, she was informed that she had not been selected for the program, but she would be placed on a waiting list of alternate candidates.

Six weeks later another school, in a less desirable area and with only an average reputation, called to tell her that she'd been admitted but without financial assistance. She was told that she had to decide within two hours.

Her heart sank, because she still had the dream of attending the University of Chicago. She called me in a panic. She was distraught and wanted to know what to do.

I explained that this was her golden opportunity, and suggested that all she had to do was to call the University of Chicago and tell them that she was under pressure to accept an offer that very day from another school, so that if they were interested in her they'd have to move quickly.

She was skeptical that this would do any good, but she called the admissions office and explained the situation to the secretary of one of the professors on the admissions committee. Within ten minutes the professor called back to inform her that they were extremely interested in her and if she would consider attending the University of Chicago, they would offer her free tuition plus a stipend of $8,000 per year for living expenses. She immediately accepted and ultimately received her doctorate there.

Why was she suddenly accepted when she'd been ignored? Because she was in demand. They probably thought that if someone else was pressuring her to accept an offer, she was an incredibly desirable candidate. This made them want her as well. It's basic human nature to want something that's a little beyond our grasp, and this is true in school or job interviews.

If you want to take advantage of the Burns Rule, you should court every suitor when you're applying for a position. Once you get an offer, even if it's an unappealing one, you're over the biggest hurdle because you're in demand. Leak this information to the people you're interested in. Let other interviewers know that you've had an offer, but that you like them very much and would be proud to consider their offer as well. If you do this in a friendly manner, I think you'll be pleasantly surprised to discover that you will suddenly get many offers.

You may object to this strategy, thinking it amounts to manipulation. In a way, you're right. I felt a little guilty when writing this section. I was concerned that I might come off as exploitative or insensitive. If I offended you, I apologize. However, I felt that this information was necessary, because the people who conduct interviews wield great power. They've got what you want, and they are intentionally playing you off against many other candidates so they can get the best possible person to work for them or to attend their university. You need a little power too, to balance the situation. I want you to get the best possible offer so you'll feel happy and excited about the opportunity just ahead of you. Then you'll do the best job you're capable of, and everyone will win.

17

•

Test and Performance Anxiety

Our culture places a heavy emphasis on competition and success. While it's healthy to want to do good work, many people believe that success is the only key to happiness and self-esteem. They believe that to be loved and respected by others, they must be outstanding in every respect. This attitude can create a crippling pressure to achieve called "performance anxiety."

You may get performance anxiety when you are studying or taking a test. This is called "test anxiety." You may get performance anxiety when you have to write a paper or a report—this is called "writer's block." You may get performance anxiety when you have to give a talk, take an oral examination, act in a play, or even just introduce yourself to a group of people.

Performance anxiety has two causes. One of them is obvious, and the other is hidden. Fear of failure is the obvious cause. And why is this failure not okay? Because you feel you will be humiliated and ostracized if you don't succeed. Your sense of self-esteem gets tied up with your achievements, and you feel convinced that others would love and respect you less if you fell short of their expectations of you.

The second, more hidden cause of performance anxiety may be that the goals you have chosen are not really the ones you want. Your anxiety may be your body's way of letting you know that you're trying to push a round peg into a square hole. You may be forcing yourself in a direction in your career or in your studies that really isn't right for you.

A troubled first-year law student recently sought treatment because of anxiety attacks in classes. Fred said he was terrified about being called on to answer questions in front of the other students. He confessed, "When the professor calls on me, I'll probably goof up." This fear is especially common among first-year law students because the professors ask intimidating questions to lead the students into contradictions and to make them unsure of themselves. This is intended to toughen the students and prepare them for the competitive rigors of a legal career, but many of them feel traumatized by the experience. I explored what Fred was really afraid of:

DAVID: Suppose you did goof up in class. Why would that be upsetting? What would that mean to you?

FRED: Well, then I'd make a fool of myself.

DAVID: Suppose you did make a fool of yourself? Why would that be upsetting to you?

FRED: Because then everyone would look down on me.

DAVID: Suppose people did look down on you, what then?

FRED: I'd feel miserable.

DAVID: Why is that? Why would you feel miserable if people were looking down on you?

FRED: Well, that would mean I wasn't a worthwhile person. It might ruin my career. I'd get bad grades, I'd flunk out, and I might never become an attorney.

DAVID: And what then? What would that mean to you?

FRED: That would mean I had failed at something I've wanted all my life.

DAVID: And then?

FRED: Life would be empty. It would mean I was a failure. It would mean I was worthless.

This brief dialogue reveals the perfectionism and fear of disapproval at the root of Fred's difficulties. He believes it would be terrible to make a mistake or to fail at achieving a personal goal. He has convinced himself that if one person looks down on him, then everybody will. It is as if the word "Reject" will be stamped on his forehead for everyone to see.

Fred's feelings of self-esteem seem to be contingent upon approval or success. He believes that his achievements have to be outstanding or else they will be no good at all. If his cravings for perfection, approval, and success are not satisfied, Fred senses that he will be an unloved nothing, because he has no true support from within. Because he feels he must be totally competent and confident, he cannot accept his own humanity or cope with the insecurities he feels as a struggling law student.

There may be another reason that Fred feels blocked and tense about his performance in law school. He may not be sure that he really wants to be there in the first place. He may be slaving away dutifully so he can make his parents proud and impress his friends. But inside he may never have asked himself, "Is a high-powered legal career what I really want? Is this *my* vision for my life, or someone else's?"

The following techniques are designed to help you confront and conquer the fears that cripple you so that you can pursue your own goals in life with greater passion and self-confidence.

CONFRONT YOUR FEARS

Some people deal with performance anxiety through avoidance. You may habitually procrastinate and put your work off to the last minute. This allows you to protect yourself from the anxiety for as long as possible. In addition, you may reason that if you don't really hustle and do your best, you won't feel like a complete failure if you do a bad job. You can tell yourself, "I didn't really try, but if I had tried, I'd be the greatest."

People with performance anxiety may procrastinate for another reason. They have the misconception that they can't concentrate or perform effectively when they feel nervous. If you believe you can't function, you will probably give up and stop functioning. Then you'll conclude that you were right: you'll think you really couldn't function. But this is just a self-fulfilling prophecy.

A college student named Henry didn't take his chemistry final because he was convinced that he'd panic and get a bad grade on the test. He was a conscientious student and had never skipped an exam before. He reasoned that only a very disturbed person would be "unable" to complete a course. Consequently he dropped out of school. Letting his anxiety get the better of him in this way was entirely unnecessary. Henry had no real evidence that he wouldn't do a good job on the chemistry final—he simply gave up because he assumed he couldn't perform well.

If you refuse to give up in spite of your doubts and fears, you will usually discover that you can perform far better than you thought. Anxiety is uncomfortable, but it need not prevent you from doing practically anything you choose to do. No matter how nervous you feel, you can write papers, study, take exams, or compete athletically. Your anxiety will try to fool you by making you believe you can't function properly. But when you call the bluff on your fears, you will discover that your "inability" to function is just an illusion, a bogey monster full of hot air.

Penny was referred to me three days before her first final exam of the first semester in law school. She said she was so panicky that she simply couldn't study. She explained that her mind raced uncontrollably and she couldn't understand a single sentence in any of her books. She was convinced she was going to flunk out and wanted me to write a letter to the dean so she could drop out of school with a medical leave of absence.

I told Penny I'd write any letter she wanted, but that I didn't believe she really did need to drop out of school. I explained that the biggest mistake she could make was to stop studying, and that if she just kept studying in spite of how she felt, she would probably do reasonably well on her exams. I told her that anxiety creates the myth that you cannot function properly, but if you refuse to give in, you'll discover that you can function even though it seems you can't.

Penny protested: "But I can't understand what I'm reading when I try to study." I told her just to move her eyes across the page, whether or not it seemed as if she was understanding anything. I said it was crucial to go through the motions and study all day long, even though she felt she wasn't getting anywhere. I emphasized that the only error she could make would be to stop studying.

Penny told me that she would get so nervous when she took the test that she might not even be able to understand the questions. I told her it wasn't at all important to feel that she understood the questions. What was important was for her to agree to keep moving her pencil across the page during the entire two hours of the exam, no matter what she wrote down. I told her she was not allowed to give up or to waste any time thinking or questioning herself.

She protested: "But what if I can't think of anything meaningful to put down?"

"Then put down *anything*. It doesn't have to seem meaningful."

"But what if I can't think of even one sentence?"

"Then just string some unconnected words together and put a period at the end. You may not think it makes sense, but you must keep moving the pencil!"

"But what if I can't think of even a single word to put down?"

"Then just write gibberish. You must agree not to give up or to stop."

Penny reluctantly agreed. She said she was annoyed and insisted that I didn't understand how confused and anxious she felt. She said she was certain she'd flunk and then I'd have to write a letter to the dean for her. I agreed.

When I saw Penny a week later, she was furious. She explained that she'd followed my advice and it hadn't worked. She studied night and day for three days before the test but only got more and more confused, just as she had told me she would. She said that when she got the test she was unable to comprehend even one question on it. She just wrote gibberish in the answer book, the way I told her to. She said she flunked the test and felt enraged and humiliated. She insisted that I call the dean to arrange a leave of absence.

I asked Penny what grade she got. Her face turned red and she said that she hadn't gotten the examination back yet, but she knew she had flunked! I suggested we wait another week and assured her I would write a letter to the dean if she still wanted me to, once she got her grade on the exam.

At our next session Penny was still annoyed with me. I was curious about how she'd done on the test. Peevishly she admitted that she'd received an A. Apparently there was a note on the front of her answer book that said that her essay was the best in the class.

I asked Penny how she reconciled this with her belief that she couldn't study or perform adequately on tests when she was anxious. She replied, "It's obvious that I flunked the exam. They simply must have confused my examination booklet with someone else's!" I asked Penny if I could help straighten this out, and even offered to call the professor to explain that there may have been a mixup and that they had gotten her booklet confused with some other, brighter student's.

She changed the subject and didn't take me up on the offer. I sure would hate to face her in court someday! She doesn't back down very easily!

Penny's story reveals how your anxiety can fool you and make you feel convinced that you can't function when you really can. It illustrates how vitally important it is not to give up when you feel anxious. Suppose that, like Penny, you're trying to study for an important exam and the pressures are intense. Every time you open the book you panic. Your mind races and it seems as if you can't concentrate on what you're reading. You may tell yourself, "I can't think straight! What's wrong with me? I can't understand a single sentence!"

One way to deal with this is to test the validity of what you're telling yourself. Is it really true that you can't think straight? Read one sentence and then see if you can write a brief summary of what it says. You'll discover that you actually did understand it, even though you thought you didn't.

You may argue, "Well, maybe I could read that one sentence, but I could never understand an entire paragraph." If so, repeat the experiment. Read a paragraph twice and then summarize what it said. Once again, you'll discover that you did understand it reasonably well.

If you're struggling to write a report, you may feel that you're too nervous to write one decent sentence. If so, find out if this is true. Force out a sentence, no matter how inept it seems. Once you get it down on paper, you'll discover that it wasn't as bad as you thought. With a little editing you can make it even better. Then you can add several more sentences, and pretty soon you'll have a decent paragraph.

THE COMPARTMENTATION TECHNIQUE

We can learn a great deal about how to cope with performance anxiety by investigating the strategies used by successful athletes. In a study of weight lifters, Drs. Michael J. Mahoney and Marshall Avener, of Penn State University, investigated the impact of anxiety on performance during the final trials for the U.S. Olympic team.* Who

*M. J. Mahoney and M. Avener, "Psychology of the Elite Athlete: An Exploratory Study," *Cognitive Therapy and Research* 1, no. 2 (1977): 135–141.

do you think experienced more anxiety before the competition— the athletes who went on to win, or the athletes who ended up losing?

Drs. Mahoney and Avener discovered that both groups of athletes experienced similar amounts of anxiety. What distinguished the winners from the losers was how they coped with it. The less successful athletes tended to pay a great deal of attention to their fears. They aroused themselves into near-panic states with exaggerated self-doubts and fantasies of impending tragedy. In contrast, the athletes who won were more likely to ignore their anxiety. They reported that they just proceeded as if it weren't there. They were aware of their nervousness, but they concentrated on what they had to do. They gave themselves helpful mental instructions, like "Now I will take a deep breath. Now I will reach up and grip the bar," and so on. Because they assumed their anxiety was nothing more than a nuisance, it didn't get in the way. They were aware of the anxiety but they didn't dwell on it.

I call this technique "compartmentation," because you put your anxiety in a mental compartment—a box—and you ignore it. Instead, you focus on what you have to do. This is a powerful way to deal with performance anxiety. To learn this technique, establish a goal you would like to accomplish. You might have to prepare for an important exam, write a paper, or act in a play. Next, break the task down into a series of small steps and proceed with the task, one step at a time. If at any point your anxiety causes a problem for you, simply develop a strategy to solve the problem. If you persist and refuse to give in to your anxiety, you'll discover that you can always perform effectively, no matter how anxious you feel. There's a double payoff: you'll perform more effectively, and your anxiety will lose its grip.

Ann is a freshman in college. She told me she got so anxious that she could never take written exams. I asked her to imagine she had just been handed a test and to describe how she felt. She said she would feel so panicky that her vision would get blurred and she couldn't even read the questions properly. I asked her how she could cope with this problem. It occurred to her that she could focus her eyes on the first word of the first question. When her eyes were clearly in focus she could read this question, one word at a time. This made it clear that her anxiety could not prevent her from reading.

Then she asked, "But suppose I don't understand the question? When I'm anxious my mind starts racing and I get totally confused. I won't even know what the point of the question is." I asked Ann to think about how she might solve this problem. She decided that she could paraphrase the question in her own words immediately after reading it. For example, if the question read "Who was the first president of the United States?" she would say this to herself: "Let's see, this question is about the first president of the United States. That must be George Washington." She could see that this process of paraphrasing each question would help her understand it. This gave her a little more relief.

The next problem Ann anticipated was that she might feel insecure if she didn't know the answer to the first question on the test. Then she'd panic. I asked her how she could cope with this problem. She thought about it and decided that she could find an easy question to answer first. Then she'd be off to a good start.

Let's review the basics of this compartmentation technique: You put your anxiety in a mental box and ignore it. If you're afraid that your anxiety will prevent you from performing adequately, ask yourself specifically how your anxiety could hurt your performance. Then you develop a method for coping with this problem. Concentrate on the task at hand. This will show you that your anxiety might make you uncomfortable or slow you down a bit, but it will not prevent you from achieving your goal.

Imagine that you have to write a report for your boss. You've been procrastinating for two weeks because you feel so anxious, and the deadline is approaching. In the left-hand column of the chart on page 348 I've listed the specific problems that are holding you back. In the right-hand column, write down how you would solve each problem. Then you can compare your solutions to the ones at the end of the chapter.

When you list the problems that make it hard for you to function, you'll see that there are ways to work around them. Once you get started, your anxiety will usually diminish. This technique is based on the philosophy that you can conquer your fears if you confront them instead of avoiding them. Suppose you have to study for a difficult test. You'll want to put it off because you feel so nervous. If you give in, you'll feel better temporarily because you'll tell yourself, "Whew! What a relief! I can put that out of my mind for a while." You'll feel a momentary mood lift, but in the long run you'll feel

Problems	Solutions
1. I'll get so nervous, I'll feel that I can't even sit down at my desk and write a single word.	1. _____ _____ _____
2. I'll feel so worried and confused that I won't know how to get started on the report.	2. _____ _____ _____
3. I'll tell myself I have to write a really fantastic first sentence. Then I won't be able to think of anything especially brilliant to say.	3. _____ _____ _____
4. I'll feel overwhelmed, thinking about what an enormous task it is.	4. _____ _____ _____
5. I'll tell myself that I'm not in the mood to get started. Then I'll get up and wander around.	5. _____ _____ _____

even more insecure and anxious. If you confront your fears instead, you'll usually discover that the task wasn't nearly as impossible as you thought it was going to be. You'll be on the road to greater self-confidence and productivity.

WORRY BREAKS

You may find that you get distracted by daydreams when you're anxious and trying to study. You may stare into space, fantasizing about being on a Caribbean island, or you may imagine going to pick up your examination after it's been graded and seeing a large red F on it. The harder you try to study, the more powerful and distracting these fantasies become. Pretty soon all the time is gone and you haven't gotten anything done.

Sometimes it helps to schedule "worry breaks" every few minutes. During these breaks, take one full minute to daydream or to fret and catastrophize about how terrible things are. Time it on your watch. Give full vent to your insecurities without trying to fight them. At the end of the minute go back to work again, and concentrate for two or three minutes until your next "worry break." After a while, the distracting thoughts and fantasies will begin to lose their power over you. Then you can sustain your concentration for longer and longer periods of time.

It's probably not good to try to study more than ten or fifteen minutes at a time without at least one "worry break." Your mind is like a finely tuned automobile engine. It just isn't built to run at full speed endlessly. If you try to do too much at once, you'll burn out.

During these "worry breaks," you might find it helpful to dictate your thoughts about how terrible everything is into a tape recorder for one minute. You can say: "I'm such a slow learner. I'm so far behind. Just think of everything else I have to do. I'm not getting anywhere. It's hopeless. Everyone else is so much smarter," and so on. Then play it back and listen to yourself. Although these thoughts might be upsetting at first, after a while they'll lose their power because they'll begin to sound ridiculous and boring.

THE DAILY MOOD LOG

The Daily Mood Log, described in Chapter 5, can help you combat performance anxiety. First, describe the "Upsetting Event," the situation that's making you feel nervous, as illustrated on page 352. Next, write down your negative emotions and rate each one on a scale from 0 to 100. You may feel frightened, anxious, irritable, worried, nervous, pressured, or tense.

In the "Automatic Thoughts" column, write down the negative thoughts that make you feel upset. Try to tune in to the messages you're giving yourself. What are you telling yourself? You may feel petrified because you're thinking: "I'm probably not studying hard enough. There's so much I don't know! Think of everything else I should be doing. I don't understand this very well. I just can't concentrate. What if I flunk?" These thoughts make you feel overwhelmed and disorganized. You may get up and wander about the house or eat compulsively.

After you write down these negative thoughts, identify the distortions in each of them, using the list on page 308. Finally, substitute more realistic thoughts that "call the bluff" on your anxiety in the "Rational Response" column.

Joan is a psychologist who was having a great deal of trouble studying for her certification examination. As you study the "Automatic Thoughts" in her log on page 352, you will see that she was giving herself a number of negative messages that were extremely self-defeating. Each time she opened a book, Joan would berate herself for not having started sooner. Instead of focusing on what she was learning at a particular moment, she would obsess about all the other material she hadn't studied yet. Instead of assuming that her hard work and preparation would pay off, she would tell herself that the material she was studying probably wouldn't even be on the test.

It's little wonder that Joan felt frustrated and overwhelmed! Once she wrote down her negative thoughts, she could see how hard she was being on herself. However, she was convinced that her negative thoughts were absolutely valid. For example, the second negative thought is "I may not pass the exam." She agreed that this was an example of "fortune-telling," since she was predicting a catastrophe, but she couldn't see that there was anything illogical or unrealistic about it. She believed she really might flunk the exam and told me she didn't want to be involved in any ridiculous "power of positive thinking" program.

I suggested we examine the evidence for her claim that she would probably flunk the exam. Joan admitted that out of the hundreds of exams she'd taken in her life, she'd flunked only one test—a health quiz in high school that she hadn't studied for. Based on her track record, it seemed more realistic to assume that if she studied consistently she could probably do well on the exam.

COST-BENEFIT ANALYSIS

Sometimes a logical demonstration that your fears are groundless will not be convincing. Joan was still hesitant to give up her pessimistic predictions. She explained that if she became too confident and stopped worrying, she might get too complacent to study. Then she really *would* blow the exam! She assumed that her constant worrying and fretting was the price she had to pay for success.

This belief that your worry will somehow help you and protect you from danger is extremely common. It's as if God expects us to suffer and we'll be punished if we become too happy or confident! You may also feel that optimism is foolish and think that it's safer and wiser to assume the worst. If so, do a Cost-Benefit Analysis: make a list of the advantages and disadvantages of feeling anxious and worrying about failure. Ask yourself how all the worrying will help you and how it will hurt you. Then make a second list of the advantages and disadvantages of feeling confident and thinking about your work in an optimistic way. Ask yourself how a positive attitude will help you and how it will hurt you. Finally, weigh the advantages against the disadvantages of each option. This may make it clear just how self-defeating your anxiety and worry can be.

Joan listed these three advantages of worrying: "(1) I'll be thinking about my examination constantly, so I won't get overly complacent. (2) People will see how important it is for me to do well, so they'll be more forgiving if I fail. (3) If I worry about failure, I may try harder and do a better job."

Joan listed only one disadvantage: "I'm crippling myself with all this worry and self-doubt." However, this one disadvantage of worrying far outweighed the three advantages in her mind. This insight made Joan more motivated to talk back to her negative thoughts, and the Rational Responses helped her feel more relaxed. She agreed to write down and answer her negative thoughts every night when she was studying at home during the next week. This helped her feel more confident, and she was able to study much more effectively. Ultimately she did quite well on the exam.

I'm not claiming that things will always turn out well simply because you believe they will. That would be just as superstitious as telling yourself that obsessive worrying will protect you from danger.

THE DAILY MOOD LOG*

STEP ONE: DESCRIBE THE UPSETTING EVENT
<u>Sitting down trying to study.</u>

STEP TWO: RECORD YOUR NEGATIVE FEELINGS—and rate each one from 0 (the least) to 100 (the most). Use words like sad, anxious, angry, guilty, lonely, hopeless, frustrated, etc.

Emotion	Rating	Emotion	Rating	Emotion	Rating
1. Anxious	99	3. Angry	75	5. Hopeless	65
2. Frustrated	90	4. Disgusted with myself	80	6.	

STEP THREE: THE TRIPLE-COLUMN TECHNIQUE—

Automatic Thoughts	Distortions	Rational Responses
Write your negative thoughts and estimate your belief in each one (0–100).	Identify the distortions in each Automatic Thought.	Substitute more realistic thoughts and estimate your belief in each one (0 and 100).
1. Just think of all the time I've been wasting! (100%) 25%	Mental filter; discounting the positive	1. I did a little studying yesterday, and I'm going to learn something right now. (100%)
2. I may not pass the exam. (100%) 25%	Fortune-telling	2. The exam has four sections. It's unlikely I'll flunk them all. If I look at the situation realistically, the worst that could happen would be that I'd flunk one section and have to

(Continue on next page)

Automatic Thoughts	Distortions	Rational Responses
		make it up. Since I've passed nearly all the exams I've ever taken, there's a good chance that I'll pass this one. (90%)
3. But I can't remember anything three days after I study it. ~~(100%)~~ 0%	All-or-nothing thinking	3. I can remember some things. I can also take notes and review them later. (100%)
4. There's too much material to cover. ~~(100%)~~ 0%	All-or-nothing thinking; "should statement"	4. There *is* a lot of material and nobody can remember all of it. I can focus on the most important ideas and learn as much as possible in the time I have. (100%)
5. I'm going to study the wrong things—they won't appear on the test. ~~(100%)~~ 0%	Fortune-telling	5. Some of the things I'm studying probably will be on the test. Some things won't be on the test, but this happens to everybody.
6. They're just going to ask a lot of trivial questions. What right do they	Fortune-telling; "should statement"	6. I have no evidence that all the questions will be irrelevant or trivial. It would be

(Continue on next page)

Automatic Thoughts	Distortions	Rational Responses
have? They're supposed to be educators! ~~(100%)~~ 0%		unfortunate if the test wasn't a good one, but it wouldn't be a catastrophe, because everyone has to take the same test. (100%)
7. I never do enough. I should be doing more! (100%) 25%	"Should statement"	7. I probably ask too much of myself as it is. If I aim to do a little less, I'll probably feel less pressured and end up doing more. (100%)

STEP FOUR: OUTCOME—Re-rate your belief in each Automatic Thought from 0 to 100 and put a check in the box that describes how you now feel:

☐ not at all better; ☐ somewhat better; ☒ quite a bit better; ☐ a lot better.

I'm not saying that you should be a "cockeyed optimist" and ignore the possibility of failure. But things usually will turn out far better if you anticipate success and adopt a positive attitude.

DEFINE YOUR GOALS

It can help to ask yourself, "Why would failure be so upsetting to me?" You might think that people would lose respect for you, that your career would come to an end, or that you'd be a terrible disappointment to your parents or friends. While these concerns may contain a grain of truth, they are frequently exaggerated. The real problem may be that you aren't clear about your own goals in life. For example, after the law students I described earlier began to feel a little less anxious, nearly all of them confessed that they didn't really know if they even wanted to be in law school in the first place. They said they didn't have a burning desire to be lawyers and were in law school because that's what their parents wanted or because they couldn't think of anything better to do. They felt resentful about having to meet their parents' expectations because they had not asked themselves, "Is this what I want for my life?"

When I asked this question, the answer was always "No." Most of them did *not* want to be Wall Street lawyers, but it had never dawned on them they had the right to pursue their own dreams for their lives. Instead of clarifying what they *did* want to do, they were rebelling against what they *didn't* want. Their anxiety was a perfect way out of a trap. Subconsciously they were telling themselves, "I'm so anxious I may have to drop out of school. This will give me a perfect excuse to quit. My parents won't really be angry or disappointed in me. I tried my best, but I just had to quit because of my nerves."

Their anxiety was the result of this conflict. They were divided against themselves, like two teams were pulling against each other in a tug of war. The side that felt they should be in school was competing with the side that didn't want to be there but couldn't admit it. Once they became aware of that struggle, they were free to do one of two things: they could leave law school and put their energies into some other career, or they could stay because they wanted to, and not just to please their parents.

When you feel anxious about your performance, you may not be aware that you have mixed feelings because you're busy telling yourself, "This is what I should want to do. I should just push harder and get through it." But if it isn't what you really want to do, then every psychological technique in the world will fail to make your anxiety go away. Your lack of commitment to a goal will sabotage any possible treatment effect. You can take a tranquilizer to quiet the two teams doing battle, but they will continue to struggle. You can give one of these teams a pep talk and try to energize it to win, but the other team will just fight back a little harder, and you won't gain much ground. You've got to call time out and tell these two opposing teams, "Hey, guys, we're stuck because we're at odds. We've got to pull together toward a common goal. What should that goal be?"

Surprisingly, none of these anxious students ever did drop out of law school. Instead, they decided to stay and pursue very different kinds of career goals that appealed to them. A black student with an interest in international law became excited about the possibility of working with emerging African nations. A woman who loved the theater decided she would like to work in the legal aspects of the entertainment business. A young man from Minnesota decided he wanted a rural law practice in a small midwestern community where his wife, who was studying agricultural engineering, could more easily pursue her career. Once they gave up the need to do what they thought they *should* do and felt free to define personally meaningful goals, their anxiety usually vanished.

FEARED FANTASY TECHNIQUE

You may be concerned that if you pursue your own goals and stop trying so hard to meet everyone else's expectations, other people will be disappointed in you. For example, you might want to take a year off from school or to change your major. How would your family react? When the law students confronted their parents with their new career plans, their parents were usually pleased and relieved that the emotional storms were over. However, there may be times when people will feel let down because you didn't live up to their expectations. You can confront these fears with the Feared Fantasy Technique. Let's pretend that I'm your son. You can pretend to be a critical, angry parent. You're disappointed in me because I've decided I'd like to practice law in the Midwest instead of going to Wall Street. Our dialogue might go like this:

ANGRY FATHER: I'm extremely upset. You say you're not going to Wall Street? You're going to practice in the Midwest? You don't want to do that! You're missing the boat. That's no career.

STUDENT: Yes, I plan to practice in the Midwest, in a rural area.

ANGRY FATHER: But you'll never make any money like that. And with your brains you could do something worthwhile with your life!

STUDENT: It sounds as if you think my choice of a career isn't very worthwhile. That makes me feel like I must fit into your mold. I feel hurt. I want you to love and respect me for the career that I've chosen.

ANGRY FATHER: I don't want you to fit into a mold, I just want you to do what's best for you. I know you'll never be happy in the Midwest.

STUDENT: I feel very committed to a general law practice in the Midwest. Can you tell me why this is upsetting you?

ANGRY FATHER: I've already told you why I'm upset! The top people go to Wall Street and they make a name for themselves. The losers go to Nebraska and grow corn. Your mother and I want to be proud of you.

STUDENT: It sounds as if you won't be proud of me if I go to Nebraska. Am I reading you right? Would you feel that I was a loser? Would you love me less?

Now the father has two choices. He can continue to be judgmental and rejecting because his son isn't doing precisely what he wants him to, or he can accept his son and love him as he is. Most fathers would not be so hostile and rejecting, but at least the son could live with himself. He would have a sense of integrity and self-respect because he pursued a vision for his life that made sense to him. Over the course of time, I suspect that his father would soften.

Let's review the methods for coping with test and performance anxiety:

1. **Confront Your Fears:** You do an experiment to test your belief that you can't function properly when you feel anxious. If you feel so nervous that you think you can't concentrate or understand what you're studying, read one sentence out loud and summarize what it said. You will usually discover that you did understand it, even though it seemed as if you couldn't.

2. **The Compartmentation Technique:** You put your anxiety in a mental box and ignore it. You concentrate on doing the task one step at a time.

3. **Worry Breaks:** You schedule one-minute worry breaks every five or ten minutes. During the worry breaks you give full vent to all your self-doubts and fantasies of failure.

4. **The Daily Mood Log:** You write down your negative thoughts, identify the distortions in them, and substitute more positive and realistic thoughts.

5. **The Cost-Benefit Analysis:** You make a list of the advantages and disadvantages of worrying and predicting failure. Then make a second list of the advantages and disadvantages of feeling confident and giving yourself positive, optimistic messages.

6. **Define Your Goals:** Ask yourself, "Do I really want to be doing this? Am I feeling coerced and trying too hard to meet other people's expectations?"

7. **The Feared Fantasy Technique:** You write out an imaginary dialogue with someone who feels let down and acts excessively critical because you didn't live up to his or her expectations.

SOLUTIONS TO THE EXERCISE ON PAGE 348

1. My anxiety really can't prevent me from sitting down at my desk. I can certainly pick up the pen. Then I can at least write one word on a piece of paper.

2. I can review my notes. Then I can outline the report. Then I can draft the introductory paragraph.

3. I can try to write an average first sentence instead of trying to write a brilliant one. Then I can do some average editing later on, and revise it and make it even better.

4. I can work on one small part of the report at a time. Then it won't seem so overwhelming.

5. I can remind myself that I don't need to "feel like it" in order to get started. Tough jobs are bound to be uncomfortable at first. Once I start to make some progress I'll probably feel more motivated.

Feeling Good Together: How to Strengthen Relationships Through Better Communication

18

•

Good and Bad Communication

Communication seems easy, and we all think we're experts. After all, you've been talking since you were a child, and it comes naturally most of the time. You just open your mouth and the words come spilling out. When you feel happy and close to someone, it is easy to communicate well. You feel good and they feel good and everything seems rosy. It's when you have a strong disagreement or a conflict with someone that you find out whether you can really communicate well. How well do you do when you're angry, or when someone is angry with you? How do you deal with criticism? What do you say when the other person is being unreasonable and refuses to listen to your point of view? How well do you communicate when you feel vulnerable and hurt?

People who can communicate effectively in these situations are exceedingly rare. But these are the situations where good communication is vital. The key to intimacy, friendship, and success in business is the ability to handle conflict successfully. People have enormous difficulty with this. Husbands and wives don't communicate well. Friends don't communicate well. Family members often handle conflicts and disagreements very poorly.

Even psychotherapists, who are presumably experts, have difficulties communicating with patients. When I teach psychiatrists and psychologists at workshops, I often ask a volunteer to role-play so we can see how effectively they can communicate with a difficult, hostile patient. Pretending to be the patient, I say something like "Dr. Smith, you don't seem to care about me. I want help with my problems, but all you ever say is 'Hmmm.' " Almost invariably the therapist responds in a defensive or evasive way. He or she might say "Hmmm" or "Tell me more" or "I do care about you." Therapists seem to have little comprehension of how annoying and inappropriate these responses might sound to an angry patient!

Would you like to become a better communicator? First, let's see if we can define good communication and bad communication. Good communication has two properties: you express your feelings openly and directly, and you encourage the other person to express his or her feelings. You say how you are thinking and feeling, and you try to listen and understand what the other person is thinking and feeling. According to this definition, the ideas and feelings of both people are important.

Just as good communication involves self-expression and listening, bad communication involves a refusal to share your feelings openly or to listen to what the other person has to say.

Becoming argumentative and defensive is one sign of bad communication. You may contradict the other person without trying to understand his or her feelings. You may project subtle messages that say "I'm not really interested in what you have to say. I'm only interested in broadcasting my own feelings and insisting that you agree with me."

Another sign of bad communication is denying your own feelings and acting them out indirectly. You may act pouty or get sarcastic. This is called "passive aggression." Active aggression is also bad communication—when you tell the other person off or threaten or issue ultimatums. The list of "Characteristics of Bad Communication" on the next page will make you more aware of what not to do when you are trying to resolve a conflict with someone. Study this list carefully!

You may recognize several bad habits that get you into trouble. Changing these tendencies can make a tremendous difference in the way you relate to people and save you endless grief!

THE CHARACTERISTICS OF BAD COMMUNICATION*

1. **Truth**—You insist that you are "right" and the other person is "wrong."

2. **Blame**—You say that the problem is the other person's fault.

3. **Martyrdom**—You claim that you're an innocent victim.

4. **Put-down**—You imply that the other person is a loser because he or she "always" or "never" does certain things.

5. **Hopelessness**—You give up and insist there's no point in trying.

6. **Demandingness**—You say you're entitled to better treatment but you refuse to ask for what you want in a direct, straightforward way.

7. **Denial**—You insist that you don't feel angry, hurt, or sad when you really do.

8. **Passive Aggression**—You pout or withdraw or say nothing. You may storm out of the room or slam doors.

9. **Self-blame**—Instead of dealing with the problem, you act as if you're an awful, terrible person.

10. **Helping**—Instead of hearing how depressed, hurt, or angry the other person feels, you try to "solve the problem" or "help" him or her.

11. **Sarcasm**—Your words or tone of voice convey tension or hostility which you aren't openly acknowledging.

12. **Scapegoating**—You suggest that the other person has "a problem" and that you're sane, happy, and uninvolved in the conflict.

13. **Defensiveness**—You refuse to admit any wrong-doing or imperfection.

14. **Counterattack**—Instead of acknowledging how the other person feels, you respond to their criticism by criticizing them.

15. **Diversion**—Instead of dealing with how you both feel in the here-and-now, you list grievances about past injustices.

Let's examine the way several of my patients communicate. They are ordinary men and women who are probably similar to you. In each case, I want you to decide if what my patient said was an example of good or bad communication.

Joanne is 26 years old and is completing her law degree. Her husband, Ted, is a surgeon. Ted and Joanne separated several months ago but have been attempting a reconciliation. They are struggling with the issue of whether they should separate permanently or try to resolve their difficulties and get back together again. Joanne complains that Ted has difficulty expressing his feelings. She says that when he's annoyed he gets pouty and gives her the icy treatment instead of telling her how he feels. Ted complains that Joanne is too close to her family. He says she's bossy and self-centered. He tells her that she puts her family and her career ahead of him. This makes him feel like a second-class citizen.

Recently Ted planned a trip to Bermuda, and they argued about whether or not Joanne would go with him. At first he wanted to go alone and Joanne felt hurt. Later he asked her to go with him, but in the meantime she had decided that she needed some time alone. When she told him she wasn't planning to go, he got annoyed and said, "You should get on with your life and not hold any hopes for this relationship!" Joanne replied, "No problem! I have already started to do that." First, let's look at Ted's comment. Would you say it was an example of good communication or bad communication?

_____ good communication

_____ bad communication

I'd say it's bad communication, because he didn't express his feelings or acknowledge hers. If you examine the list on page 365, you will see that he's involved with "Denial." He probably felt rejected and angry but he tried to hide his feelings. He could say, "I'm disappointed and hurt. I care for you and I really wish you'd go with me." Instead, he simply rejects her and puts her down. This is consistent with her image of him as someone who acts pouty and cold when he's upset.

Ted also failed to acknowledge her feelings. Why did she decide not to go? How is she feeling? When he doesn't ask these questions, Ted projects a lack of love and interest in her.

Now let's look at her comment. Would you call this an example of good communication or bad communication? Think about it a little bit and review the list on page 365 before you answer this and read any further.

_____ good communication

_____ bad communication

Her comment is another example of bad communication, because she hasn't acknowledged his feelings or expressed her own. She's involved in "Sarcasm" and "Denial." It seems pretty clear that he feels hurt, angry, and rejected, but she appears to be ignoring his feelings. This will make her seem self-centered and uninterested in him. Joanne is not expressing her own feelings either. She felt stung and wounded by his comment. Instead of expressing this, she simply responded in a cold, rejecting manner.

This denial of the way you really feel is extremely common. Many people have a terrible fear that something awful will happen if they simply state, in an open and direct way, how they feel. I have a strong hunch that you may have this problem too!

Joanne could express her own feelings and acknowledge Ted's by saying something like this: "I feel very bad right now because you told me that I should get on with my life. I feel hurt and angry. I still care for you and I don't want our relationship to be over. You're telling me not to hold out any hopes in this relationship. Your voice has a sharp edge to it. I wonder if you're feeling annoyed because I decided not to go to Bermuda? Can you tell me how you feel about this?" This would make him aware of how she's feeling and would encourage him to talk about his own feelings. That's good communication. It isn't a put-down, it isn't a denial, and she wouldn't be playing the role of a martyr or victim. The response would make Joanne vulnerable, because she would disclose her feelings in a non-defensive way and would invite him to express his anger directly. But at the same time, her response would be powerful because she urges him to open up and come out of his shell, and she has set aside the impulse to get back at him.

Let's look at another example of a separated couple with problems communicating. Henry is a management consultant in New York City. He separated from his wife, Denise, several months ago because of conflicting goals about marriage. Henry very much wants children, but Denise does not want a family and would prefer to pursue her own career instead. Henry has been very disappointed by Denise's lack of interest in sex. Denise complains that Henry is married to his career. She says she wants a husband with a nine-to-five job who would come home in time for dinner so they could spend their evenings together. This is far more important to her than having him put in long hours so he can make lots of money. Henry feels rejected and unappreciated. He takes great pride in all his hard work and has developed an outstanding career and a good salary. Henry's father, an immigrant from Russia, worked long hours as a tailor. When Henry was growing up, the importance of ambition, hard work, and success were stressed. Henry wishes Denise would respect his accomplishments so they could enjoy the good life together.

Henry and Denise have always had a great deal of difficulty discussing conflicts or dealing with angry feelings. Henry sometimes plays the role of a martyr. He feels resentful that Denise doesn't love and appreciate all the sacrifices he's made to raise their standard of living, and he's afraid to tell her how badly he wants to have children. He also is afraid to tell her how unhappy he feels about her lack of interest in sex, because he doesn't want to hurt her feelings. As a result his resentment built up, until he finally moved out and began to date other women.

Like the previous couple, Henry and Denise have not decided whether they should get a divorce or try to work their problems out. Recently they went out on a date, and afterward they were talking about a couple they know who were about to get married. Denise mentioned that the woman in that relationship was "making all the sacrifices." She explained that "to maintain a relationship, people must sacrifice." Henry found this statement annoying because he felt that Denise's definition of "sacrifice" was to submerge all your desires and needs entirely to another person. Since this is exactly what Henry felt he had been doing, and since it had worked out poorly for him, he felt infuriated. He said, "No. Sacrifice causes resentment." Is Henry's statement an example of good communication or bad communication? Review the list on page 365 before you answer this question.

_____ good communication

_____ bad communication

I would say this is an example of bad communication. Henry is not expressing his own feelings openly, and he is not encouraging Denise to express hers. Henry's communication error is "Truth." His statement will only provoke an argument. Can you think of a better response? What could Henry say? Put your ideas here:

_____

_____

_____

_____

My suggestion would be along these lines: "Denise, I feel resentful right now. I think you're talking about our relationship. Maybe you think you've done all the sacrificing. I know this is how I feel. I feel I've done all the sacrificing and it really bothers me. Tell me how you feel about this." If Henry said this, he would be sharing his feelings in a straightforward way, and he would be encouraging Denise to tell him how she feels about their relationship, rather than talking about some other couple.

You might be interested in Henry's response when I suggested this. He said he thought it would be an excellent approach, but he was terribly afraid to be so open with Denise. He said, "It would make me vulnerable. If I expressed my feelings and opened myself up to her left hook, I don't know what would happen!" This fear of making yourself vulnerable is one of many attitudes that can cause poor communication. You end up living in a box and having to communicate by tapping on the wall in Morse Code.

Husbands and wives are not the only ones who have difficulties expressing their feelings. Mildred's 25-year-old son, Jerry, is attending medical school in San Francisco. He is very close to Mildred and they talk frequently on the telephone. He does well in his classes and seems to have lots of friends. However, he tells Mildred that he's going nowhere and that his life seems empty and has no meaning. He sometimes says that if it weren't for the fact that she's still alive, he would commit suicide.

When Jerry says these things, Mildred feels panic and anguish. She tells him that he has a great deal to live for. She emphasizes that he's intelligent and has many friends. She reminds him that he's good-looking and that women like him. Is Mildred's response an example of good communication or bad communication? Review the list on page 365 before you answer.

_____ good communication

_____ bad communication

I would say this is an example of bad communication. Her communication errors include "Truth" and "Helping." Mildred is not encouraging Jerry to express his feelings, and she is not expressing her own. How does Mildred feel when he says these things? She feels shocked, frightened, concerned, frustrated. But she does not say this to Jerry. Instead, she tries to cheer him up by contradicting him. Essentially, he says "My life stinks" and she says "No, your life is good." This will frustrate Jerry. He will feel that she doesn't understand how bad he feels, so he will continue to complain even more persistently. He'll point out five things in his life that stink. She'll try to cheer him up by pointing out five good things. They will both end up feeling anxious and exasperated.

Bad communication nearly always involves some type of argumentative response. We don't listen to what the other person says because it upsets us to hear how they feel. Mildred feels so frightened that she isn't aware she's being contradictory. She loves Jerry and desperately wants to make him feel better. That's understandable, but there are far more effective ways to do this.

The tendency to argue and contradict the other person when you feel upset is practically universal. You may not be aware that you are doing this. It seems to be a deeply ingrained part of human nature. If you believe that intimacy involves emotional closeness and a sharing of feelings, then this habit of contradicting others will defeat you. It always creates distance and prevents intimacy.

Jerry is looking for some understanding. He wants his mom to understand how bad he feels. He must want to communicate with Mildred because he calls her so frequently. If you were Mildred, what would you say to Jerry? Think about it for a moment before you read on, and then put your ideas here:

Mildred could respond like this: "Jerry, I want you to know how bad I feel right now. I get alarmed when you say that your life is empty and that there's no point in being alive. I love you and it breaks my heart to hear so much sadness and despair in your voice. I want to understand you better. Can you tell me why you feel the way you do? Maybe there's something missing from your life that's very important to you. Maybe there is a problem that you've been afraid to share with me. Can you tell me more about how you feel?" This response would be more honest, because she's admitting how frightened and concerned she feels instead of denying her feelings and acting "helpful." She would also be encouraging him to open up. Most people want to be understood and accepted more than anything else in the world. If she tries to understand and gives up the urge to help, she will be helping him. It's a paradox.

Let's look at a mother/daughter interaction. Marilyn is about the same age as Mildred. Her daughter, Susan, is about Jerry's age. Susan lives with Marilyn and they manage a chain of clothing stores that Marilyn founded after her husband died. They do well and have a beautiful home. However, Marilyn's daughter is often bossy and domineering. She puts Marilyn down, and Marilyn simply takes it because she sees herself as a "nice, sweet person."

Recently Marilyn was having her kitchen redone. One evening when she was washing the countertop after work, Susan made the following statement in a very irritable tone of voice: "Mother! I can't believe you're doing this! The workers told me specifically that we're not to run the dishwasher or get any water on the floor until they finish putting in the tiles!" Marilyn's face stiffened, and angry tears welled up in her eyes. She stormed out of the room muttering, "I can't believe she said that!" Would you call this an example of good communication or bad communication? Examine the list on page 365 before you answer.

_____ good communication

_____ bad communication

This is an example of bad communication, because Marilyn is not expressing her feelings and she is not acknowledging what Susan is saying. Holding your hurt feelings inside is called "Passive Aggressiveness." Marilyn is expressing her anger passively and indirectly by walking out and saying nothing. What could she have said to her daughter instead? Remember that good communication has two components: you express your feelings openly, and you acknowledge how the other person is feeling. Put your ideas here:

_____

_____

_____

_____

Look at the response you wrote down. Was it sarcastic or aggressive? Did you tell Susan off or put her down? Active aggression is not the antidote to passive aggression. Marilyn's aim is to communicate with her daughter and to improve their relationship, not just to hit back.

Marilyn needs to point out that her daughter sounds condescending and nasty. Marilyn can tell Susan that she feels put down and annoyed. She doesn't need to say this in an antagonistic or sarcastic way, because then she would be accepting her daughter's invitation to be childish and to have a fight. She would be giving Susan the power to set the tone of the interaction.

Marilyn could say, "I didn't know we weren't supposed to use the kitchen tonight, and I will be careful not to get the floor wet. I'm quite upset right now because I feel talked down to. Your tone of voice sounds condescending, and that makes me angry. I want you to treat me with respect. It sounds like you might be annoyed with me. If you are, I want you to tell me. Are you angry or upset about something?'' This response will call attention to Susan's insulting tone of voice and will encourage her to communicate in a more direct way.

Susan probably is annoyed with Marilyn. Instead of bringing the problem up and talking it out, she acts hostile and insulting. When Marilyn runs out of the room, this makes Susan feel very powerful. Marilyn's "sweetness" and her habit of avoiding conflicts hurts both of them. But if Marilyn sticks up for herself, they will both benefit.

Brothers and sisters frequently have trouble communicating. Janice recently discovered that her brother Tom was involved in a homosexual relationship. Janice learned that Tom's lover wanted to be included as co-owner of a house Tom was buying, without helping to pay for it. Janice was disturbed on several accounts. First, she felt that she had never really been close to Tom. She was concerned that she and Tom had never really gotten to know each other very well. Second, she was upset that Tom was gay and she worried about AIDS. Finally, she was concerned that Tom's lover would get half ownership of his house without helping to pay for it.

Janice told Tom that she was afraid that the man he was living with might be taking advantage of him. Tom responded: "He's not!" He said this in a very defensive, irritable tone of voice. If you were Janice, what would you say next? Put your ideas here:

_____

_____

_____

_____

_____

Janice said, "I was concerned because he asked for half ownership of the new house without offering to pay for it." Would you say this is an example of good communication or bad communication?

_____ good communication

_____ bad communication

I would say it's an example of bad communication, because she's ignoring his defensive tone and she is not revealing her feelings about the matter. She's being argumentative. Her communication errors include "Truth" and "Denial." She is pushing the idea that Tom's lover may not be completely fair and honest. Although she may be right, she'll get nowhere. Tom will simply get defensive and they'll end up arguing. Are you familiar with this pattern? Does this ever happen to you?

Janice could respond this way instead: "I hope you're right. I'm worried because I care for you and I don't want anyone to take advantage of you. I noticed a sharp edge in your voice just now. I wonder if you feel that I don't understand the situation. Maybe you think I'm talking down to you. Maybe I'm sticking my nose in where it doesn't belong. If so, I apologize. I really do want to feel closer to you. Can you tell me more about what's going on? I would appreciate it." This response gives Tom the chance to talk about his feelings and encourages him to tell her if he's annoyed instead of arguing defensively.

You may not always like the responses I have suggested. A different style and tone may suit you better. We all have different personalities, and what works for one person isn't always the same as what works for someone else. What I do hope is that you are beginning to comprehend what bad communication is and how enormously common it is. Bad communication is almost as automatic and natural as breathing! Bad communication has two characteristics. What are they?

1. _____

_____

_____

2. _____

_____

_____

They are not expressing your feelings openly, and not acknowledging how the other person is thinking and feeling. Instead you argue and get defensive.

Good communication also has two characteristics. What are they?

1. _____

_____

_____

2. _____

_____

_____

They are expressing your feelings openly and directly, and acknowledging the other person's feelings.

In the next chapter I will describe three powerful listening skills and two self-expression skills that will help you communicate more effectively and more intimately.

◆

19

Five Secrets of Intimate Communication

The five communication techniques described in this chapter can change your life. Three are listening skills and two are self-expression skills. You will learn to listen with your "third ear" so you can understand precisely what the other person is thinking and feeling. They will also help you express your feelings more clearly and effectively. Once you have learned each of the five techniques, I will show you how to put them all together so you can communicate more effectively.

Listening Skill #1: The Disarming Technique

This is the most difficult—and the most powerful—listening skill. You find *some* truth in what the other person is saying and agree with them, even if you think that what they're saying is wrong. This is a particularly effective tool when you feel criticized and attacked. It takes the wind out of the other person's sails and has a profound and sudden calming effect. Regardless of how unreasonable their criticism might seem, find some grain of truth in it. When you resist the urge to argue or defend yourself and you instead agree with the other

THE FIVE SECRETS OF EFFECTIVE COMMUNICATION*

LISTENING SKILLS

1. **The Disarming Technique.** You find some truth in what the other person is saying, even if you feel convinced that what they're saying is totally wrong, unreasonable, irrational, or unfair.

2. **Empathy.** You put yourself in the other person's shoes and try to see the world through his or her eyes.

   - **Thought empathy:** You paraphrase the other person's words.
   - **Feeling empathy:** You acknowledge how they're probably feeling, given what they are saying to you.

3. **Inquiry:** You ask gentle, probing questions to learn more about what the other person is thinking and feeling.

SELF-EXPRESSION SKILLS

1. **"I feel" statements.** You express your feelings with "I feel" statements (such as "I feel upset") rather than with "you" statements (such as "You're wrong!" or "You're making me furious!").

2. **Stroking:** You find something genuinely positive to say to the other person, even in the heat of battle. This indicates that you respect the other person, even though you may be angry with each other.

person, you will paradoxically end up a winner. He or she will usually feel like a winner too, and will be much more open to your point of view.

Here's an example. Suppose you told me: "I'm suspicious about these communication techniques. I don't think they will work for me." What could I say to you? How could I respond, using the disarming technique? Put your ideas here:

_____

_____

_____

_____

Answer: I could say, "You're right to be suspicious. I'm not convinced these methods will be helpful to you either. People sometimes find it extremely difficult to change. I'd like to hear more about why the methods don't seem useful to you."

Can you see the value in this response? There is nearly *always* some truth in what another person is saying. When I agree with you, it will be hard for you to keep up the argument.

You may not want to use this disarming technique because when you are criticized you will feel angry, and a voice inside you will be screaming, "I'm right and I have the right to defend myself!" If you give in to this voice—and the temptation will be almost overwhelming—you'll be off to the races in a pointless, frustrating battle. Arguing with a critic almost never works. Agreeing with a critic almost always builds rapport. The effects can be quite magical!

Now let's try it again. Let's assume your spouse says, "You're always late and I'm sick of waiting for you." How would you disarm him or her?

_____

_____

_____

_____

You could say: "It's true. I *am* late and you have the right to be angry." Can you see the value in this response? When you admit that you're late, your spouse will feel listened to and respected and won't feel nearly so mad. But if you get defensive and make excuses for yourself, it will enrage him or her even more.

Let's try another example. Your boss says: "This proposal stinks. Were you daydreaming when you wrote it?" Let's assume you put a great deal of effort into the proposal and you felt proud of it. You know it's not *that* bad, and you'd like to kill your boss. In spite of this, how could you disarm your boss? Put your ideas here:

_____

_____

_____

_____

Answer: You could respond: "It sounds like I really missed the boat on the proposal, even though I worked hard on it. Could you tell me what you liked and disliked about it?" This will calm your boss down, and he or she will probably communicate in a more tactful manner.

When you use the disarming technique, you must be genuine in what you say or it will backfire. You can always find some valid way to agree, no matter how illogical the person's accusations might seem to you. If you agree with them in a sincere way, they will generally soften and will be far more willing to listen to you.

Suppose I say to you, "That green shirt looks awful on you." Let's assume that you're wearing a bright turquoise shirt and everyone's been telling you how great it looks. How could you disarm me?

_____

_____

_____

_____

You could say, "Green may not be my best color. What color would you like to see me wearing?" Notice that this response avoids an argument and puts the ball back in my court. I've invited you to get into a stupid argument about what color your shirt is, and you've tactfully declined by finding some little morsel of truth in what I said. What's the point in arguing with me about the color of your shirt?

Of course, some people seem to love pointless debates. That's perfectly okay—you can argue with people endlessly if that's what turns you on! But if you're tired of arguing and find that people never listen to you, and if you'd like to feel closer to people, then the disarming technique could change your life!

Some readers may resist and think, "I shouldn't have to agree with someone who's being unreasonable." The answer to this is that you don't have to. However, you'll probably be far better off if you do. When you disarm someone who's being unreasonable, you'll often win them over to your point of view. Instead of arguing, look for a common framework so you can begin to understand each other and work together as a team. When you listen more deeply and try to grasp where the other person really is coming from, the relationship will be transformed. No longer are you enemies fighting each other to "win." The other person will frequently do a sudden turnabout and agree with you. This is because you have made a basic decision to build a relationship based on trust instead of doing battle in an effort to tear the other person down.

There are several reasons why this can be so remarkably effective. When two people argue, they always polarize each other and take extreme positions because they both feel they're not being listened to. Inside, the other person knows there's another side to the issue, but they feel you don't appreciate their point of view—you're both being dogmatic and defensive. Once you disarm them, they will recognize that you respect them, and they won't feel so dogmatic and have such an urge to insist that they're right and you're wrong. They will usually soften and acknowledge your feelings and ideas.

Let's try some more disarming. It's a terribly important technique, and you will need to practice it over and over before you catch on. Keep in mind as you practice that I'm only asking you to use this one technique. In an actual conversation, you would combine the disarming technique with the other methods described in this chapter, so that you will come across in a natural and effective way.

But right now, you need to concentrate all your efforts on this one technique.

Let's assume you're a little overweight and your spouse says, "You're a fat slob! You've got no self-control." How could you disarm him or her? Put your ideas here:

_____

_____

_____

_____

Answer: You could say, "You're absolutely right. I *do* need to lose weight and I need better self-control." Keep in mind that you are only using the disarming technique just now. In an actual conversation, you would also want to express your feelings and acknowledge how your spouse is feeling. In this instance, you would probably be feeling hurt and put down. Your spouse, too, sounds angry and frustrated. You would want to encourage him to express his feelings more directly and openly so he doesn't have to resort to hostile jabs. The other methods in this chapter, when combined with the disarming technique, will allow you to do this.

Your husband says, "You're too emotional about things. You get too upset. You're so irrational. You overreact. Why don't you use a little logic? The world won't come to an end!" How could you disarm him?

_____

_____

_____

_____

Answer: You could say, "I agree with you. I often overreact and get illogical, and it turns out later on that I wasn't being realistic."

Your wife says, "You're too logical and rational about everything!" How could you disarm her?

_____

_____

_____

_____

Answer: You could say, "You're right. I tend to be too logical instead of sharing my feelings."

Your husband says, "You get pouty and irritable when you get upset." How could you disarm him?

_____

_____

_____

_____

Answer: You could say, "I think I do act like that when I get mad."

Many readers may be thinking, "These techniques stink! I wouldn't agree with any creep who talked to me like that! Who does he think he is?" You are quite right in thinking this. When someone beats up on you, it's important to express your feelings.

Remember, though, that there is always a grain of truth in what the other person is saying, even if it sounds obnoxious and insulting. Even if their criticism seems very off base, there's still something valid about the way they feel. If you acknowledge this, they'll be more willing to listen and less likely to argue and put you down. They need to be listened to just as much as you do. In fact, the reason most people get so dogmatic and unreasonable is because they feel frustrated. And why do they feel frustrated? Because they think—quite rightly—that nobody's really listening or caring about what they're trying to say.

We will get to your side of things shortly. I do want you to be a winner. But sometimes you have to lose in order to win. You have to give in order to get. If you want respect, you have to give respect first. If you want to be listened to, then listen to the other person first. When you surrender, you will suddenly achieve victory. This is a paradox, but it's a practical, powerful reality.

Epictetus stated this idea nearly 2,000 years ago when he wrote, "If someone criticizes you, agree with them at once. Tell them that if only they knew you well, they would not bother to criticize only that!"

Most people are so preoccupied with standing up for their own ideas that they have trouble grasping the disarming technique. I am treating a businessman from Dallas named Al who is so brilliant that he memorizes every therapy session and then sends a perfectly typed memo the next day, summarizing everything that was said. In addition, he enters this information into a computer so he can cross-reference everything he learns. If he calls and talks to my secretary to change an appointment, I receive a memo the next day that contains a verbatim transcript of the conversation.

Al does a lot of legal work and loves to fight in court. He's extremely competitive and takes great pride in his ability to poke holes in the testimony of his opponents. He's a kind of white-collar cowboy and prides himself on being the fastest gun in town. So why is he in therapy? Al feels lonely and at odds with his wife, and he's concerned that he can't get close to people. His great logical mind is a two-edged sword: he is a success in business, but he is so aggressive that he sometimes drives people away.

His wife, Claire, is often quite timid. She feels angry and intimidated by Al, and she's terribly afraid to express herself. Recently they had their second therapy session as a couple. I told Claire to express her feelings and instructed Al to disarm her:

CLAIRE: You're a totally controlling person. You try to control who I meet, where I go, and what I do.

AL: That just isn't right at all. I don't try to control you in any way! There was a time when I did, but I don't do that anymore and I haven't in a while.

CLAIRE: Yes you do!

At this point I interrupted them because they were off to the races. Instead of disarming Claire by finding truth in her comment, Al couldn't resist the urge to argue that she was "wrong." Of course, by insisting Claire was wrong, he proved that she was right, because his argumentative response was very controlling. Al is putting a wall up and saying, "I don't want to pursue this topic."

If you were Al, how would you have disarmed Claire?

Answer: He could have said, "You're right. I *am* very controlling and I can see that this has really hurt you and angered you." This response would make Claire feel less angry because she would feel listened to. In addition, by agreeing that he was overly controlling, Al would show that he wasn't as controlling as she thought. Do you see this?

There's one caveat. When you disarm someone and you agree with their criticism, it will be effective only if you maintain a sense of self-esteem. For example, suppose you tell me, "You're a jerk." If I feel threatened by the criticism, I might answer you in a defensive or sarcastic way by saying, "Oh, sure. I'm a jerk! Look who's talking!" This hostile response will instantly make things deteriorate. Alternatively, if I feel depressed and believe that I am a worthless loser, I may sigh and sadly say, "Yes, I really am a worthless jerk." This comment probably won't gain many friends either! But if, with a twinkle in my eye, I say, "Yes, I've suspected that about myself for some time now," you will probably feel less irate. My sense of humor and lack of defensiveness may win you over and transform a potential battle into a friendly and productive discussion of the real problem. I have projected the message "I'm not afraid of criticism and I'm willing to listen to what you have to say." This attitude is likely to melt the hostility and win the day.

Let's practice the disarming technique again. Suppose I say, "You'll never understand these methods. You're such a stupid reader—I can't believe it!" How could you respond, using only the disarming technique?

_____

_____

_____

_____

_____

You could say, "As a matter of fact, I don't understand these methods as well as I'd like. I'm sure there are many readers who are much smarter than I am." Of course, you would also want to express your feelings and learn more about mine. You could add, "I feel really put down and I don't like being talked to like that. It sounds like you're frustrated with me. Are you?" This statement illustrates the next skill.

Listening Skill #2: Empathy

Empathy means that you try to put yourself in the other person's shoes and understand what they are thinking (called "thought empathy") and feeling (called "feeling empathy"). Thought and feeling empathy are crucial to practically any conversation.

Thought empathy. Repeat out loud what the other person is saying so they will know you got the point. You can ask a question to see if you got it right. Let's assume your lover has been acting distant and he says, "I feel our relationship has no real future. There's too much of an age difference." Reflect it back to him in a quiet manner. "No real future? Apparently you feel the age gap is too great. Can you tell me more about how you feel about this?" Don't say this sarcastically or defensively. Try to convey a spirit of genuine curiosity. Your goal is to understand where he's coming from and not to argue or state your own point of view. Instead, you mirror what he is saying in a nonjudgmental way so as to grasp the essence of what he is feeling.

This strategy will enable you to develop a much sharper understanding of his mind-set. Try to grasp the meaning behind the words.

Feeling empathy. Once you have paraphrased what the other person said, acknowledge the feelings he or she might have and ask a question to see if you are reading his or her emotions correctly. Suppose your husband suddenly jumps on you by saying: "Why don't you ever listen? Trying to talk to you is like beating my head against a brick wall!" Using feeling empathy, you could respond: "It sounds like I've been closed-minded and stubborn. I can imagine that you might be feeling fed up and frustrated with me. Do you feel that way?" As he begins to ventilate about how he feels, accept his feelings instead of reacting in a critical or hostile way (the aggressive response) or withdrawing and playing the role of wounded victim (the passive response). If he says, "Damn right I'm upset!" you can then say, "I'm glad you told me that, even though this is upsetting to me. I get pretty frustrated when people don't listen to me, so I can understand how you're feeling." This response involves resisting your all-too-human urge to lash out and fight back. You'll probably be feeling just as hurt and angry as he is, and you'll understandably want to prove that he's wrong. Don't.

Let's practice thought and feeling empathy. Remember that you don't have to agree or disagree with the other person. Instead, you repeat what they said and acknowledge how they might be feeling. It may help if you begin with one of these expressions in a gentle tone of voice:

- "What you seem to be saying is . . ."
- "It sounds like . . ."
- "I take it that you think . . ."
- "Let me see if I'm getting this right."
- "I just want to make sure that I understand what you're saying."

Then you can paraphrase what they said and ask a question to see if you grasped their meaning.

I urged Claire to tell Al just how angry she was. I told her to let him have it. She hesitated, but after some cajoling on my part, she said, "Okay. Al, here's my fantasy about you. I often imagine that I'm in a room with ten strong men and you're tied to a chair. I remind you of one of the times you've hurt me, and one of the men comes and smashes you in the face. You mutter, 'I'm sorry, I'm sorry, I'm sorry!' Then I tell you about another time when you humiliated me, as the second man comes up and lets you have it, and you apologize again. We do this again and again." If you were Al, how could you respond using thought empathy and feeling empathy? Put your response here:

_____

_____

_____

_____

Answer: Al could say, "It sounds like there have been many times that I've hurt you and you want to even the score and get back at me [thought empathy]. You must be awfully furious with me [feeling empathy]. It also sounds like you're afraid to tell me how you feel unless I'm tied down and you have ten strong men to protect you when you tell me how upset you feel [feeling empathy]. Perhaps you want me to feel remorse and to apologize for how badly I've treated you."

During a recent session with a separated couple, the woman mentioned some bills that her husband hadn't paid. He became enraged and said, "You're trying to provoke me and get sympathy from Dr. Burns. You're trying to make it look like it's my fault! I won't stand for this bull!" How could she respond, using thought empathy and feeling empathy? Put your ideas here:

_____

_____

_____

_____

Answer: She could say, "It sounds like you're really upset with me for bringing that up [feeling empathy]. You say I'm trying to provoke you and blame you and get Dr. Burns to side with me [thought empathy]. That would make me angry, too [feeling empathy]. It's no fun to be blamed or ganged up on [feeling empathy]."

Let's try it again. Suppose I tell you, "I'm ticked off. You're reading my *Handbook* but you're not filling in the blanks and doing the exercises. Are you looking for magic? How do you expect me to help you? You can't change without doing the written exercises. It just won't work!" How could you respond, using thought empathy and feeling empathy? Put your ideas here:

_____

_____

_____

_____

Answer: You could say, "Dr. Burns, you say that it's important to do the written exercises [thought empathy]. It sounds like you're frustrated because I haven't been doing them [feeling empathy]. You believe that if I really want to change, I'll have to do them [thought empathy]."

At first you may find that you cannot grasp these communication methods very well. Like many of my patients, you may argue when you think you're disarming, and you may preach and attack when you think you're empathizing with the other person. If you really want to change, you'll have to work at it persistently for many weeks. If you do, things will begin to fall into place. And then, Eureka! You'll have the ability to use some incredibly powerful tools that can transform the way you relate to others.

Now suppose you're thinking, "That's a lot of hype. And besides, this is much too complicated and manipulative. I could never keep all this stuff straight and I don't think I'd even want to." How could I respond, using thought empathy and feeling empathy?

_____

_____

_____

_____

Answer: I could say, "You're absolutely right [disarming]. I'm probably bragging too much about how wonderful these methods are, and they don't sound realistic or genuine to you [thought empathy]. You seem a little put off [feeling empathy]. You feel there's too much to learn and it's all a little overwhelming [feeling empathy]. In addition it sounds like you think I'm sounding phony and manipulative, and that turns you off [thought and feeling empathy]."

Many people do feel a little intimidated by these methods at first. They may seem artificial and confusing, and they will go against the grain. During a marital spat, you will tell yourself, "I don't want to agree with the S.O.B.! After all, he's wrong and I'm right!" These and many similar thoughts will get in the way. But if you persist and practice every day, it will start to come together.

Good communication can be extremely powerful. Like any source of power, these methods can be used for good or evil purposes. If your goal is to manipulate others and to "win," then these techniques will not enhance genuine intimacy. However, if your goal is to feel closer to others, then you don't need to fear any awkwardness you may feel when you first try these techniques, because your positive intentions will be obvious.

Remember that we're focusing on single methods which are likely to sound artificial if you say nothing else. If your spouse calls you a jerk, you might respond, "You say that I'm a jerk." This is a technically correct example of thought empathy, but you sound more like a parrot than a real human being. Your spouse will probably feel infuriated because you're not being genuine or real. You can avoid this problem if you express your feelings with "I feel" statements. An "I feel" statement is a simple statement of how you feel. We'll talk more about this later, but I'll give you an example now. You could tell your spouse, "You say I'm a jerk, and you're probably pretty annoyed with me [thought empathy, feeling empathy]. This bothers me. I feel put down ['I feel' statement]. Maybe I have been acting like a jerk [disarming technique]. Can you tell me what I did that turned you off?" This last response also illustrates the next skill.

Listening Skill #3: Inquiry

Inquiry is the use of gentle, probing questions to learn more about what the other person is thinking and feeling. You can ask them to tell you more about their negative feelings, since that's what most people are afraid to talk about. You can also encourage them to tell you more about what you've done or said that turned them off or hurt their feelings.

It's very hard for most people to express angry feelings. They don't want to admit that they feel hurt. That's why the inquiry technique is so important. You give the other person a direct, explicit invitation to criticize you and to tell you how annoyed they feel.

If you use the inquiry technique and get the other person to lay the cards on the table, you can deal with the problem and you'll know where you stand. To give a simple example, if I sense that a patient is uncomfortable with me or with their progress in therapy and I don't encourage them to talk it over, there's a good chance they'll express their dissatisfaction indirectly. They may be argumentative and "forget" to do their self-help assignments between sessions. They may not show up for their next session and drop out of therapy prematurely. They may not pay a bill. I end up feeling frustrated and shot down. On the other hand, if I use the inquiry technique and ask them if they feel turned off, it nearly always leads to an honest exchange of feelings that makes the therapy far more satisfying and useful. The same principle holds for any relationship, whether it's with your spouse, your child, your boss, your customer, or your best friend.

Most of my patients are afraid to use the inquiry technique. They don't want to open Pandora's box and let all the nasty monsters out. They like to avoid anger and conflict. They are often afraid of being criticized. They may argue that "nice" people don't fight or get mad at each other. Do you ever feel like that? Are you afraid of hearing angry criticism from someone you care about?

I know I used to be like that. So was a patient of mine named Sarah. Sarah is separated from her husband, David. David has a great deal of pent-up anger toward her, so I urged Sarah to ask him to tell her about his angry feelings whenever he was acting nasty. But Sarah didn't want to hear about how furious David was. She told me that what he was saying wasn't right; she told me that David was to blame; she told me that it wasn't fair for David to be so mean and angry with her; she told me that it was too upsetting to hear all those awful things.

Sometimes she got defensive and argued with David when he seemed annoyed. That shut him up. Sometimes she would apologize and promise to be a better wife in the future if only he would come back to her. She would tell David what a wonderful relationship they could have if he would just forget about the past. That shut him up. She also learned to change the subject when David appeared angry. That also shut him up.

David got more and more icy and distant. He called less and less frequently. He began to speak more often about divorce. Sarah complained that the therapy wasn't helping.

One Sunday, out of desperation, Sarah decided to ask David about all his negative feelings. She agreed to listen to what he had to say. She used the disarming technique to find some truth in his criticisms. She used the inquiry technique and asked him to tell her about his dissatifactions with their marriage. She used thought and feeling empathy to try to see the world through his eyes and understand how he was feeling. At last David opened up. It wasn't pleasant. He began to rip into her. She disarmed him and asked for more criticisms. He ventilated more. This went on and on. It was rather traumatic. He raged at Sarah and finally stormed out of her apartment. Sarah went to bed discouraged and tearful and alone. She was convinced of what she'd been telling me all along—the stupid communication techniques had only made things worse.

When I saw Sarah two days later, she was elated. On Monday David had called her. He was affectionate and said that she seemed changed. After he left the apartment he began to realize that a lot of what he'd said wasn't entirely fair. He said he had also contributed to their problems and he thought he was beginning to fall in love with her again!

Although the effects of the three listening skills are not always so magical, they often are. A similar thing happens to me frequently in psychotherapy sessions. At the beginning and the end of every session I say, "Please tell me what you liked and disliked about our last session [or the session we had today]. Let's start with the negative things. Was there anything I said that hurt your feelings or turned you off?" Then, regardless of what the patients tell me, I look for the truth in their criticisms.

Let's assume the patient says, "You laughed and made fun of me." Now I might feel that I had been laughing at myself, but that's irrelevant because the patient felt laughed at and is hurt. If I defend myself, it will only alienate the patient. I might say, "I'm glad you said that. I feel bad that it hurt your feelings when I made a joke [feeling empathy]. I would feel angry if I felt someone was laughing at me [feeling empathy]. Do you feel that way [inquiry]? It's not my intention to make fun of you. You deserve my support and my respect [disarming]."

The purpose of a response like this is to make it safe for patients to express their feelings. If they're afraid to tell me when they're angry, my efforts will be sabotaged. If they tell me when they feel turned off and I respond with respect, feelings of trust and rapport will nearly always develop.

You're probably not a therapist and you may be wondering, "What does all this have to do with me?" Answer: Everything! I don't care if you're talking to your spouse, your son, your boss, or your customer. Everyone gets hurt and angry from time to time. Most people won't tell you—they feel too inhibited. If you make it your responsibility to encourage people to open up, you can deal with these negative feelings and they won't rob you of joy, intimacy, and success.

When you use inquiry, your tone of voice will be crucial. If you ask a question sarcastically or defensively, the method won't work. To state an extreme example, if someone accuses you of being selfish, you could get sarcastic and say, "Oh, I'm being selfish, am I?" This sounds like a question, but it's not. It's a rhetorical question. It's a thinly disguised put-down. What you're really saying is, "How dare you say such an insulting, unkind thing to a wonderful and innocent person like me!" Don't be surprised if the other person doesn't respond in the kindly, agreeable way you were hoping! A more valid use of inquiry would be: "Can you tell me what I've done or said that seemed selfish?" If you say this in a spirit of genuine curiosity, it will prompt the other person to open up in a more direct way.

Inquiry is not only used to learn more about how the other person is thinking and feeling, it can help transform vague negative reactions into concrete problems that you can deal with in a more productive manner. Suppose you are trying to get a promotion and your supervisor tells you he has some doubts because of your lack of experience. Don't succumb and feel defeated for the next six months.

Instead, use the inquiry technique: "Just what kind of experience do you feel I lack?" When your boss describes the qualities or experience you lack, respond with empathy and use the disarming technique: agree with your boss and show you understand his or her point of view. Make a plan to get that experience. Learning precisely what your boss is looking for will help you improve your marketability and will demonstrate your ability to listen and learn. Your boss will respect you more and will be more likely to help you. He or she might eventually give you the promotion you want or suggest another interesting option you hadn't considered.

Let's practice the inquiry technique. The man you've been dating says, "I need more space. I need my freedom." How could you respond?

_____

_____

_____

Answer: You need to focus on his feelings. What's he really saying? What's the message behind the words? You could say: "You say you need more space, more freedom [thought empathy]. It sounds like you feel trapped and dissatisfied with our relationship [feeling empathy]. Maybe you want to date other people [feeling empathy]. Can you tell me what some of the problems in our relationship are [inquiry]? I'd like to know what you like and don't like about it [inquiry]."

Your spouse says, "You're always leaving your socks around the house." How can you respond?

_____

_____

_____

Answer: "It's true. I have [disarming]. Are there other things I've been doing that you feel annoyed about [inquiry]?" Notice that you're not defending yourself or apologizing and promising to do better. Maybe you *should* try to be more consistent about throwing your dirty socks in the clothes bin. However, it would be unwise to focus prematurely on the solution to the problem because then the exchange of feelings will be cut short. Your spouse needs to talk about how he or she feels. Your spouse probably has *ten* complaints, but underneath all of them there's only one: "I feel hurt and angry because I feel unloved." It isn't terribly important if you think that some of these complaints are unreasonable. What is important is that you give your spouse a chance to tell you how he or she feels. Show that you're willing to listen and want to understand. Encourage your spouse to talk about the angry feelings. Respond with openness and show that you care. Then you've hit the jackpot. This is infinitely more important than picking up a pair of socks. This is the real secret of intimacy.

The three listening skills—disarming, empathy, and inquiry—capture the essence of effective listening. These skills are frequently overlooked, even by professionals whose very work demands expert communication. In a recent study at Presbyterian Medical Center in Denver, more than 300 clinical interviews by physicians were observed and evaluated. The investigators commented: "To our surprise all did not seem as it should be. Physicians at all levels [of training] who had previously been thought quite competent appeared defective in their interaction with patients. Our initial reaction was to distrust our observations, but repeated observations have shown great consistency." One of the problems: Doctors did not listen carefully to patients.

Sensitive listening skills are rare. Responding with empathy is especially difficult when you feel frustrated and upset, and when you feel you are being criticized or not listened to. But this is when you need listening skills the most, because your attempts to defend yourself and get your point across will just infuriate the other person. They have their heels dug in, and the more intently you try to contradict them, the more stubbornly they will insist that you are "wrong."

If you don't want to be involved in an exasperating no-win war of wills, find truth in what the other person is saying. You can often put the lie to their criticism without ever putting up a single argument in your own defense. It sounds like a paradox, and I call it the "Persuasive Law of Opposites": Agree with your critic, and you will disprove what he or she is saying about you. Try to disagree with your critic, and you will increase his or her conviction that the accusations are absolutely valid.

This startling phenomenon is illustrated on page 396. As you can see, when you respond to a harsh attack with a combination of empathy, disarming, and inquiry (the "persuasive answer"), the critic will soften and will revise his or her entrenched ideas about you. In contrast, if you become defensive or insist on contradicting the critic (the "defensive answer"), this will be about as helpful as throwing gasoline on a fire. He or she will feel certain that every accusation is true.

Persuasion through effective listening captures a form of verbal power that might be viewed as Eastern. I like to think of the method as "zeroing in," because you allow yourself temporarily to become a zero. Instead of being preoccupied with promoting your own ideas and forcing the other person to listen to your feelings, you *zero* in on the other person's thoughts and feelings. The moment you give up your urge to control or to convince the other person you are right, you will paradoxically gain enormous influence.

Let's assume you have listened and are ready to express your own point of view. How do you proceed? You can use two self-expression skills, "I feel" statements and stroking.

Self-Expression Skills #1: "I feel" Statements

Instead of arguing or getting defensive, you can express your feelings with "I feel" statements. The method is incredibly simple. All you do is say "I feel" and add a word that describes how you feel. You can use a word like annoyed, hurt, worried, frustrated, concerned, or sad. For example you can say, "I feel nervous" or "I feel angry."

There are several types of feelings that you can express with "I feel" statements:

1. **Negative feelings.** Examples include "I feel angry," "I feel criticized," "I feel put down," "I feel frustrated," "I feel coerced," "I feel misunderstood."

2. **Vulnerable feelings.** "I feel sad," "I feel rejected," "I feel hurt," "I feel unloved," "I feel disappointed," "I feel ignored," "I feel intimidated," "I feel attacked," or "I feel inadequate."

THE PERSUASIVE LAW OF OPPOSITES

If you agree with an angry critic by finding a grain of truth in what is said, you will paradoxically put the lie to the criticism. This is illustrated as the "Persuasive Answer." In contrast, if you defend yourself or disagree with the criticism, you will frequently make the critic more upset and convinced about his or her accusations. This is illustrated as the "Defensive Answer."

EXAMPLE #1

Your partner attacks you by saying:	"You obviously don't care about anyone but yourself."
Persuasive answer:	"What you're saying upsets me ['I feel' statement]. I guess I've given you the impression I don't care about you [thought empathy]. You certainly don't deserve to be treated like that [disarming]. I don't like to be ignored either, and I can understand that you might feel pretty irritated with me [feeling empathy]. Do you [inquiry]?"
Why you disprove the criticism:	You have demonstrated a genuine concern for the other person and expressed a regard for his or her feelings. You have avoided defending yourself in a self-centered manner. This demonstrates that you *do* care about him or her. Hence, the accusation is invalidated. By agreeing with the criticism, you have disproved it!
Defensive answer:	"That's a lie. I *do* care about you and when I don't give in, you whine and accuse me of not loving you. You're the one who's selfish!"
Why you confirm the criticism:	You sound angry and blaming. Your message doesn't convey the love and warmth you claim to feel, so the response sounds phony. Your partner will see you as cold, critical, and defensive and will feel justifiably convinced that you don't care about anybody but

	yourself. Your attempt to contradict the accusations will backfire. By contradicting the criticism, you have proven that it's valid!
EXAMPLE #2	
Your partner attacks you by saying:	"It's all your fault. I'm right and you're wrong. Why don't you just admit it, and stop being so stubborn?"
Persuasive answer:	"I probably have been acting stubborn [disarming]. You say things are my fault, and I'm willing to accept my share of the blame [thought empathy, disarming]. There is truth in what you're saying, and I want to understand your point of view a little better [disarming, inquiry]. I'm frustrated too, because I'm not getting my ideas across ['I feel' statement]. I want you to try to understand how I feel ['I feel' statement, feeling empathy]."
Why you disprove the criticism:	Because you are assuming some responsibility for the problem, you are rising above your partner's childish blame-casting. By showing your flexibility and willingness to listen, you have proven that you're not as "stubborn" or as "wrong" as your partner claims.
Defensive answer:	"You can blame me until kingdom comes, but you'll just be proving how childish you are. It's sheer stupidity to insist you're entirely right and I'm entirely wrong. The fact is, you're just as much to blame. Why don't you just admit it!"
Why you confirm the criticism:	Because you are contradicting your partner in an argumentative way, he or she will feel even more convinced that you are stubborn and inflexible. Your partner will feel attacked and will counterattack. The war of words will continue.

3. **Wishes and desires.** "I would like to spend more time with you," "I want us to work out this problem and feel close to each other," "I really want you to be on time," or "I would like you to try to understand my point of view."

"I feel" statements are in sharp contrast to "you" statements, like "*You're* making me mad" or "*You've* got no right to say that" or "*You're* wrong about that." These "you" statements sound critical, blaming and judgmental. They will always trigger a fight or an argument.

The three listening skills will help you deal with someone else's negative feelings. The self-expression skills will help you express your own. People have the greatest trouble expressing anger. We learn to attack when we're angry or we act our feelings out instead of stating them openly. We fear sharing our angry feelings because this makes us vulnerable. It's far easier to say, "Screw you!" and to reject someone rather than to tell them, "I feel annoyed about this. Let's talk it out."

"I feel" statements are crucial when you find yourself getting defensive or argumentative. I've observed hundreds and hundreds of times that when people are angry they start arguing instead of saying how they feel. They defend what they believe to be the "truth." You will tell yourself, "I'm right about this." You will argue and try to convince the other person that they are "wrong." But they are just as certain that they are right, so you will get locked into an argument. And no one will ever win!

The solution to this is simple. What you call the "truth" is, in reality, a disguised form of anger! Let me repeat that: TRUTH is just a form of hostility! And if you don't mind being shocked, then I'll tell you this: Your TRUTH is your ENEMY! Don't ever defend the "truth" again! Instead, simply say, "I feel angry" or "I feel frustrated right now." These statements will be a whole lot more honest and a whole lot more effective than arguing about the TRUTH!

Now, let's see if you can get the hang of it. Let's assume a family member says, "You're wrong about this. You're such a stupid jerk!" How would you respond, using "I feel" statements? Put your ideas here:

_____

_____

_____

_____

Answer: You could say, "I'm feeling attacked and put down. I feel defensive and hurt." This is infinitely better than, "Oh no I'm not! *You're* the one who's wrong about this! You're a jerk if I *ever* saw one!" This will just lead to an argument. Can you see this?

Suppose a friend says, "I'm ticked off at you." You feel annoyed because you feel they're blaming you for something that was primarily their fault. How would you respond, using "I feel" statements?

_____

_____

_____

_____

Answer: You can say, "I feel angry, too." This is infinitely preferable to getting defensive and criticizing them. The idea is to *share* your feelings rather than to *attack* with your feelings. The "I feel" statements simply provide information about how you feel. You tell them how you feel instead of arguing about who's right and who's wrong.

You're an attractive college student talking to your professor about your paper. He's an inspiring teacher, but he has a lecherous reputation. He says, "I think there's a special chemistry between us." You feel confused, embarrassed, upset. What can you say, using "I feel" statements?

_____

_____

_____

_____

Answer: You could say, "I'm feeling really pressured and uncomfortable right now. I came to get some help with the paper."

Although these ideas may sound quite straightforward, most people have an intense fear of expressing their feelings directly and openly. When they feel upset or annoyed, they deny their feelings and act them out instead. A patient became annoyed with me during a conference with several staff therapists who were all involved in her treatment. She felt I was discussing problems that were quite personal and she didn't feel ready to talk about them in the group setting. Her concerns were valid, but instead of saying "I'm not comfortable with this and would prefer to work on other problems," she suddenly stood up, complained of a headache, and stormed out of the room.

Although she felt and acted helpless, this was in reality a powerful maneuver that stunned everyone in the room. She projected the message "Don't mess with me or I'll make you pay!" Later on she denied that she was angry and claimed to be unaware that her actions might have been upsetting to others! This "passive-aggressive" behavior seems obvious when you see it in others, but it's all too easy to get sucked into it when you feel hurt, because you don't want to admit how you feel. You may pout, slam doors, play the role of the martyr, or gossip about people behind their backs instead of telling them how you feel face to face. You may express your feelings in a disguised form—being critical, or getting sarcastic and defensive and argumentative. You may express your feelings with judgmental body language like frowning, crossing your arms in front of you, or shaking your head to signal "no" while the other person is trying to talk.

The problem with this behavior is that although you let people know that *something* is going on that you don't like, you're not really clear about what it is. If you openly and honestly share how you're feeling, you and the other person will have the opportunity to deal with what's bothering you.

Self-Expression Skill #2: Stroking

More than anything else, people want to be cared about and appreciated. What we fear the most is being rejected or put down or judged. Therefore I always try to express a positive regard for the other person, even in the heat of battle. I try to let them know that I respect them and that they're important to me. This can relieve unspoken fears that someone is going to get rejected.

Many people have the hidden assumption that anger and caring are opposites. You may jump to the conclusion that if two people are mad at each other, it means they don't respect each other or care for each other. This makes you overreact, and any difference of opinion becomes a federal case. You may feel the need to reject the other person before you get rejected, so you can save face. You can often prevent this if you let them know that although you're at odds, you still think highly of them. This will make it easier for them to open up and to listen, because they will feel less threatened.

If a patient is angry with me and I also feel annoyed, I might say, "It seems that we're both frustrated with each other. I believe we can talk this out, even though it's uncomfortable to feel angry and to be criticized. I'm convinced that in the long run, this will make our work together more rewarding." The purpose of this message is to acknowledge honestly that we both feel angry and to let them know that I think it's okay to feel this way. I want it to be crystal clear that my agenda is to make things better and not to reject them.

You can express this same message in slightly different language to your spouse or to a friend or to someone you're doing business with. You might tell your spouse, "I'm mad as hell, but I do care about you." If you're having an argument with a close associate at work, you could say, "We have a strong difference of opinion about this, and I'm not at all comfortable with your point of view. However, I know we'll work this problem out, and I want you to know that I respect you and like working with you." The purpose of this is to keep the machine well oiled so it doesn't overheat and blow up. Most of us can tolerate considerable frustration if we feel cared about. It's easy to get that message across if you're willing to.

The philosophy behind stroking is that you can still respect someone even when you feel furious with something they did or said. This is similar to the philosophy of unconditional self-esteem that's behind so much of cognitive therapy. You can dislike what a person is *doing*, you can disagree with what they're *thinking*, and you can be uncomfortable with what they're *feeling*. But you won't gain anything if you judge or condemn them *as a person*. Remember that they are a collection of strengths and weaknesses, just as you are. If you maintain an attitude of respect or liking, the other person will sense this and will be far easier to deal with.

You may be thinking, "But what if that person really *is* a bum and I don't like them and I don't even want to have anything to do with them?" There will be many times when you will choose not to have anything to do with someone. They may be too exploitative, too self-centered, or too insensitive to be worth the effort. The costs of maintaining the relationship will simply outweigh the benefits. The only question is how to part ways with them. When you express your negative feelings, it may be a good idea to say something positive about them as well. If you allow them to salvage some self-esteem, they'll be less likely to get defensive and more likely to hear at least some of what you have to say. Your message will be more realistic and have a more powerful impact.

Communication Exercise #1

Now let's see if you can integrate good listening skills with good self-expression skills. A man named Harry runs a dry cleaning establishment. He has a tendency to feel irritable and harassed by customers. Last Saturday, several people complained about spots on their slacks. By the time the third customer complained, Harry felt he'd had it. A lot of four-letter words were flying through his mind as he explained in an icy tone of voice that *some* spots *cannot* be removed and that they simply become more obvious when the garment is *properly* dry cleaned. Would you call that an example of good communication or bad communication?

_____ good communication

_____ bad communication

Why?_____

_____

_____

_____

_____

I would say it's bad communication, because Harry's defending himself and alienating the customers. They will feel put down and take their business elsewhere. Then Harry will get even more irate as his business dwindles. He'll complain about how unreasonable and ungrateful people are. He sees himself as a victim, and this mind-set operates as a self-fulfilling prophecy.

Although your life is probably very different from Harry's, there may be times when people complain when you feel you've done a good job. If you were Harry, how could you respond to the complaining customer, using the techniques you've been learning?

_____

_____

_____

_____

_____

Answer: You could say, "I'm disappointed that the slacks aren't satisfactory to you ['I feel' statement]. I know how frustrating it can be to have a bad spot like that on a nice pair of trousers [feeling empathy]. Your business is important to me and I want you to be pleased [stroking]. Sometimes a spot like that will show up more when a garment is cleaned, and it may not be possible to remove it without ruining the slacks ['I feel' statement]. What would you like me to do [inquiry]? I don't want you to leave here feeling annoyed or thinking you're not getting the very best service [thought and feeling empathy]." The purpose of this statement is to create an attitude of friendliness and cooperation. Harry might offer to clean another pair of slacks free as a gesture of goodwill, even though he's not at fault. Over the years, he'll make the money back a hundredfold if he has a happy customer. If he empathizes and shows some genuine concern for the customer's frustration, the customer will probably accept Harry's explanation and not demand any compensation at all.

Some readers may raise the question: "But what if the customer is totally unreasonable and insists that Harry ruined the slacks? What if the customer demands $100 for a new pair?" I'm curious about your answer to this question. If you were Harry, what would you say, using the listening skills and self-expression skills?

_____

_____

_____

_____

Answer: Harry could say, "I know how annoying it is not to be able to wear a fine pair of slacks because of a stain [feeling empathy]. It sounds like you're pretty angry, and I would be, too [feeling empathy]. I'm not comfortable paying for the slacks, because they were cleaned properly ['I feel' statement]. If we ruin a garment because of negligence, we do pay for it, because that's only fair [disarming]. I value you and don't want to lose you as a customer [stroking]. Is there any other way I could compensate you as a token of my goodwill [inquiry]? I'd be happy not to charge for this bill, since the slacks are no good to you, and I'd also be willing to give you a credit for another cleaning."

Communication Exercise #2

A teenage girl named Linda was shopping with her boyfriend, Ray, in a record store. Linda told him she was going next door to use the ladies' room at a fast-food restaurant. As she left she said, "I'll meet you at the car in five minutes." Ray misunderstood and thought Linda said "I'll meet you here."

On the way out of the restaurant, Linda bought Ray a milkshake. She waited for him at the car in the hot sun. After five minutes she got furious, dumped the melting milkshake on the ground, and stormed into the store. Linda glared at Ray. He said, "What's wrong?" She refused to talk and pouted. Ray became upset and pleaded for her to tell him what was wrong. She still refused to talk. They left the store and went for a drive. Linda ignored him and he begged her to talk to him.

You can see that her passive-aggressive reaction has many payoffs.

Linda's pride was hurt and she can make Ray pay! In addition, she gets loads of attention from him! She gets to take out her frustration on him by glaring while he says all the right things, such as "I love you! I want to talk to you!" This makes Linda feel enormously powerful and important.

Why shouldn't she behave like this if it's so rewarding? One danger is that she may get into this pattern with friends who may not be so willing to put up with her. As her relationship with Ray progresses, he too may begin to get sick of her, once he realizes he's being manipulated and is jumping through a hoop like a trained dog. Finally, Linda's selfish, self-righteous behavior is not consistent with her value system, with her personal happiness, or with real sharing and intimacy.

How could she have expressed her feelings, using "I feel" statements, when she went into the store?

_____

_____

_____

_____

Answer: She could have said: "I'm feeling ignored and annoyed. I said I was going to wait at the car and I thought you'd be right out. I bought you a milkshake. I've been waiting out there in the sun and the milkshake has almost melted."

How could Ray have expressed his feelings, using "I feel" statements, when she was pouting at him and glaring and refusing to talk?

_____

_____

_____

_____

Answer: He could say, "You seem real upset with me, and I don't know what you're upset about [feeling empathy, inquiry]. It bothers me when you glare at me and refuse to talk ['I feel' statement]. I feel punished ['I feel' statement]. I don't like it ['I feel' statement]. If I did something to make you mad, I want you to tell me what it was so we can clear it up [inquiry]."

Sometimes when people pout, they don't want to talk. They want to be left alone for a few minutes. How could Linda express this, using "I feel" statements?

_____

_____

_____

_____

Answer: She could say, "I'm upset and I don't want to talk right now. I need to be left alone for a few minutes. Then it will be easier for me to talk about it."

Summary of Communication Skills

LISTENING SKILL #1: THE DISARMING TECHNIQUE

1. Find some truth in what the other person says. They have to be right to some extent, since no one is ever 100 percent wrong. Usually, when you agree with the other person they will then stop arguing and agree with you! This remarkable phenomenon is called the "Law of Opposites."

2. If you feel angry or attacked, express your feelings with nonchallenging "I feel" statements, such as "I feel upset that . . ." Avoid the temptation to argue or strike back. Don't get defensive.

3. Answer in such a way that your dignity and self-esteem are maintained, even if you agree with the other person's criticism.

4. Give up your desire to lash out or blame the other person. Try to maintain an attitude of mutual respect so that nobody has to lose face or feel put down.

5. Avoid getting into who is "right" or "wrong." This serves no purpose!

LISTENING SKILL #2: EMPATHY

1. Put yourself in the other person's shoes. Listen carefully and try to understand accurately what they are thinking as they are talking. State what you think the other person is thinking by saying something like "It sounds like . . ." and then paraphrase respectfully what you understood them to say.

2. Also try to understand what the other person is feeling. Listen with your "third ear." Notice their body language. Do they appear tense? Angry? Hurt? Acknowledge what the person is feeling, based on what they said and the manner in which they said it.

3. Ask a question to confirm how they are feeling, such as "I can imagine you must be feeling frustrated with me. Is this true?" Ask them if you have accurately understood what they are thinking and feeling.

4. Use an "I feel" statement to let them know how you would feel if you were in their shoes. You might say, "I would be feeling the same way if this had happened to me."

5. Accept the other person's feelings. Do not be hostile, critical, or defensive. Let them know that you are willing to hear what they have to say.

LISTENING SKILL #3: INQUIRY

1. Most people have an intense fear of expressing their feelings openly. They are always afraid of conflict and will avoid telling you they're angry with you. They deny their feelings, and then act them out. You can prevent this if you ask the other person to tell you more about their negative feelings.

2. You can also ask the other person to tell you more about the specific problem that makes them feel upset. What are the

details? How often does it happen? How do they feel about it? What did you do that turned them off?

3. Ask the person to tell you directly what you did or said that hurt their feelings. When they tell you, don't get defensive. Instead, use empathy and the disarming technique. Find some truth in what they have to say. If you feel upset or irritated or put down, express your feelings with an "I feel" statement.

4. Use a tone of voice that is respectful, not challenging, when asking what made them unhappy or angry. Do not use any form of sarcasm.

5. Don't be afraid of anger and conflict. They are healthy. Don't let the other person's unhappy feelings go unexpressed. That makes the feelings much more intense.

SELF-EXPRESSION SKILL #1: "I FEEL" STATEMENTS

1. When expressing your feelings, use "I feel" statements, such as "I feel upset." Avoid "you" statements, such as "You're making me upset." These "you" statements sound critical and judgmental and always trigger fights and arguments! Here are some examples:

"You always" or "You never . . ."
"You are wrong."
"You shouldn't . . ."
"You've got no right."
"It's your fault."
"You're making me angry."

2. Don't act out your feelings! State them! Use "I feel" statements. Acting out emotions can take the form of:

Pouting	Being sarcastic
Stony silence	Being critical
Gossiping	Being argumentative
Door slamming	Frowning
Martyr playing	Being rude
Drinking too much	Negative body language

3. Negative feelings can be expressed by saying, "I feel . . ." with words like:

concerned   pressured
frustrated   misunderstood
angry   uncomfortable
coerced

4. Vulnerable feelings can be expressed by saying, "I feel . . ." with words like:

sad   nervous
rejected   ignored
hurt   inadequate
unloved   intimidated
disappointed

5. Wishes and desires can be expressed by saying something like:

"I would like to spend more time with you."
"I really want us to work out this problem and to be closer."
"I really want to feel close to you."
"I want you to try to understand my point of view."

SELF-EXPRESSION SKILL #2: STROKING

1. Generally speaking, most people want to feel cared about and appreciated. The greatest fear that people have is being put down, rejected, or judged.

2. Reassure the other person by clearly letting them know that you respect them and that they are important to you, even if you are angry or disagreeing with them at the moment.

3. Let the other person know that you want to work out the problem in a mutually satisfactory way.

4. Don't criticize or condemn them as a person. Nothing is ever gained by doing this. Attacking them personally is very different from commenting negatively on something they are doing or thinking.

5. The listening and self-expression skills are only techniques. Real communication results from the spirit of genuine respect for yourself and for the other person. If your goal is to prove

yourself right, to blame the other person, or to get back at them, any communication technique will fail. But if your goal is to resolve the problem and to understand how the other person is thinking and feeling, these powerful methods will help you resolve conflicts and enjoy greater intimacy.

20

•

How to Change the Way You Communicate

So far you've learned what good and bad communication are and how to listen and express your own feelings more effectively. I have devised a three-step written exercise that can help you make these ideas a natural part of the way you communicate. This exercise can make the difference between intellectual understanding and actual changing. If you read a book on dieting or jogging, you would learn a great deal about losing weight and getting in shape, but your body wouldn't actually change a great deal unless you began to eat less and exercise regularly. By the same token, if you do the written exercise in this chapter over a period of weeks, the insights you've gained will be transformed into a new and more effective way of communicating with others.

I decided to change the way I communicated in the late 1970s. I found that I sometimes got into conflicts with uncooperative patients, and I wasn't always satisfied with the outcome. If an angry patient expressed feelings of hopelessness and said that I didn't really understand his or her problems, I often got defensive. I would say that I thought I could understand their problems reasonably well and that I felt convinced they weren't hopeless. I would urge them to start doing more of the self-help assignments between sessions. The patient might reply, "That won't work! I've already tried it." Then I might point out that the one time he or she tried it, the symptoms of depression actually improved. Then the patient would say it was a fluke and it didn't count. On and on the argument went!

Going home on the train at night, I would write out a little script of what the patient and I had said to each other. Although my statements always appeared valid and logical, I could see that they weren't especially effective. The conflict usually hadn't been resolved, and the patient and I felt frustrated with each other.

I got tired of these logjams and asked myself, "What could I have said instead? How might I have handled it differently?" I started rewriting those scripts. If I felt stuck, I showed the scripts to colleagues and asked what they would say. After revising my statements several times, I usually found a new approach that I was more comfortable with. Then I tried this out the next time I saw the patient—with a much better result. The patient felt understood, there was a meeting of the minds, and we began to work together effectively.

The disarming technique and the "I feel" statements were especially helpful, but I sometimes resisted the disarming technique because I felt that I was "right" and the patient was "wrong." I also sensed that a kind of battle was going on, and I didn't want to back down or lose face. I found that it helped enormously if I told myself, "Win by losing, remember to surrender," during these confrontations.

I worked at these written scripts every day for several months, and the method was extremely helpful. I really did change the way I communicated with patients. The change was dramatic, not subtle, and it became second nature after a while. Now when a patient becomes annoyed or uncooperative, I switch into the listening skills and the self-expression skills almost as if I'm going on automatic pilot. The plane usually navigates through the storm and lands safely.

You can master these same skills. First, think of a conflict you had with someone that didn't work out well. In the left-hand column of the Revise Your Communication Style form, write down what they said that was upsetting to you, as shown in the sample on page 413. David, one of my patients, had an argument with Terri, his wife. Terri said, "You criticize every single thing I do." As you can see David wrote this down verbatim.

REVISE YOUR COMMUNICATION STYLE		
S/he says	**I ordinarily say**	**Revised version**
In this column record something your partner typically says that you find upsetting.	In this column record what you usually say. Point out why your statement is self-defeating.	Substitute a more effective statement.
Terri: "You criticize every single thing I do."	David: "Terri, I don't! That's a stupid thing to say!" (This sounds critical and disrespectful. I dismissed what she said and contradicted her. It's a put-down. She'll feel hurt and frustrated.)	David: "I've got to agree with you [disarming]. I do feel angry and left out of your life ['I feel' statement]. I often feel hurt ['I feel' statement] and I criticize you to get back at you [disarming]. And it only makes things worse [disarming]."

In the middle column, write down what you said to the other person. (If you pouted and said nothing, just put "I said nothing.") David responded by saying, "Terri, I don't! That's a stupid thing to say!" Once you write it down, think about why this response didn't work very well. You will notice that your responses are often an example of bad communication because you're not expressing your own feelings with "I feel" statements and you're not acknowledging how the other person is thinking and feeling. You will find that your comments are nearly always argumentative and that you are preoccupied with your version of the "Truth." When you analyze your middle-column responses, review the list of "Characteristics of Bad Communication" on page 365. This list will help you figure out why your statement precipitated an argument instead of a good exchange of feelings.

You can see how David analyzed his comment. By insisting that Terri was wrong, he proved that she was right! His statement was critical, and this provoked an argument. Arguing or avoiding each other is just about all David and Terri have done for several years.

Finally, in the right-hand column, labeled "Revised Version," write down what you might have said. Try to use the three listening skills and the two self-expression skills. Remember to express your feelings and to paraphrase what the other person is saying. Try to find some truth in it.

You can see that David has been doing his homework. He was able to apply those methods skillfully. You will probably agree that his revised response would have a markedly different impact.

There are two blank Revise Your Communication Style forms at the end of this chapter. Practice with one of them, and save the other one to copy. If you have trouble coming up with good "revised versions," or if you can't see why your middle column answers aren't satisfactory, think it over for a couple of days. Reread the previous chapter. Then come back to the form and read over what you wrote. Usually the light bulb will suddenly come on, and you will think of a better response! I often find it useful to ask a friend or colleague. They frequently have the objectivity I may lack when I'm overly involved in a situation.

Let's look at another example. Joanne is the woman described in Chapter 18, who was separated from her husband, Ted. When she finally encouraged Ted to express his anger, his interest in the relationship was rekindled. They were having a good time on a date when Ted suddenly said in an irritated tone of voice: "Why are you being so sweet? Why are you being so fake? This is how you were when we were first dating! Everything was 'fine.' " Joanne replied: "That's how I feel. I have missed you. I'm not being fake." This led to an argument. Later Joanne wrote his comment in the left-hand column of the form and put her response in the middle column, as illustrated on page 415.

Can you see why her comment triggered a bad response? She forgot to express her feelings or to acknowledge his. That's the definition of bad communication. She responded defensively and contradicted him. This tendency is nearly universal, and it never works well. This is the most important thing for you to understand about communication! It may seem obvious when you see these argumentative reactions in other people, but when *you* do it, you won't notice. You'll think you're being reasonable.

REVISE YOUR COMMUNICATION STYLE		
S/he says	**I ordinarily say**	**Revised version**
In this column record something your partner typically says that you find upsetting.	In this column record what you usually say. Point out why your statement is self-defeating.	Substitute a more effective statement.
Ted: "Why are you being so sweet? Why are you being so fake? This is how you were when we were first dating. Everything was 'fine.' "	Joanne: "That's how I feel. I have missed you. I'm not being fake." (I'm being defensive. I'm contradicting Ted. This triggered an argument.)	Joanne: "I feel upset right now ['I feel' statement]. I feel put down ['I feel' statement]. You seem annoyed with me [feeling empathy]. Have I been acting fake [inquiry]? Were you uncomfortable with me when we were first dating [inquiry]?"

There's something else about Joanne's middle column remark that I find amazing. Do you remember the "Persuasive Law of Opposites" from the previous chapter? If you agree with a criticism you will put the lie to it, but if you argue with the critic, you will always prove that he or she is right. You can see that Joanne argued with Ted. She insisted she wasn't being "fake." She insisted she did feel "sweet." Can you see that these argumentative responses proved that Ted was right? In reality, she felt hurt and put down at that moment. By insisting that she felt loving and that she had missed him, she came across in a way that was quite "fake." She wasn't being honest with herself or with Ted.

In the right-hand column Joanne put a revised version of how she might have responded. You can see that she expresses the annoyance she feels when Ted attacks her. She doesn't do this in a blaming or defensive way—she's simply sharing her feelings by using "I feel" statements. She also asks about his feelings and urges him to tell her what he's thinking. This will be more likely to lead to an honest exchange of feelings that will bring them closer together.

REVISE YOUR COMMUNICATION STYLE*

S/he says	I ordinarily say	Revised version
In this column record something your partner typically says that you find upsetting.	In this column record what you usually say. Point out why your statement is self-defeating.	Substitute a more effective statement.

REVISE YOUR COMMUNICATION STYLE*

S/he says	I ordinarily say	Revised version
In this column record something your partner typically says that you find upsetting.	In this column record what you usually say. Point out why your statement is self-defeating.	Substitute a more effective statement.

THE FIVE SECRETS OF EFFECTIVE COMMUNICATION*

LISTENING SKILLS

1. **The Disarming Technique.** You find some truth in what the other person is saying, even if you feel convinced that what they're saying is totally wrong, unreasonable, irrational, or unfair.

2. **Empathy.** You put yourself in the other person's shoes and try to see the world through his or her eyes.

   - **Thought empathy:** You paraphrase the other person's words.
   - **Feeling empathy:** You acknowledge how they're probably feeling, given what they are saying to you.

3. **Inquiry:** You ask gentle, probing questions to learn more about what the other person is thinking and feeling.

SELF-EXPRESSION SKILLS

1. **"I feel" statements.** You express your feelings with "I feel" statements (such as "I feel upset") rather than with "you statements" (such as "You're wrong!" or "You're making me furious!").

2. **Stroking:** You find something genuinely positive to say to the other person, even in the heat of battle. This indicates that you respect the other person, even though you may be angry with each other.

21

•

How to Deal with Difficult People

In this chapter we will talk about dealing with difficult people, including:

- People who are "passive-aggressive." Instead of telling you they're upset, they pout and refuse to talk to you.
- People who are actively aggressive. They put you down and sound hostile, sarcastic, or condescending.
- People who are stubborn and argumentative.
- People who are critical and judgmental.
- Pushy people who put you on the spot and make excessive demands on you.
- Chronic complainers.
- People who need help.
- People who are boring and superficial.

How to Communicate with Someone Who Refuses to Talk to You

Many people ask me, "Dr. Burns, the listening skills you describe are all well and good, but what do you do when someone refuses to talk to you?"

Here are some examples:

- Steve's 14-year-old son misbehaved. When Steve tried to discuss this with him, he threw a tantrum and slammed the door to his room.
- Mary has had an argument with her friend Susan. They both flew off the handle and made a lot of inflammatory statements. A few days later Mary suggested it might help to talk things out. Susan replied: "There's *nothing* to talk about. You're not the kind of person I care to have anything to do with!"
- Harold's wife seemed sullen. Harold didn't know what the trouble was, so he asked her if she was upset with him. She bristled: "Of course I'm not upset. Why don't you get off my back and leave me alone!?"

Steve, Mary, and Harold have been thwarted. Thwarters rely on passive-aggressive tactics. They stone you with silence and insist they're not upset. They relish their power to frustrate and upset you. If you try to persuade them to talk to you, they'll just continue to thwart you.

So what's the solution? It's easy. You can neutralize their "thwarting" with the potent "anti-thwarting maneuver."

Step 1: Empathize. Instead of insisting they talk, ask in a friendly way why they don't want to. This often opens up the communication immediately. Eventually Steve's son will have to come out of his room. Steve could say, "It must be hard to talk things over when you feel criticized. Is that how you feel?" Mary could use a similar technique to respond to Susan's thwart: "I'm not the kind of person you care to have as a friend? Maybe you'd be willing to tell me some of the ways I've let you down. Would you?" Harold could say this to his wife: "I see that you don't much feel like sharing your feelings with me. Maybe you think I'm not an easy person to talk to. Is this the case?"

If you empathize in an accurate and nonjudgmental way, the chances are good the other person will soften up and talk. Use the inquiry technique to probe gently for more information about how he or she thinks and feels. If the other person says something critical—which probably will happen, because he or she feels angry with you—make sure you use the disarming technique to find some truth in the criticisms. This will set the other person more at ease.

Good listening skills are especially important in dealing with thwarters, because their thwarting habits show that they lack good assertive skills. They're annoyed and they don't know how to express their feelings in an effective manner. When you disarm them, empathize, and use the inquiry technique, it will be much easier for them to say what's on their mind.

Step 2: The Anti-Thwart. Let's assume the worst. Even when you empathize, they still refuse to talk. This frequently happens, especially if they're boiling. What can you do? It's quite simple. You zap them with the Anti-Thwart.

Here's how it works. Briefly agree that this isn't a good time for them to talk. Emphasize that you feel some communication is needed and suggest that you can talk things over later, when they're more in the mood. That's all you have to do.

Suppose Steve's son refuses to open up and says, "I've already told you, I'm not going to talk about this. Leave me alone!" Steve can say: "I can see you're not in the mood to talk now, and you shouldn't have to. I respect that. Every man needs to be alone at times. Nevertheless, we *do* have something we need to talk over. We can do this sometime in the next day or two, when you're more in the mood."

Typically, the other person will respond to our Anti-Thwart with another desperate attempt to thwart you. Steve's son might say, "Don't hold your breath" or "I won't talk to you now *or* later! Leave me alone, dammit!" In this case, just stick to your strategy and repeat your position gently—like this:

STEVE: You've got the right to be alone now, and you need to be alone. That's why I'm not going to talk to you any more right now. Nevertheless, we do have some things we need to talk over later. Even though you don't want to just now, eventually we will find a time. Tomorrow or the next day, I'll ask you if you're in the mood. In the meantime, if the spirit hits you and you want to talk, let me know.

SON: I'll *never* be in the mood. Not *now*, not *ever*!

STEVE: I know exactly how you feel. But never is a long time. I'll check with you in a day or two. When you feel ready, we'll work this problem out. We do have some things that we need to look at.

Essentially, this anti-thwarting strategy allows Steve to avoid getting caught up in a power struggle, and it leaves the ball in his son's court. His son is acting childish—and probably knows it—and Steve reminds him that sooner or later he'll have to deal with the problem. Steve wins because he doesn't try to control his son—he gives him his freedom. At the same time, Steve doesn't have to compromise on the principle that ultimately the problem must and will be talked out.

The anti-thwarting maneuver accomplishes a lot for you. It allows both parties to withdraw temporarily without losing face. You have responded to the other person's adolescent tactics in an adult way— they'll have to come up to your level if you don't descend to theirs. You have refused to accept the invitation to feel frustrated, to act pushy, or to get involved in a nonproductive battle of wills. You relinquish the urge to control. You avoid blaming, making demands, or polarizing the other person.

The thwarter may *want* you to get uptight and combative. This gets them off the hook so they can focus on your irrational behavior. Why give in to this? By reminding them that you do need to talk, but only when they're ready, you've left the ball in their court. The onus is on them, not you, and they know it!

THE ANTI-THWARTING DO'S AND DON'TS

- *Don't* insist they talk to you right now. They have a right to be alone. Respect that right. You'll only lose by trying to control them.
- *Don't* thwart them by saying, "Okay, then I won't talk to you, either." In this case, you're buying into the rejection.
- *Don't* blame yourself or judge what you're doing by the other person's haughty and childish reactions. They're refusing to talk. It's a reflection on them, not on you.
- *Don't* get judgmental. Although they are behaving in a hostile and immature way, keep your eye on your two goals—empathy and a postponement of the discussion.
- *Don't* allow yourself to get frustrated by insisting they talk right now, because you will give them the gratification they crave. They want you to feel upset so they can switch the spotlight onto your irritation. Keep your cool. Don't get sucked into their trap.
- *Do* empathize with their reasons for being unwilling to talk things over. They may think you're overly critical or judgmental; they may think you're not a sympathetic listener; they may be feeling ashamed or embarrassed about something they did; or they may be clamming up because they feel it's inappropriate to express angry feelings. Ask them about these possibilities in a gentle, nonjudgmental way. This will frequently open them right up.

- *Do* postpone the discussion if they still refuse to talk. Emphasize the importance of discussing things later, and give them permission to back off temporarily. This prevents a polarization. If they continue to thwart you later on, simply empathize and postpone again.

How to Deal with Someone Who Is Hostile

Sometimes, instead of refusing to communicate, the other person may be aggressive and give you a verbal blast. He or she may talk down to you or use a condescending or sarcastic tone of voice. Your first reaction will usually be to get defensive and blast right back, or to feel hurt and to blame yourself. In both cases, you're letting the other person call the shots. You're putting him or her in charge. Either response will just make the unpleasantness escalate.

So what can you do? Good listening and self-expression skills are nearly always the key to the resolution of any conflict. You need to listen and hear the truth in what the other person is saying, and to acknowledge how he or she is feeling. At the same time, you need to express your feelings about the way you are being treated. I call this method "changing the focus," because you draw attention to the hostile way the feelings are being expressed.

Changing the focus is a listening skill: you acknowledge the other person's anger and you describe the hostile way they are expressing it. Changing the focus is also a self-expression skill: you let them know that you feel upset about the way you're being treated. This technique can soften a hostile exchange and bring about greater feelings of trust. For example, if someone puts you down you can say, "I'm feeling put down right now ['I feel' statement]. Your tone of voice has a sharp edge [changing the focus]."

When you draw attention to the way you are being treated, don't get hostile. Think in terms of sharing the way you feel instead of attacking the other person. You don't want to say "You're putting me down." It makes you sound like a self-pitying victim, because you're blaming the other person. It will infuriate the other person. He or she can say, "What a pity! Little baby feels put down!"

You will also want to use the three listening skills to learn more about what the other person is feeling. If a family member calls you an idiot, you could say, "It sounds like you're pretty annoyed with me [feeling empathy]. I want you to tell me what I did that turned you off [inquiry]. I suspect you've got a good reason to feel ticked off [disarming]."

The other person undoubtedly has a valid point. The only problem is that the two of you are battling. Use the inquiry technique to prompt the other person to become more direct with you. Try to maintain a spirit of respect when you do it. Use the disarming technique and try to put yourself in the other person's shoes to see if you can grasp why he or she is acting in such an aggressive way.

Debbie was enraged when she discovered that her husband, Tom, a Wall Street investment banker, had been having an affair with a colleague for many years. After several months of turbulence, they got divorced. Tom subsequently married this woman, and Debbie maintained custody of their 12-year-old son, Bob.

Debbie felt devastated and intensely jealous. She had difficulties letting go, and the hope that Tom would leave his new wife and return to her kept her from getting genuinely interested in any of the men she dated. To make matters worse, Tom and his new wife purchased the very house that Tom and Debbie had once dreamed of owning. When Tom's new wife got pregnant, he seemed to gloat and Debbie felt crushed. She felt that Tom had everything—a successful career, good looks and charm, and an attractive wife—and that she had nothing but bitterness and loneliness.

One night when Tom was on the phone telling his son Bob about his new wife's pregnancy, an argument ensued. Bob blurted out that Tom seemed more interested in his new baby than in him or Debbie. Then Bob hung up on his dad. Tom called back and Debbie answered. Tom was enraged and demanded to talk to Bob. Debbie explained that Bob was in his bedroom sobbing, too upset to come to the phone. Tom became abusive, hurling four-letter words at Debbie. He even accused her of being an unfit mother and said he was going to sue for custody of their son.

If you were Debbie, how would you have handled this? Would you defend yourself? Would you fight back? Debbie's best bet may be to change the focus. Remember that the essence of the technique is to change the focus of the conversation from the content of the discussion to the style of the interaction.

First, Debbie must empathize with Tom's angry feelings. She needs to draw him out, using the three listening skills, so she can try to see the world through his eyes.

Debbie could say, "I know you love Bob a lot and it hurts you that he won't come to the phone [feeling empathy]. You two do need to talk this over, and I'm willing to support you in this [disarming]. I'm sure Bob feels just as hurt and threatened by the new baby as I do ['I feel' statement]. After he's settled down a bit, I'll encourage him to call you back so the two of you can talk things over." This response would mean that Debbie is giving up the urge to get revenge. Her goal becomes to work with Tom toward a solution rather than allowing their son to become a pawn in the struggle. She validates his concerns instead of opposing him and doing battle.

Next, Debbie needs to share her feelings about the way she is being treated. She could say, "I feel put down, and it bothers me greatly that we're fighting like this over Bob. ['I feel' statement]. You've got a valid need to talk to him [disarming], but when you swear at me and threaten me, it makes it hard to work together."

This concept is not new to you, since I've repeatedly emphasized the vital importance of good listening skills throughout the last several chapters. These skills are *exceptionally* important in hostile interactions. Tom does not feel respected or understood. That, in fact, is the very reason that he feels so hostile and acts so aggressive.

Aggressive individuals like Tom are generally just as afraid of intimacy and sharing as are the passive-aggressive people described in the last section. It just doesn't seem that way because they blast their negative feelings at you with full intensity. Tom lashes out instead of sharing his negative feelings because he feels afraid. He fears being vulnerable and saying, "Debbie, I feel hurt and frightened. It seems like I'm losing my son's respect. I need your support." Instead, he intimidates Debbie and provokes a fight. This keeps Debbie on the defensive and he doesn't have to risk feeling vulnerable or appearing weak and inadequate.

Notice that when you change the focus, you point out how you feel about the hostile style of relating instead of arguing about the issue at hand. One reason this is so difficult is that you'll get distracted by the content of what the other person is saying and you'll overlook the hostile style and tone in which they say it. Tom sounds self-righteous and intimidating, and it's easy for Debbie to get confused and to fight back.

When should you apply this technique? When you feel threatened, put down, or exasperated, you can use these emotions to your advantage if you take them as signals that you need to change the focus. Changing the focus calls attention to Tom's hostility and shifts the tone if Debbie is willing to hear what he has to say. He obviously feels frustrated and probably thinks she doesn't respect him. That is why he's acting so hostile in the first place. She needs to acknowledge his concerns in a sympathetic way, and to let him know that she also wants to be treated with greater respect. This conveys an attitude of self-esteem as well as a basic respect for Tom. Neither of them will have to lose face or be reduced to the status of an object.

Does this mean she's supposed to like Tom after he betrayed her and left her in so much anguish? No. She has every right to feel angry and hurt. But she has a basic decision to make, the same decision we all have to make during an angry encounter. There's a fork in the road, and we have to go down one road or the other. One is the road of hostility and defensiveness. You are intent on winning because you are so afraid of being the loser. You feel beaten down and have the overwhelming desire to even the score.

The other road is based on self-esteem and respect for the other person. Although you may feel angry, your goal is to share your angry feelings in a way that will enhance your chances of being heard, and to listen to the truth and the hurt feelings behind the other person's angry blasts. You are working from the assumption of "us," as opposed to "me versus you." Your goal is not to wage war but to work together to resolve the problem.

How to Communicate with Someone Who Is Stubborn and Argumentative

One of the commonest complaints I hear is "My spouse always has to be 'right.' He [or she] is never willing to listen to my point of view." The biggest mistake you can make in this situation is to promote your own ideas and try to persuade the other person that they should listen to you. This never works. You need to give in order to get. If you want to get some understanding, you may have to give some understanding first.

First, ask yourself why the other person is being so argumentative and stubborn. Maybe part of the problem is that you're not listening to them! Why would they keep harping away at you if they felt you had gotten the point? They wouldn't! Every stubborn, argumentative person has an equally stubborn partner who is defensive and argumentative and who refuses to listen to them.

This problem will disappear if you use the three listening skills: the disarming technique, empathy, and inquiry. Of the three, disarming is probably the most powerful and important. The moment you find the truth in the other person's point of view, they will soften and suddenly become more open to your point of view. In order to do this, you must give up the notion that you are the only one who's right and that what they have to say is pure and utter nonsense. There's always something important and valid about what the other person is saying that's being ignored and resisted. That's precisely why they get dogmatic and furious.

Linda and Fred participated for several weeks in our intensive program for depression at my clinic in Philadelphia. Part of the treatment included therapy sessions with them together because they both admitted their marriage had been cold and unfulfilling for decades. Linda had caught Fred in an affair thirty years earlier, and she had never forgiven him. She felt he was an untrustworthy, narcissistic liar, and she wasn't about to open up and become vulnerable and let herself get hurt again. They'd practically never had sex ever since. Linda's feelings of chronic depression, bitterness, and unfulfillment were the price she gladly paid to get back at Fred and to protect herself from the risk of trusting him.

During their sessions, Linda would frequently say, "I can't trust you. You don't tell the truth. You betrayed me and showed your true colors when you had the affair." Then Fred would defend himself and insist this wasn't the truth and that it wasn't fair. He would explain that he'd learned his lesson and he'd never had any more affairs. He insisted that had been faithful to her ever since. Then Linda would repeat that he was basically dishonest and untrustworthy. On and on the argument raged. They both admitted that they'd been trying unsuccessfully to resolve this for decades.

Now, put yourself in Fred's shoes. Assume that you have been faithful and trustworthy ever since. How would you get Linda to see your point of view? How would you get her to agree with you? What can you say when she accuses you of being unfaithful? Put your ideas here:

_____

_____

_____

You must acknowledge the truth in her point of view before she will soften and open up to you. You could say, "You know, you're right [disarming]. I did have an affair and I betrayed you [disarming]. I hurt you terribly [feeling empathy]." Notice that instead of trying to defend his innocence—which will annoy her and make him seem even more dishonest—he admits his guilt. Paradoxically, Linda may suddenly sense the possibility of forgiving him. As they talk, he may also want to express his feelings—he feels punished and rejected— instead of arguing that he's "right." This will have a far more powerful impact than insisting that he's been faithful. That's because sharing his feelings *is* intimacy. In contrast, when he argues about what a good guy he has been, he simply sounds phony and dishonest. Furthermore, he *is* dishonest when he defends himself, because he's hiding how annoyed and put down he feels!

With considerable encouragement, Fred did begin to communicate more openly with Linda. When he acknowledged her feelings and shared his own feelings of anger and rejection, she wept and admitted how lonely she felt and how much she wanted to feel close to him again. She said she knew that she'd been punishing him because of her fears of being let down. She asked him to be patient with her because the process of forgiveness and building trust would take some time.

How to Deal with People Who Are Critical and Judgmental

Recently I was having a therapy session with a businessman named Frank who tends to be rather overbearing when he is upset. Frank told me that I was too preoccupied with money and that he shouldn't have to pay at each session. He said he wanted to be billed monthly. I felt annoyed because I told myself "He always has to have things his own way." I also felt guilty because I told myself, "He's probably right. Maybe I *am* too preoccupied with money." I got defensive and explained in a terse, polite voice that I had tried a monthly billing system, but it hadn't worked out very well because some patients had run up substantial bills without paying. He didn't appreciate this comment and argued that he had impeccable credit and knew much more about credit and billing than I did. Then we launched into a frustrating debate about billing systems.

Notice how my negative thoughts and feelings functioned as a self-fulfilling prophecy. I felt attacked and had the urge to defend myself. This caused me to be attacked! Suddenly I told myself, "Whoa! I don't need to be so defensive about this." Then I decided to try a different approach. I turned to him and said, "You know, I think you're right. I've been too concerned about getting paid and I'm being defensive. You have every right to feel annoyed and I owe you an apology. We should focus on the problems in your life and not worry so much about money." He immediately softened and told me how much he appreciated working with me. He began to share his feelings of insecurity and started to talk about what was really bothering him. The next time we met, he handed me a check for twenty sessions in advance!

Many people have a great deal of trouble dealing with criticism. It's natural to feel hurt and to get defensive. Since most of us are programmed to base our self-esteem on how much other people like and approve of us, criticism feels like a blow to our egos. Part of the solution involves learning to communicate more effectively when you are criticized, and part has to do with a basic change in your attitudes and values.

The most important principles to keep in mind when you are being criticized are these:

1. Disarm the person who is criticizing you. Find some truth in the criticism instead of getting defensive. There is always truth in a criticism. When you acknowledge it, the person who is criticizing you will usually back off and calm down. This is the single most important technique in dealing with criticism.

2. Use the empathy and inquiry techniques. Encourage the other person to express all their criticisms and negative feelings.

3. Express your feelings with "I feel" statements instead of arguing.

You may be thinking, "But how can I disarm someone if their criticism is unfair and wrong?" If so, it's even more important to find some truth in it. Do you remember the "Persuasive Law of Opposites," described in Chapter 16? When you agree with a criticism, you will immediately put the lie to it. On the other hand, when you argue and contradict the criticism, you will prove that it is valid. To understand this concept a little better, review pages 396 to 397.

People who are judgmental and critical often have a lot of unexpressed anger or dissatisfaction. They may act that way because they never have the chance to get their feelings off their chest. You will contribute to this problem if you are argumentative and defensive. Instead, encourage the other person to say everything bad they can think of about you. If they open up and tear you to shreds, don't defend yourself. Instead, find truth in what they say. Acknowledge how they feel. Urge them to tell you more. This can work wonders.

When you are criticized, you will probably feel upset. You may feel defensive, inadequate, annoyed. You may not want to admit these feelings openly. Instead, you get defensive. This is a huge mistake. It makes you appear phony and culpable. Instead, tell the person how you feel. If you feel put down, say "I'm feeling put down." If you feel defensive, say "I'm feeling defensive." If you feel inadequate, say "I'm feeling inadequate." If you feel angry, say "I feel angry." But when you do, add "But I know there's a lot of truth in what you're saying, and I want you to tell me more."

Your ego can get in the way of this. You may tell yourself you're not supposed to feel the way you do. I see this problem frequently in the therapists I train. Some patients have an uncanny ability to sense their therapists' greatest vulnerabilities and they "go for the jugular" when they're angry. The therapist generally feels tense and becomes more formal and more "professional." This alienates the patient, because the therapist doesn't appear genuine. Instead, he or she sounds condescending.

To take a simple example, suppose an angry patient says this to a student therapist: "Aren't you a little on the young side? Do you have your license yet, or are you just a novice?" The therapist may feel annoyed and threatened by the question. He or she *does* feel insecure— that's quite natural. Instead of owning up to this, the therapist may get defensive and begin to look like a *real* jerk.

What could the student therapist say that would be effective? Put your ideas here:

_____

_____

_____

_____

The therapist could say, "As a matter of fact I *am* a novice, and I do feel like a beginner at times [disarming, 'I feel' statement]. I know that I will feel more comfortable once I get to know you better and once we're working together productively ['I feel' statement]. You may feel awkward about this and wonder if I will be able to help you or understand your problem [thought and feeling empathy]. Do you [inquiry]?"

Many readers will resist the approach I'm describing. You may feel you have a right to defend yourself when you are criticized. You may feel that something terrible will happen if you use the disarming technique, the inquiry technique, and "I feel" statements. Agreeing with a critic goes against the grain of human nature. We feel we're supposed to be competitive and to stand up for what we believe. Try to resist this urge. You will discover that these techniques are tremendously powerful—far more so than you might imagine.

A patient of mine named Hal has a short fuse, and he frequently gets angry while driving. Last week he inadvertently cut in front of another car in traffic. When Hal pulled up to a stoplight, the other driver pulled up next to him and started screaming obscenities, telling him in four-letter words what a lousy driver he was. If you were Hal and you were subjected to all this humiliation and abuse, what would you do? Put your response here:

_____

_____

_____

_____

Hal decided to use the disarming technique. He simply turned to the other driver and said in a friendly voice: "You're right [disarming]. It *was* my mistake [disarming]. I shouldn't have cut in front of you [disarming]." The driver was dumbfounded and turned bright red. Hal smiled inwardly, and as the light turned green he drove off in triumph!

This example illustrates that the disarming technique alone is usually enough to deal with criticism, especially when the other person is irate and trying to put you down in an extremist, childish way. Suppose someone says, "You're ugly!" How would you disarm this criticism?

You could simply say, "I'm not the best-looking person in the world, that's the truth!"

Suppose someone says, "You're a jerk!" How would you disarm this criticism?

You could say, "Yes, I am a bit of a jerk. In fact, I've probably done quite a few jerky things you don't even know about yet!"

The critic says, "You're to blame for this. It's your fault!" How could you disarm him or her?

"I think I *have* contributed to the problem. I feel bad and I'm concerned that I've let you down."

As an exercise, make a list of several sincere or insulting criticisms that have been leveled at you at one time or another. Then see if you can write down a brief disarming response. I have done this exercise on many occasions, and it has made a huge difference in the way I relate to people who are critical of me.

How to Deal with People Who Put You on the Spot and Make Unreasonable Demands

It's easy to get overcommitted and become overwhelmed by all you have to do. You may be constantly driving your children from place to place and trying to keep up with the cooking and the housework and dozens of other chores that never seem to end. Your boss may tell you to do this and do that and it seems it would take an army to keep up with all the demands. You go home each night feeling drained and exhausted and guilty. You feel even further behind than when you went to work that morning.

One of the reasons we get overcommitted is because of guilt and the feeling that we should always say yes to people. The real problem isn't that people make demands on us, but that we don't know how to deal with these demands in a tactful way. A method that I've found extremely helpful is called "punting." You tell the person you need to think about their request and that you'll get back to them. In the meantime, you can figure out what you want to do. If you feel overwhelmed and their request does not seem reasonable, you can practice how to say no.

I'm often asked to give lectures or workshops. There are times when I enjoy lecturing, but at other times when I am committed to my writing, patient care, and research, lecturing seems like too much of a burden. Let's suppose a colleague calls and pressures me to give a lecture at his university. I've learned to say, "I'm really flattered that you thought of me. Let me check my schedule and see if it will be possible. I'll call you back in a day or two." This gives me time to think about the proposal and deal with any feelings of guilt. If in my heart of hearts I know it's better to say no, I think about what I will say when I call back. Usually it turns out to be easy. I just say, "I really appreciate being asked but I find that my schedule is overcommitted right now. Please think of me again in the future."

Now you might think, "That's so simple! But why not just say no right away instead of 'punting'? You'd save yourself two days of worry." I have a tendency to believe I must always say yes and please everybody. Saying no when someone puts you on the spot can sometimes be difficult. If you're like me, you'll find it far easier to "punt" when you feel pressured. This gives me the time I need to regroup and to rehearse a friendly, assertive response.

How to Cope with a Complainer

Do you know anyone who always bitches and complains? Whatever you do to try to cheer them up, they just complain louder. When you try to give them some helpful advice they just say, "that won't work," and they continue to complain. Then you get frustrated because you don't know what to do.

You need to recognize that complainers usually don't want any advice, they simply want to be listened to. All you have to do is to use the disarming technique and *agree* with them instead of trying to "help" them. They nearly always feel better and they quiet down. It works like a charm! This is because you've given them what they really want—a little T.L.C. and some understanding.

I want you to try it. Suppose an elderly parent tells you, "No one spends any time with me anymore." You feel a sudden pang of guilt and annoyance. How could you respond?

_____

_____

_____

_____

Answer: You could say, "I think what you're saying is true [disarming]. People don't spend much time with you, and it sounds like you've been feeling pretty neglected [feeling empathy]. Have you [inquiry]?"

Notice that you find some way to *agree* with a complainer. Do *not* argue or give advice or try to help in any way! The disarming technique alone is frequently the most effective approach.

Suppose a complainer says, "Oh, my hemorrhoids are aching and the doctors never do me any good." How could you disarm him or her?

_____

_____

_____

_____

Answer: "It sounds like your hemorrhoids are real sore and the doctors aren't giving you *any* help [thought empathy]. Doctors really can be a waste [disarming]!"

Suppose an associate moans that, "Nobody respects me! I work my fingers to the bone and nobody ever cares or notices." You suddenly feel resentful. How can you respond?

_____

_____

_____

_____

Answer: "You're right [disarming]. You work awfully hard and you don't get the credit you deserve [disarming]. Everyone takes you for granted [disarming]. It's not fair [disarming]!"

Now, you might resist this approach. You might say, "I don't want to be phony. I shouldn't have to agree with someone who's complaining." The answer to this is that you don't "have to." It's just an option. But it works wonders. The complainer will nearly always calm down and stop complaining. Every other approach I'm aware of will fail, and you'll both end up feeling frustrated.

When should you use this approach? The tip off is that you're starting to feel frustrated because you're hearing the same complaints over and over and you notice that the complainer simply isn't listening to you. You feel irritated, and you can't wait to get away from the complainer. Concentrate on the listening skills and stop trying to be helpful. The complainer just wants his or her feelings validated. He or she only wants you to agree with him or her. I used to hate complainers because I never knew what to do. I felt guilty, inadequate, and frustrated. Now I love complainers because the disarming technique works like magic. Give it a try. I think you'll be amazed.

How to Help a Troubled Loved One

If you are having difficulties helping someone who is upset, ask yourself the following questions:

1. Is this person really asking for my help?

2. Is it appropriate to help him or her?

3. Is this person asking me to help solve problems, or is he or she simply asking me to be a good listener and to provide emotional support?

The first question may make you aware that you are trying to help someone who hasn't really asked for help. This may be due to an irrational attitude I call the "help addiction." You may feel it is always your duty to help friends and loved ones find solutions to their problems. You try to help even when help hasn't been asked for. As a result, you may appear intrusive and controlling.

Mildred was upset because her son, Jack, a 28-year-old stockbroker, had left his wife and two daughters to live with an 18-year-old girl whom Mildred described as "low class." Mildred lamented: "I just don't understand it. He met her at a bar and she smokes marijuana. He was always such a lighthearted, model boy when he was growing up. He was so poised, and everybody loved him. What's happened to him now? I thought I raised him right."

Mildred refused to let Jack's girlfriend set foot in her home, and she repeatedly urged him to straighten out. She warned him that he was ruining his career, breaking his poor mother's heart, and damaging his daughters. She complained that Jack didn't spend enough time with her. She was bewildered by how selfish and insensitive he'd become.

Mildred felt it was her duty to make sure he changed his ways. She felt accountable for his actions and afraid that her friends would look down on her because of Jack's affair. She blamed Jack for her misery and was determined not to feel any better until Jack repented.

What are the consequences of Mildred's attitude? She will drive Jack away because he feels judged and guilty whenever he is around her. Then she will complain that she feels lonely and abandoned!

Jack may be going through a "crazy period," a delayed adolescent rebellion, but Mildred's blaming attitude will only feed the fire. She will lose his respect. Although she insists she loves him and only wants to help him, the message Jack hears is "I will punish you until you do exactly what I want you to. I am determined to control you. I will not accept you until you fall in line."

What could Mildred do? Her feelings are important, and she would have a far greater chance of being heard if she expressed them with "I feel" statements instead of trying to "help" Jack. She could say, "I feel upset that you have left your wife to live with this young woman. I feel terribly disappointed and ashamed and hurt." These "I feel" statements convey direct information about her feelings without implying that Jack is entirely responsible for them. At the same time, she could express a genuine concern for Jack if she asked him about his feelings in a nonjudgmental manner. Why did he leave his wife? What were the problems they were having? How does he feel about the separation? Communication, rather than helping, would be the goal because Jack has not asked for help.

One reason we may jump in and "help" is because our egos are on the line. We may link our self-esteem with the happiness of others. We may get upset if a loved one is having difficulties because we think this is a reflection on us. We feel we have failed.

The second question to ask yourself is whether it's appropriate to help someone. There are times when people would benefit more from working things out for themselves.

Ned dropped out of college impulsively. He persuaded Harry, his father, to lend him $7,000 to start a business. Harry felt uneasy about this but gave in because he told himself "A loving father should be willing to help his son." Ned had poor judgment and soon squandered the money. Harry felt manipulated and angry, but he was reluctant to discuss this with Ned for fear of hurting Ned's feelings.

A short while later, Ned persuaded his dad to give him a credit card. Ned explained that he couldn't get his own because he had no previous credit record. He said that if his dad would help him, he could establish a line of credit, which would be useful for a new business venture. Several months later, Harry started getting calls from a collection agency: the card was overextended and no payments had been made.

You can probably see how Harry's efforts to help backfired in his dealings with his son. He felt that a caring father should be ready and willing to be supportive when his children need something. He behaved as though the message "I will help you" means "I care about you." But this message is a two-edged sword because it also implies "You need me and you can't do it on your own." If someone really *can* do it on their own, the impact of your help can be destructive. If you reward people with love and attention every time they get upset or act sick, they may learn to manipulate you. This can rob them of the motivation to become more self-reliant.

If you decide that you do want to help someone, the third question to ask yourself is *how* you are going to help them. There are two very different ways to offer help. You can help simply by listening, or you can help by doing favors or giving practical advice. You can think of these approaches as the "listening mode" and the "problem-solving mode." If you and the other person are on the same wavelength, there's no problem. However, you will have difficulties if you are in the problem-solving mode while the other person only wants you to be a good listener. Your message is: "Why don't you pull yourself up by your bootstraps? Think more positively. Try doing X." The other person may resent all this "logical" advice. He or she just wants you to say, "I hear how lousy you feel. I know how awful it can be." Unfortunately, you may not know that some emotional support is all that's needed, so you offer advice that sounds intrusive and insensitive to the other person.

You may wonder when you should be a good listener and when you should be more active in helping someone solve a problem. Sometimes you simply have to ask them. Many of my patients genuinely want help, and they will work actively to solve their problems along the lines I suggest. But others simply want to be listened to. They don't want help or advice. If I try to help them, they get annoyed and start complaining. That's when it's time to listen and to avoid trying to be helpful by solving problems.

I'm just like everyone else, and when I feel upset, I want someone to listen to me as well. There are times when I come home from the office and I feel like complaining about how unreasonable the world is. I don't want my wife to give me advice—if I want advice I generally ask for it. I just want her to say, "There, there, you're right. People shouldn't be so irrational." Then I feel relieved because somebody understands. I cheer up right away and I stop complaining!

How to Instantly Transform a Boring Conversation into an Exciting One

This week a young man asked me what he was supposed to do when he was on a date with someone who was uninteresting or when he was stuck at a party, talking to someone who seemed boring. This problem can also come up in your relationships with friends or professional colleagues. You may know someone who talks too much about nothing very interesting. He or she drones on and on and all you can think is, "How can I get away from this person?"

There's only one cause of boring interactions, and there's always one instantaneous solution. Before I reveal the secret, you will first have to decide if you *want* to have a more exciting interaction with the person who seems boring. You always have the right to excuse yourself and look for someone you naturally feel more attracted to. There's no rule that says that you're obligated to be interested in everyone. If the chemistry's not there, you can pass.

However, you have another option. You can transform the most boring interactions into incredibly exciting ones within less than thirty seconds with a 100% success rate if you use this simple but bold technique: Comment, in a tactful and friendly way, on the fact that you feel bored. Ask the other person if they feel the same way. That's all you have to do!

If you're chatting about trivia with someone at a party and you're crawling out of your skin, you could say: "Have you ever noticed how easy it is to get involved in really boring small talk at parties like this?" They'll probably say yes. Then you could say, "Well, that's how I feel right now ['I feel' statement]. Do you feel the same way [inquiry]? We're just talking about nothing at all. I don't know why, because I'll bet you're an interesting person and I'd like to get to know you a little better [stroking]." The moment you admit that you feel bored there will be a certain electricity in the air. It's a fairly daring statement, and your boredom will be history! The compliment "I'll bet you're an interesting person" is included to reassure the other person that you don't want to put them down and that you simply want to get to know them better.

You may be *afraid* to use this technique. Lots of people go through life playing games, censoring their own feelings and being petrified about being open and honest with others. Your boredom is just your way of reminding yourself that you're not being honest with yourself or with the other person. You're pretending. You're lying. If you're willing to be honest and to step out from behind your mask, your boredom will vanish.

Dave, a divorced man in his thirties, told me about a woman he'd dated several times. He said she was attractive but he didn't like her very much because she seemed superficial and "not very deep." He wondered whether he should stop taking her out. What could Dave say to her? Put your ideas here:

_____

_____

_____

_____

Dave could say, "Sarah, you're a really attractive woman [stroking], but when we go out I have trouble because I feel I'm not getting to know you very well ['I feel' statement]. We seem to stick to superficial topics ['I feel' statement]. Have you noticed this [inquiry]? It makes me uncomfortable ['I feel' statement]. I don't know why that is, and I'd like to get to know you better as a person [stroking]."

Dave tried this approach after we rehearsed it during a session. The next week he was euphoric. To his amazement, Sarah opened up immediately. They began to talk about past disappointments in romantic relationships. He told me that Sarah was a "very exciting" and "very deep" person with all kinds of feelings and ideas. He couldn't imagine how he'd ever thought she was superficial or boring.

There's actually no such thing as a boring person. Boring interactions exist, but boring people do not. There's only one cause of boring interactions, and there's one cure. Inassertiveness is the cause, and assertiveness is the cure. This method always works. It never fails. Do you have the guts to try it?

22

•

Why People Can't Communicate with Each Other

In the last several chapters we've talked about the difference between good and bad communication, and you've learned how to listen and express your feelings more effectively. It will take some work to master these skills, but with effort it can be done. Patients of mine find that it takes a good five or six sessions, with a reasonable amount of homework and practice between sessions. Those who work at it consistently get good results, and many report that the techniques are astonishingly effective.

However, many people find that they resist these methods. They can see that they do not communicate well, and yet they stubbornly dig in their heels when it's time to try something new. I predict that you will have to battle with some powerful feelings that could sabotage your efforts to communicate more effectively. See if you can recognize yourself in any of the attitudes described on pages 443 and 445.

How Your "Truth" Keeps You Stuck

"Truth" is probably the greatest barrier to good communication. During an argument with a friend or your spouse, you may have such a powerful conviction that you are right that you don't try to see the

TEN ATTITUDES THAT KEEP YOU FROM EXPRESSING YOUR FEELINGS*

1. **Conflict phobia.** You are afraid of angry feelings or conflicts with people. You may believe that people with good relationships shouldn't fight or argue. You may also believe that the people you care about would be hurt and couldn't take it if you told them how you felt or what was really on your mind. I call this the "ostrich phenomenon," because you bury your head in the sand instead of dealing with the problems in your relationship.

2. **Emotional perfectionism.** You believe that you shouldn't have irrational feelings like anger, jealousy, depression, or anxiety. You think you should always be rational and in control of your emotions. You are afraid of being exposed as weak and vulnerable. You believe that people will look down on you if they find out how you really feel.

3. **Fear of disapproval and rejection.** You are so terrified by rejection and ending up alone that you'd rather swallow your feelings and put up with some abuse than take the chance of making anyone mad at you. You feel an excessive need to please people and to meet everybody's expectations. You are afraid that people would not like you if you expressed your own ideas and feelings.

4. **Passive-aggressiveness.** You pout and hold your hurt and angry feelings inside instead of sharing them openly and honestly. You give others the silent treatment and try to make them feel guilty instead of sharing your feelings.

5. **Hopelessness.** You feel convinced that your relationship cannot improve no matter what you do, so you give up. You may feel that you've already tried everything and nothing works. You may believe that your spouse is just too stubborn and insensitive to be able to change. This acts as a self-fulfilling prophecy. Once you give up, things get stuck and you conclude that things really are hopeless.

*Copyright © 1989 by David D. Burns, M.D., from *The Feeling Good Handbook*

6. **Low self-esteem.** You believe that you aren't entitled to express your feelings or to ask others for what you want. You think you should always please other people and meet their expectations.

7. **Spontaneity.** You believe that you have the right to say precisely what you think and feel when you are upset. You may feel that any change in the way you communicate will sound phony and ridiculous.

8. **Mind reading.** You believe that people should know how you feel and what you want without your having to express yourself directly. This gives you a perfect excuse to hold your feelings inside and to feel resentful because people don't seem to care about your needs.

9. **Martyrdom.** You are afraid to admit that you're angry, because you don't want to give anyone the satisfaction of knowing they've upset you. You take enormous pride in controlling your emotions and suffering silently.

10. **Need to solve problems.** When you have a conflict with someone, you go around and around in circles trying to solve the problem instead of sharing your feelings openly and hearing how the other person feels.

TEN ATTITUDES THAT PREVENT YOU FROM LISTENING*

1. **Truth.** You believe that you are right and the other person is wrong. You are preoccupied with proving your point instead of expressing your angry feelings more directly or trying to grasp how the other person is thinking and feeling.

2. **Blame.** You believe that the problem is the other person's fault. You feel overwhelmingly convinced that you're completely innocent and tell yourself that you have every right to blame him or her.

3. **Need to be a victim.** You feel sorry for yourself and think that other people are treating you unfairly because of their insensitivity and selfishness. Your stubborn unwillingness to do anything assertive to make the situation better gives people the impression that you like the role of a martyr.

4. **Self-deception.** You cannot imagine that you contribute to a problem because you cannot see the impact of your behavior on others. For example, you may complain that your wife nags you, but you don't think about the fact that you repeatedly "forget" to follow through on your promise to repair the fence. You may complain that your husband is dogmatic and stubborn and unwilling to listen to your ideas, but you don't notice that you constantly contradict everything he tries to say.

5. **Defensiveness.** You are so fearful of criticism that you can't stand to hear anything negative or disagreeable. Instead of listening and trying to find some truth in the other person's point of view, you have the urge to argue and defend yourself.

6. **Coercion sensitivity.** You are afraid of giving in or being bossed around. Other people seem controlling and domineering, and you feel that you must dig in your heels and resist them.

7. **Demandingness.** You feel entitled to better treatment from others, and you get frustrated when they do not treat you as you expected. Instead of trying to understand what really motivates them, you insist that they are being unreasonable and have no right to feel and act the way they do.

8. **Selfishness.** You want what you want when you want it, and you throw a tantrum if you don't get it. You are not especially interested in what others may be thinking and feeling.

9. **Mistrust.** You put up a wall because you believe you will be taken advantage of if you listen and try to grasp what the other person is thinking and feeling.

10. **Help addiction.** You feel the need to help people when all they want is to be listened to. When friends or family members complain about how bad they feel, you make "helpful" suggestions and tell them what to do. Instead of being appreciative, they get annoyed and continue to complain. You both end up feeling frustrated.

other person's point of view. Instead, you argue and try to force them to agree with you. This never works. You've probably noticed that the more you try to persuade the other person to agree with you, the more argumentative he or she becomes. This is because you're not really listening to their viewpoint. They believe their feelings are being ignored, and they'll argue louder and longer to try to get you to listen. You both end up feeling angry and frustrated.

You may be completely unaware you're doing this. A woman's husband recently said, "Sarah, you always do exactly what you want without considering my needs. You put your career and your needs first." Sarah replied, "No, I don't. You are my priority, Harold, but sometimes my studies have to take precedence if I have a big exam coming up." Although Sarah might think she's being honest and reasonable, she has made the mistake of suggesting that she's right and he's wrong about this. The moment she contradicts him, she proves that he's right. In point of fact, she's not trying to understand his point of view, she's only tuned in to her needs and her own view of the situation. That's exactly what he's complaining about!

So what's the alternative? She could express her feelings with "I feel" statements. How does she feel? She feels ticked off! So why not just say this instead of being argumentative? She could also try to understand what he's thinking and feeling. How does he feel? He feels shut out and ignored. She could say, "I feel put down and angry ['I feel' statement], but I know there's some truth in what you say [disarming]. Apparently you think I've put my career first and you feel rejected [thought empathy]. Is this the way you feel [inquiry]? If so, I could understand why you feel hurt and angry [feeling empathy]."

I've worked with hundreds of people with troubled relationships, and practically every one of them has made the same mistake of arguing about the "truth." This strategy never helped anyone resolve a problem. When you feel upset, you will have a tremendous urge to explain why your ideas and feelings are valid. *Don't do it!* You will have a tremendous urge to defend yourself and argue. *Don't do it!* What usually happens when you try to point out the truth to someone? When you argued and got defensive, did your spouse ever stop arguing and say, "Thank you, thank you for opening my eyes. I see now where I was so wrong"? Of course not!

The key to resolving an argument is often to back off and try a different approach. The bottom line is that you must never defend the "truth"! Your "truth" is your enemy! When you give up the idea that you have a monopoly on the truth and you try to understand the other person's point of view, you will find that people will be much more willing to listen to you and to understand your own point of view.

Now you may be thinking, as so many of my patients do, "But what if I *am* right and my partner *is* wrong? Doesn't the truth count? I don't want to be a liar. I *won't* be a liar." There are two difficulties with this position: It won't work, and it's not valid. The reason it won't work should be clear to you by now. Whenever you're having a dispute with someone, you will both feel upset. Any attempt on your part to insist that you are right and the other person is wrong will only fan the flames.

The second difficulty is that the other person's feelings are just as valid to him or her as your feelings are to you. Defending your "truth" is foolish because there really isn't any one truth in a situation. People have feelings that need to be accepted and understood. These feelings are neither true nor false.

In a session recently, Erika told her husband that he was always talking down to her and treating her as though she was inferior. Erika had been battling a long-standing drinking problem and had purchased a book on Alcoholics Anonymous. Before she had a chance to read it, John had read it and presented her with a computer printout highlighting all the ideas in the book. She said she was furious because she felt that he was trying to control her and was implying that she was unable to understand the book on her own. John replied that this wasn't true and insisted he was just trying to help her.

Now, who is "right"? Is Erika "right" that he's talking down to her and trying to keep her under his thumb? Or is John "right" that he's trying to help her so they can feel closer? There are worlds of truth in what each of them has to say. She's right that he's overly aggressive and intellectual. She felt inferior in school and resentful of her domineering father when she was growing up. She feels intimidated by John's active mind. Erika would feel more comfortable with him if he were a little warmer and more low-key.

John is also right. She does have a drinking problem and she needs to do something about it. He feels lonely and he desperately wants to feel closer to her. If either one of them tries to develop a sympathetic and accurate understanding of how the other one feels, the conflict will probably disappear, because they will both feel respected and cared about.

What could John say to break the stalemate? Instead of defending himself he could say, "I understand how you feel [feeling empathy]. I must have seemed kind of thoughtless and controlling to have gone through the whole book like that [disarming]. I know that probably made you angry [feeling empathy]. At the same time I'm feeling kind of frightened about your drinking, and lonely, and I really want to be close to you ['I feel' statement]. Maybe we need to talk about what's going on between us. Are you feeling upset with me now [inquiry]?"

What could Erika say to break the stalemate? She could say, "I felt resentful when you outlined the book ['I feel' statement]. I feel like you're the brilliant, impatient teacher and I'm the dumb student ['I feel' statement]. But I know you feel lonely and rejected by me, and you're trying to be helpful [feeling empathy]. Is that how you feel [inquiry]?" This response would shift the focus away from who's right and who's wrong. John will learn what she's feeling, and he will see that she's trying to understand his point of view.

When you argue and defend the "truth," it becomes nearly impossible to feel close to your partner or to resolve any conflict. You'll simply fight on and on. If, instead, you reveal your feelings and encourage your partner to share his or hers, you will be on the path to greater intimacy.

How Self-Deception Keeps You Stuck

Another great barrier to communication is the tendency to blame others and to deny that we are contributing to the problem. Part of the difficulty is that during an argument we can literally see what the other person is doing to us—we see them being hostile, self-centered, defensive, and narrow-minded—but we cannot see what we are doing that may be contributing to the problem. That's because there are usually no mirrors or television cameras around when we're having a fight with someone, so we literally cannot see ourselves in action. This blindness to the impact of our own actions on others can be quite profound.

A depressed woman named Molly complained bitterly that her

husband, Frank, never expressed his feelings. Molly told me she had had the bad luck to marry a cold fish. She said Frank was like a lot of men—he didn't care about intimacy or about talking about feelings. She was feeling discouraged and hopeless about their relationship and spoke about her marital problems at nearly every session.

To find out what was really happening, I encouraged Molly to invite Frank to come with her so I could observe firsthand what was going on. I proposed that we work on improving the way they communicated. Possibly I could help Frank get over his inhibitions about expressing how he felt. Molly was quite enthusiastic about this plan, and Frank was very willing to participate in the therapy.

During a session with the two of them together, I summarized Molly's feelings of loneliness and asked Frank if he'd be willing to take a stab at opening up and sharing some of his feelings with her. Frank said he spent most of his time working and avoiding Molly. He said he would have no inhibitions about sharing his feelings, but he felt pretty sure that Molly didn't really want him to communicate more openly.

Molly seemed annoyed and insisted that what Frank was saying wasn't true! I was puzzled and asked Molly if she wanted Frank to open up. She reassured me that indeed she did. I told Frank to go ahead.

Frank told Molly that he, too, felt lonely and hurt. He said he felt she was quite critical of him and put him down a great deal. He told her that he often tried to express his feelings and ideas, but that she jumped all over him whenever he did. He said it just didn't seem worth it. He said he felt just as angry and rejected as she did.

As he was speaking, Molly got more and more agitated and finally interrupted him. She was furious and said he had "no right" to say things like that. She said what he was saying was "unfair" and "untrue." She began sobbing and stormed out of the office, slamming the door behind her.

I was quite taken aback. Molly was so fragile and threatened by Frank's negative feelings that she couldn't stand to hear what he had to say. When he did try to open up, her punishment of him was instantaneous and severe. She hit him with her most powerful weapons—anger, depression, and rejection. But Molly was totally unaware of the way Frank might feel about her behavior. She couldn't see that she was partially responsible for their poor communication and was convinced the difficulties were entirely due to his shortcomings. On pages 451–452 you can see several additional examples of how people unknowingly create the very problems they complain so loudly about.

How Blame and Mistrust
Keep You Stuck

A woman from Cleveland named Laura told me what an insensitive lover her husband, Dave, was. She complained that she'd never once experienced an orgasm in over thirty years of marriage. I asked Laura to tell me specifically about the problems she and Dave were having in the bedroom. One of Laura's main complaints was that Dave, a strong and athletic man, pinched her nipples tightly and constantly during intercourse. She told me that her nipples were quite sensitive and she didn't want them touched, at least not like *that*!

I asked Laura whether she had ever talked this over with Dave and told him what she liked and disliked sexually. She seemed shocked and protested, "I shouldn't have to! Don't you think he'd get the idea after thirty years?" Like Molly, Laura saw herself as the victim of someone else's insensitivity. She had never stopped to ask, "What am I doing to contribute to this problem?"

You might be thinking, "Okay, that's interesting, but it's not really so serious. All you have to do is encourage Laura to be more open with Dave. Encourage them to have some sessions together so they can talk about their sexual problems. Once she tells Dave where and how she likes to be touched, he'll probably respond differently. They both have a lot to gain and nothing to lose."

If that's what you are thinking, you took a page out of my book! I encouraged Laura to bring Dave to the sessions for that precise reason. She agreed, with some reluctance, but warned me that she thought the situation was "hopeless."

After several sessions with them together, I got to know Dave. He agreed that something important was missing from their marriage. For years he had been troubled by Laura's dissatisfaction with him. He felt he wasn't sufficiently manly to excite her sexually, and told me with embarrassment how he'd taken up long-distance running to try to build up his stamina. He was jogging over 60 miles a week and had competed in numerous marathons. He thought that if he

ARE YOU CONTRIBUTING TO THE PROBLEM?

Problem	How you may explain the problem	How you may be contributing to the problem
1. Your partner is uncommunicative and won't talk to you about how he or she feels.	You tell yourself that your partner is a cold fish who doesn't care or know how to express his or her feelings.	When your partner does try to express feelings, especially negative ones, you may feel put down and act hurt. You may get defensive and criticize him or her. Your partner feels attacked and reluctant to talk about his or her feelings.
2. Your partner seems rigid, dogmatic, and argumentative and won't listen to your point of view.	You tell yourself that your partner is stubborn, closed-minded, and controlling. You think that he or she has to be "right" all the time. You tell yourself that he or she doesn't care about your feelings and ideas.	You may be equally argumentative. You may insist on getting your ideas across without truly listening or trying to find truth in what your partner is trying to say.

Problem	How you may explain the problem	How you may be contributing to the problem
3. Your spouse and family seem selfish. They constantly make demands on you and rarely take your needs into account. You feel more like a hired maid than a wife and mother.	You tell yourself that your husband and children are insensitive to your needs and care only about themselves.	You may be unassertive and afraid to say no or to tell others what you want. You may think people should be sufficiently sensitive to be able to read your mind and know how you feel without your having to express yourself. You may have low self-esteem and feel you don't deserve to be happy or treated well by others. You may fear disapproval and think you have to be "nice" all the time to keep from being rejected.

became more athletic, that might please her and turn her on. With tears in his eyes, he admitted that no matter how hard he worked at it, he simply couldn't excite her. He felt like a real "loser" at sex.

I felt we were on the verge of a real breakthrough, so I asked Laura if she'd be willing to tell Dave about some of her sexual needs and feelings. I suggested she might tell him specifically what she liked and disliked about his lovemaking.

There was a long, tense moment of silence. Then Laura turned to me and said, "Dr. Burns, you're just like Dave. You really don't understand! I won't stand for this ridiculous conversation any longer!" She got up and bolted from the room.

Why did Laura walk out instead of talking about the problem that we had agreed to discuss? One reason has to do with Laura's feelings of fear and mistrust. She may have never felt loved or lovable. She may have never learned that it was possible to be open with the people she cared about. She may have never discovered that although these problems can be painful at first, there can be a reward after you confront your fears and resolve the problem. She may not have believed that she and Dave could feel close as a result of working things through. Laura is much like someone with a severe phobia. She is terribly afraid of talking about a conflict openly, in much the same way that some people are terrified of elevators. She believes that if she opens up, something awful will happen.

Reality often reinforces these fears. When people try to work through a problem, it usually *is* stressful at first. For one thing, Laura may have always felt ashamed of her sexual impulses. Talking about her feelings may make her feel embarrassed, vulnerable, and unfeminine. In addition, she may not express herself well at first, and Dave might feel hurt or he could get defensive. This might make her all the more convinced that expressing her feelings just won't work. She might conclude it isn't worth all the grief and pain it causes.

Since Laura is extremely angry at Dave for not loving her as she wants to be loved, there may be another motivation for storming out of the room instead of staying to work on the problem. Laura may feel so angry with him that she prefers to punish him and sabotage the therapy.

I am always amazed when I see people choosing the road to revenge over the path to intimacy. It seems that there is something seductive and appealing about our hostility, and it can be very difficult to let go of it. It can be hard to admit that we're choosing to hang on to our anger instead of resolving the problem. There's something strangely comforting about blaming another person and imagining that they are the sole cause of our unhappiness. Let's face it, revenge fantasies are enormously appealing. And if we have to choose between what seems like the outside chance of being loved and the virtual certainty of perpetuating the war, it can be awfully hard to resist the temptation of inflicting further pain.

How Your Conflict Phobia Keeps
You Stuck

The desire to get back at others can prevent you from opening up and getting closer to them. Many people have the opposite problem—they are afraid of anger and conflict. They think they should be nice all the time and never have any negative feelings. I call this a "conflict phobia." People with this attitude will go to great lengths to avoid talking openly about disagreements or hurt feelings.

Many of us were raised with the belief that negative emotions like anger are bad. This attitude can make it hard for you to express your feelings. You may be afraid to say "I feel angry right now" or "I feel lonely," because you think you shouldn't feel this way. This attitude may also make it hard for you to listen. If someone you respect is angry with you, you don't want to hear it because you feel you have failed or that your relationship is less than what it should be.

The following is an excerpt from a therapy session with Andy, a businessman who has suffered from chronic anxiety, depression, and loneliness for much of his life. Andy doesn't feel nearly as close to his wife, Mary, or to his daughters as he would like. Every time he tries to raise this issue at home, he gets nowhere.

As the session unfolds, Andy is telling me how bad he feels because Mary and his youngest daughter, Betsy, ignore him at the dinner table. The problem is especially poignant for Andy because his other daughters are away at college in California and this is Betsy's last year at home.

ANDY: I got into a hassle with Mary about our youngest daughter, Betsy. Betsy and Mary usually ignore me at the dinner table. I feel like Betsy excludes me from the conversation. What really hurts is—I feel alone. I tried to talk to Betsy but it didn't work out too well. She cried and said she was unhappy and felt guilty. She said she felt she was trying her best and that nothing more could be done.

DAVID: If Betsy is ignoring you, maybe she's angry with you. You need to find out how she feels and to share your feelings with her. Otherwise you're not connecting with her.

ANDY: I didn't realize it was important to do that. I've never done it, and I'm not sure I can handle a lot of negative emotions. I can try to draw her out but I'm afraid if I do I'll feel like I've screwed things up by causing all this conflict.

DAVID: How does it follow that you've screwed things up?

ANDY: I feel those negative emotions wouldn't have been there if I hadn't stirred them up.

NOTE: Andy's tendency to blame himself makes him fear conflict. If Betsy gets upset, he feels like he's done something wrong. Do you ever feel this way?

DAVID: Let me see if I understand. Prior to the conversation, Betsy had nothing but sweet emotions for you?

ANDY (*Laughs*): Right! Yes! That's correct. And then when I got angry it stirred up all these negative feelings that weren't there. That's what I was thinking. I guess I tend to blame myself when Betsy gets upset. I feel I caused her to feel that way. When I was growing up my mother used to say, "If you want to talk about something bad, I don't want to hear it." Maybe my whole family has the belief that people shouldn't talk about negative feelings. If someone expresses negative feelings, then I feel I've failed. It seems there's something wrong if someone is angry. I dislike conflict, and so I must project that attitude to the kids.

DAVID: Yeah, they're obviously avoiding conflict just like Dad and Mom do.

ANDY: How can I change this? How can I get Betsy to open up? When I told Betsy I wanted to talk, she said, "Yeah," in a cool way, as if to say, "Dad's here. Ugh!"

DAVID: What was your response?

ANDY: I said, "I'd like to talk to you about what happened yesterday when the three of us were talking at dinner."

DAVID: Okay. Now, what's wrong with that? Let me remind you about the two principles of good communication: you express your own feelings and acknowledge how the other person is feeling. Can you see that you failed to tell her how you were feeling or to acknowledge where she was coming from?

ANDY (*Laughs*): Oh, *I* see! Yeah, sure. Whenever I walk into the room, it's always the same. She acts cold, as if she doesn't want to talk to me. I don't comment on that. I ignore it.

DAVID: Yeah—and how does it make you feel when she treats you like that?

ANDY: Not good. She's real cool. I feel defensive.

DAVID: Exactly! Now instead of intellectualizing about what happened yesterday, could you tell her how you feel? What would you say?

ANDY: I could tell her that I feel defensive and uncomfortable and shut out, and that I really *do* want to talk.

DAVID: That would be a good statement of how you feel. That's quite good. You might also want to ask her about her feelings, like this: "Betsy, when you said 'Yeah' you seemed so cool. You seem annoyed, and that tone of voice hurts me. I feel real put down. This happens between us an awful lot. This is what I wanted to talk to you about. If you feel upset with me, I want you to tell me how you feel more directly. Do you feel annoyed?"

ANDY: Yeah . . . that's good.

DAVID: I don't think you need to go any further than this. Ask her how she's feeling, and tell her how you're feeling. That's the solution, to focus on how you both feel.

ANDY: I try to talk about my feelings, but I get intellectual and confused and I don't know what's going on.

DAVID: The reason you get confused is because you're not really paying attention to your emotions. Your feelings need to be shared, and her feelings need to be expressed as well. But instead, you kept trying to solve the problem of being excluded at the dinner table. You failed to get together emotionally.

ANDY: I guess she was unhappy with me and I was unhappy with her.

DAVID: Exactly! And instead of dealing with that, you probably kept focusing on your so-called agenda.

ANDY: Right! But how do you deal with being unhappy with each other?

DAVID: All you have to do is say, "It sounds like you're feeling a little unhappy with me. I'm not comfortable either. Tell me a little more about how you feel right now." The purpose of a close relationship is simply to share your feelings with someone you trust. But that's the one thing that many people have great difficulty doing.

ANDY: Okay, but *then* what do you do? She may say she's unhappy with me. What then?

DAVID: Be a good listener. Find some truth in what she's saying. Empathize with how she feels. Be curious and ask her questions so you can learn more about her feelings. Be open and friendly and let her know how you feel.

ANDY: So she's unhappy with me, and I'm unhappy with her because I feel alone.

DAVID: There you go. That's it! That's what needs to be said—and heard.

ANDY: I *told* her I felt ignored. She came out with all these reasons she was acting that way. I can't deal with that crap.

DAVID: Of course not. But you do need to listen. You can tell her that you feel lonely and hurt and that you want to feel close because you care about her. And you need to hear that she's unhappy too. You don't need to look for a solution, because the moment you share your feelings in a spirit of trust and caring, you will feel closer to each other. That's the real meaning of intimacy.

The next week Andy told me that the session made a strong positive impact on him. He saw that he had to take a risk and open up emotionally in order to feel close to his wife and daughter. He also saw that his lifelong struggle to intellectualize and to avoid conflict had become more uncomfortable than simply dealing with the negative feelings that are inherent in any close relationship. Although revealing these feelings may be painful and frightening in the short run, it can provide an opportunity for real sharing and growth.

How Martyrdom Can Keep You Stuck

Marge is a 52-year-old woman who decided to start dating after being divorced for many years. She's a sweet, petite, spunky woman who's done well in business, but she sometimes strikes people as being a little too formal and too "nice." For several months we talked about how to flirt and how to dress in a more casual and appealing way. Marge was an enthusiastic student and her phone was ringing frequently. Lots of men wanted to date her.

One fellow, Nate, was attracted to Marge, but he seemed a little bit unstable and irresponsible. One thing he did that was annoying was to call her late at night after he'd been drinking, to brag about his real or imaginary sexual exploits with various women. Marge was turned off by this obnoxious behavior, but she was nevertheless attracted to him because she felt inhibited and he seemed wild and exciting.

One Friday, Nate called at midnight to invite Marge to have

dinner with him and a business associate on Nate's yacht the next evening. He told Marge to meet them at the dock at 6:00. Although it was a last-minute invitation, Marge accepted. She showed up at 6:15 because of a traffic jam, and Nate's yacht was nowhere in sight. She was perplexed and waited several minutes. No Nate. Then she asked a man who worked on the dock if he'd seen Nate's boat. Marge learned that Nate and another man had taken the boat out two hours earlier. Marge felt furious and embarrassed for being stood up.

She left and didn't contact Nate. Several days later he called at 3:00 a.m. Marge was away and her daughter took the call. Nate was intoxicated and demanded to know why Marge had stood *him* up. Marge's daughter explained that her mother wouldn't do something like that, and said that Marge was gone for the weekend.

During the next session, a student co-therapist asked Marge what she wanted to do about the situation. Marge said she really wanted to call Nate and tell him he was acting like a jerk. I asked Marge if she would be willing to do that. Marge pulled back and turned red and said she wouldn't *dream* of doing something like that! Her reasons? She had many excuses, including:

"I'm supposed to be a nice person."

"It's my fault for choosing the wrong kinds of guys."

"When I was raised, I was told that you shouldn't make yourself vulnerable by letting someone know that you're angry or that they hurt you."

Marge told us that when she was growing up, her mother, a bitter and unhappy woman, always told her she should *never* show her feelings. A girl Marge knew constantly picked on Marge and Marge wanted to tell her off. Marge's mother told her to "rise above it." She said she should never let this girl know she was getting to Marge.

While there's some value in turning the other cheek and not letting someone get your goat, playing the role of a martyr can be destructive. Marge learned to blame herself and to hide all her feelings. This is unfair to her *and* to other people. In the first place, she comes off as too sweet and doesn't seem genuine. In addition, how can people know how she feels if she doesn't tell them?

This type of interaction occurred repeatedly while I was seeing Marge. Acting sweet and ignoring people's hostile behavior was as natural to her as breathing. The most recent incident involved an exciting and successful lawyer who proposed to her after they'd been dating for several months. Marge was thrilled with his proposal. The only problem was that she never heard from him again. Marge finally began to realize that her "niceness" simply wasn't working, and that she was just a doormat and was getting used. It took considerable courage and persistence for her to express herself. She finally took the risk of being more open and assertive, and she's feeling a lot happier with herself and more satisfied in her relationships.

Men are just as frequently afraid of expressing angry feelings. I have just started treating a 30-year-old architect named Ben who developed a severe depression after he and his wife separated. Ben separated from his wife because he had an affair with a lady client whom he found terribly exciting. Ben told me that he had lost interest in his wife and the excitement and the romance just weren't there any longer. However, the real problem in Ben's marriage wasn't the absence of romance, but the inability to deal with anger. Ben believed that it was "wrong" to feel upset, and he took great pride in the fact that he never displayed any angry feelings. Since he never let his negative feelings out, they simply built up and sabotaged the sexual and tender ones. He had recently lost his job for a similar reason: his boss, an aggressive man, told him, "You have no blood in your veins. You're too cold and calculating. I never know what you feel."

During his third therapy session, Ben discussed yet another problem—a conflict with his parents. He felt annoyed with them but told himself, "I have no right to be angry with them, because they're trying to help me. I shouldn't feel angry with them." This thought made him feel inadequate and guilty. He said he felt like a failure in his marriage, in his work, and as a son.

Ben insisted that he was being realistic. He said he felt strongly that he should never get angry. Although he acknowledged that most people feel angry at times, he said he took great pride in the fact that he always hid his anger and suffered silently. He could see that this was rather self-defeating, but said he didn't want to give in and lower his standards and end up like any other "average" man who lost his cool and got mad. This reveals the tremendous sense of pride that often lurks beneath our pain.

To help Ben deal with his problem, I asked him to list the advantages and disadvantages of believing he should never get angry. You can see in his Cost-Benefit Analysis (page 461) that there are many benefits, as well as a number of disadvantages, to this mind-set.

Probably the greatest benefit is a sense of self-righteous perfectionism. By refusing to express his anger, Ben can stay in control and keep people at a distance, in a one-down position. "I'm just a tad better" is the message he projects, "so I won't let you get to me." In spite of all the misery he feels, he can tell himself, "I'm one cut above the rest." The disadvantages include constant stress, loneliness, and depression, because Ben can never feel close to himself or to other people. Is it worth paying such a heavy price?

How Your Need to Solve Problems
Keeps You Stuck

One attitude that gets in the way of good communication is the need to solve problems. I often tell troubled couples that they must refuse to solve the problems in their relationship if they hope to experience greater love and closeness. This may sound like a paradox, but it's really not. If two people are upset with each other and are arguing about some "problem," they will usually go round and round in circles when they are trying to solve it. This bickering will continue as long as they feel angry with each other. Their feelings need to be expressed in a nondefensive way—and listened to. But if their anger isn't shared openly—and it almost never is—all their attempts to solve the problem will fail. As long as they feel angry and at odds, they will need to get back at each other. This makes it impossible to solve the problem. In contrast, if they share their feelings and listen in a spirit of trust, and feel cared about and respected once again, they will find it far easier to solve the problems that bother them.

To take a simple example, let's say that Marilyn wants to go out Thursday nights to attend a class at the local college. Ron, her husband, is uncomfortable about having to make dinner that night and eat alone with their daughter. They have been arguing about this problem and they just can't seem to find a solution that would be fair to both of them.

Marilyn argues that it's her right to go out one night a week. She

COST-BENEFIT ANALYSIS

The attitude or belief I want to change:

I should never get angry

Advantages of Believing This

1. I'll avoid confrontations and conflicts with people.
2. When I'm aware that I'm getting angry, I'll be able to criticize and scold myself.
3. That way I'll never be out of control.
4. The world, other people, and outside stimuli won't be able to exert any influence over me.
5. I'll be able to deceive myself into thinking I have risen above mere average people and I'll think that I'm somehow better.
6. I'll feel like Mr. Cool.
7. It makes life simple because I'll always know what to do.
8. I can keep people at a distance.

Disadvantages of Believing This

1. The anger will come out in some other way that may be destructive.
2. I will deny myself a part of being human.
3. I'll set a bad example for my daughter.
4. I'll set an impossible standard for myself. This will lead to further frustration and pain as I reprimand myself for not being perfect.
5. I won't feel comfortable with myself.
6. I may not come across as genuine to other people.
7. I may deprive myself of a source of self-esteem and intimacy.
8. My anger could help me deal with many situations more effectively.
9. Life loses its complexity and richness.

(40)———————(60)

Revised Attitude: Anger may be uncomfortable but there are times

when it's better for me and for the relationship to tell the other person

how I feel.

says that Ron needs to spend more time with their daughter, so it shouldn't be a problem. Ron half-heartedly agrees with this but says he feels uncomfortable with the arrangement because he and Marilyn don't ever have much time together anymore.

Can you see why their attempts to solve this problem might fail? Marilyn feels controlled and housebound. Ron has had a successful career and she's dutifully raised their children. Now she would like to make her life a little more interesting and complete her undergraduate degree. If Ron recognizes this and listens to her feelings, Marilyn will feel respected and cared about. But if he criticizes her plans and only complains about being alone every Thursday, he'll appear selfish and insecure. This will make her angry and she'll get more and more demanding, because she doesn't want to feel controlled.

By the same token, Ron has slaved away at his career and developed a good income, and he would like to feel closer to Marilyn and to his daughter. He wants to spend more time with them. He feels lonely and needs greater intimacy. If she listens and shows concern for how he feels, then Ron will feel respected and cared about. But if she just proclaims her right to do her thing, she will appear selfish, and this will make him feel even more hurt and lonely. Ron doesn't want to feel rejected and cast aside.

If they attempt to solve the problem of what to do on Thursday night, failure is almost guaranteed. No external arrangement can ever meet their needs to feel loved and respected by each other. But if they refuse to solve this problem and try instead to listen to each other in a spirit of trust and caring first, their problem will no longer exist. The problem of what to do on Thursdays doesn't really need a solution. What they are craving is intimacy and self-esteem.

You may protest. You say, "All that touchy-feely stuff is missing the point. The bottom line is that they have to figure out what they're going to do on Thursdays. Will she go to her class or won't she? They've got to compromise and find a solution." I don't believe that a compromise is indicated, and I think that looking for a solution would be a mistake. Ron and Marilyn need to express their feelings and be heard. If Ron feels loved and respected, I doubt that he'll mind cooking and spending a couple of hours on Thursdays with their daughter. He might see cooking as an expression of his love for Marilyn and for his daughter and not as an imposition. By the same token, if Marilyn feels loved and cared about, she will take Ron's needs into account as she plans more time outside the home to complete her studies and to develop her own career. She will view her relationship with Ron as a haven and as a complement to her independence rather than as a restriction of her freedom. It will be important to spend time with him and to make sure he feels loved and happy.

I have written this chapter to warn you that even though you may be hurting a great deal and desperately want to make your personal relationships better, you may find it exceedingly difficult to change. When you're annoyed with someone, it's natural to focus on what the other person is doing wrong and to hide the many things you are doing that may contribute to the difficulties. This is a trap from which very few can escape. Over and over, patients are extremely enthusiastic when they first learn about the two principles of good communication—sharing your own feelings and drawing out your partner. But when it's time to put these principles into practice, they suddenly have a change of heart. They find that they can't resist a good argument about the "truth," in much the same way that an alcoholic can't resist the urge to take a drink.

People always have lots of reasons why they shouldn't have to express their feelings with "I feel" statements or to draw out how the other person feels. They may insist that their situation is hopeless and tell me that these techniques wouldn't do any good. They may explain that their spouse "really *is* wrong" and emphasize that it's terribly important to point this out to him or her. The list of reasons not to share your feelings openly or to listen goes on and on. Arguing and blaming your partner may feel good in the short run, and it's awfully tempting to pout and to lash out. Making yourself vulnerable by listening and by sharing your feelings in a spirit of trust frequently gets forgotten in all the sound and fury. When it comes to a choice between love and hatred, between sharing and attacking, between working together or doing battle, it's hard to resist the more hostile approach.

Learning to listen and to share your feelings more openly will not come easily, but I believe that with persistent determination, you can experience greater intimacy.

PART FIVE

Mood-Altering
Medications

23

◆

Everything You Need to Know About Commonly Prescribed Psychiatric Drugs

In this book we have emphasized drug-free treatments for depression and anxiety. You may be wondering whether or not you would also benefit from an antidepressant medication or from a tranquilizer. At my clinic, about half the patients receive psychotherapy alone and half receive psychotherapy plus a medication. In this chapter I will tell you about the medications that are currently used to treat anxiety, panic attacks, phobias, depression, mania, and personality disorders.* You will learn:

- whether you should be treated with drugs only, with psychotherapy only, or with a combination of both;
- what you can expect from medications, and what kinds of medications are most likely to help you;
- how you can find out if a medication is really working;
- how to decide when you are ready to go off a medication and when you should switch to another drug;
- correct dose ranges, side effects, and dangers of all the currently prescribed drugs;

*Some of the information in this chapter was obtained from: A. F. Schatzberg and J. O. Cole, *Manual of Clinical Psychopharmacology* (Washington: American Psychiatric Press, 1986). I am grateful to the authors for their permission to use portions of this excellent reference.

- common errors in prescribing that you should be aware of; and
- blood tests that can help you determine the correct dose and monitor untoward reactions.

You may be thinking, "Why should I have to deal with all these complicated issues? Isn't it my doctor's responsibility to know which drugs I need and to inform me about them?" In an ideal world that would be true, but in the real world we live in, it may not always be a safe assumption. It pays to be well informed about any medications you are taking, and it doesn't hurt to be assertive with the physician who prescribes them for you.

I don't mean to stir up conflict between you and your physician. Quite the contrary. The dialogue you have with your doctor about drugs and side effects is a crucial part of therapy. Your knowledge can enhance the feeling of teamwork and increase the chances for a positive result.

Who would be most likely to benefit from a medication in addition to psychotherapy? The following guidelines are not rigid. They are intended to provide a general framework.

- People who are out of touch with reality and who have delusions or bizarre hallucinations.
- If you are so severely depressed or anxious that you cannot function or do anything to help yourself, you may need the help of an antidepressant medication.
- If you feel suicidal, you should probably be treated with the best of everything available, including a good antidepressant medication and intensive psychotherapy.
- If you have been working hard in your psychotherapy for a couple of months and you feel stuck, you may benefit from a medication. Often the right antidepressant will get things moving forward more rapidly.

How long should you continue to take a medication? As a general rule, I don't keep a patient on any drug unless it is having a fairly dramatic beneficial effect. Minor tranquilizers work rapidly; usually you will feel substantially less anxious and depressed in a few days. If this does not occur, I would raise the dose and wait another few days. If there's still no response, I would consider switching to another type of medication.

Antidepressants usually have a more delayed effect, so you may need to wait three to five weeks before you know whether the medication is helping. If there's no obvious reduction in your scores on mood tests like the Burns Depression Checklist or the Burns Anxiety Inventory (see Chapter 2), I would switch to another more promising antidepressant. Usually you can find one that will be beneficial.

When a medication does help, how long should you stay on it? Minor tranquilizers like Valium or Xanax can be extremely addictive when taken in large doses for over two months. I encourage my patients to taper off these drugs after they have been feeling better for a few weeks. Since most antidepressants are not addictive, your doctor may suggest a treatment period of six to twelve months before you taper off.

Some medications may be prescribed for much longer periods of time. Patients with manic-depressive illness (see page 57) usually require ongoing treatment with lithium, which helps to stabilize the abnormal highs and lows and can prevent future mood swings. Efforts to discontinue the lithium may result in severe mood swings, so some patients with this problem continue to take lithium indefinitely. The situation is somewhat analogous to diabetes, where daily insulin may be needed to stabilize the metabolism of blood sugar.

We will discuss the major classes of drugs that have been used in the treatment of mood problems, including barbiturates, minor tranquilizers, antidepressants, lithium, and others. If you are taking one of these medications, pay particular attention to that section. If you have questions about the dose, the side effects, or the effectiveness of any drug you are taking, review your concerns with your physician.

For your convenience, the following list indicates where the medications you are taking are discussed:

BARBITURATES

These drugs were introduced in the early 1920s and were first used in the treatment of insomnia and epilepsy. Thirty to forty years ago barbiturates were the only drugs available to sedate anxious and agitated patients. They include Amytal (amobarbital), Butisol (butabarbital), Mebaral (mephobarbital), Nembutal (pentobarbital), phenobarbital, Seconal (secobarbital), and Tuinal (secobarbital and amobarbital). These drugs have calming properties, but they can be quite dangerous. High doses can produce intense sleepiness, anesthesia, coma, and even death. Barbiturates can be very intoxicating and are commonly sold in the streets by junkies, who call them "downers." They are very addictive. Except in rare or unusual situations, they are no longer used in the treatment of mood problems such as anxiety, panic, or depression.

MEPROBAMATE (MILTOWN)

This drug was first marketed in the mid-1950s, when it received substantial media attention as the first true tranquilizer. It is about as effective as the newer tranquilizers like Valium, but it will produce sleepiness and a loss of coordination in high doses. Miltown can also cause addiction and physical dependence. Strong withdrawal effects, such as convulsions and delirium, can occur if you suddenly withdraw from doses of only 3,200 mg/day, or twice the recommended upper dose range. It is not in widespread use today, but it is occasionally prescribed for the rare anxious patient who becomes restless and agitated when taking the minor tranquilizers. Some practitioners prescribe Miltown at bedtime in doses of 400 to 800 mg for patients with insomnia.

MINOR TRANQUILIZERS

When these drugs were introduced in the 1960s, they dramatically changed the treatment of anxiety. The minor tranquilizers account for over 80 percent of the prescriptions written for anxiety. Only 20 percent of these prescriptions are written by psychiatrists. The vast majority are written by internists, family practitioners, and obstetricians. These remarkable statistics reflect the fact that most patients who suffer from anxiety and panic attacks do not know that their symptoms are the result of stress and conflicts in their lives. Indeed, many are overwhelmingly convinced that a medical problem accounts for their symptoms. Although most physicians are aware that many of these patients have marital or personal problems that are causing the symptoms, they may be pressed for time and lack the professional training to do any extended counseling. This may create an unfortunate tendency to rely excessively on prescription medications. In addition, both the doctor and the patient may see the need for psychotherapy as a somewhat stigmatizing and threatening sign that the patient is deeply disturbed. Even in this day and age, a referral to a psychiatrist or a psychologist may be seen as a last resort. As a result, the patient's personal problems frequently get overlooked entirely.

The real danger is that you might rely on tranquilizers as an escape from your problems or as a way of camouflaging your feelings. This tendency to avoid upsetting situations is almost universal, and tranquilizers can sometimes feed into it. Instead of facing up to your fears and grappling with conflicts at work or with your spouse, you may simply increase the dose in the hope that you will feel better.

The most widely prescribed minor tranquilizers are the *benzodiazepines*. Their chemical and brand names and dose ranges are listed on page 473. They are used mainly for stress and anxiety. One of the newer tranquilizers, Xanax, also has some antidepressant properties and is often beneficial for patients who suffer from anxiety plus depression.

These tranquilizers are not as dangerous as the barbiturates. They are also less likely to be abused, because they don't cause so much sleepiness and intoxication. In fact, most of these minor tranquilizers have very few or no side effects aside from slight sleepiness, and the sleepiness can usually be reduced or eliminated by lowering the dose. Excessively high doses can impair mental concentration and coordination and slow down your heart, especially when combined with other sedative agents such as alcohol. That's why high doses of tranquilizers can be quite dangerous when mixed with large amounts of alcohol. Side effects such as dizziness, weakness, decreased coordination, nausea, and forgetfulness have been reported, but small or moderate doses rarely cause significant side effects.

The minor tranquilizers can be extremely habit-forming. If you take high doses over a long period of time, your body may become dependent on them. Then when you try to get off the tranquilizer, you may experience withdrawal symptoms such as insomnia, anxiety, extreme restlessness, shakiness, sweating, racing of the heart, upset stomach, or diarrhea. You may also feel confused and be overly sensitive to light and sound. These withdrawal symptoms may make you think that you still need the drug, and you can easily get hooked. The sudden withdrawal from high doses of minor tranquilizers can even lead to epileptic seizures and death.

You will note that two of the drugs, Xanax and Ativan, are of higher potency than the others and require lower doses. These two drugs may have particularly intense withdrawal symptoms and are especially likely to cause addiction if taken in large doses for a prolonged period of time. There are reports that Serax, which is less potent and requires a higher dose, may produce fewer withdrawal symptoms.

The *Physician's Desk Reference* emphasizes that minor tranquilizers have no proven effectiveness beyond four months' use. They are most useful if you need temporary relief for severe anxiety or insomnia while you are making constructive changes in your life. The minor tranquilizers can be used in one of two ways. You can take them occasionally as needed for anxiety or insomnia. For example, I have a number of patients who take the smallest dose of Xanax, 0.25 mg, or even a half a pill, if they feel stressed or if they have difficulty getting to sleep. They take only one to three pills per week. The other approach is to take a minor tranquilizer regularly, on a fixed schedule throughout the day, for a maximum of three months and then to slowly taper off the drug entirely.

The following guidelines will be helpful if you are taking a minor tranquilizer:

1. You should not stay on a minor tranquilizer for more than a week or two unless it proves to be tremendously helpful. Since there is a small but real danger of addiction, the corresponding benefit must be great. If the drug isn't doing you any good, there's simply no reason to keep taking it.

2. Any adjustment in the dose—whether it's an increase or a decrease—must be gradual.

3. No matter how effective the drug is, you cannot stay on it indefinitely. The longer you stay on it, and the higher the dose, the more likely it is that you will become addicted. This can make the withdrawal extremely difficult. Therefore, it is best to limit the length of treatment to one to three months. Use this time to work hard on the problems in your life.

ANTI-ANXIETY DRUGS

Generic name	Brand name	Total daily dose range (mg/day)*	Available sizes (mg)
MINOR TRANQUILIZERS (BENZODIAZEPINES)			
alprazolam	Xanax	1–4	0.25/0.50/1.0
chlordiazepoxide	Librium	15–40	5/10/25
clonazepam	Klonopin	0.5–5.0	0.5/1.0/2.0
clorazepate	Tranxene	15–60	3.75/7.5/15
diazepam	Valium	2–40	2/5/10
halazepam	Paxipam	60–160	20/40
lorazepam	Ativan	1–6	0.5/1/2
oxazepam	Serax	45–120	10/15/30
prazepam	Centrax	20–60	5/10/20
OTHER TRANQUILIZING AGENTS			
buspirone	Buspar	10–60	5/10
meprobamate	Equanil	1,200–1,600	200/400
	Miltown		200/400/600
ANTIHISTAMINES			
diphenhydramine	Benadryl	50–300	25/50
hydroxyzine pamoate	Vistaril	200–400	25/50/100
hydroxyzine hydrochloride	Atarax	200–400	10/25/50/100
BETA-BLOCKING AGENTS			
atenolol	Tenormin	50–150	50/100
nadolol	Corgard	40–240	40/80/120/160
propranolol	Inderal	40–160	10/20/40/60/80/90

*The total daily dose of medication is usually given in divided doses at meals and at bedtime.

4. Alcohol must be taken minimally or not at all. The effects of the alcohol will be more potent when you are taking any minor tranquilizer.

5. I have frequently observed an increase in aggressiveness in mild, unassertive patients who are taking minor tranquilizers such as Xanax. They suddenly become quite courageous and begin telling people off, including me! A little bit of increased assertiveness can be therapeutic, but too much can be a bad thing. Watch out for sudden hostile outbursts if you are taking any minor tranquilizer.

6. Do not drive or operate dangerous machinery until you find out how the drug affects you. This precaution applies to any medication that affects your mind.

7. Inform your physician if you are pregnant or planning to become pregnant. The use of tranquilizers during early pregnancy should almost always be avoided because of the risk of congenital malformations. Since these drugs can be present in human milk, you may have to stop nursing if a tranquilizer is prescribed.

8. Do not take more than your physician has prescribed. If you feel the urge to take more and more pills to cope with personal problems, or to get high, inform your physician immediately. Some good counseling could prevent the development of addiction.

This approach seems to me to be conservative and sensible. You should be aware that some psychiatrists might prescribe large doses of tranquilizers for much longer periods of time for patients suffering from anxiety or panic attacks. For example, daily doses as high as 10 mg or more of Xanax have been prescribed, and these high dose levels are often maintained for a year or more. I strongly prefer to keep the dose low and the duration brief, so that the chances of a serious addiction problem with dangerous withdrawal symptoms are minimized. I do not claim that the use of high doses is always wrong, but I do question this trend, especially when patients are not exposed to helpful forms of psychotherapy which can speed recovery and make the use of medications unnecessary.

CLONAZEPAM (KLONOPIN)

This drug is a minor tranquilizer, but it is listed in the *Physician's Desk Reference* as an anticonvulsant. It has been used for many years by neurologists in the treatment of epilepsy. Recently psychiatrists have begun using clonazepam in the treatment of anxiety disorders, including panic attacks. It also appears to have antimanic properties, and can be used along with lithium in the treatment of manic-depressive illness.

Clonazepam is excreted very slowly; it takes thirty to fifty hours for half a dose to be eliminated from the body. For this reason, the drug provides a very smooth effect throughout the day—in contrast to a drug like Xanax, which leaves the body quite rapidly. Since clonazepam can be given just once or twice a day, it is more convenient. Preliminary reports by Dr. Jerold F. Rosenbaum, who studied over 400 patients with panic attacks or with agoraphobia who were treated with clonazepam, have been extremely favorable.

Initially, a dose of 0.25 mg of clonazepam at bedtime may be started. This can be gradually increased to a total daily dose of 1.0 to 5.0 mg, which is given partly in the morning and partly at bedtime. The main side effect of clonazepam is sleepiness, particularly as the dose is raised. A dose reduction will correct this. Excessively high doses could produce slurred speech and impaired coordination, as with any tranquilizer. Some patients (less than 10 percent) may develop symptoms of depression while taking the drug. In this event, an antidepressant can be added or the clonazepam can be gradually discontinued. Another occasional side effect is headache. This may respond to a reduction in the dose.

The risk of withdrawal effects is thought to be lower with clonazepam than with the shorter-acting drugs like Xanax. Nevertheless, clonazepam must be withdrawn very slowly, just like any minor tranquilizer.

BUSPIRONE (BUSPAR)

This is a new anti-anxiety drug which is chemically distinct from the minor tranquilizers. It has some potential advantages over the minor tranquilizers:

- In moderate doses, Buspar does not cause significant sleepiness or impaired alertness or coordination.
- It does not cause addiction, because it does not make you euphoric.
- You can go off Buspar, unlike the minor tranquilizers, without experiencing any withdrawal effects.
- It does not appear to be especially dangerous when mixed with alcohol.

The usual starting dose of Buspar is 5 mg twice daily. This can be gradually increased by 5 mg/day every two to three days, as needed, up to a maximum dose of 60 mg/day. The optimal dose for most patients appears to be between 20 and 30 mg per day in divided doses. The drug should begin to work in one to two weeks and will become maximally effective in three to four weeks. The most commonly reported side effects include dizziness, lightheadedness, nausea, headache, nervousness, and excitement. However, if Buspar is helpful for you, and the side effects for you are minimal, the fact that it will not cause addiction makes it an attractive alternative to the minor tranquilizers.

Since Buspar is a new drug, further clinical experience will help psychiatrists determine just how effective and safe it is. It seems to be quite promising, but it has not been on the market long enough to permit a fair and complete evaluation. Answers to the following questions will emerge as more and more clinicians prescribe Buspar:

1. How effective is it? Does it eliminate anxiety, or does it simply reduce the symptoms?

2. How well does Buspar work for the different types of anxiety, such as panic attacks, agoraphobia, social phobia, or anxiety that is mixed with depression? It is known that some forms of anxiety do not respond to Buspar.

3. How common and severe are the side effects, such as nausea?

4. Does Buspar have any dangerous toxic effects that have not yet been reported?

5. Will the drug have good long-term effects? Most of the preliminary studies have been of short duration—about four weeks. The drug may prove to be more or less effective when taken for longer periods of time.

There are several precautions if Buspar is prescribed. It is not known if Buspar affects the metabolism of other drugs so you should inform your physician of any other prescription or nonprescription drugs you are taking. Although you can drink alcohol when you are on Buspar, you should do so only in moderation. Do not drive or operate dangerous machinery until you find out how the drug affects you. Inform your physician if you are pregnant or planning to become pregnant or if you are breastfeeding an infant.

BETA-BLOCKERS

Some people with anxiety, panic attacks, or phobias experience uncomfortable physical symptoms such as rapid heartbeat, tingling fingers, tremors, sweating, or rapid breathing. These symptoms are caused by stimulation of the autonomic nervous system, which controls the internal organs such as the heart, sweat and salivary glands, and digestive system. Drugs such as propranolol (Inderal), nadolol (Corgard), and atenolol (Tenormin) are called "beta-blockers" because they inhibit part of the automatic nervous system. These drugs are used primarily by cardiologists to slow the heart, to reduce high blood pressure, and to prevent angina (a type of chest pain associated with poor blood flow to the heart). Beta-blockers are also sometimes used in the treatment of migraine headaches.

These drugs can block some of the physical symptoms of anxiety, such as palpitations, sweating, and tremor. Although the Food and Drug Administration has not yet officially approved the beta-blocking agents for the treatment of anxiety in this country, propranolol has been used to treat anxiety in England since the mid-1960s. Some American physicians are also beginning to prescribe propranolol for anxious patients. Propranolol is also used to treat the tremor that some patients experience when taking lithium. However, this is often unnecessary, since the tremor can usually be managed simply by lowering the dose of lithium.

The usual starting dose of propranolol is 10 mg twice daily. This can be gradually increased to 80 to 160 mg per day. Patients receiving propranolol for the treatment of high blood pressure may receive doses as high as 240 mg per day, but anxious patients rarely need this high a dose. As with the minor tranquilizers, it is probably best to limit the length of treatment to a relatively short period and to slowly taper off the drug after taking it for several weeks. If you are taking propranolol, for anxiety or for lithium tremor, your doctor may keep you on the drug for a much longer time, and so far there have been no reports of major side effects or toxic reactions. However, the beta-blockers can cause a drop in blood pressure along with weakness and fatigue, mental confusion, and gastrointestinal upset in some patients. In addition, they can cause spasm of the airways and must not be given to patients with asthma or with Raynaud's disease, a disorder in which the toes and fingers get cold, pale, and painful. Finally, you might become depressed while taking beta-blockers.

These depressive reactions may possibly be triggered by the feelings of fatigue.

Although the beta-blockers do not cause intoxication or addiction they could be hazardous if you have a cardiac problem because they cause a slowing down of the heart. For these reasons, they should be used only under careful medical supervision.

Blood tests are not necessary to monitor the beta-blockers, but it is necessary for your physician to take your blood pressure, to determine your heart rate, and to listen to your heart and lungs with a stethoscope before you start these drugs. Your doctor should check your heart and blood pressure periodically when you are taking the drug.

ANTIHISTAMINES

Antihistamines, such as Vistaril and Benadryl, are ordinarily prescribed for the itching associated with skin allergies. They have mild sedative and anti-anxiety properties, but they are not widely used for anxiety because they are not especially potent. They cause dry mouth and may make other sedative drugs, such as alcohol, more potent. One significant advantage of antihistamines is that they are not habit-forming and there are no significant withdrawal symptoms. Thus they may be quite useful for people with mild anxiety. Some of my patients with insomnia have found that Benadryl is a mild and safe sleeping medication.

MAJOR TRANQUILIZERS

The so-called major tranquilizers (including Compazine, Haldol, Loxitane, Mellaril, Moban, Navane, Prolixin, Quide, Serentil, Sparine, Stelazine, Taractan, Thorazine, Tindal, Trilafon, and Vesprin) are used for the treatment of psychotic states. These include mania (an uncontrollable "high" not caused by drugs and often requiring hospitalization) and schizophrenia (which is characterized by delusions, hearing voices, or the belief that others are plotting against you). The major tranquilizers are not particularly effective in the treatment of depression, anxiety, panic disorders, stress, or phobias. They should usually not be used for these disorders because they have a number of uncomfortable and dangerous side effects which far outweigh any potential benefits.

ANTIDEPRESSANTS

The names and dose levels for all the currently used antidepressant drugs are listed on page 480. The original patents on some of these drugs—such as imipramine (Tofranil) and amitriptyline (Elavil)—have expired, so that inexpensive generic brands are available.

The antidepressant drugs are used for a number of disorders:

- Any form of depression, including major depressive episodes, the depressed phase of manic-depressive illness, and chronic mild depression;
- generalized anxiety;
- agoraphobia with panic attacks;
- obsessive-compulsive disorders;
- headache and chronic pain syndromes;
- bulimia (this is an eating disorder consisting of compulsive binging followed by vomiting);
- childhood bed-wetting;
- insomnia (several antidepressants, especially doxepin, amitriptyline, trazodone, and imipramine, have sedative properties and compare favorably with sleeping pills. They have the advantage that they are usually not habit-forming.)

There is very little difference and considerable overlap among the antidepressants listed here in terms of safety, effectiveness, and side effects. Most clinicians have several antidepressants they use most often, and this is primarily a matter of personal choice. I like to start with imipramine (Tofranil) because it has relatively mild side effects and the generic brand is quite inexpensive. It has been on the market the longest, and its track record indicates that it is effective and quite safe. The doses of all these antidepressants are important. They will be ineffective if the dose is too low, and toxic if the dose is too high. In addition, different people will require different doses of these drugs. Therefore, you must work closely with your physician to make sure that the dose you are taking is the right one for you. Your physician may want to do a blood test to see if your dose is too high or too low. The blood must be drawn eight to twelve hours after you took the last pill. I usually ask my patients to get their blood test the first thing in the morning, before they take their morning dose.

The newer drugs do not have any clear-cut advantages over the older antidepressants, and unanticipated toxic effects sometimes show up within the first few years after new drugs are marketed. For

ANTIDEPRESSANT DRUGS

Generic name	Brand name	Total daily dose range (mg/day)*	Available sizes (mg)	Therapeutic plasma level (ng/ml)
TRICYCLICS				
amitriptyline	Elavil Endep	150–300	10/25/50/ 75/100/150	100–250†
desipramine	Norpramin Petrofrane	150–300	10/25/50/ 75/100/150	150–300
doxepin	Sinequan Adapin	150–300	10/25/50/ 75/100/150	120–250†
imipramine	Tofranil Janimine Sk-Pramine	150–300	10/25/50	150–300†
imipramine pamoate	Tofranil-PM (sustained release)	150–300	75/100/125/ 150	150–300†
notriptyline	Pamelor Aventyl	50–150	10/25/75	50–150
protriptyline	Vivactil	15–60	5/10	75–250
trimipramine	Surmontil	150–300	25/50/100	Unknown
TETRACYCLICS				
amoxapine	Asendin	150–450	25/50/100/150	Unknown
maprotiline	Ludiomil	150–200	25/50/75	150–250
OTHER ANTIDEPRESSANTS				
trazodone	Desyrel	150–300	50/100	Unknown
fluoxetine	Prozac	20–80	20	Unknown

*The dose ranges are approximations. Some patients will respond to less than the minimum doses on this table; others may require more than the maximum doses.
†Total concentration of the drug plus its demethylated metabolite.

example, amoxapine (Asendin), trazodone (Desyrel), and maprotiline (Ludiomil) were released several years ago with great enthusiasm. They were hailed as potentially superior antidepressants with fewer side effects. However, clinical experience has not borne this out. These drugs are no better and may even be less effective than the older ones.

Some patients receiving the newer drugs have experienced extremely adverse effects. Maprotiline can occasionally cause epileptic seizures. Wellbutrin (bupropion) was released in 1987 and then withdrawn after it was discovered that it also caused an unacceptably high incidence of seizures, particularly in patients with bulimia. Some patients taking amoxapine have experienced unexpected milk production by their breasts, and others have been troubled by the development of abnormal involuntary body movements. Desyrel, when taken on an empty stomach, can cause nausea, dizziness, or fainting. An even more recently released drug, nomifensine, was suddenly withdrawn from the market because of a number of deaths in Europe due to hemolytic anemia. For these reasons, it may be wise to avoid newly released drugs until their safety and effectiveness are clearly documented through widespread clinical use. If you are depressed, I would recommend a thorough trial with one or two of the older antidepressants first. If this is not successful, then you might want to try one of the newer drugs.

The following would be a typical dose schedule for imipramine (Tofranil):

Week 1:	Day 1	25 mg at bedtime
	Day 2	50 mg at bedtime
	Days 3–7	75 mg at bedtime
Week 2:	Day 8	100 mg at bedtime
	Day 9	125 mg at bedtime
	Days 10–14	150 mg at bedtime
Week 3:	Day 15	150 mg at bedtime; 25 mg the next morning
	Day 16	150 mg at bedtime; 50 mg the next morning
	Days 17–21	150 mg at bedtime; 75 mg the next morning

You can see that for this hypothetical patient, the drug was gradually increased to a maximum dose of 225 mg over a three-week period. Doses up to 150 mg can be given at bedtime. If more than

150 mg is required, it can be given in divided doses throughout the day. If the side effects are not severe, and if the patient has not yet begun to respond clinically, the dose could be slowly increased to 300 mg in the fourth week. The drug should be maintained for at least six weeks before concluding that it is not helpful. If the patient is not improving, the physician will probably want to try another antidepressant.

Elderly individuals may not tolerate such high doses, and many patients will respond to lower doses. Doxepin (Sinequan, Adapin) and trimipramine (Surmontil) appear to have gentler side effects and are often recommended for individuals over 60 years of age.

I ask all my patients to monitor the effects of the antidepressant by taking a mood test like the Burns Anxiety Inventory and the Burns Depression Checklist (see Chapter 2) once or twice a week. At the beginning of each therapy session, I ask them to give me their most recent scores and I record them in the chart. This is an infinitely more accurate way of judging the degree of improvement than simply asking if they feel any better. To justify continuing with any antidepressant, there should be a fairly obvious and sustained improvement in your depression and anxiety scores. For example, a reduction in your score on the Burns Anxiety Inventory from 60 (indicating a severe anxiety) to 30 (indicating moderate anxiety) would be quite encouraging and I would definitely want you to continue the drug. This pattern of improvement should continue until your scores drop below 10 (normal) or below 5 (indicating you are absolutely free of anxiety). If this improvement does not occur, I would switch to another medication.

The same principles would apply in the treatment of depression. You may begin with a score of 30 (indicating a severe depression) on the Burns Depression Checklist. By the fourth week your score might drop to 18, indicating substantial improvement, and within several more weeks the score could drop below 10 or even 5, indicating that the depression is mostly gone. Of course these scores are hypothetical, and there is tremendous variation among different individuals—but these tests do provide an excellent way of determining whether or not a particular drug is doing any good.

I do not think that you should take any antidepressant for more than one or two months unless it's having an obviously beneficial effect. This means, in simple terms, that you feel a lot better because of the drug. This will nearly always be reflected by a substantial and sustained drop in your scores on the Burns Anxiety Inventory or the Burns Depression Checklist. If you're not getting fairly dramatic relief, you shouldn't continue to take that drug! This may seem obvious, but I can tell you that many patients who are referred to me have been on an antidepressant for several years without any obvious benefit.

The antidepressants have little potential for abuse because they do not make you feel "high" or intoxicated. Unlike the minor tranquilizers, which can often relieve anxiety within a few hours, antidepressant drugs usually require several weeks to be effective. If an antidepressant works for you, your doctor may want you to continue taking it for six to twelve months. Then you can slowly taper off and your depression or anxiety usually will not return. This suggests that these antidepressants may have more of a "corrective" effect on your brain chemistry than the tranquilizers, which are more likely to lead to relapses when you attempt to go off them.

When you discontinue an antidepressant, either because it isn't working or because it did work and you've been free of symptoms for a period of time, you should taper off it slowly. Going off an antidepressant too abruptly can cause insomnia, anxiety, and upset stomach. If you were taking 225 mg per day of imipramine, I would suggest that you reduce it by 25 mg every one to three days. If you have improved a great deal and then relapse when you go off the antidepressant, you can raise the dose again and continue it for another month or two. Then you can try tapering off again. Getting off an antidepressant usually is not a problem, and I've had very few depressed or anxious patients who required indefinite treatment with these drugs.

The most common side effects of the antidepressants include:

- Dry mouth (common), constipation (common), or difficulties starting the flow of urine (uncommon). These effects are related to the dose. If they are severe, they can be helped by a reduction in the dose. I tell my patients to expect some dry mouth, because this indicates the dose is getting into the therapeutic range.
- Dizziness when you stand up suddenly. This can be corrected by getting up more slowly or by running in place when you have this sensation. The dizziness occurs because blood temporarily pools in your leg veins when you stand, causing a temporary loss of blood supply to the brain. Running in place pumps the blood back to your heart and to your brain.

- Skin rashes (especially with Ludiomil). This can usually be eliminated by switching to another antidepressant.
- Sleepiness, especially with amitriptyline (Elavil), doxepin (Sinequan, Adapin) or trazodone (Desyrel). This will often improve over time and can sometimes be corrected by taking the drug only at bedtime. Alternatively, you can switch to a less sedating and more stimulating antidepressant, such as imipramine (Tofranil), desipramine (Norpramin, Petrofrane), or protriptyline (Vivactil) or fluoxetine (Prozac).
- Feeling "spacey." Some antidepressants, especially doxepin (Sinequan, Adapin) and amitriptyline (Elavil), seem to make patients feel strange the first day or two. I strongly encourage patients to continue the drug, because these symptoms nearly always disappear.
- Nausea, twitches, or tremors. These symptoms may indicate an excessively high dose and are usually improved by a dose reduction.
- Weight gain. Any antidepressant can cause weight gain, but amitriptyline (Elavil) and doxepin (Sinequan) are probably the worst. The weight gain usually occurs only because you're eating more, since the antidepressants stimulate appetite. This problem can be managed by careful dieting, or switching to trazodone (Desyrel) or fluoxetine (Prozac). These drugs are often associated with weight loss.
- Impotence and sexual changes. Any psychiatric drug can impair sexual functioning in some patients. You might experience a loss of interest in sex, difficulties maintaining an erection, or delayed orgasm. Most of these problems can be resolved by lowering the dose or by switching to another drug. The new drug trazodone (Desyrel) can on rare occasions cause a condition known as priapism. This is a prolonged erection which can become irreversible and require emergency surgery. Although this unfortunate complication is rare, I avoid using Desyrel in male patients since so many other equally good drugs are available. Any male patient taking Desyrel who experiences a prolonged erection should immediately stop taking the drug. If the erection persists for more than an hour, go to an emergency room for treatment.

Although this list of side effects may sound intimidating, my experience with the antidepressants has been good. For most patients, a slightly dry mouth and mild constipation are the only noticeable problems. Most of the other side effects tend to be mild and easily managed. If the drug is helpful, the benefits usually far outweigh the side effects.

If you have anxiety and panic attacks, you may have unusually strong reactions to antidepressants. You may complain of palpitations and feel panicky and speeded up during the first few days that you take a drug like imipramine. Obviously you will want to stop taking the drug, because you will feel it is making you worse. Usually, if you persist, these symptoms will diminish and the drug may ultimately prove to be very beneficial once you have been in the therapeutic dose range for several weeks. One way to cope with this is to start with a very low dose, such as 10 mg per day of imipramine, and then to build up slowly. Another alternative would be to switch to a more sedating, calming drug like doxepin (Sinequan, Adapin), amitriptyline (Elavil), or trimipramine (Surmontil) and to take the drug at bedtime.

What should you do if you do not respond to the antidepressant? First, make sure you've been on it long enough. It often takes two to four weeks to start to work and as many as ten weeks to be fully effective. Second, make sure the dose is adequate by having a blood test. You may begin to respond if the dose is raised. An overly low dose is probably the most common prescribing error. You may also prefer a low dose because of feelings that drugs are "bad" or fears of becoming addicted. These concerns are usually unwarranted. I think you will be much better off if you take a full, effective dose and get better. Then you can taper off the medicine and be drug-free. If you take a low dose that does you no good, you may not improve and end up being on the drug for a prolonged time.

If you have been on an adequate dose for a sufficient time and you are not improving, you can either switch to another antidepressant or you can add another drug that may potentiate the effects of the antidepressant you are taking. Lithium at relatively low doses (900 to 1,200 mg per day) can sometimes make antidepressants more potent; the antidepressant may suddenly become effective within one or two weeks after lithium is added. (Lithium is discussed on page 495.)

Some clinicians may add a small dose of thyroid to a tricyclic antidepressant drug to potentiate the response. A typical dose would be 25 to 50 micrograms per day of L-triiodothyronine (Cytomel). This combination should be continued for seven days to see if it is effective. There are few side effects, although some patients may feel warm or develop headaches.

I frequently see depressed or anxious patients who are taking many different kinds of drugs at the same time. This practice is called "polypharmacy." For example, I have seen patients who were simultaneously taking two different antidepressants, plus lithium, plus a minor tranquilizer, plus sleeping pills, plus painkillers. When I ask why, they generally say that nothing was working but the doctor thought this particular combination of drugs might work. For the most part, the practice of prescribing many drugs is frowned on by more knowledgeable specialists. There are many problems with polypharmacy. You don't know which drug is causing what, and you can greatly increase the number of side effects and drug interactions. More often than not, polypharmacy is ineffective. It may be based on a shotgun approach rather than a careful, systematic analysis of your personal problems along with a thoughtful blueprint for solving them. It is usually preferable to take only one drug at a time, and to take it at the correct dose so you can carefully evaluate its effect. If it doesn't help, switch to a different drug. If you take one drug at a time, you will be most likely to find the drug that will be right for you.

Like any rule, this one has a few exceptions. One would be the combination of lithium plus an antidepressant described previously. In addition, patients who experience mania as well as depression frequently need antidepressant drugs or major tranquilizers in addition to lithium to control their extreme mood swings.

FLUOXETINE (PROZAC)

This drug was first marketed in 1988 as a new and chemically different type of antidepressant. At the time this chapter was finalized, fluoxetine (Prozac) was "taking off" in sales. Hopefully, this initial optimism will be maintained as clinicians gain more experience with the drug.

Fluoxetine acts specifically by potentiating the activity of serotonin in the brain. Serotonin is a chemical which certain nerves use to transmit messages to one another. For many years, it has been suspected that a decrease in the levels of serotonin in the brain may cause depression. Since fluoxetine boosts brain serotonin activity and also improves the mood and outlook of some depressed patients, this supports the serotonin theory. Although this theory has not yet been proven, fluoxetine is obviously of great interest to researchers and clinicians.

Fluoxetine is not more effective than other antidepressants, such as imipramine (Tofranil), which have been around for many years.

However, its side effects are quite different from the tricyclic antidepressants described in the last section. It is less likely to cause dry mouth, constipation, and dizziness. It does not stimulate the appetite, like so many antidepressants do. In fact, some patients taking fluoxetine experience weight loss. This may be a real benefit to depressed patients who need to lose weight. Most patients on fluoxetine do not complain of sleepiness. In fact, many experience some stimulation and insomnia, and for this reason, the drug is usually given only in the morning and at noon. Other common side effects include headache, nervousness, anxiety, tremors, fatigue, nausea, diarrhea, and sweating. These side effects are reported by 5% to 20% of patients who take fluoxetine. Keep in mind that between 2% and 15% of patients taking a placebo will report similar side effects. Therefore, the "real" side effects of fluoxetine are rather minimal for most patients.

Fluoxetine comes in only one size, 20 mg, and may be taken once a day (in the morning) or twice a day (morning and noon). The normal dose is one to four pills per day. Like nearly all antidepressants, fluoxetine requires two to four weeks to be effective.

If you are taking fluoxetine, you should be aware that the drug is excreted from your body exceedingly slowly. Once you stop taking the drug, it will take as many as five weeks before it has cleared out of your system. This is important because fluoxetine can have dangerous interactions with some other drugs such as L-tryptophan (which is sold in health food stores as a treatment for insomnia), or MAO inhibitors (which are given for depression and are described in the next section). The combination of fluoxetine plus L-tryptophan can cause agitation and gastrointestinal distress. The combination of fluoxetine plus MAO inhibitors can be potentially fatal. Therefore, you must *not* take these drugs for at least five weeks after going off fluoxetine. In addition, if you have been on an MAO inhibitor and your doctor switches you to fluoxetine, allow a minimum of two weeks for the MAO inhibitor to clear out of your blood.

Several additional precautions should be noted by patients taking fluoxetine:

- Because fluoxetine (or any other psychiatric drug) may affect your thinking, alertness, or coordination, do not drive or operate heavy machinery until you are reasonably certain the drug does not affect your performance.

- Inform your physician of any other prescription or non-prescription drug you are using. Fluoxetine may affect the blood levels of some drugs such as Coumadin, digoxin, or Valium.
- Notify your physician if you plan to become pregnant or to breast-feed an infant.
- Notify your physician if you develop hives or a rash.

Like other new antidepressants, fluoxetine should probably be used after one or two of the older, better established antidepressants have been tried first, since it is not clearly superior in terms of effectiveness. One clear disadvantage of fluoxetine is its extreme cost. In Pennsylvania, 100 tablets of a generic brand of imipramine can be obtained for as little as $5.00. In contrast, 100 tablets of fluoxetine costs in excess of $100.00! However, fluoxetine has few side effects and may hold real promise for some patients who have not responded adequately to the older medications.

MONOAMINE OXIDASE INHIBITORS (MAOIs)

Phenelzine (Nardil), tranylcypromine (Parnate), and isocarboxazid (Marplan) are the most widely prescribed MAOIs. These were the first antidepressants developed, but during the past two decades they were largely replaced by the tricyclic and tetracyclic antidepressants because the MAOIs require strict dietary precautions. However, the MAOIs are becoming popular again because they can be helpful for depression, anxiety, agoraphobia, panic attacks, obsessive-compulsive disorders, and certain personality disorders. When the MAOIs work,

MONOAMINE OXIDASE INHIBITORS			
Generic name	Brand name	Total daily dose range (mg/day)*	Available size (mg)
isocarboxazid	Marplan	30–50	10
phenelzine	Nardil	45–90	15
tranylcypromine	Parnate	30–50	10

*Some patients may respond to smaller doses, especially if they have responded successfully to the drug in the past; some clinicians will give higher than the maximum doses to severely depressed or anxious patients who are carefully supervised.

they often have a dramatic effect. Some patients tell me they "glow" and feel the best they've ever felt. Another advantage is that many patients report that these drugs have very few, if any, side effects, especially when the dose is low.

The MAO inhibitors are usually given after an unsuccessful trial with one or more of the tricyclic antidepressants. I have seen great success with MAO inhibitors in patients with long-standing severe problems with depression and anxiety tracing back to childhood. They have often not been treated successfully in the past, in spite of years and years of psychotherapy and medication therapy. One particularly difficult diagnostic category, called the "borderline personality disorder," often responds amazingly well to MAO inhibitors. Patients with this problem can be especially challenging to work with. The symptoms include:

- Chronic severe depression and anxiety, often since childhood or early adolescence.
- Intense loneliness, along with severe difficulties getting close to others. You may distrust people, anticipate rejection, and push others away. Then you may feel bitter, unloved, and alone.
- A tendency to act out your anger instead of verbalizing it, because you may have deep feelings of shame and find angry feelings unacceptable and overwhelming. Paradoxically, the fact that you can't express your anger sometimes makes you appear hostile, because you have difficulties expressing your feelings openly and directly.
- When you feel depressed and frustrated, you may experience intense self-loathing. You may express this in self-destructive behavior such as wrist-slashing or burning your arms with cigarettes. These are frequently not suicidal attempts but efforts to distract yourself from the feelings of low self-esteem, frustration, and anger toward others.
- Sudden emotional changes: You may be polite and articulate and appear well-adjusted at the beginning of therapy. Within a week or two, you may have switched to the opposite—you feel angry, desperate, hopeless, and suicidal. You may appear manipulative, because you are unable to deal with your intense feelings of disappointment in others.
- You have intense dependency and desires to be taken care of, along with a powerful reluctance to take the initiative to cope with your problems actively and independently.
- You have a poor sense of who you are, a lack of identity, and feelings of emptiness and boredom inside.

If you have these symptoms and you respond to a MAO inhibitor, your depression and anger may be dramatically reduced and will frequently disappear entirely. Your personality may become brighter, and the self-hatred will be replaced by feelings of self-esteem and greater trust and liking for others. You will feel happier and more self-reliant. Although all of this may sound too good to be true, I do see this result in approximately 50 percent of my patients who receive a MAO inhibitor.

Certain foods, such as cheese and pickled herring, are strictly prohibited because they contain an amino acid called tyramine (see page 491). If you eat any food containing tyramine while taking a MAOI, you may experience a sudden and potentially dangerous elevation in blood pressure. Most of us can tolerate a temporary increase in blood pressure without any adverse effects. For example, if you work out with weights or exercise strenuously, your blood pressure may temporarily go up from 120/80 (a typical level) to 180/100 or even higher. When you stop exerting yourself, your blood pressure comes down again. This is normal. However, if your blood pressure remained elevated indefinitely, it would cause problems. You could conceivably get a stroke due to the rupture of a blood vessel in your brain. This is why you must watch your diet faithfully while you are taking a MAOI. You don't want to eat a food with tyramine and cause a temporary increase in your blood pressure. Any time you discontinue a MAO inhibitor, you must stay on the special diet for two more weeks to prevent a blood pressure problem. This is because the effects of a MAOI persist for up to fourteen days after you stop taking the drug.

You may find the list of foods to be avoided somewhat confusing. What most of these foods have in common is the breakdown of protein, which causes the formation of the amino acid, tyramine. Fresh fish or meat has no tyramine and is quite safe. However, partially decomposed meat, such as smoked fish or strong sausages, or strong cheese, contains large amounts of tyramine and is dangerous. Therefore, pizza is definitely out while you are taking a MAOI! Similarly, an overly-ripe banana or avocado would contain some tyramine, especially in the rotten areas.

Good doctor-patient teamwork is vital if you are taking a MAOI. I ask all my patients who take MAOIs to purchase a blood pressure cuff (usually for under $30 at the local drugstore) so they can monitor their blood pressure regularly. Blood pressure cuffs are relatively easy

FOODS AND BEVERAGES TO AVOID IF
YOU ARE TAKING A MONOAMINE OXIDASE INHIBITOR*

Foods to avoid completely

Cheese, particularly aged or strong cheeses (Cottage cheese and cream cheese are allowed.)

Beer and red wine

Brewer's yeast or yeast extracts (Breads and cooked forms of yeast are safe. The yeast extracts from health food stores are dangerous. Yeast extracts may be found in certain soups.)

Pods of fava beans, also called Italian green beans (Regular green beans are safe.)

Smoked or dried fish or unrefrigerated fish

Pickled or salted herring

Liver

Caviar or pâté

Fermented sausages such as bologna, pepperoni, salami, and summer sausage

Overripe bananas or avocados

Foods that may cause problems in high doses

White wine

Clear alcohol, such as vodka or gin

Sour cream

Yogurt

Soy sauce

NutraSweet (the artificial sweetener found in diet sodas and other diet foods)

Foods once thought to cause problems but which are probably safe in moderate quantities

Chocolate

Figs (avoid overripe figs)

Meat tenderizers

Caffeine in beverages like coffee, tea, and soda

Raisins

*Modified from: B. McCabe and M. T. Tsuang, "Dietary Considerations in MAO Inhibitor Regimens," *Journal of Clinical Psychiatry* 43 (1982): 178–181.

to learn to use. If you get symptoms suggesting increased blood pressure, such as nausea, vomiting, sweating, neck stiffness or a severe headache, you can check your blood pressure immediately. It is a relief to know that you have a blood pressure cuff available so you can monitor any potential problem. I advise all my patients to take their blood pressure two hours after their morning dose for the first two weeks they take the medication. In my experience, midmorning is the time when a blood pressure elevation is the most likely to occur.

After the first two weeks, you should monitor your blood pressure once a week. If your blood pressure rises above 150/95, check it every ten to fifteen minutes. If it continues to go up and reaches 180/105 or above, go to a hospital emergency room for observation. In the past ten years, I've had about six patients who have had blood pressure elevations at or above the 180/105 range. In all these cases, their blood pressures came down spontaneously within thirty minutes without any treatment. However, these episodes can be alarming. You and your physician should monitor the medication and your diet carefully, and you should take your blood pressure regularly.

How dangerous is it to eat any of the "forbidden" foods? Foods can vary in their tyramine content, and individuals on MAO inhibitors can vary in their responses to foods containing tyramine. When in doubt, if you do slip up and eat one of these foods, get your blood pressure cuff and check your blood pressure! You might get away with eating a mild cheese or drinking beer on a few occasions and conclude that you are relatively immune to the blood pressure increases. However, you may be fooling yourself, because on another occasion you could unexpectedly have a dangerous blood pressure elevation after eating the same forbidden food that you got away with in the past. You were lucky, but it wouldn't be smart to assume that it's safe to continue to violate the diet.

The MAOIs are usually taken only in the morning and at noon, because they are somewhat stimulating. They can cause insomnia if you take them later in the day. This stimulation can be helpful if you feel depressed and sluggish and low on motivation. Parnate is the most stimulating MAOI. Some patients taking Nardil have reported daytime sleepiness and restlessness at night.

You must avoid certain medications if you are taking a MAO inhibitor (see the list on page 493). Decongestants, asthma drugs, and cold preparations should not be taken. You should also avoid stimulants, such as weight loss pills, amphetamines, Ritalin, and cocaine. These stimulants have powerful effects on the cardiovascular system, and taking them in combination with a MAO inhibitor could trigger an extremely dangerous abnormal heart rhythm or an increase in blood pressure. You should also avoid the narcotic pain-killer Demerol. However, aspirin and Tylenol are quite safe.

If you should require elective surgery while on a MAO inhibitor, it is best to discontinue the drug for two weeks prior to the surgery. You should inform any doctor you work with that you are taking a MAO inhibitor. You may want your doctor to consult with your psychiatrist if there is any doubt about a drug he or she may want to prescribe. You should also inform your dentist, because local anesthetics containing epinephrine can be dangerous.

MEDICATIONS TO AVOID IF YOU ARE TAKING A MONOAMINE OXIDASE INHIBITOR

Cold tablets or drugs

Nasal decongestants (tablets, drops, or sprays)

Hay fever medications

Most sinus tablets

Asthma inhalants

Weight-reducing pills

Stimulants such as cocaine, Ritalin, or amphetamines

Other antidepressants, including tricyclics such as imipramine or desmethyimipramine, as well as flouxetine (Prozac) or other MAO inhibitors

Demerol (meperidine)

Epinephrine, Adrenalin, pseudo-epinephrine

Local anesthetics

L-DOPA

L-Tryptophan

Oral hypoglycemia agents (they may have a more pronounced effect)

Tegretol (carbamazepine)

Flexeril (cyclobenzaprine)

You should carry a special card in your wallet, which explains that you're taking a MAOI. The card lists all the foods and medications that you should avoid. (The drug manufacturers provide these cards free of charge to physicians.) If you are in an accident or you require emergency surgery, or if you have a hypertensive reaction, the card will inform the hospital staff that you have been taking this medication so that they will know how to treat you.

I generally start patients on one pill per morning of Parnate (10 mg each), Nardil (15 mg each), or Marplan (10 mg each). After a few days I increase the dose to two pills. Although the *Physician's Desk Reference* suggests a starting dose of three pills per day, I find that some patients respond so positively to one or two that it's not necessary to raise the dose any further. In the absence of significant improvement on a dose of two pills per day for two weeks, I would increase the dose to three pills (two in the morning and one at noon). I only occasionally increase to a dose as high as four to six per day. Some psychiatrists will go as high as eight pills per day for people with severe mood problems, but I avoid these very high doses because they are usually not necessary.

When higher doses are required, some side effects do begin to appear. In the lower doses I prescribe to most patients, the side effects are usually nonexistent. The most troublesome side effect as the dose is raised is a drop in blood pressure when you stand up suddenly. As with the tricyclic antidepressants, this is caused by blood pooling in the legs. This creates the sensation of lightheadedness or dizziness, and your vision may go black momentarily. One way to compensate for this is to rise more slowly or to walk or run in place when this occurs. It may also help if you maintain adequate fluid intake by drinking eight glasses of fluid daily, and if you eat more salty foods such as potato chips. Some psychiatrists report that wearing support stockings can help, but I've had no experience with this.

Another side effect I have seen on rare occasions is delayed orgasm. This isn't necessarily a bad thing. One young man who had a problem with premature ejaculation reported making love for hours shortly after starting Parnate. He was perplexed, but he said his girlfriend was thrilled. He advised me to buy stock in the company that manufactured the drug!

Weight gain can be a problem with MAO inhibitors, as with any antidepressant. Exercise and calorie counting may be needed. Some patients may report dry mouth, constipation or a loose stool, muscle cramps or twitches, or difficulties starting the flow of urine. These side effects are far less frequent than with the tricyclic antidepressants and can be minimized by lowering the dose. If you receive an extremely high dose of a MAOI, you might begin to feel drunk and confused and have trouble with your coordination. Obviously the dose must be reduced immediately. If you develop muscle pains, cramps, or tingling fingers—side effects that have been reported but which I have never observed—a daily dose of 100 mg of vitamin B_6 (pyridoxine) may help. This is because MAO inhibitors may interfere with pyridoxine metabolism.

Finally, people on MAO inhibitors have on rare occasions developed a high fever along with confusion, nausea, and a sensitivity to light. These are called "hyperpyrexia" states. ("Hyper" means higher and "pyrexic" refers to fire, or fever.) These reactions are dangerous if untreated and can lead to coma. They require immediate discontinuation of the drug along with emergency medical care. Fortunately, these reactions are quite rare.

LITHIUM

Lithium chloride is a salt which is very similar to ordinary table salt, or sodium chloride. In 1949 an Australian psychiatrist discovered that lithium had a calming effect for manic patients who suffered from uncontrollable mood swings. Since then, another form of lithium called lithium carbonate has become the primary drug used in the treatment of manic-depressive illness. (It is also available in a liquid form as lithium citrate.) As you may recall from Chapter 3, this disorder causes extreme highs characterized by euphoria and hyperactivity, which are often followed by severe states of depression. Lithium can help manic-depressive patients in several ways:

- It can control manic excitement and agitation. It is usually given along with other calming drugs such as the major tranquilizers.
- It can be taken prophylactically (preventatively, when there are no symptoms) to prevent or minimize future episodes of mania as well as depression.
- It helps some patients with chronic depression or with recurrent depressions who have never experienced any symptoms of mania.

Lithium has a number of other uses as well:

- It can be given along with the tricyclic antidepressants or the MAOI antidepressants. Lithium often makes these antidepressants more potent.
- It is sometimes given to patients with impulsive personalities who become episodically violent.
- It can sometimes help individuals who suffer from schizophrenia plus mood problems. For these patients, lithium is usually combined with a major tranquilizer such as Thorazine.
- Lithium can help some emotionally unstable individuals who have the borderline personality disorder (see page 489).
- Lithium has been helpful for some alcoholics with a history of depression.

The usual starting dose of lithium is 300 mg three or four times daily. (There are new timed-release versions which can be taken twice daily. Lithobid is available in 300-mg capsules, and Eskalith CR is available in 450-mg tablets.) Based on the level of lithium in your blood, your doctor may raise or lower the dose. When lithium is used between episodes to help to prevent a recurrence of depression or mania, levels of 0.4 to 0.6 mEq (milliequivalents) per liter may be sufficient. During an episode of depression or mania, a blood level of 0.6 to 0.9 mEq per liter is optimal. Blood levels above 1.0 are generally considered undesirable because of the greater risk of side effects and toxic effects. At these high levels, you could experience excessive fatigue, nausea, slurred speech, mental confusion, severe tremor, and a loss of coordination. If you have these symptoms, stop taking the drug at once and seek immediate medical attention.

The lithium blood test must be taken first thing in the morning, before you take your first morning pill. Since the blood test must be taken eight to twelve hours after your last pill, if you take your last daily dose at 10:00 p.m. and you have a lithium test the next morning at 9:00 a.m., eleven hours will have passed. This is optimal, and the results of the test will be valid. You must be scrupulous about observing these rules. Otherwise the results will be misleading and your doctor may put you on a dose that is too high or too low.

Initially you must have a lithium blood test every week for the first month. Then you will need a blood test every month. Eventually a lithium test every two months will be sufficient. A few of my patients who are very reliable and who have been on lithium for many years get serum lithium tests every three or four months, and that seems to be satisfactory.

When you go on lithium for the first time, your doctor will probably also order the following tests:

1. Serum creatinine test: This is a test of how well your kidneys function. Some patients who have been on lithium for many years experience some impairment in kidney function. This is usually not dangerous, but the creatinine test should be repeated once a year so your doctor can monitor any effect on your kidneys.

2. Serum electrolytes (sodium, chloride, potassium, and carbon dioxide) if you are taking a diuretic or if you are on a low-sodium diet for high blood pressure. This is because certain diuretics may cause your blood potassium level to fall and will cause an increase in serum lithium levels. Because of the diuretic, you will probably require a lower dose of lithium to maintain a therapeutic blood level, and you will need careful frequent monitoring of your serum lithium level.

3. Tests of thyroid functioning: T_3, T_4, and TSH. Lithium can sometimes cause a decrease in thyroid functioning, along with an enlargement of the thyroid gland. Your doctor will want to repeat these tests once a year while you are taking lithium.

4. A complete blood count (CBC): Lithium stimulates an increase in white blood cell production in some patients, so your doctor may want a baseline white cell count around the time you first go on the drug.

In addition, if you are over 40 years old or if you have any heart problems, your doctor may order an electrocardiogram (EKG) before you start to take lithium. He may repeat the EKG after you have been on the drug, to make sure that there are no adverse effects on your heart. This test is optional.

In the first week you take lithium, you may experience some fatigue, diarrhea, or an upset stomach. These side effects usually disappear. The nausea may be minimized by lowering the dose, by taking the lithium with meals, or by using a sustained-release brand of lithium, which is possibly less irritating to the stomach. Remember, though, that the sustained-release capsules such as Eskalith CR or Lithobid are more expensive, and they are usually unnecessary.

Twenty percent of the patients who take lithium get thirsty and urinate more frequently. Usually this can be managed by reducing the dose.

A tremor of the hands is the most common side effect of lithium. The tremor will often improve if the dose is reduced. The lithium tremor occurs primarily in the fingers. It may affect your handwriting, and you may shake when you hold a cup of coffee. Most of my patients simply put up with the tremor as a small price for a vastly improved outlook on life that lithium has provided. Some psychiatrists treat the tremor with the beta-blocker propranolol (Inderal). A total daily dose of 40 to 160 mg per day is generally used. I do not prescribe propranolol for lithium tremor because I am uncomfortable giving my patients too many drugs at the same time.

Lithium, as well as other antidepressants, can sometimes cause memory problems. Some patients become somewhat forgetful and may have difficulties remembering names. These effects are reversible and usually disappear when the dose is lowered.

Increased appetite and weight gain can be problems on lithium, as on any antidepressant, but in my practice this has not been a common problem. Some patients develop rashes as well as flare-ups of psoriasis. Although rare, this may require a consultation with a dermatologist, a change to another brand of lithium, or going off the lithium temporarily. Another rare complication is hair loss, but the hair usually grows back. I've never observed this side effect.

If possible, lithium should be avoided, as should any psychiatric drug, in pregnant women. It has been associated with birth defects involving the heart. In addition, lithium is secreted in human milk and should be avoided by nursing mothers. If the lithium is needed, breastfeeding should be avoided.

Anti-inflammatory drugs such as indomethacin and phenylbutazone may cause your lithium level to go up. In contrast, excessive amounts of coffee (or anything containing caffeine) may cause increased urination and your lithium level may fall, requiring significantly higher doses of lithium to maintain the proper blood level.

CARBAMAZEPINE (TEGRETOL)

This drug is an anticonvulsant that was first introduced in the 1960s as a treatment for temporal-lobe epilepsy. In the 1970s, Japanese investigators discovered that Tegretol was often helpful for manic-depressive patients who did not respond to lithium. Although it has not yet been officially approved for the treatment of mania and depression by the FDA, it is often quite helpful. In addition, some psychiatrists have found that Tegretol can be helpful for the so-called atypical depressions, in which severe anxiety and depression co-exist with self-destructive behavior such as wrist slashing. (This is also called the "borderline personality disorder," as described on page 489.)

The beginning dose of Tegretol is 200 mg twice daily for two days. It may then be raised to 200 mg three times a day for five days. After this, the dose is gradually increased to 200 mg per day every five days up to a total daily maximum of 1,200 mg to 1,600 mg.

You will receive a blood test every week for the first two months. After that, you will need a blood test every one or two months. The results will guide your doctor in the amount he prescribes. Most patients with depression or mania will respond to a blood level of 6 to 8 mg/liter.

Tegretol usually takes one to two weeks to be effective, as do many psychiatric medications. If the Tegretol is helpful, your doctor will probably suggest you stay on the drug for a longer period of time to prevent a relapse.

Sleepiness is the most common side effect of Tegretol, especially at the start of treatment. This can be minimized by raising the dose more slowly. Usually the drowsiness will wear off. You may also experience some nausea and vomiting at first, as well as other side effects similar to those caused by the tricyclic antidepressants—dry mouth, constipation, and dizziness when standing up suddenly.

A more serious concern is that Tegretol may cause a drop in your white blood cell count. To monitor this, your physician will order frequent complete blood counts along with the Tegretol blood test. A normal white cell count is around 6,000 to 12,000. If your white cell count falls below 3,000, your physician will stop the drug immediately and obtain a consultation with a hematologist. On rare occasions, Tegretol can cause a dangerous and potentially fatal bone marrow suppression. When the drug was first introduced, this possibility frightened many physicians. Now that Tegretol has been prescribed extensively and careful blood testing is in widespread use, it is gaining in popularity. However, because there is a small risk, it should probably not be used for psychiatric problems unless other drugs have been tried first and have proved ineffective.

For Therapists (and Curious Patients) Only: How to Deal with Difficult Patients

24

◆

The Ingredients of Therapeutic Success—and Failure!

Several years ago, I became curious about the reasons why some patients felt so much better at the end of therapy sessions. What was the key to the more successful sessions, in which there was an improvement in mood and self-esteem and a decrease in depression, anxiety, or anger? Dr. Jacqueline Persons—who was then a student and is now a colleague practicing in Oakland, California—and I designed an experiment to learn more about this. We hypothesized that patients would feel better at the end of a session if they felt cared about and understood by their therapist, and if there was an actual change in their negative thinking patterns during the session. These two dimensions reflect the degree of empathy and rapport (the "nonspecific" aspect of therapy) as well as the effectiveness of the cognitive interventions (the "specific" aspect). We also hypothesized that patients with certain diagnoses, such as "borderline personality disorder" (see page 489), would experience relatively less improvement in any particular session because of their chronic feelings of resentment and difficulties with trust.

We studied the degree of empathy, the percent of reduction in belief in Automatic Thoughts, and the degree of emotional improvement in a randomly selected group of patients at the beginning and end of their therapy sessions. As we had predicted, patients who felt cared about and understood by the therapist, and those who reported the greatest decreases in the amount they believed their negative, self-critical thoughts, reported the greatest improvement in feelings of depression, anxiety, guilt, and anger at the end of their sessions. Patients with personality disorders in addition to depression and anxiety reported significantly less improvement.

The magnitude of these effects was large. Together, these three factors—empathy, the percent of change in the degree of belief in negative thoughts, and the presence or absence of a personality disorder—accounted for 89 percent of the variance (or variability) in the degree of emotional change during sessions. This meant that we had almost entirely accounted for the reasons why patients felt better, worse, or unchanged during therapy sessions.*

This result was surprising. We sometimes think of human emotions and the therapeutic relationship as mysterious, sacred, unmeasurable, unknowable. It doesn't seem that what goes on during psychotherapy sessions could be precisely measured or that the results could be predicted in the way we can make accurate predictions in the "hard" sciences like biology or astronomy.

From a clinical perspective, the results were *not* so surprising. I had had a strong hunch that there were usually only two reasons why patients did not feel they were being helped: Either they didn't feel cared about and understood—indicating a lack of empathy and trust—or they weren't making any real headway in modifying the negative, self-critical thoughts that were making them feel so depressed. The research indicated that these two causes of therapeutic failure—a lack of empathy or a lack of successful technique—operated independently of each other. This means that some patients may feel you have lots of brilliant techniques to help them, but they may feel a lack of warmth and caring, which makes them annoyed and mistrustful. They may feel that you are talking *at* them rather than truly comprehending how awful they feel. Other patients may feel you're the most wonderfully sympathetic person in the world—there's really good chemistry between you—but they aren't helped much in their sessions because you aren't giving them the tools they need to modify their pessimistic thinking patterns.

*Therapists interested in learning more about this study can consult: J.B. Persons and D.D. Burns, "Mechanisms of Action of Cognitive Therapy: Relative Contributions of Technical and Interpersonal Interventions," *Cognitive Therapy and Research* 9, no. 5 (1985): 539–551.

Empathy. A failure of empathy can occur for one of two reasons. Patients may think you haven't really listened and heard how bad they feel, or they may feel angry because of something you did or said that rubbed them the wrong way. They may feel annoyed because:

- You were late for a session or answered the phone during a session.
- You charged for a missed visit.
- You made a comment that sounded sarcastic or hurtful.
- Your therapeutic strategy struck them as dishonest, phony, or superficial.
- You seemed rushed and uncaring.

Patients are often extremely inassertive and may not express these negative feelings. This will sabotage the therapy. These patients may need to make the therapy fail, as a way of thwarting you and letting you know indirectly how let down and hurt they feel.

Some patients may feel belittled because you are trying to problem-solve prematurely, at a time when they still need emotional support and caring. Since the newer therapies—such as cognitive and behavioral therapy—are rich in technology, the human dimension can get lost in the shuffle. Therapists may be too eager to swoop in and help patients turn things around. Patients may not be ready for this. They may need you to listen and to show concern. This is a potential problem at the beginning and throughout therapy.

There are two ways to tune in to the lack of empathy. At the beginning and end of every session, I try to ask each patient for positive and negative feedback. At the beginning I might say, "I'd like to hear your positive and negative feelings about the therapy so far. Let's start with the negatives first. Was there anything about our last session that turned you off? When you listened to the tape of the session, was there anything I said that was confusing or that rubbed you the wrong way?" After I hear what the patient has to say, I go on to ask, "I'd also like to hear if there was anything that was helpful to you." I ask similar questions at the end of each session.

If the patient appears tense but denies any negative feelings, I might say: "I have the feeling you might be a little uncomfortable, even though you say there were no problems during the session. Let me ask you this: If you *were* a little annoyed with me or dissatisfied with the therapy, would it be easy or difficult for you to tell me?" If the patient says "Difficult," then you can say, "I wonder, then, if you're having some difficulty right now. I know it can be hard to tell someone when you feel ticked off, but I believe that this can make our work much more rewarding and effective."

In addition, I ask the patients to fill out the Empathy Scale after each session and to give it to me at the beginning of the next session. I would urge you to copy this form, which appears on page 507, and to give copies to your patients. The first ten questions are similar to the Empathy Scale which Dr. Persons and I used in our research. Answers of 3 on questions 1, 3, 5, 7, and 9 as well as answers of 0 on questions 2, 4, 6, 8, and 10 indicate that the patient feels liked and understood by you. Other answers usually indicate negative feelings which need to be explored and expressed so the therapy doesn't get stuck. If you don't get all 0's and 3's on the report, I would explore the patient's feelings about you. If you get a 2 on questions 1, 3, 5, 7, or 9, you may think, "That's not so bad." However, you may be lulled into complacency if you think this way. Even slightly less than optimal responses can reveal strong negative feelings. This may be condemnation through faint praise!

I've noticed a strong reluctance among therapists to use this form with patients. It's as if we don't want to hear the bad news. If you don't believe me, ask yourself this question right now: "Do I plan to copy the Empathy Scale and hand it out to my patients starting this week?" I guarantee that the form will provide surprising, unexpected information that is vital to successful treatment, and that you cannot get this information in any other way. Furthermore, the form is quick and easy to fill out and interpret.

If you don't plan to use it, or if you feel ambivalent and uncommitted, ask yourself why. It may be that you are afraid of conflict and criticism. This is a very human reaction, and many therapists do feel this way. I know that there are times when I find it difficult to be criticized by an angry patient. It's particularly upsetting when I know that I haven't done as good a job as I'd like. Maybe I was annoyed and sounded cold or judgmental and made a sarcastic remark. It hurts to have this pointed out! You can get used to criticism by eliciting it over and over. The fear tends to diminish, in much the same way that an elevator phobia will diminish when you finally get on the elevator and stay on it for a while. Once you become comfortable with patients' negative reactions, the therapy will become more effective and more rewarding.

Some therapists think they are too sophisticated and sensitive to

EMPATHY SCALE*

Using the scale from 0 to 3 below, rate the EXTENT TO WHICH YOU FEEL EACH OF THESE STATEMENTS IS TRUE TODAY.

0—I do not feel this statement is valid
1—I feel this statement is somewhat valid
2—I feel this statement is moderately valid
3—I feel this statement is extremely valid

_____ 1. I feel that I can trust my therapist.

_____ 2. Sometimes my therapist does not seem to be completely genuine.

_____ 3. My therapist thinks I'm worthwhile.

_____ 4. My therapist pretends to like me more than he or she really does.

_____ 5. My therapist is friendly and warm toward me.

_____ 6. My therapist does not seem to care what happens to me.

_____ 7. My therapist usually understands what I say to him or her.

_____ 8. My therapist does not understand the way I feel inside.

_____ 9. My therapist is sympathetic and concerned about me.

_____ 10. My therapist sometimes acts condescending and talks down to me.

PATIENT'S REPORT OF THERAPY SESSION

Was there anything that was said during the session which irritated you, rubbed you the wrong way, or which you disagreed with? Describe any negative feelings you had during the session:

_____

_____

_____

_____

_____

_____

_____

Was there anything in today's session that was particularly helpful or useful? Was there anything you learned or would like to develop further? Outline any key points that were covered:

_____

_____

_____

_____

_____

_____

_____

_____

need a tool like the Empathy Scale. They believe, wrongly, that they can sense intuitively when patients feel angry or uncared about. Nothing could be further from the truth. Studies have indicated that therapists' estimations of how empathetic and caring they are during therapy sessions are poorly correlated or completely uncorrelated with patients' ratings how empathetic and caring their therapists are.* This means that although you feel that you were being extremely supportive and that you listened with sensitivity and compassion during a particular session, there may be no greater than a random chance that the patient will feel cared about or will report that you listened and understood how he or she was feeling.

These surprising findings have intriguing theoretical and practical implications. First, they indicate that our patients' thoughts—rather than our actual behavior—dominate the way they feel about us. A depressed college student named Ted once asked if I cared about him. I told Ted that I did like him and respected him greatly. He began sobbing and appeared enraged. When I asked Ted what he was thinking, he said: "Even my shrink can't see what a fraud I am!" Even though I thought I had expressed genuine caring, Ted did not feel cared about. His self-esteem was so low, and his feelings of mistrust and resentment were so strong, that he did not accept what I said.

The practical implication is obvious—you have to *ask* patients repeatedly about their positive and negative feelings about you, and you have to look at ratings on the Empathy Scale. You will discover many negative reactions that you were not aware of, and you will have a chance to deal with them. But if you are a therapeutic ostrich and you keep your head buried in the sand, you won't know how the patient really feels about you. The therapy will get stuck and you will get frustrated because no matter how hard you try, the patient just won't seem to respond.

Good therapists dance back and forth constantly between technique and empathy, depending on the signals they receive from the patient on a moment-by-moment basis throughout the session. There are times when patients just want to ventilate. You may see a sudden change in the facial muscles as tears well up: the patient is looking for a signal—"Is it okay for me to cry?" If you are sensitive to this,

*For a review article, see: P. E. Orlinsky and U.I. Howard, "Process and Outcome in Psychotherapy," Chap. 8 in *Handbook of Psychotherapy and Behavior Change*, 3rd ed., S. L. Ossfield and A. E. Bergin, eds. (New York: Wiley, 1986).

you will encourage the patient to let the tears flow. You will listen and provide support.

Some patients are angry at the world. It makes no difference if their complaints appear to be irrational—they need to get these feelings out. They feel inadequate, panicky, desperate, hopeless, and bitter. They want you to see the world through their eyes without judging them or insisting that their feelings are illogical or distorted. This process creates bonding and feelings of trust that are crucial to the success of the therapeutic process. Once you can grasp the world through your patients' eyes and fully comprehend the traps that they feel caught in, your subsequent interventions will be more sensitive and successful. You can help them from *within*, rather than attacking their faulty cognitions from *without*.

Patients will often feel angry with you. Some of their reasons may be valid. You may have inadvertently made a mistake or said something that upset them. You may have made a comment that had a sharp edge because you felt frustrated. Some of the reasons for their anger may be distorted. Many patients have difficulty trusting and getting close to others, and these feelings may get projected onto you. A man may have the belief that he is unlovable and will inevitably be rejected. He may filter all your actions through this lens and constantly look for little signs of rejection and dislike. He may act hostile and provoke fights because he is so sure you will ultimately reject him.

To make matters worse, many patients fear conflict. They are unassertive and extremely reluctant to express these feelings openly and directly. Instead, they become evasive or argumentative. They may cancel sessions at the last minute, fall behind in paying their therapy bills, or "forget" to do their self-help assignments between sessions. They may complain that you aren't helping and insist that they are hopeless. All these can be signs that the patient is angry with you. If these feelings are aired and worked through, they won't sabotage the therapeutic process. Indeed, they can enhance the therapy greatly.

The matter is even more complicated because therapists, being human, are also imperfect. We bring our own vulnerabilities and shortcomings to the therapeutic process. There's a popular myth that people who pursue careers in psychology or psychiatry are neurotic and insecure and are looking for help. I think this is often true. Most of us have fears and wounds from the past which may make us vulnerable to criticism and personal conflict. I have seen these reactions in most of the therapists I have trained, and I have seen them in myself. We're all human, and therapy can be extraordinarily stressful at times. It's easy to get frustrated and anxious and to feel inadequate and threatened. We share many of the same inhibitions and irrational beliefs that plague our patients. We fear criticism. We fear anger. We feel ashamed of our shortcomings. Right? These emotional barriers can interact with a patient's fears and create a negative emotional climate that will interfere with the therapeutic relationship. Learning to deal with these difficulties can make the therapy far more effective.

Technique. Even when the feelings of rapport are adequate, therapy can fail when the technical aspect of treatment is insufficient. A patient could come to sessions for months and months, complaining about depression and anxiety. He or she could tell you how dissatisfying life is. You could listen and understand and express great caring and emotional support. The patient might like and respect you greatly. But if there are no specific, effective interventions to help the patient change these negative patterns of thinking and behaving, there will be no tangible improvement in his or her mood and outlook.

There are three reasons for a technical failure. First, you may not have negotiated meaningful goals for the therapy or developed a specific, workable agenda at the beginning of each therapy session. This is the commonest reason why therapy fails, and therapists are frequently unaware that this is the source of the difficulty. The patient may vaguely want to feel less depressed, without having defined any concrete problems—such as a troubled marriage or career—that he or she wants help with.

A second reason for a technical failure is that even when there is a specific problem, you and the patient may not yet have come up with the best strategy for resolving it. The patient may procrastinate at work or at school. You may try a few interventions and discover that none of them work. Then you may give up and conclude that the patient doesn't really want to change, so you succumb to a more passive role as a friend and listener.

Suppose your patient has a self-defeating belief such as "I deserve to suffer because of the abortion I had many years ago," or "I will never again feel truly happy or fulfilled because I was rejected by someone I loved," or "I must be perfect in everything I do," or "It is terribly dangerous to express my inner feelings to others," or "I'm basically inferior because other people are so much more intelligent and attractive and successful than I am." You may try one, two, three, four, or more cognitive techniques and discover that the patient is still trapped in the same belief system. Helping the patient modify dysfunctional attitudes and negative thinking patterns requires creative, persistent therapeutic effort. In Chapter 6 I described numerous cognitive techniques that can help patients modify negative thoughts and self-defeating attitudes. You may need to be relentless in trying a myriad of approaches until you finally discover the combination to the lock. If you give up prematurely, the door to the safe may never open.

Motivation.   A third reason why therapy can fail is that patients may have mixed motives about getting better. Often what we see as a "problem"—such as the patient's obesity, depression, and excessive dependency on her parents—may actually be a "solution" to her fears of intimacy, sexuality, and growing up. Helping her to resolve these "problems" through dieting and other self-help exercises may be met with resistance if you have not conceptualized her deeper concerns and fears of change. You need to ask what her life would be like if she *did* get better. Is she prepared to deal with men's sexual advances? Does she really want to leave home and face the world alone? Her despair and overeating may be painful and humiliating, but these habits may also be old friends that are familiar and reliable. We do not readily say good-by to dear friends. The predictable pain of obesity, loneliness, and low self-esteem may in some ways be preferable to the terrifying fear of taking risks and moving forward with one's life.

In the following chapters I will describe techniques that my associates and I have developed for dealing with difficult patients. We are excited by the clinical and theoretical challenges these patients present. When therapy is stuck, the solution often involves substantial growth for the therapist and for the patient. I hope that you will share the excitement we feel and that your eyes will be opened to new ways of understanding and dealing with these challenges!

25

◆

Empathy:
How to Establish Rapport with the Critical, Angry Patient

Therapists at all levels of experience seem to have one overwhelming concern: How can I deal with difficult patients? The cognitive, behavioral, and interpersonal techniques illustrated in *The Feeling Good Handbook* work well for about two thirds of the patients that my colleagues and I see in our clinic. These patients describe their problems and share their feelings openly. The therapist listens and shows concern and proposes a variety of approaches that might help. The patient and therapist respect each other and work productively toward a solution.

For the other third of the patients, it's not nearly so easy. Therapy gets bogged down. These patients may complain that their therapists aren't helping or don't care or don't understand. They may feel hopeless, and they are often unclear about what they want from therapy. They frequently feel unmotivated and may appear to resist their therapist's efforts.

I suspect that you can think of many difficult patients you have treated through the years. You may have felt frustrated with these patients, disappointed in the results and insecure about your own level of skill.

These therapeutic impasses frequently result from a lack of therapeutic empathy. Although most therapists feel that they have good interpersonal skills and believe they communicate well, this is often not the case. Whenever I do workshops or teach groups of psychiatrists and psychologists, I ask therapists to demonstrate in a role-play how they would respond to an angry, evasive, critical patient. The therapists almost invariably get defensive. They appear stiff and formal. This is not something I have occasionally observed, but something I nearly *always* observe. It makes no difference if the therapist is a novice or a full professor with an international reputation as an expert in communication! When you see how therapists actually relate to difficult patients, the deficiencies sometimes become uncomfortably obvious.

I once did a full-day cognitive therapy workshop for a small group of highly experienced psychiatrists and psychologists in New York, along with one of my colleagues, Tony Bates. The participants all had illustrious careers in teaching, research, and clinical practice. At the beginning of the workshop, I decided to quickly review basic interpersonal skills before we moved on to specific cognitive and behavioral techniques. I asked if the participants felt comfortable dealing with critical, demanding, angry patients. They all indicated that this was familiar territory. Several of them had written and taught extensively on the subject. I told them I thought that one important principle was not to get defensive but to empathize and draw patients out so they would feel it was safe to express their angry feelings. The workshop participants unanimously agreed that this was crucial. I suggested that I could pretend to be a hostile patient and I would criticize each of them, one at a time. I told them that all they had to do was to use the three listening techniques described in Chapter 19:

1. **The Disarming Technique:** You find some truth in what the patient says, even if the criticism seems somewhat irrational. For example, if an angry patient says that you "don't understand," you could sincerely agree that you don't understand him or her as well as you would like and ask for more information in a friendly way.

2. **Thought and Feeling Empathy:** You show that you understand how the patient is thinking by paraphrasing what the patient tells you. You try to grasp how the patient is feeling, and you reflect this back. To continue with the previous example, you might say,

"Feeling understood by someone who cares is one of the most important things in the world. It sounds like I haven't really understood you very well yet. You might be feeling mistrustful and frustrated with me. Are you?"

3. **Inquiry:** You use gentle, probing questions to draw the patient out and validate your interpretation ("Are you?"). You can encourage the patient to share more of his or her angry feelings and you can indicate your willingness to listen and to try to comprehend. You want to convey an attitude of curiosity rather than defensiveness.

In addition, the three self-expression skills described in Chapters 19 and 21 can be useful:

1. **"I feel" statements:** Let the patient know how you feel about what he or she is saying. This will make you appear more genuine and real. For example, if the patient says he's ticked off because the therapy is a waste of time and money, you can let him know that you feel concerned. You might say that you also feel frustrated because the therapy seems to be at an impasse just now.

2. **Changing the focus:** Instead of focusing on the content of the patient's criticisms, you draw attention to the dysfunctional interpersonal process and share your feelings about this. For example, if a patient is excessively aggressive and hostile, you might say, "I'm feeling attacked right now. I sense that we're arguing instead of working together. Your criticisms and feelings are important, and I want to hear what you have to say, but I feel there's a lack of trust and teamwork between us. I wonder if you also feel this way. Do you?"

3. **Stroking:** You can remind the patient that you do respect him or her and that you feel optimistic that you can work together successfully, even though you may both be feeling some tension or annoyance with each other. This will let the patient know that it's okay to be angry with you and will relieve any fears of rejection, which could make the conflict escalate.

The participants all agreed that these techniques made good sense. They emphasized that this was precisely how they ordinarily responded to angry, critical patients. I asked them to demonstrate these listening and self-expression skills. I walked around from person to person, saying things like "Dr. Smith, I feel as if you don't care about me. All you seem to care about is getting paid."

I was amazed—as were the participants—that *not one* of the therapists was able to respond effectively. Every one of them got defensive! Dr. Smith got tense and said, "But I *do* care about you." This, of course, is argumentative; he contradicted me instead of drawing me out. At first I thought this was a fluke, so Tony Bates and I demonstrated the listening and self-expression skills. The participants continued to have rather serious difficulties. What would you have said if you were the therapist? Put your response here:

_____

_____

_____

_____

Here's one approach. You might say: "It sounds as if you feel that I don't care about you, and that I seem more interested in getting paid than in helping [thought empathy]. That must be really upsetting [feeling empathy]. I wonder if you might be annoyed with me [inquiry]. I know I'd be upset if I felt someone was exploiting me to make money [disarming]. Can you tell me more about this [inquiry]?"

The therapists agreed this was a more effective response, and they all wanted to try again. I continued playing the role of an angry patient and came up with more criticism and accusations. I said, "Dr. Jones, I don't feel as if I'm getting any help with my problems. All you do is nod your head and say 'Hmm' or 'Tell me more.' " The results were similar. Dr. Jones sounded stiff and defensive. He nodded and said, "Mmm . . . tell me more"! What would you say if you were the therapist? Put your ideas here:

_____

_____

_____

_____

You might say, "You don't feel you're getting any real help with your problems [thought empathy]. I think you're right—things do seem bogged down [disarming]. I'm frustrated, too ['I feel' statement]. It seems like we're arguing instead of working together [changing the focus]. Can you tell me a little more about the problems we're not solving [inquiry]? I'd also like to hear more about things I've said that have turned you off [inquiry]."

We ended up working for half the day on the basic listening and self-expression skills that we had planned to review in ten minutes! And even then, it seemed as if we were still just scratching the surface.

This group was not unique. Psychologists, psychiatrists, and therapists from a variety of persuasions have all had similar difficulties. Unless you are extraordinarily gifted, your communication skills could probably be improved as well.

You can enhance your skills with a method I have developed, called script writing. In the late 1970s it dawned on me that there were many moments in therapy sessions that I was not handling in a satisfactory manner. A patient would complain, and by the end of the session it was clear that the problem was still unresolved. Although I often felt I was handling the difficulties in a reasonable way, the patient still felt annoyed and we both left the session feeling dissatisfied.

On the train coming home from work, I would reconstruct from memory a brief excerpt of what had gone on. I wrote down what the patient said, what I said in response, what the patient said next, and what I said. This amount of dialogue—two consecutive statements by the patient and two of my responses—was sufficient to illustrate the conflict. The patient was generally frustrated and annoyed with the therapy. Although my statements initially seemed quite helpful and logical, I could readily see that I was not using good listening and self-expression skills. I often discovered that my statements were subtly sarcastic or defensive, or that I was "helping" when I should have been listening. I would revise the dialogue and try to write down more effective responses.

The next day, I would study the revised dialogues again. I often discovered that my revised responses were equally ineffective, so I revised them again. I would often consult with a colleague and ask, "How would you have handled this? What would you have said?" Eventually I would come up with an approach that I was more comfortable with. The next time I saw the patient, things usually went much better. I did this over a period of months, and the exercise proved to be extremely helpful. The listening skills and self-expression skills became more and more naturally my way of responding to these difficult moments in therapy.

If you use the script-writing method, I strongly encourage you to show your responses to a colleague. It's an inherent part of human nature to be blind to our own foibles. You may come up with a response to a patient's criticism that you think is just wonderful, and you may not tune in to the fact that it sounds phony or subtly controlling. You may be invalidating the patient's feelings. I cannot emphasize this enough.

Let's practice this technique now. Suppose a patient says, "I didn't like it when you answered the phone during the last session." What would you say?

_____

_____

_____

_____

_____

Some therapists might get defensive ("I don't usually take the phone, but my secretary buzzed me because it was an emergency"). Others would try to solve the problem by saying, "In the future, I can ask my secretary to hold the calls during your sessions." These responses have two serious flaws. First, the therapist may be feeling somewhat tense and is trying to disguise this by sounding "professional." This will irritate the patient. Second, the therapist hasn't drawn the patient out and given him or her the chance to express the negative feelings. The therapist indicates that the discussion has ended and there's nothing more that needs to be talked about. The therapist has suddenly cut off the communication and appears to be protecting him- or herself from the patient's anger. The patient may conclude that negative feelings are too upsetting to talk about.

You may think, "Oh, I wouldn't do that! Only a novice would do that!" But I know of very few therapists who don't unwittingly fall into this trap.

A more effective reply might be, "You may feel that I'm ignoring you and not putting a high priority on your problems [thought empathy]. I know if someone interrupted my sessions to answer the phone, I would feel a little ticked off [feeling empathy]. Do you [inquiry]?" This would encourage the patient to share his or her feelings and would acknowledge that you have feelings too. In the discussion that follows, you could ask the patient what he or she likes and dislikes about you. This may help the patient get over the hurdle of expressing anger to another human being. These feelings often provide a window to the patient's deeper fears and feelings of inadequacy.

Now I want you to try. First, think of a difficult, hostile patient who's dissatisfied with the therapy. Have you thought of someone? Good. Now write down an upsetting comment the patient made that you felt you didn't handle as well as you would like:

_____

_____

_____

_____

Now write down what you said next:_____

_____

_____

_____

_____

Analyze your statement. Can you see why it was ineffective? Ask yourself if you were argumentative and contradicted what the patient said. Did you sound defensive? Sarcastic? Phony? Critical? Rejecting? Show your response to a colleague who will be honest and who's not afraid to criticize you. Ask him or her to point out why your statement was ineffective and to suggest an alternative one.

Finally, substitute a revised response. What could you have said instead? Try to utilize the listening and self-expression skills described earlier. Try to draw the patient out and to create a safe emotional environment so that he or she can express angry, desperate feelings without shame and without the fear of being judged or rejected by you. Try to see the world through the patient's eyes. You may need to express your feelings tactfully, genuinely, and openly. If you feel put down or inadequate or frustrated, say so, but do it in a friendly way. Your goal is not to elicit sympathy or to make the patient feel guilty, but to give vital information that will be helpful to him or her. You use your own reactions as a mirror, so the patient can see how he or she is affecting you.

Put your revised response here:_____

_____

_____

_____

_____

The other day I had a long session with a critical, intelligent woman named Ronda, who has felt depressed and bitter for many years. She was on the attack during most of the session. No matter what I said, it didn't seem to work. As the session wore on, I felt more and more drained and inadequate. I felt embarrassed and humiliated. I felt inept and lame. Just before she left, she indicated that the session had been a waste of time and money.

As the therapist, what would you have said?

_____

_____

_____

_____

I told Ronda that I felt inadequate. I said I felt as if every sentence that came out of my mouth was wooden and useless to her. I said that although I usually felt I had something to offer, it didn't seem that way today. I told her I felt excluded and shut out, and that I felt angry with her. I said I wanted to give her something positive and I believed that the therapy could be successful, but I felt thwarted in my efforts. I said that she also seemed angry and mistrustful and I wondered if she ever had a similar problem with other people, or if it just happened with me.

My motive was not to get back at her but simply to share my feelings. She left in a huff and didn't make another appointment. I was too embarrassed to ask if she wanted to schedule one. I wondered if I would ever see Ronda again.

The next day she called the office to set up a session. She asked the secretary to tell me that she'd made the decision to keep trying. The next time I saw her, she reported that her depression score had fallen by more than half (indicating a substantial improvement in her mood) when she was waiting to catch the train after the session. She gave me a note describing her reaction to what I thought was a terribly inept session. In the note, she said the session had been helpful because she was able to deal with her anger in an up-front way. Although we were fighting, she felt she was being direct and holding her own. She said that simply being angry and open with me was a relief, and that she had had a flash of insight when I said that I felt excluded and shut out. She said that she felt vulnerable and wounded and needed greater emotional support from me. She said that if I would explore the pain she felt in a gentle way, it would be easier for her to open up.

We often feel ashamed of these moments when therapy seems to fail, because we feel that we are supposed to be successful. But there's really no such thing as a "failure." Those moments of desperation and frustration are an inherent and necessary part of the creative therapeutic process. When you and your patient feel the angriest and the most defeated, you may be the closest you have ever been to each other and to the source of the difficulty. Often when you immerse yourself in the patient's desperation and allow yourself to experience the hopelessness the patient perceives, you are just a stone's throw from the solution. Sometimes you have to see and touch the wall of impossibility before you discover how to slip around it or climb over it or tunnel underneath it.

A second way to enhance your interpersonal skills is to role-play with a group of three or more therapists who want to learn together. You can make a list of barbed comments that you have heard from patients, such as:

"Of *course* I'm not angry with you!"

"Aren't you a little young, doctor?"

"I feel as if you don't care about me."

"The therapy seems a little superficial."

"I read in the paper that some people have chemical depressions. Maybe that's why I'm not getting better."

"You don't seem to understand what's really bothering me."

"You always seem to be in a rush."

"You seem to be siding with my spouse."

"You're one of the best 'mechanics' in the business."

I'm sure you can come up with lots more of these! One of you can play the role of the patient and one can play the role of the therapist. The others can watch. After a minute or so of role-playing, the "patient" can provide feedback about what he or she liked and disliked about the therapist's communication techniques and interpersonal style. Did the therapist express a concern for the patient? Did he or she encourage the patient to express the angry feelings? Did the therapist seem genuine? Was the therapist accurately tuned in to what the patient actually said and felt? Did the patient feel cared about? The therapists who observe the role-play can also provide constructive suggestions.

You will be shocked to find that you will usually get poor ratings from the "patient" and from your peers who are watching! If your ego can't take it, then this approach is definitely not for you! But if you dare to expose your shortcomings to the scrutiny of other therapists, then you will have the chance to enhance your therapeutic skills and to grow.

When I do this exercise with a group, I make it abundantly clear that we're working together in a spirit of mutual trust to reveal our insecurities and shortcomings to each other. The goal is to feel closer and more comfortable with our humanity and with our limitations. We are there to talk about our failures, not to show off. If you confront your fears of being judged, the process can be exhilarating, and your therapeutic skills will develop enormously!

26

•

Agenda Setting:
How to Make Therapy Productive
When You and Your Patient
Feel Stuck

At a workshop I conducted recently at the annual meeting of the American Psychiatric Association, one of the participants asked this question: "Dr. Burns, I have this patient named Susan. I've been working with Susan for eighteen months, but we don't seem to be getting anywhere. She's depressed and she has a terrible self-image. She has a real problem with her weight. Sometimes she binges and then she starves herself. Susan is very resistant and won't follow any of my suggestions. What can I do to help her?"

How would you answer this question? It's the most common question I hear from the therapists I train and from those who attend professional workshops. I won't ask you to write out your answer to this one, but I want you to stop and think about it for a moment before you read on.

Have you thought about how you'd answer the question? I asked the doctor what specific problem Susan asked for help with in their most recent therapy session. He replied, "I don't know. I don't think I've ever asked Susan that question."

This may explain why the therapy is bogged down. He may want to help Susan lose weight or develop better personal relationships, but she may not have the same agenda. She may feel bad because she's unpopular and can't get the boys at school to pay attention to her. She may be interested in learning how to flirt and getting the boys to chase her. She may feel angry and bossed around by her parents and want help in dealing with them. She may feel she's fine and is in therapy only because her parents are pressuring her to be there. If you and your patient are on different wavelengths and are not working on a common problem, the therapy has little chance of success.

This is an incredibly common therapeutic pitfall. The patient complains that you aren't helping, but it may not be clear to you, or to the patient, what problem you're supposed to solve. How can you possibly help someone if the two of you haven't agreed on whether the patient really wants help and, if so, what he or she wants help with? As basic as this might seem, these issues are frequently overlooked.

At the beginning of each therapy session, I encourage patients to set an agenda for the session. I ask what problems they want to work on that day. Usually this is straightforward. Patients may want to review the Daily Mood Logs they have been working on between sessions, or they may want suggestions about how to deal with specific problems in their lives. Sometimes it is not so easy. Patients may be evasive or vague about what they want help with. If you let this go unnoticed and unchallenged, the therapy is almost certainly doomed to failure.

This difficulty can be overcome with a technique called "agenda setting." Agenda setting has two components. First, you and the patient need to agree on the specific problem he or she wants help with in each session. Second, you need to agree on the methods you will use to solve the problem.

The problem must be specific and concrete, or it cannot be dealt with. For example, a woman may want help with her depression. She says her goal in therapy is to feel better about herself. This sounds specific, but it really isn't. I would ask her to tell me about the problems in her life that she feels bad about. Is she worrying about her marriage? School? Her career? Let's suppose she has a career problem. I would want to know more about it. What is the problem? Is her boss too critical? Does she procrastinate? Does she get panic attacks at work? I would want to know:

- What day did the problem occur? What time of day was it?
- Where did the problem occur? Whom was she with? What was going on?
- What her life would be like if the problem was solved—what would be different?

Once you have defined the problem, you need to agree on the methods you will use to attack it. What are you expected to do? To listen? To teach communication skills? To help her identify and to talk back to her negative thoughts? Does she want you to prescribe a medication? All these issues need to be spelled out and negotiated. After all, therapists aren't magicians, and we don't just say "presto" to make problems disappear. We have certain skills to offer. Patients have the right to know what these skills are and to decide if they want to make use of them.

As a part of this negotiation, it's important to agree on what the patient is expected to do during the sessions and between sessions. You might expect her to keep a daily journal of her negative thoughts between sessions, to fill out the depression and anxiety tests weekly and to show the results to you, and to bring a cassette tape so that each session can be recorded and she can listen to the tapes between sessions. Your list of requirements may differ, depending on your therapeutic orientation and the type of problem the patient wants help with.

Some patients are vague and not used to defining problems in a precise way. I recently saw a 22-year-old woman from New York. Sue is single, very attractive, slim, and intelligent. She's lonely and says her life is dull. Sue was referred by her mother, who'd read *Feeling Good.* She felt that Sue was unhappy and would benefit from cognitive therapy. That, of course, was one strike against me: Sue didn't come because she had made the decision herself and felt strongly motivated to change. Therefore her basic mind-set seemed to be: "I'm not really sure I want to be here. You've got to prove that you can help me."

During the sessions Sue was quiet and asked appropriate questions, but she rarely talked about herself. I found that I was easily seduced into talking a great deal and answering all her questions. She appeared interested but played the devil's advocate. She asked questions like "What makes you think cognitive therapy can help me?" If you were the therapist, how would you answer this question?

_____

_____

_____

_____

I might say, "I'm not sure the therapy can help you. I'm hopeful we can work together, but I need to find out specifically what you want help with first. Then we can discuss a variety of approaches that might appeal to you." The purpose of this response is to avoid getting into a salesman's role. If you try to persuade her that you can help her, you will almost surely fail. For one thing, you don't know yet if you can help her because you don't have the vaguest notion of what, if anything, she wants help with!

I encouraged Sue to describe a specific problem. Eventually she came up with several:

1. Fears about the future.

2. Obsessing too much about things.

3. Not having any fun in life.

As the therapist, what would you say next? Put your ideas here:

_____

_____

_____

_____

I asked Sue to choose one problem to work on first. I was unwilling to make that choice myself, because that would be my agenda rather than hers. She reluctantly chose "Not having any fun in life." She didn't seem especially happy with her decision. What

would you do next? Check the strategy that makes the most sense
to you:

———————   Explore her reluctance.

———————   Suggest ways she might have more fun in life.

———————   Explore conflicts that might make it hard for her to have fun.

———————   Ask her to tell you more about the problem—for example,
          what kinds of fun is she missing out on?

———————   Ask how she thinks you might help her.

———————   Other:

_____

_____

_____

_____

I believe that each approach has merit, but I explored her reluctance first. Why is she reluctant? If we don't talk about her negative
feelings, she may dig in her heels and resist me. That's precisely what
I'm trying to avoid.

Sue said she was reluctant because she didn't want to work on
trivial, day-to-day problems but wanted to get to the "deeper issues
at the heart of the matter." She said she wanted to know why she was
"like this." However, she had no idea what these "deeper issues"
might be and she left that up to me. What would you say next?

_____

_____

_____

_____

There could be many effective responses. You could ask what she
meant by the "heart of the matter" or "being like this." I decided not

to do this, since I'd covered that territory a number of times already and her answers had tended to be vague. She would usually say that she was basically fine but wasn't always quite as happy as she wanted to be, and she would add that she obsessed about the future too much.

Instead, I said: "The deeper issues are important, but I've found it works better to work on a specific, practical, concrete problem first. As we solve one problem, we may begin to understand what some of these deeper issues are. If we try to work immediately on the deeper issues, we may ramble on and on in a vague way that won't be helpful to you." Once she agrees to work on a specific problem, I might show her how to fill out a Daily Mood Log, and I would illustrate the "Vertical Arrow Technique" (see page 122). This might help us unearth the "silent assumptions" at the root of her difficulties.

I asked Sue if what I said made sense, and if she wanted to continue working on the specific problem of "not having enough fun in life." She agreed to pursue this theme. As the therapist, how would you proceed? How would you help her work on "not having enough fun in life"?

_____

_____

_____

_____

I would want her to be more specific. The problem is still far too general. I might ask:

- What type of fun is she missing?
- Whom would she like to have more fun with?
- What happens when she tries to have fun?
- When would she like to have more fun?

I suspect you can think of a number of equally good questions that would help to clarify the problem.

I asked *when* she wanted to have more fun. She looked puzzled and then said, "Today." I asked, "What time today?" She seemed taken aback, and said "Right now." I replied, "Right now? You mean that the problem is that the therapy sessions aren't any fun? Should we play cards, or what?" This admittedly sarcastic response was intended to jar her into being more specific. If she laughed, I would know it's okay to use a little humor. If she appeared hurt, I would apologize.

Sue said she wanted to have more fun when she took the train back to New York that evening after her session. What would you say next?

_____

_____

_____

_____

I would still want more specific information. What is her idea of having fun on the train? Are there times when taking the train isn't any fun? We generated a list of activities that people might consider to be fun on a train:

- talking to some interesting people;
- reading a good book;
- getting work done;
- drinking cocktails in the club car.

She decided that it would be fun to find some interesting people to talk to. What would you say next?

_____

_____

_____

_____

I would still want her to make the problem more specific. Does she want to talk to *anyone*? Or does she really mean that she wants to meet a cute and eligible young man? How would she go about talking to someone who interested her? What problems would she encounter? How could I help her with these problems? Would she be willing to follow through with some of my suggestions, even if they might make her a little anxious?

Sue is not difficult in the sense that she's hostile or argumentative or defensive. However, she is difficult in the sense that she's not used to dealing with real problems in a practical, direct way. She tends to be vague and unfocused. If you allow her to talk on and on, she might be in therapy for months or years without making any real changes. Can you see how easy it would be to fall into this trap with her? In contrast, if you gently but forcefully encourage her to define a real, tangible problem that she wants help with, the chances for rapid and significant improvement are great.

Sue said that sometimes when she tried to talk to people, the conversation got dull and she couldn't think of anything to say. She was worried that this would happen to her on the train. I suggested that she could tell the other person they seemed interesting and admit that she couldn't think of anything to say. She could also tell them that she wanted to learn more about them. Sue agreed that this statement would be rather bold and would probably open things up quickly, but she said it would take courage to be so direct. We role-played various ways of flirting and talking to cute guys. Sue did a good job and grasped all the ideas I proposed. We talked about the importance of being less serious and a little more outrageous in the way she related to men. She seemed to enjoy the session.

As you can see, most of these interventions focused on communication training. The next time I see Sue we may need to use cognitive techniques to deal with any fears and inhibitions that make it difficult for her to open up to others. She may be perfectionistic and have rigid expectations for herself that make it hard to lighten up and have fun. These are probably some of the "deeper issues" that she wants to deal with. However, we will be moving from the specific problem—such as feeling anxious when she talks to a cute guy on the train—to the more general problem, such as the fear of making a fool of herself or the belief that she should always be poised and in complete control of her feelings.

The point of this example is to illustrate that therapy can become productive and meaningful when you push for a specific agenda. This session was admittedly an easy one because Sue was motivated and cooperative. As long as I provided the appropriate guidance, she was willing to follow my lead.

Let's assume that you're my patient and you want help with procrastination. Our session might proceed like this:

DAVID: So you'd like help with your procrastination? Can you tell me what you're procrastinating about?

YOU: Oh, everything, Doctor!

DAVID: Well that's a tall order for me—to help you with "everything." I'm afraid I may not be quite up to it. Now if there's one thing you're procrastinating on, maybe I could help you with that. Then you could use the same tools to get more motivated and productive in other areas of your life.

YOU: Well, one thing would just be a drop in the bucket. What good would that do?

DAVID: Possibly no good at all. I think you're saying that helping you with one thing is not really very appealing to you. Is there anything else I could do to be helpful to you?

YOU: Are you saying you can't help me with my procrastination?

DAVID: No, I'd love to work with you on this problem. But I've never figured out how to work on more than one thing at a time. I really wouldn't know how to help you with "everything." After all, we only have forty-five minutes to work together today. But we might make a start if you were willing to work on just one problem.

Notice that I'm beginning to negotiate with you about how we will work together. I'm not going to jump in and try to help you until it becomes clear that what we're doing makes sense. I won't buy into your agenda of solving *all* your procrastination problems today. We only need one problem to work on. We might continue like this:

YOU: Okay. Well, how about my problem of not going to classes? I've skipped so many that I'm on probation. I've just got to get out of bed and get to classes.

DAVID: That's a problem we could work on together. Are you sure you want help with it?

YOU: Oh, yes. Oh, absolutely!

DAVID: What time would you like to be helped?

YOU: Oh, all the time! I almost never go to classes.

DAVID: Once again, "all the time" is a pretty tall order, and it's probably too much for an old man like me. You might need a younger and more energetic therapist. But if you'd like help going to *one* class, I'd be interested in helping you.

YOU: Okay, I need to go to history class. Can you get me to go to history?

DAVID: I doubt I could make you do anything you didn't want to do, and I can assure you I wouldn't dream of trying. But if you really want me to help you get to your history class, I'll be glad to see how I might help. But tell me, history class is probably really boring to you, and I'll bet you have some very good reasons for not going. Can you tell me why we should be working on this problem?

Can you see the reason for this intervention? I'm not sure yet that you really want to solve this problem. Maybe your real agenda is to take a year off from school. Maybe you feel stubborn and coerced by your parents. You may express your anger indirectly, by rebelling and refusing to make a commitment to school. If I don't clarify your motivations, I may become like a parent who pressures you while you resist. This won't be helpful for you or rewarding for me! We'll just end up feeling frustrated with each other.

Let's assume that we have dispelled these concerns and you have convinced me that you really do want help going to history class. Then I would continue like this:

DAVID: Okay, I can see that you genuinely want help with this. When would you like me to help you go to history class? When is the next class scheduled?

YOU: At 8:00 tomorrow morning.

DAVID: Eight a.m.! That's awfully early in the morning. You'd have to get up by 7:00 or 7:30. Are you sure you want to do that?

YOU: Oh, yes. I've just got to go.

DAVID: Okay, what kind of help would you like?

YOU: I don't follow.

DAVID: I don't know what kind of help you need. Do you need help waking up? Getting out of bed? Do you need help walking to class?

YOU: Well, I just can't seem to get motivated. I get up but I get distracted by other things. I just read novels.

DAVID: It makes good sense to read a novel, because going to class will be upsetting when you're so far behind. I can see why you don't feel motivated. I'm still not sure what kind of help you'd like. Would you like to hide your novels so you won't feel so tempted? Should we make a list of the advantages and disadvantages of going to class in spite of the fact that you don't feel like it? Or should we look at some of your negative thoughts so we can find out why going to class is so upsetting to you? Do any of these ideas make sense to you?

Notice that I've presented you with a menu of methods we might use in dealing with the problem. These are the two essential components of agenda setting—selecting a specific problem the patient wants to solve, and agreeing how we will tackle the problem. When these two criteria are not fulfilled, therapeutic failure is probable. When they are fulfilled, the chances for success are high.

Some patients will resist establishing a meaningful therapeutic agenda because they are mistrustful and have mixed feelings about being in therapy. They may project the message "Help me, I'm desperate! By the way, I will resist you and fight you every step of the way."

These individuals are often reluctant to ask for help and unclear about the problems they want help with. Agenda setting may be traumatic for them, but it's absolutely essential. The following dialogue illustrates this process. The patient is a moderately difficult adolescent girl who is demanding and uncooperative. She feels angry and depressed but isn't clear on the problem she wants help with.

DAVID: Can you tell me what you'd like to work on in today's session? Are there some problems you'd like help with?

NATALIE: I've just been feeling really depressed and I don't know what to do.

DAVID: So you've been feeling depressed and you don't really know what to do. Can you tell me what you've been feeling depressed about?

NATALIE: Well, I seem to have a lot of problems with . . . like . . . everything. My whole life seems pretty awful.

DAVID: That sounds pretty upsetting. You feel depressed, and everything seems just awful. I'd like you to tell me more about the way you feel.

I am empathizing with Natalie. She may need some time to ventilate and to share her feelings. I would encourage her to tell me how awful her life seems. I would be sympathetic and I would not challenge her. This might go on for five or ten minutes, or for a full session or two.

After Natalie has had sufficient time to get her feelings out and she sees that I am trying to understand her and am not judging her, we would come back to the issue of agenda setting. I would want to know what particular problems Natalie wants help with. I might introduce this by saying, "Well, Natalie, we have been talking for a period of time about some of the problems in your life. I think I can understand how bad you feel. One way we can work together would be for you to pick out one of the problems you'd like some help with. Then I can teach you some techniques that might help you solve this problem. In time, we'll work on all of your problems. Does this appeal to you? Is there a particular problem you might like to work on in today's session?"

NATALIE: I guess that sounds fine. One problem, I think, would be the one with my boyfriend 'cause it's the most confusing one.

DAVID: Okay, that's a good one to start on. Tell me about the problem with your boyfriend. Can you be a little bit more specific? What's going on? What is it that bothers you?

NATALIE: Well, we are always fighting. Nothing seems to work. We never get along. There's always something to fight about.

DAVID: Oh, I see. I guess you fight an awful lot and you have trouble getting along. Can you tell me about a recent fight that you've had that you'd like some help with?

NATALIE: Well, on Friday my parents told me I had to baby-sit and I couldn't go out. He got really upset because we planned to go out that night. Then I felt really helpless.

DAVID: Oh, I see. You were caught in kind of a no-win situation. On the one hand, your parents were putting pressure on you to baby-sit, and on the other hand your boyfriend was putting pressure on you to go out with him. Am I reading you right?

NATALIE: Yeah, I guess that's it.

DAVID: Is this something you might want to work on?

NATALIE: I don't know.

DAVID: Perhaps we could work on how you negotiate your duties with your parents or how you talk to your boyfriend when you both feel upset.

NATALIE: No. I just want it to be better.

DAVID: Let's see. You want it to be better but you don't want to work on how to talk to your parents or your boyfriend when you feel upset?

NATALIE (angrily): *You're* the therapist! *You* tell me what to do!

Natalie is getting a little hostile and evasive. I would empathize for a period of time and try to find out why she's annoyed with me. Once I have explored her angry feelings, I would encourage her to zero in on the problem she wants help with.

DAVID: You say that I'm the therapist and I should know what to do. In fact, I do have lots of ideas about how to solve different kinds of problems, and I'd really love to tell you about them. I'm a little confused because I'm not sure what problem you'd like help with. I'm puzzled because I don't know if you want some help on how to communicate with your boyfriend or with your parents, or if you'd like some help dealing with your negative feelings, or if you just want to talk so I can be a good listener.

NATALIE: Tell me how to talk to him so that we don't fight. I can't do it myself and I need help.

Now Natalie is being cooperative. She is saying that she does want help with communication. I might teach her the self-expression and listening skills that are described in chapters 16 through 18.

Let's assume that Natalie isn't so cooperative. She may keep complaining and thwarting my suggestions. She may be vague about what she wants help with.

NATALIE: Well, I don't really know. Why don't you just help me? You should know what will work best.

DAVID: Okay. Well, one thing that might help would be some communication training. Another thing might be for me to help you turn some of your negative thoughts and feelings around. Do any of these ideas appeal to you?

NATALIE: I don't even know what those things are. Why don't you just help me with my problems?

DAVID: Okay. Can you tell me about the problem that you'd like to have some help with? What is the problem as you see it?

NATALIE: I already told you! You must not be listening to me very well. Are you?

As the therapist, what would you say to Natalie at this point? Put your ideas here:

_____

_____

_____

_____

At this point I would empathize. She has told me that I am not listening to her feelings. I might say something like this: "You're telling me that I am not really listening to you [thought empathy]. You seem frustrated with me [feeling empathy]. Are you [inquiry]? Maybe that happens when you talk to your parents and your boyfriend, too. I understand that you are upset because your boyfriend and your parents were mad at you and they were making demands on you. Is there something that I might not have understood [inquiry]?"

NATALIE: Well, I *told* you I am having problems with my boyfriend and my parents. I don't know what to do and I just need some help.

DAVID: Yes, you want some help with your boyfriend and with your parents. I think you might feel like you weren't treated very fairly. That part is very clear to me. It's a good problem and I think we can work on it together. I need you to help me break it down into smaller pieces so I can know the best way to help you. We could talk about how you feel, or we could talk about some solutions to these problems with your boyfriend and your parents. Do any of these suggestions appeal to you?

NATALIE: I think you really are a stupid therapist. You're really annoying me a lot. How come you can't just give me some help with my boyfriend or my parents? How am I supposed to know what we should do?

What would you say to Natalie at this time? Put your ideas here:

_____

_____

_____

_____

I might say, "You say that I'm a stupid therapist. Once you get to know me better, you may see that I'm even stupider than you think! I would like to help you, and I think I have some tools that can help you, but I am feeling a little unsure of what you want. I admit that I am perplexed. You seem annoyed with me, and I'm not sure how you would like to proceed. For example, if you told me you wanted help cooking, I might ask if you wanted help with cakes or with roasts. Once I knew what the trouble was, I could suggest a solution. By analogy, I need to know if you want to work on the problem with your boyfriend or your parents first. Can you tell me a little bit more about this? I need your help."

NATALIE: Well, I don't want to hear about cooking, I want to hear about my boyfriend and me. We're just not getting along and I don't know what to do. We're always fighting and it's stupid.

DAVID: You know, that's a common problem. A lot of people fight with people they care about because they don't know how to deal with angry feelings and conflicts. I think this is something we could work on together. Maybe we could talk about what goes on when you and your boyfriend are fighting. Would that appeal to you?

NATALIE: Fine. If you think *that* will work! Is that what *you* want to do?

What would you say to Natalie at this point? Notice that she still seems to be on the attack. Her voice has a sharp edge. What is going on? What would you say to her now? Put your ideas here:

_____

_____

_____

_____

I would comment on her tone of voice instead of dragging her along reluctantly. I might say, "You still sound pretty annoyed with me, and you seem to have some doubts about my suggestions. It may not be the way you really want to proceed. I don't want to push you into something you don't feel good about. Maybe you're not sure that you want to learn how to communicate with your boyfriend any differently."

NATALIE: Well, how will that help me? What will that do? What is this technique?

DAVID: I believe that good communication involves learning to express your feelings and learning to listen to what the other person is trying to say. That's good communication. Bad communication is when people argue and get defensive and go around and around in circles and never get anywhere. This is what most people do. In fact, that's kind of what we've been doing. We're both feeling frustrated because we're not working together as a team. We're bickering. Communication training shows you how to change this. It would take a number of sessions to teach you how to express your feelings in a more effective way and to listen better when your boyfriend expresses his feelings. This might help you deal with your angry feelings more effectively. I am not saying that you *should* do this, I'm just saying that this is one thing that might be helpful. You'd have to work hard, but I believe you could learn it. Does that appeal to you?

NATALIE: But why should I have to, when the problem isn't my fault? I'm not doing anything wrong. I get blamed for everything, but it's not my fault! It was unfair for him to get mad. My parents shouldn't make me baby-sit at the last minute. My parents are hopeless.

At this point, the reason for Natalie's angry resistance becomes more obvious. Write down your hypothesis about why Natalie is reluctant to engage more productively in the therapy:

_____

_____

_____

_____

I believe that Natalie feels scapegoated and blamed unfairly. As a result, she's got her heels dug in. I reflected this to her.

DAVID: So, you think that the problems aren't your fault. There's clearly some truth in that. You may feel that if we did some communication training it would mean that some of the problems *are* your fault. You don't like that idea very well. That probably annoys you. Your parents sent you in for treatment, so it looks like you're the sick one who's to blame for everything. Am I reading you right? I know I'd be real ticked off if that happened to me.

NATALIE: How can it be my fault? My boyfriend is such a stupid asshole. He doesn't let me do anything I want to do. He's always telling me to do this and do that, just like my parents.

DAVID: It sounds like you are really frustrated with all of them. They're all bossing you around. Is this true?

NATALIE: Of course! I already told you that!

As a therapist, what would you say now?

_____

_____

_____

_____

I would ask about the annoyance in her voice. She was just beginning to open up, and now she suddenly sounds angry and mistrustful again.

DAVID: I feel like you're a little frustrated with me again. Are you?

NATALIE: It doesn't have anything to do with you!

DAVID: I see. You say that your problems don't have anything to do with me. That's certainly true.

NATALIE: When you say something, you always agree with me. I don't know what you're doing to help me!

DAVID: I feel frustrated because it seems like I'm not connecting with you in the way I'd like to. I'm trying to get you to zero in on a problem so that we can work together. I feel pushed away. I would like to help you, but I feel like you won't let me. Are you aware of that? You seem annoyed with me. Maybe we need to talk about that a bit more and see if we can clear the air before we work on your problems at home. Could you tell me more about this? Are you uncomfortable with me?

It may be a mistake to rush prematurely to a specific agenda. It may be better to back off and listen to Natalie's complaints about me, her boyfriend, and her parents. Her core conflict seems to be "Nobody treats me right." Her response is to get mad and to pout, and she's mistrustful and reluctant to change.

The therapist must dance back and forth constantly between active, empathetic listening and gentle, persistent agenda setting. She will predictably get angry every time I ask what the problem is and how she wants to work on it. The very question is a challenge to her defense. Her posture toward the world may be "You don't love me. It's all your fault. I will punish you until you love me more. I will complain angrily and withdraw until you admit your wrongdoing and give me the love and respect I deserve."

It's possible that Natalie will not come around. She may get so frustrated that after two or three sessions she'll drop out of treatment. On the other hand, if the therapist combines warmth and gentleness with a firm, persistent request for her to define a problem to work on, the chances for success will be enhanced.

She may drop out of therapy prematurely. You may be disappointed, but the termination may be therapeutic. You have laid your cards on the table and said, "Here are some ways we may be able to work together. There are many other ways as well. Do any of these ideas make sense to you? Is there a chance that we can work together? If you would like to be in therapy with me, then I'm convinced we can find a way to work together successfully. Would you like to?" I think this message should be presented in a kindly, flexible, and encouraging way.

Premature dropout could be due to several reasons, and you can review them with patients who seem uncommitted. They may dislike you and find it difficult to tell you. The ideas and strategies you are suggesting may not appeal to them. There may be something embarrassing that they are afraid to talk about. They may be frightened and mistrustful. They may find the therapy sessions upsetting, or they may have financial difficulties and feel the therapy is too costly.

As you review these possibilities, you can ask if any of them sound correct. If so, you can offer to help the patient find a solution. Several additional ideas might help:

1. You might consult with a colleague and role-play how you interact with the patient. You might discover that you were missing

the boat or coming across in a sarcastic or defensive way. It might be that you're missing a powerful positive or negative transference reaction that needs to be explored. The consultation might give you an idea of how to approach the situation differently.

2. You might ask the patient's permission to allow another therapist to sit in as a co-therapist on one or more sessions. This could be a more experienced colleague or a student therapist. The co-therapist might also have individual sessions with the patient. Two heads can be better than one, especially when working with difficult patients. However, it's important that the two therapists respect each other and work together as a team so that the patient's efforts at splitting and playing people off against each other are not successful. In addition, you need to make it clear that you would like to remain the primary therapist. Emphasize that you're not trying to get rid of the patient by shuffling him or her off to a colleague.

AGENDA-SETTING EXERCISE

In Chapter 25, I described how a group of two or more therapists can learn cognitive and behavioral techniques. One therapist can volunteer to play the role of the patient, and a second therapist can volunteer to be the therapist. The others in the group can observe and provide feedback.

The "therapist" begins by asking what specific problem the "patient" would like to work on in today's session. The "patient" is instructed to be purposefully vague. The therapist's job is to try to get the patient to describe a specific, real problem, and to determine what kind of help the patient wants. This could involve modifying a dysfunctional attitude like perfectionism or a communication problem like getting defensive when criticized. You can stop the action every minute, so that the "patient" and the observers can give specific positive and negative feedback.

You will be surprised to discover that most people in the therapist role will do quite poorly. They will be unable to define an adequate therapeutic agenda with a patient who is only moderately difficult. You will see right away that some therapists will get tense or defensive. Others will fail to listen and will respond to something the patient didn't really say. Some therapists will get nervous and talk too much. Once the error has been pointed out, try again or do a role reversal.

In setting the tone for the group, it's important to remind the participants that most of us have clay feet and that we all fantasize that other therapists are far more talented and effective. The purpose of the group training is to grow and to reveal our inadequacies without having to feel ashamed. If we can trust each other and share our vulnerabilities, the group experience can be exhilarating.

I enjoy the process of group training because it makes me feel more human and much closer to my students and colleagues. And, of course, the potential for rapid learning is enormous. There's also another reward: When you play the role of the patient, you can pretend to be one of your most difficult patients, one you feel annoyed with. You can act just as whiny and uncooperative and hostile as you want! This can be cathartic. You can get your frustration and aggression out of your system. In addition, by putting yourself in the patient's shoes, you will see the impact of the therapist's efforts to respond to you. This will make you more aware of effective and ineffective therapeutic interventions.

Let's review some of the principles illustrated in this chapter. First, what did you like or dislike about the techniques and concepts that I illustrated? List what you disliked or disagreed with:

_____

_____

_____

_____

Were there some ideas you found helpful? List them here:

_____

_____

_____

_____

What communication techniques can you use when a patient gets angry and critical of you?

1._____

2._____

3._____

4._____

5._____

These are empathy, the disarming technique, inquiry, "I feel" statements, and stroking.

After you have empathized and allowed the patient to ventilate, you will need to agree on an agenda. What are the two most important aspects of agenda setting?

1._____

2._____

You need a clear and specific description of the problem the patient wants help with, and a consensus about which therapeutic methods you will use to solve the problem.

27

•

Self-Help Assignments:
How to Motivate Patients Who
Sabotage the Therapeutic Process

One of the most common problems that cognitive and behavioral therapists encounter is the patient's lack of compliance with self-help assignments between sessions. These assignments can take many forms, including:

- taking a mood test, such as the Burns Anxiety Inventory or the Burns Depression Checklist, each week to monitor one's progress;
- bringing a cassette tape to the session and listening to the tape of the session at home;
- keeping a journal of negative thoughts with the Daily Mood Log;
- bibliotherapy—reading articles or book chapters that may be relevant to one's problems;
- practicing self-expression skills or listening skills with friends and family members;
- scheduling more productive and satisfying activities;
- confronting a feared situation or a phobia through gradual exposure or flooding;
- doing an experiment or conducting a survey to test the validity of a dysfunctional attitude;

- taking an antidepressant medication and obtaining necessary blood tests to monitor the dose.

Some patients seem to "forget" these assignments, while others wage a more open rebellion and angrily refuse to participate in them. Solving this problem is of vital importance. In a recent study published in the journal *Cognitive Therapy and Research,* Dr. Jacqueline Persons and I reported a strong positive correlation between compliance with these self-help assignments and therapeutic improvement. By the time of completion of therapy, patients who regularly did at least some self-help assignments had an average 80 percent reduction in Beck Depression Inventory scores. In contrast, those who did not do these assignments averaged zero percent improvement. This striking finding suggests that compliance with self-help assignments may be the most important predictor of therapeutic success.

The problem of compliance is also of great interest because it brings cognitive and behavioral therapists back to the old, unresolved issue of resistance. Why do some patients come for help and then sabotage the therapeutic process? How can we motivate these patients to collaborate more actively with us?

The first thing to ask yourself when a patient isn't doing the self-help assignment is whether the purpose, nature, and importance of these assignments have been spelled out adequately. Many people think of psychotherapy as something that occurs in the therapist's office. You sit or lie on the couch and share your feelings with a therapist who listens and asks questions. You presumably improve because of the insights you gain and the emotions you express during these sessions. The idea that you would be asked to do self-help assignments between sessions may seem strange to some people.

At my unit, all new patients receive a copy of the "Concept of Self-Help" memo at the completion of their intake evaluation (see page 560). They are asked to read and fill out this memo and give it to their therapist at their first session. The memo emphasizes the importance of self-help assignments and describes the types of assignments that may be utilized in the course of therapy. The memo asks whether or not patients are willing to participate in this aspect of the therapy ("yes," "no," or "needs discussion" are the response options). They are also asked how many minutes per day they are willing to spend on the self-help assignments, how many days per week they are willing to do them, and the number of weeks they are willing to keep it up. The answers to these questions can alert the therapist right away that compliance may be a problem. For example, some patients are evasive and do not fill out this section of the memo. I gently confront them with this so we can negotiate the issue of self-help assignments prior to the beginning of the actual therapy.

The memo concludes with a list of reasons why they may not want to do these self-help assignments. They are asked whether each reason describes them "not at all," "somewhat," "moderately," or "a lot." A review of the responses can make the therapist and patient more aware of why the self-help assignments might be a problem. Since I made it a policy that every patient at my clinic must complete the memo and review it with his or her therapist at the beginning of therapy, the degree of adherence of self-help assignments seems to have increased substantially.

A lack of homework compliance may occur because you did not make it clear precisely what you wanted the patient to do or why you asked him or her to do it. Toward the end of a session, I will frequently make a written list of what I've asked the patient to do. I review this list with the patient to make sure there's no miscommunication. At the beginning of the next session I review the list and go over the patient's homework, so they'll know I am serious about it and am interested in what they've done. I try to accentuate the positive, and I compliment them on what they've done so they won't feel ashamed or fearful of my criticism.

If the self-help homework was clearly assigned and the patient failed to comply, you can ask why. Maybe you haven't properly identified the problem the patient wants help with. Maybe the patient was uncomfortable with the methods you advocated. During one of her first therapy sessions a woman told me that she wanted to work on the problem of whether to continue to build her own interior decorating business or to work full-time for a local company that had repeatedly asked her to join their firm. I asked her to list the advantages and disadvantages of each possibility so we could review it during the next session.

She seemed sheepish at the next session and had not completed the assignment. She said she was annoyed with me and ambivalent about being in treatment. She said that the career problem was not at all crucial, and she felt that she needed to talk about her dissatisfaction with her husband. She owned up to the fact that she'd been having an affair with her neighbor. She said that rationally she knew he wasn't good for her, but she didn't feel ready to give up this relationship. She was afraid I'd judge her and tell her she had to be faithful to her husband.

Part of the problem, as you can see, is the need to negotiate what she most wants to work on. In addition, a transference issue may be emerging. She seems concerned that I may look down on her and tell her what to do, and she may not trust me. I will need to explore why she is dissatisfied with her husband. What are the problems in her marriage? What therapeutic methods will we use to deal with these problems? I will also need to do some active listening. Can she tell me about her negative feelings about the therapy? Are there things I said or did that turned her off? Are there other people who have tried to boss her around and tell her how to run her life?

Some patients may be clear about the problem they want help with, but they may have mixed feelings about the therapeutic methods you advocate. In Chapter 8 I described a severely depressed nurse who felt angry and frustrated with the way she was treated by the hospital staff, the physicians, and the patients. When I listened to her description of several problems at the hospital, it seemed to me that her complaints were valid. I felt her anger was frequently a healthy and appropriate response to a genuinely irritating situation.

I suggested that we might work on communication skills so she could learn to express her feelings more effectively. I explained that if she opened up a little more, she wouldn't have to go around being resentful because of all the feelings she kept bottled up. She reacted very negatively. She said that she didn't want to be angry with people. She said she wanted me to use cognitive techniques so she could achieve greater emotional control and not react so angrily.

I was uncomfortable with her request. I was concerned that she was already overcontrolled and inassertive. Although cognitive techniques could help her change the way she thought and felt during conflicts with others, this didn't seem to be the whole answer, because it might just feed her belief that she should never be upset with anyone. She had an intense fear of conflict and was convinced that any expression of her feelings would be inappropriate and would get her into trouble.

It took us several sessions to reach a compromise on this point. She agreed to tell people a little bit about how she felt, as an experiment. Fortunately she got positive responses from her co-workers, which boosted her mood and made her more animated and committed to the therapy. She saw that being more open with people, though frightening, could be important and helpful to her.

Sometimes failure to do self-help assignments may be a form of passive aggressiveness. The patient is saying, "I don't like you. I don't feel cared about. Therefore I'll go on strike. I won't play ball with you." The quickest way to find out is to ask them to fill out the Patient's Report of the Therapy Session (see pages 507–508). Low ratings for warmth and trust will tip you off that they feel annoyed with you. You can encourage the patient to talk about these negative feelings with the communication techniques described in Chapter 25. Once these feelings are aired, the patient will often be willing to cooperate and work with you again.

Sometimes patients won't do the self-help assignments because they feel hopeless and convinced that they cannot get better. This attitude operates as a self-fulfilling prophecy, because once they give up, the therapy gets stuck. It's important to identify feelings of hopelessness because they can also lead to suicidal impulses.

If your patients fill out the Burns Depression Checklist weekly (or an equivalent self-assessment instrument, such as the Beck Depression Inventory), you can simply glance at item 2, which assesses hopelessness, as well as item 15, which assesses suicidal thoughts. If the responses indicate that the patient feels hopeless or suicidal, then you can explore these feelings during the session. (Ways of assessing the seriousness of suicidal impulses are described on page 40.)

Let's assume that a patient says there's no point in doing the self-help exercises because nothing could possibly help. You have asked the appropriate questions and determined that the patient isn't actively suicidal. What would you say next? Put your ideas here:

_____

_____

_____

_____

_____

You could say, "It sounds as if you feel that your problems are so severe that nothing could help you [thought empathy]. Is this true [inquiry]? It's also possible that you're not comfortable with me or with the therapy [inquiry]. Maybe I did or said something that made you feel turned off. Does any of this ring true [inquiry]?"

Note that I am emphasizing the listening skills. Patients are frequently very unassertive. They may be afraid to tell you how they feel, and they may communicate indirectly—by missing a session, by coming late, by failing to do the self-help exercises, or by insisting that they're hopeless. You need to lift the rock so you can see what's lurking underneath. Often you will find resentment hidden in the shadows.

Now suppose the patient feels hopeless and discouraged, but he or she is not angry with you. What would you say or do next? Remember that the patient is not doing any self-help assignments. Put your ideas here:

_____

_____

_____

_____

Answer: I can think of three strategies, and there are undoubtedly many more. One suggestion would be to tell the patient to *maintain* the belief that he or she is hopeless, but to test this belief over an appropriate period of time, such as ten weeks. During that time the patient can agree to do the self-help exercises and to fill out the Burns Depression Checklist every week as a way of assessing progress. Ask the patient how much the score on the test would have to improve to prove that he or she *is* getting better. The advantage of this strategy is that you and the patient can work together productively instead of getting involved in a debate about whether or not the therapy can be helpful.

A second strategy involves agenda setting. Ask the patient what he or she *specifically* wants help with, and how he or she would like to proceed. Is there a marital problem? What kind? Is there a problem with procrastination? With the career? You must spell out precisely what the patient wants help with before you can decide whether you can be of help.

It's important that you both agree that the therapeutic methods are appropriate. Maybe the patient is asking for something you're not comfortable with. If a man asked me to explore his childhood to find out why he had an elevator phobia, I would say that I wasn't an expert in psychoanalysis and I couldn't do an adequate job. I would let him know that I did want to work with him. I would be eager to find a way that we could work together that would be mutually satisfactory, but I would not agree to any approach that didn't make sense, given my theoretical orientation and skills. I might tell him that if we got on the elevator together, and stayed on it for about thirty minutes, he might get anxious at first and then he would probably start to feel better. The anxiety might even disappear completely. I would say that this made a lot more sense to me than probing for causes. I would add that nobody even knows the cause of elevator phobias, but that the problem can usually be corrected. If the method I suggested made sense we could proceed.

A third response to a hopeless patient would be to ask why he or she is coming to therapy. What does he or she want from you? There's something basically illogical about coming to a therapist, paying a good fee for the time, and then announcing that the therapist cannot help. What's going on? I would caution you to pursue this line of inquiry *cautiously*, and to express concern for the patient, because this line of inquiry could sound flippant or disrespectful. I would say that I was committed to the patient and felt confident that we could work together successfully, but that I felt puzzled and needed to know why the patient was there and what he or she wanted. Maybe the patient doesn't want to be in therapy but feels coerced to come. You could explore this dynamic and help the patient decide if he or she wants to continue working with you.

You may discover that the patient has no real desire to be in therapy with you. A psychiatry resident at the University of Pennsylvania was asked to treat a hostile young man with a diagnosis of schizoid personality disorder who had been referred by a dermatologist. Apparently, the patient had been to numerous dermatologists for a skin problem and the referring doctor sensed that there were significant emotional problems. I would suspect that the patient was angry and was compulsively going to dermatologists because of a fixation with his skin instead of dealing with the problems in his life.

He was resentful and uncooperative and told the psychiatric resident that she couldn't help him. She felt annoyed and frustrated with him and didn't know how to proceed. If you were the therapist, what would you say next to the patient?

Answer: I would say, "Can you tell me what it is you want help with?" The patient's response was, "I've got an itch." If you were the therapist, what would you say next?

Answer: I would say, "I can imagine that an itch would be quite uncomfortable [feeling empathy]. Can you tell me what type of help you're looking for? [inquiry]" This is the crux of the issue. What in the world *is* he looking for? Did he want her to scratch it? I apologize for my sarcasm, but I want to emphasize how crucial it is to negotiate a specific agenda. The issue is, how will you and the patient work together?

You could ask the patient if there were tensions at home or problems in his life that he wanted to talk about. More than likely, he will reject this and terminate therapy. If so, at least you have tried to clarify what kind of help he wants and attempted to find some common ground.

Another attitude that can get in the way of doing self-help assignments is the fear of change. Some patients are ambivalent about getting better. They vaguely want to feel better, but they are terrified of what this might mean. A new patient suddenly quit doing homework assignments after the first couple of sessions. She told me: "Dr. Burns, when you said the patients who do the assignments have an average of 80 percent improvement as compared with zero in those who don't, I suddenly got cold feet. I couldn't motivate myself to do the assignments anymore. I got scared that the therapy would work and that things would start to change." If you were the therapist, what would you say next? Put your ideas here:

_____

_____

_____

_____

I would ask, "What is it that frightens you about getting better [inquiry]? What do you think might happen [inquiry]?" It turned out that she was afraid of getting too close to people, including her husband. She said she was "a closed person" and didn't feel comfortable opening up. Her intake diagnoses confirmed this, since in addition to chronic depression she had a diagnosis of "avoidant personality disorder." She said, "My family never thought I'd actually marry Hal. They thought I'd cancel out at the last minute. I like freedom, and Hal and I do our own thing. If we get too close, it might cause problems. If I maintain a distance, I can stay in my own little world. People tell me I should communicate more openly, but I don't really want to let the walls down."

If you were the therapist, what would you say next?

_____

_____

_____

_____

I would explore her fear. What does she think would happen if she got too close to her husband? I might ask if there are some problems we could work on together that would be a little less threatening to her.

Some patients may resist doing self-help assignments because of strong dependency needs and feelings of entitlement. This is especially true of those with a diagnosis of borderline personality disorder. They may have strong needs to be loved and cared about, and they may feel angry and entitled to better treatment from the world. They may resist doing self-help assignments because they do not believe that they can learn to be happy and to function in a more self-reliant manner. They may feel that they should not have to assume any responsibility for their negative feelings and unsatisfactory relationships. Their personal lives may reveal a pattern of loneliness and rejection, and they are often excessively dependent on others for emotional and financial support.

These patients may be extremely ambivalent toward you. They may idealize you at first and then become angry when you do not meet all their needs for love and affection. Because they have difficulties expressing these feelings openly and directly, they may act them out instead. They may miss sessions, stop doing self-help assignments, make suicidal threats, slash or burn their wrists, legs, or stomachs, or engage in other impulsive, self-destructive activities.

The angry, coercive motivation behind these actions is usually pretty transparent. A young man named Sam described how threatening and self-destructive he got whenever he was frustrated. He told me that once, while holding a gun to his own head, he had called a prior therapist and made admittedly unreasonable demands. He told the therapist that he would pull the trigger if the demands were not met.

Sam called me once, just as I was about to jump in a taxi to appear on a local television show. I was tense because I was on the verge of being late. Sam knew of this appearance because it had been announced in the *TV Guide*. Sam said, "Dr. Burns, I want to thank you for all the help you've given me. You've been great and I've really appreciated all your efforts. I'm just calling to say good-by. I finally realized I was hopeless, and so I've decided to commit suicide while you're on the show. I know you need a twenty-four-hour notification to cancel appointments, so I wanted to let you know not to expect me at tomorrow's session. By the way, I'm out of town, in a phone booth, with a hose from my car's exhaust pipe into the front window, so there's nothing you can do to stop me. It will be useless to call the police, so you don't need to worry about me. Good-by and have a terrific show."

I was furious and told Sam I expected him to keep his appointment and that I wanted him to come in for an emergency session right away. However, he wouldn't stay on the line and hung up on me. On the way to the show I felt intense guilt and panic. I thought, "I must be a terrific phony. How can I talk about *Feeling Good* when my patients are dropping dead like flies?" This reaction illustrates how uncanny these patients can be when they are angry. They sense our greatest vulnerabilities and stick the dagger in the bull's-eye! But my anxiety turned into anger as I thought about the situation. I told myself, "I'm not going to let Sam do this to me. I'm going to have a great show in spite of him." During the show, I told the audience that we are all subjected to great stress at the times we least expect it and described what had just happened to me. This revelation made it easier for the people in the audience to open up about the problems in their own lives. The show went unusually well.

When I returned to my office, the phone was ringing. It was Sam. He congratulated me and said he had watched the entire show. He said it was my best TV show so far. He let me know he would be there shortly for his emergency appointment.

Patients like Sam often make therapists feel guilty and insecure. You may make the mistake of trying too hard to please them. They tell you that the therapy cannot help, that you do not care about them, and that there's no point in doing the self-help assignments. They insist you just don't understand. So you try harder. You propose a new strategy. They complain that they have already tried it and insist that it "just won't work." On and on the battle goes, and you get more and more frustrated. No matter how hard you try, they just won't cooperate or respond to your efforts.

It's important not to buy into this common power struggle. Suppose a woman who has failed to do the homework says, "These silly assignments won't do me any good anyway. I don't think you can help me. You don't really care about me." How would you respond?

_____

_____

_____

_____

You could say, "It sounds like you feel I don't care about you and you think the self-help exercises won't be helpful to you [thought empathy]. You may be upset with me and disappointed in the treatment [feeling empathy]. Are you [inquiry]?" Notice that you're drawing her out instead of defending yourself or trying to be helpful.

Suppose she says, "I know you can't help me. Nobody can. I'm a horrible human being." What would you say next?

_____

_____

_____

_____

"You seem to be really pessimistic that we can work together, [thought empathy], and extremely unhappy with yourself [feeling empathy]. I'm concerned about how desperate you seem to feel ['I feel' statement]. I'm committed to you [stroking], and I hope we can work together ['I feel' statement]. I wonder if you do want to work with me [inquiry]. Do you [inquiry]? The self-help exercises are an important component of therapy ['I feel' statement]. Do you think this is something you will be willing to do [inquiry]? Is this the type of therapy you want [inquiry]?"

Notice that instead of trying to sell yourself to her, you're asking if she wants to work with you. The implication is that therapy is a negotiated relationship which must be satisfactory to both parties. If she says she doesn't want to do her part, and if she will not make a minimal commitment to the therapy, then it may be appropriate to question whether ongoing therapy with you is indicated. It's never wise to pursue people who are playing hard to get and putting you at a distance. This leads to endless grief and frustration, If, however, you *agree* that the therapy may not make sense, then you reverse the dynamics. You toss the ball back into her court. Let her try to persuade you that you should work together.

Now suppose she tells you that she just "can't" do the self-help assignments. She says that writing down her negative thoughts is too upsetting. She tells you she just can't do any self-help assignment at home. If you were the therapist, what would you say to her? Put your ideas here:

_____

_____

_____

_____

You might say, "You couldn't write down your negative thoughts because you got too upset when you tried [thought empathy]? When did this occur [inquiry]? Can you show me the written exercise you started when you got so upset [inquiry]?"

The purpose of this statement is to pin her down. I suspect that she really didn't try to do the self-help assignments. She just assumed the exercise would be upsetting, so she avoided it. In the unlikely event that she did begin a Daily Mood Log, you could help her complete it in the office. If she didn't even try, she might protest that she just "can't" fill out a Daily Mood Log on her own. She might explain that it's too difficult or protest that she can't think of any negative thoughts. What would you say next if you were the therapist? Put your ideas here:

_____

_____

_____

_____

I would ask her if she "can't" do the exercises or if she doesn't want to. I would explain that I could help her with any difficulties she's having, to make sure she understands each step of the self-help exercise. I would add that I was concerned that this may not be the real issue, and that we might be missing the point. She may not be strongly committed to doing the self-help exercises, and she may simply have difficulties telling me this for fear that I'll be angry with her.

Let's assume she acknowledges that she doesn't want to do self-help exercises at home. She says she doesn't think they'll help, or she thinks she "can't remember" to do them, or she makes some other excuse. What would you say next?

_____

_____

_____

_____

I would ask if she is committed to working with me, but I would be careful not to sound too rejecting. I might make a statement like this: "Jane, I'm hopeful that we can find an answer to this problem, because I would like to work with you. I believe we can work together successfully, if that's what you want. Most therapists would only ask you to come to sessions and talk, and they wouldn't ask you to do self-help assignments between sessions. That may be the type of therapy that you want and need. However, that's not my forte. The success of the therapy that I do strongly depends on whether you're willing to do things to help yourself between sessions. You certainly have every right not to do the self-help assignments, but I doubt that we will make any tangible progress. Tell me, do you think I'm the person you want to work with? Does this type of therapy make sense to you, given how hard it is for you to help yourself?"

Now she has to persuade you that she does want to work with you. She may *not* want to work with you. If so, you can refer her to a colleague with a different style and orientation. But if she does decide to stay, you've made it clear that the two of you will have to negotiate this issue in a way that makes sense to both of you.

Some patients refuse to do the self-help assignments because they don't like to be told what to do. You may have to resort to a little reverse psychology to turn this problem around. A 32-year-old man named Jerold was referred to me after ten years of unsuccessful psychotherapy for chronic depression. He felt resentful toward the world. During the first session Jerold told me he had difficulties attracting women. He complained bitterly about how lonely and unhappy he was. He insisted he was a "hard-boiled egg" and a hopeless loser no woman would want. His previous psychiatrist had suggested he read my first book, *Feeling Good.* Jerold said the "gimmicks" in the book couldn't possibly help him. He said he didn't want to do any "homework" exercises between sessions. He said I was probably just another "rip-off artist" like the two other "shrinks" who took his money and did nothing for him.

I felt a little uneasy after the session! I dreaded seeing him again, because it seemed the treatment was going to be a real uphill battle. I imagined trying to drag him forward while he sat back, refusing to cooperate and complaining that my efforts were no good. The scenario I foresaw was this: Jerold holds up the hoop and I jump through. Jerold says, "That's no good!" and holds it up a little higher. I jump through again! Then he says, "That wasn't any good, either!" Eventually I get exhausted, and ask myself, "Why in the world am I jumping through this hoop?"

I felt that Jerold's resentful, stubborn style might be protecting him from something he was afraid of. As long as he refused to cooperate, he wouldn't have to take a chance of getting his hopes up and risk getting hurt. If I rejected him or if the therapy was unsuccessful, he wouldn't feel let down because he could say, "I knew this all along."

After thinking about this problem, I called him at home very early on the morning of his second session. I told him I had thought about what he had said and concluded he was right. I said it sounded as if he didn't really want to work with me, and if he wanted, he could cancel that day's session and he wouldn't be charged for it. I told him I was willing to work with him, but he should know that I was an extremely demanding therapist and I insisted that all my patients had to work their fingers to the bone doing homework assignments between sessions. I told him it sounded as if this didn't appeal to him and that it might not make sense for him to have such an aggressive and demanding therapist. I explained that I would ask him to do all kinds of things he might not really want to do, like asking women for dates and keeping a journal of his negative thoughts. I told him I could refer him to a number of fine therapists who would be happy to listen to him without making any demands on him whatsoever. I told him I was also a "hard-boiled egg" and I felt that he deserved a better and more patient therapist.

Jerold begged me to continue my work with him! He told me he would be one of my hardest-working patients if only I'd give him a chance!

This was the start of what turned out to be a challenging and rewarding therapeutic experience. Jerold worked feverishly and faithfully at anything I asked him to do between sessions. His depression was greatly reduced after three sessions, and he began work on the tougher problem—his difficulties forming intimate relationships. He continued faithfully in his therapy and made great strides in his career and in his personal relationships.

When my second book, *Intimate Connections,* was released, I had to go out of town for two weeks for a promotional tour. When therapists go out of town, some patients feel hurt, rejected, and angry, and they may act out these feelings. Leaving for a book tour can seem particularly selfish and insulting, because it can appear as if I'm trying to promote myself and ignoring the needs and feelings of my patients. When I said good-by to Jerold, he simply shook my hand and said, "I'll miss you." There were tears in his eyes and he wished me success. I was touched by his vulnerability. Not bad for a couple of hard-boiled eggs!

THE CONCEPT OF SELF-HELP*

The purpose of treatment is to *feel* better, to *understand* why you got depressed or anxious, and to learn to *master your moods* so you can cope with your problems more effectively in the future.

There are several reasons why you may feel better as a result of your therapy:

1. You may experience a mood lift because you learn something that helps you solve a personal problem.

2. You may appreciate the support of a therapist who understands you and approves of you.

3. You may benefit from an antidepressant medication.

4. You may do things to help yourself between therapy sessions, such as scheduling more productive or pleasurable activities, becoming more assertive with people, writing down your negative thoughts and substituting more positive ones, or reading a self-help book.

Some of the newer forms of therapy are unique in emphasizing a structured self-help program to help you feel better, to become more productive, and to improve your relationships with people. Research and clinical experience have confirmed that the speed of your improvement can depend on your willingness to do self-help assignments. People who are unwilling to help themselves are often very slow to improve. In contrast, people who make an effort to participate in a systematic self-help program generally make the most rapid gains.

For this reason, it's crucial for you to decide whether you are willing to make an effort to help yourself as part of your treatment. Please answer the following questions and return this memo to your therapist so you can review it together.

1. I understand that my therapist emphasizes a self-help program as a key to personal growth.
   _____ yes _____no _____needs discussion

2. I am willing to do things to help myself between therapy sessions.
   _____ yes _____no _____needs discussion

3. The amount of time between sessions I agree to spend is _____ minutes per day (fill in).

4. I am willing to do this _____ days per week, and to continue working in my own behalf for at least _____ weeks (fill in).

*Copyright © 1984 by David D. Burns, M.D., from *The Feeling Good Handbook*, copyright © 1989

Self-Help Forms and Methods

The following is a brief review of some of the types of self-help forms and methods that are commonly used by patients involved in therapy. It is not comprehensive but is just intended to give you an idea of what is available.

1. **Activity Schedules:** A variety of forms are available to help you organize and utilize your time more productively.

2. **Daily Mood Log:** This form will help you change negative thoughts that lead to sadness, anxiety, anger, guilt, and frustration.

3. **Checklist of Cognitive Distortions:** This is a list of the ten types of twisted thinking that most frequently give rise to painful feelings. You can use it in conjunction with the Daily Mood Log to help you pinpoint the distortions in your negative thoughts.

4. **The Pleasure-Predicting Sheet:** This is a form for predicting and assessing the amount of satisfaction you get from various activities that have a potential for pleasure, achievement, learning, or personal growth. This can help you test and modify certain self-defeating attitudes that can make you vulnerable to depression and anxiety, such as:

   • I cannot feel happy and fulfilled if I'm alone.
   • I cannot feel satisfied unless I do things perfectly.
   • I cannot be truly happy unless there's someone in my life who loves me.

5. **The Anti-Procrastination Sheet:** This form can help you overcome procrastination. You break a task down into its smallest component parts and predict how difficult and satisfying each part will be, between 0 (the least difficult or satisfying) and 100 (the most). Then you do each part and record how difficult and satisfying it actually turned out to be. Things you've been putting off frequently turn out to be considerably easier and more enjoyable than you predicted.

6. **Bibliotherapy:** Many useful self-help books and pamphlets are available which can speed up your recovery. Some of these have to do with self-esteem, sex, assertiveness training, or other topics relevant to personal growth. Your therapist might be able to suggest some titles that would be especially valuable to you.

7. **The Burns Depression Checklist (BDC):** This is a 15-question multiple-choice inventory that acts as an "emotional thermometer" to measure the amount of depression you are experiencing. It can be filled out and scored in two or three minutes. While you are in therapy for depression, you can take the BDC test once a week to monitor your progress.

8. **The Burns Anxiety Inventory (BAI):** This is a 33-question multiple-choice inventory that measures the symptoms of anxiety and panic. Like the Burns Depression Checklist, it can be filled out and scored in several minutes. Taken weekly, it can help you monitor your progress in therapy.

9. **Communication Training:** During therapy sessions, your therapist can teach you specific verbal skills by role-playing difficult situations with you and demonstrating appropriate responses. Common areas of difficulty include dealing with people who are angry and excessively critical, as well as with complainers and people who make excessive demands on you. You might need to work on how to say no graciously, how to ask for a date, how to interview for a job, how to listen better, how to flirt, how to handle rejection, or how to communicate with people who refuse to talk to you. Once you have mastered a specific verbal skill in the office, your therapist can help you devise actual practice experiences outside the office.

10. **Decision-Making Form:** This form allows you to weigh the advantages and disadvantages of various options in a systematic manner when you are faced with a difficult decision.

11. **Empathy Scale:** This form allows you to give your therapist positive and negative feedback about each therapy session. You can fill it out after a session and give it to your therapist at the beginning of the next session. This will bring any negative reactions to the attention of your therapist so they won't build up and undermine your treatment. The resolution of these conflicts can improve your relationship with your therapist and give him or her valuable information about the best way to be helpful to you.

12. **Taping of Sessions:** Many patients find it very beneficial to tape their sessions so they can listen to the tapes at home between sessions. During a productive session you may discover many exciting insights about yourself or learn to solve problems that

have been troubling you. During the session these new ideas may all seem perfectly clear, but an hour or two later you may have trouble recalling what seemed so important and useful at the time. As you listen to the tape, you will have the opportunity to review these ideas again. Many patients listen to the tapes of especially good sessions numerous times. They report that the tapes can be more helpful than the actual sessions themselves.

When you listen to a tape, you may discover that you had a tendency to ignore or discount what the therapist said, even though you felt convinced during the session that you were listening carefully. At times it can be uncomfortable to hear yourself, because you will notice certain negative habits that you weren't aware of. Listening to yourself takes courage, but it can be an important growth experience. You may also become aware of mistakes your therapist is making. Be sure to share this feedback at the next session.

Twenty-Five Reasons for Not Doing Self-Help Assignments

The following are some of the reasons why you may have difficulty doing self-help work between sessions. There is some overlap between a number of the categories, and you will probably discover that several of them apply to you. These same attitudes may make you less productive and successful in other areas of your life. Once you pinpoint the problem that is holding you back, you can work with your therapist to develop a strategy for overcoming it.

After each of the following descriptions, put a check (√) in the box that indicates how accurately it describes the way you feel.

1. **The love addiction:** You may feel convinced that love and closeness are the keys to happiness, so you can't conceive of finding satisfaction as a result of learning to cope with your problems on your own. Self-help techniques may seem cold and mechanical. You may resent having to help yourself because you feel convinced that the best way to overcome your depression involves sharing your feelings with a therapist or friend who cares about you and supports you.

   This problem or attitude describes me:

   _____ not at all; _____ somewhat; _____ moderately; _____ a lot.

2. **Perfectionistic thinking:** You may feel that if you don't do things perfectly, there's no point in doing them at all. This attitude can defeat you in several ways. You may feel you have to do your self-help exercises so thoroughly and perfectly that you feel too overwhelmed to try. In fact, even five to ten minutes a day of self-help work can contribute enormously to your improvement. You may be afraid that if you make a mistake or don't complete an exercise properly, you will appear incompetent or stupid. In fact, you're permitted to make as many mistakes as you like, because your therapist is teaching you something new. You can learn from your mistakes. You may also feel that a particular exercise must lead to a dramatic change in the way you feel, or else it wasn't successful. Actually, you can learn a lot from self-help exercises that don't make you feel better, if you will review your efforts with your therapist.

   Perfectionism describes me:

   _____ not at all; _____ somewhat; _____ moderately; _____ a lot.

3. **The fear of disapproval:** You may be afraid that your therapist will think less of you when s/he reviews your self-help efforts. You may think your negative thoughts and feelings are shameful or foolish. Paradoxically, this attitude may bring about the disapproval you're trying so hard to prevent. Since your therapist's primary job is to help you design and carry out a self-help program that will help you get in better control of your life, s/he might feel frustrated about your unwillingness to try to help yourself. This could make you feel disapproved of, and even less like doing the assignments.

   The fear of disapproval describes me:

   _____ not at all; _____ somewhat; _____ moderately; _____ a lot.

4. **Putting the cart before the horse:** You may have the belief that motivation comes before effective action, so you wait around until you feel like doing something. Since the motivation doesn't come, you end up doing nothing.

   Actually, action must frequently precede motivation. Since depressed people often feel lethargic and unmotivated, you may have to make a decision to do something constructive whether or not you feel like it. Once you get started, you will often feel more motivated.

   Putting the cart before the horse describes me:

   _____ not at all; _____ somewhat; _____ moderately; _____ a lot.

5. **Unexpressed anger:** You may resent something your therapist said or react negatively to his or her personality. Instead of expressing these feelings in a direct and open fashion, you may avoid the problem and express your feelings indirectly—by cancelling sessions at the last minute, by being argumentative, or by not completing the self-help assignments you agreed to do. This can make the feelings of tension worse, and you may eventually drop out of treatment entirely.

   Avoiding conflicts when I feel angry describes me:

   _____ not at all; _____ somewhat; _____ moderately; _____ a lot.

6. **Hopelessness:** One of the most painful aspects of depression and anxiety is the illogical sense of hopelessness that many patients experience. You may feel as if your problems and suffering will go on forever, no matter what. In spite of the fact that your therapist is convinced that your prognosis for recovery is excellent, you may believe that all your efforts are pointless and doomed to failure. Then you give up and do nothing. Consequently, nothing changes. This reinforces the belief that you're hopeless.

   Hopelessness describes me:

   _____ not at all; _____ somewhat; _____ moderately; _____ a lot.

7. **Coercion sensitivity:** You may at times feel that people are trying to force you to do various things. You may think that friends or family members are being pushy and bossy or are trying to control you. Consequently you may dig in your heels and resist them, because you don't want to give in. Then they get frustrated and put more pressure on you. You, in turn, feel stubborn and even more determined not to let them control you.

   I sometimes feel as if people are bossing me around:

   _____ not at all; _____ somewhat; _____ moderately; _____ a lot.

8. **Fatalism:** You may be convinced that your moods are governed by forces that are beyond your control, such as hormones, drugs, biorhythms, fate, God, or the way other people treat you. Consequently there seems little point in trying to learn to master your moods. If you become passive and don't try, you will continue to feel that you can't control your feelings or solve your problems.

   Fatalism describes me:

   _____ not at all; _____ somewhat; _____ moderately; _____ a lot.

9. **Fear of blame:** Some people believe that if they accept the idea that they are responsible for their emotions, it follows that they will be blamed for them. Since they don't want to feel blamed, they resist assuming any responsibility for their feelings or their problems, and they refuse to do anything to help themselves.

I am afraid of accepting responsibility for my negative feelings:

_____ not at all; _____ somewhat; _____ moderately; _____ a lot.

10. **Internal vs. external expectations:** You may feel the need to meet the expectations of your parents, your spouse, your boss, etc. You might base your self-esteem on the amount of praise or criticism you get. When you're criticized, you might feel inadequate, resentful, guilty, or anxious. This is so uncomfortable that it seems preferable to adopt a low profile and do nothing at all. The less you do, the less you can be criticized for. You try to keep everybody's expectations at an absolute minimum, so that no one will get their hopes up and then be disappointed.

The fear of letting other people down describes me:

_____ not at all; _____ somewhat; _____ moderately; _____ a lot.

11. **Resistance to a structured fast-acting approach:** Some people feel that personal growth and insight must involve a long process of disclosing your feelings and childhood memories to a therapist over a period of years. The idea of trying to achieve your emotional goals in a limited period of time, using a structured training program, may strike you as gimmicky and superficial. You may tend to write off cognitive and behavioral techniques that focus on the here-and-now as "fads" or as psychological "Band-Aids" rather than as new developments that could speed up the process of psychotherapy, just as penicillin improved the treatment of pneumonia.

I believe that any rapid treatment for a mood problem will be superficial:

_____ not at all; _____ somewhat; _____ moderately; _____ a lot.

12. **Self-labeling:** Some people justify putting things off because they think of themselves as "lazy" or they call themselves "procrastinators." These labels set up the expectation that you will continue to be unproductive because of a deeply ingrained and irreversible aspect of your personality. You may even find that your family and friends buy into the passive, helpless role you

play. During a marital therapy session, a severely depressed woman announced: "I think I need a cigarette." Her obedient husband immediately picked up her pack of cigarettes from the table, took one of them out, placed it in her mouth, and lit it for her. His behavior rewarded her for acting as if she couldn't do anything for herself and had to be waited on.

I think of myself as "lazy" or as a procrastinator:

_____ not at all; _____ somewhat; _____ moderately; _____ a lot.

13. **Different priorities:** Some people are genuinely overcommitted and either forget to do their self-help assignments or feel that they can't budget any time for them. You may feel overwhelmed and believe that the exercises your therapist suggests will only add to your burdens instead of helping you solve your problems.

I feel overwhelmed by everything I have to do:

_____ not at all; _____ somewhat; _____ moderately; _____ a lot.

14. **Entitlement:** Some people feel they're entitled to happiness and fair treatment from others. They deeply resent the implication that they are responsible for the way they feel, and they think they shouldn't have to work hard to improve a difficult situation. They often think that other people don't treat them right. They resist therapy because it seems "unfair" that they should have to put out any effort to feel better. As one woman put it, "Why should *I* have to change? My husband is the one making me miserable!"

I believe that I am entitled to feel happy and that I shouldn't have to work on my problems:

_____ not at all; _____ somewhat; _____ moderately; _____ a lot.

15. **Fear of change:** Some people, in spite of their misery, fantasize that any change in the status quo might be even worse. The anxiety associated with change appears so great that the current painful state of affairs seems preferable. You may think that your personal identity depends on feeling depressed, angry, or inadequate, and so you may feel reluctant to give up your symptoms. As one woman put it, "I think I *like* being depressed and feeling sorry for myself."

I sometimes feel afraid to change my life:

_____ not at all; _____ somewhat; _____ moderately; _____ a lot.

16. **Shame:** You may have a number of painful feelings and problems that you find it difficult to share with your therapist, such as alcoholism, a sexual indiscretion, or an angry reaction to something the therapist said. The therapy may not seem relevant if you don't share this information with your therapist.

There are problems that I might feel ashamed to share with my therapist:

_____ not at all; _____ somewhat; _____ moderately; _____ a lot.

17. **Emotional reasoning:** This is one of the commonest distortions that can undermine your self-help efforts. You might reason: "I feel worse. Therefore, I must not be getting anywhere in my therapy." You might also tell yourself, "I *feel* hopeless. Therefore, I must *be* hopeless." The tendency to reason from the way you feel can be quite unrealistic and self-defeating, because your emotions will often result from distorted thoughts that have no more validity than the grotesque images in the curved mirrors at an amusement park. Virtually all patients have setbacks and feel hopeless or unmotivated at times, but this doesn't mean they can't improve.

When I feel bad, I often give up on things:

_____ not at all; _____ somewhat; _____ moderately; _____ a lot.

18. **Low frustration tolerance:** Many individuals find it difficult to stick with a task if they don't get immediate results. If they reach a plateau, or if they experience a setback, they give up. Since a number of ups and downs are an inevitable part of treatment, or practically any activity, it would be to your advantage to learn to increase your frustration tolerance so that you can have the persistence required for optimal results.

I often give up on things when I feel frustrated with my progress:

_____ not at all; _____ somewhat; _____ moderately; _____ a lot.

19. **Superman/Superwoman:** You may think that if you ask for help, it means that you're "weak" or "inferior." If your therapist tries to help you, you may feel the urge to resist and come up with something entirely different that you alone thought of. This is just as illogical as going to a tennis coach and then refusing to follow through on his or her suggestions. If you insist on hitting

the ball in your own way, your style may be quite original, but you may not win as many matches!

This attitude describes me:

_____ not at all; _____ somewhat; _____ moderately; _____ a lot.

20. **Lack of direction:** During periods of depression, some individuals experience slowed thinking and have difficulty concentrating. At these times you may have trouble figuring out what's bothering you and find it difficult to think of anything positive to do to help yourself.

This problem describes me:

_____ not at all; _____ somewhat; _____ moderately; _____ a lot.

21. **The "realism" of depression:** Some people who are depressed are reluctant to work at getting better because they are convinced their problems are real and that their misery is inevitable. They may feel there's no point in writing down their negative thoughts or trying to learn to think more positively because they think this means ignoring reality or getting involved in the "Power of Positive Thinking."

I believe that psychotherapy cannot help me because my problems are real:

_____ not at all; _____ somewhat; _____ moderately; _____ a lot.

22. **Reluctance to give up negative feelings:** Some people are reluctant to give up feelings of anger, guilt, depression, or anxiety because they believe that these emotions are healthy or beneficial to them. A psychologist who was petrified about failing her licensing examination didn't want to give up worrying because she was convinced it was helping her in some way, even though she was so nervous that she couldn't study. A woman who was considering separating from her husband didn't want to give up her anger and depression and suicidal urges because she felt that if she did, she'd get complacent and stuck in a bad marriage.

Sometimes I feel that I don't really want to let go of my negative feelings:

_____ not at all; _____ somewhat; _____ moderately; _____ a lot.

23. **The medical model:** If you go to a doctor because of a cough or a fever, you generally expect him to diagnose the problem and

prescribe a medicine that will correct it. All you have to do is get plenty of bed rest and wait for the cure to take care of itself. Similarly, many people feel that a chemical imbalance has caused their mood problems and that only a drug could make them better. Therefore, the idea of dealing with their problems or doing self-help assignments does not appeal to them.

I am convinced that only a medication can make me feel better:

_____ not at all; _____ somewhat; _____ moderately; _____ a lot.

24. **Passivity:** Some people feel that just talking to a therapist every week should be enough to make them feel better. This expectation may lead to disappointment. Your therapist can help you pinpoint the causes of the problem and develop a step-by-step plan for solving it, but ultimately you will have to work actively on your own to carry out that plan.

I sometimes feel that just going to therapy and talking about my problems should be enough to make things better:

_____ not at all; _____ somewhat; _____ moderately; _____ a lot.

25. **Summary:** After reading this memo, you may have a better understanding of the advantages and disadvantages of doing self-help assignments in therapy. Please indicate how you now feel about this.

I feel convinced that doing self-help assignments will be an important part of my recovery:

_____ not at all; _____ somewhat; _____ moderately; _____ a lot.

Index

ABOUT THE AUTHOR

DAVID D. BURNS, M.D., was graduated magna cum laude from Amherst College, received his M.D. from the Stanford University School of Medicine, and completed his psychiatric residency training at the University of Pennsylvania, where he is now clinical associate professor of psychiatry in the school of medicine. Dr. Burns has been one of the prime developers of cognitive therapy, a fast-acting treatment for depression, anxiety, and marital problems. Among his many honors was the A. E. Bennett Award, one of the top psychiatric awards for research on the chemistry of emotional distress. He is the director of the Behavioral Sciences Research Foundation and the acting chief of psychiatry at the Presbyterian Medical Center of Philadelphia.